1001

BEST THINGS TO SEE AND DO IN

NEW ZEALAND

Peter Janssen

Hodder Moa

To my Mum and Dad who taught me to be curious about the world.

Credits — region opening images
North Island: p.9 Destination Northland; p.27 Suburban Newspapers, Auckland; p.57 Peter Janssen; p.66 Driving Creek Railway; p.81 Ngaruawahia Regatta; p.99 White Island Tours with PeeJay; p.108 Waimangu Volcanic Valley; p.123 Tourism Eastland; p.134 Army Museum, Waiouru; p.144 Govett-Brewster Art Gallery Collection; p.155 Paul Gibson/H&A Design & Print; p.160 Peter Janssen; p.170 Napier Prison Tours; p.184 www.nzballoons.co.nz; p.193 Postively Wellington Tourism
South Island: p.219 Wither Hills Vineyard; p.228 WOW® Gallery, World of WearableArt & Collectible Car Museum, Nelson; p.236 www.seakayaknz.co.nz; p.243 Buller Fest; p.255 Ian Gill, Department of Conservation; p.269 Whale Watch Kaikoura; p.276 Coronet Peak, www.nzski.com — Miles Holden; p.284 World Buskers Festival; p.300 Black Cat Cruises; p.310 Michael Linton; p.322 Ewan Fordyce; p.332 Mt Difficulty Wines Ltd; p.355 The Olveston Experience; p.373 Peter Janssen; p.381 Powernet Tour of Southland; p.393 Peter Janssen

National Library of New Zealand Cataloguing-in-Publication Data
Janssen, Peter (Peter Leon)
1001 best things to see and do in New Zealand / Peter Janssen.
Includes bibliographical references.
ISBN-13: 978-1-86971-067-5
ISBN-10: 1-86971-067-3
1. New Zealand—Description and travel. 2. New Zealand—
Guidebooks. I. Title.
919.304—dc 22

A Hodder Moa Book
Published in 2006 by Hachette Livre NZ Ltd
4 Whetu Place, Mairangi Bay
Auckland, New Zealand

Reprinted 2007

Typeset by Jazz Graphics
Printed by Everbest Printing Co. Ltd, China

Front cover — clockwise from top: Real Journeys, www.nzski.com (Miles Holden), Napier Prison Tours, Destination Northland, Whale Watch Kaikoura, www.seakayaknz.co.nz
Back cover — clockwise from top left: Tourism Eastland, White Island Tours with PeeJay, Maruia Springs Thermal Resort, Suburban Newspapers Auckland, WellingtonNZ.com

Contents

Acknowledgements

Travelling through New Zealand, I have realised that the world is full of really nice people despite the impression the news reports might give. I want to say thank you to all the helpful, enthusiastic folk at all the visitor centres and Department of Conservation offices, to front-counter people and to everyone who provided me with advice, information and photographs.

In particular, I want to thank Jane Hingston at Hachette Livre for being patient, persistent and polite, Sue Hall and Eva Chan for checking my work, and to Tony Moores for planting the idea for the book in the first place. And finally, thanks to Geoff for all the driving, and backing up almost as much as driving forward.

The author

Born and raised in the Waikato, Peter Janssen has also lived in Southland, Canterbury and Wellington before moving to Auckland. Working for many years in the publishing industry he has also tried his hand at artificial insemination, bus driving, pumping petrol, and farming with varying degrees of success.

The book was inspired by his extensive travels throughout the country and the need for a guidebook that would appeal to New Zealanders as well as visitors. He now lives in Auckland with his three gold fish (originally there were eight but the cat from across the road ate the other five).

New Zealand

Kaitaia

NORTHLAND
Whangarei

AUCKLAND
Auckland
Coromandel

Hamilton
Tauranga
WAIKATO
Whakatane
Rotorua
BAY OF
PLENTY
Taupo
EAST CAPE
Gisborne

New Plymouth
TARANAKI
HAWKE'S
BAY
Wanganui
WANGANUI
& MANAWATU
Napier
Hastings

Palmerston
North

Masterton
WAIRARAPA
& WELLINGTON
Nelson
WELLINGTON
Blenheim
TASMAN MARLBOROUGH

Greymouth
Kaikoura
WESTLAND

CANTERBURY
Christchurch
Ashburton
Timaru

Queenstown
Oamaru
OTAGO
SOUTHLAND
& FIORDLAND
Dunedin
Invercargill
STEWART ISLAND

Note: This is a general map of New Zealand and does not reflect the regions described in this book

5

How to use this book

*** Worth a trip

** Worth a detour

* If you are passing

A guide book is just that, a guide, and any book with a rating system is, by its very nature, subjective. Travelling is all about making choices and the aim of this book is to help the reader make those choices, taking into account personal interests and time considerations. In writing about the places I visited I have endeavoured to replicate the experience the ordinary visitor can expect. When I visited I never phoned ahead to make an appointment, so no one was able to make any special arrangements just for me, and, in most cases, I visited anonymously — as a sort of 'travel mystery shopper'.

In order to be as fair as possible, there have been no payments of any kind made to the author or anyone associated with publishing this guide, apart from the occasional free entry.

An important factor in deciding what to include or leave out was the degree to which a sight or event is actually interesting to visit today. Many places are visually dull though they may be historically fascinating. Nothing is worse than to drive for hours to briefly stare at a five-line plaque on the side of the road, or to tramp in the wet and mud to some bleak place that was fascinating 100 years ago.

One difficult area was deciding on value for money. Some places are fantastic value for money by my standards, and other places seem outrageously expensive. As a rule of thumb, the more popular and commercial the operations, the more expensive they are — so it would pay to have an idea of the entrance fees before turning up with the family, then choking on the price. I haven't included entry prices as these can change frequently, but websites are included so you can check the latest prices before you arrive. Under the Queenstown Adventure Activities, for example, I have given a checklist to help ascertain value for money — and I endeavour to do this throughout the book.

Likewise, double-check opening times. I find it hard to believe the convoluted opening times some places have, and, like prices, they change quickly. Many places, particularly in the South Island, have significantly reduced winter hours, and some close altogether, so avoid disappointment and check ahead.

This book has not attempted to cover accommodation and food for two very good reasons. The first is that most people, when deciding on where to travel, base their decisions primarily on what there is to do and see, and not on where they will sleep and eat. The second reason is that accommodation and food places change hands very quickly and what was a great place to eat one week could be terrible the next (and vice versa).

In the last 10 years New Zealand has developed a great network of Visitor Centres that are staffed by extremely helpful people. If you want help with accommodation or more detailed information on a local attraction make the Visitor Centre your first stop when coming into town, (the same applies to the Department of Conservation Information Centres).

Choosing the best time to travel is a hard decision. There is considerable pressure on activities and accommodation from mid-December through to mid-March (and mid-winter for ski resorts). Moreover, many places hold sports events and festivals through the summer which can quickly book out accommodation months ahead. If you have your heart set on doing or seeing a particular attraction it really pays to book ahead. New Zealand weather can be fickle at any time of the year so always be prepared for the extremes, blistering hot, or bitterly cold.

On a rather sad note, I am hugely embarrassed as a New Zealander to see so many signs warning of theft, and car theft in particular. Broken window glass litters many of our visitor carparks so don't leave valuables in your car, or belongings unattended. Fortunately, most New Zealanders are nice people!

This is the first edition of this book and I am sure I have missed good things that should have been included and made the odd mistake (some of my notes I couldn't even read). So, to help, I have set up a website for updates, additions and changes or any comment a reader would like to make. Visit **www.1001bestthings.com**

Peter Janssen
August, 2006

North Island

NORTHLAND

Bay of Islands

Cape Brett/Hole in the Rock **

Numerous tour operators feature boat trips in the bay with various combinations to suit most tastes and interests, including island visits, beach stops and fishing opportunities. Nearly all include the fascinating 'Hole in the Rock', a sea cave that cuts right through Piercy Island off Cape Brett and is big enough to accommodate large boats. For the more energetic there is the Cape Brett Walkway, a 16-km track from Rawhiti to the Cape. Walks can be guided or independent, and boat transport can be arranged for those just wanting to walk one way. Visit www.capebrettwalks.co.nz

Fishing ***

The Bay of Islands is world renowned for its superb sea fishing and in particular deepwater fishing. The bay holds the world records for both broadbill swordfish (369 kg) and striped marlin (243 kg), and American author Zane Grey used Russell as his base and caught his first marlin here. Numerous fishing tours operate out of the bay catering for both beginners and more experienced fisher folk.

Russell ***

Beginning life as Kororareka, the early settlement known as the 'Hellhole of the Pacific' was notorious for grog shops, brothels and general lawlessness, and was even the capital for a brief nine-month period. While now a popular tourist destination (accessible by a short ferry ride from Paihia), the town still retains enough of its early character to remain charming, especially along the waterfront appropriately known as The Strand.

Christ's Church ***
Corner Robertson and Church Streets, Russell

Built in 1836 this is New Zealand's oldest church, and both Charles Darwin, who visited the area on the *Beagle* in 1835, and Samuel Marsden contributed to the building fund. In 1845 Hone Heke attacked the town, and fierce fighting took place around the church between men from the HMS *Hazard* and Hone's men. The church still bears the visible scars of bullet and cannonball, despite repairs. In the graveyard, in which the oldest headstone is dated 1836, are graves of Tamati Waka Nene, a local chief who supported the British, and men from the *Hazard* killed in action.

Flagstaff Hill *

As tensions grew between Maori and British Ngapuhi chief Hone Heke was well aware of the symbolic nature of the British flag flying over Russell. Four times he cut down the flagpole above the town despite extensive British attempts to protect it. After the fourth time, the town itself was attacked and captured by Hone. A modern flagpole still stands and the view over the bay is worth the walk up the hill.

Pompallier House ***

The Strand, Russell

Open December to April daily 10 a.m. to 5 p.m., May to November daily guided tours 10.15 a.m., 11.15 a.m., 1.15 p.m., 2.15 p.m., 3.15 p.m.

www.historic.org.nz/pompallier

Entrance fee

This exceptional building is unlike any other in New Zealand. Constructed in 1841–42 of pisé de terre (clay and ash), the building was originally a printery for producing Catholic texts in Maori and is the only remaining building of the once extensive mission complex. The mission was set up in 1838 by the first Roman Catholic bishop in the Pacific, Bishop Jean Baptiste Pompallier, though it eventually moved to Auckland after Russell was sacked in 1845. Later radically remodelled so that it looked nothing like the original printery, the building was finally restored in the 1990s to what can be seen today.

Cape Reinga/Te Rerenga Wairua ***

Often described, mistakenly, as the most northerly point (which honour belongs to Surville Cliffs at North Cape), Cape Reinga is renowned for the spectacular and wild seascapes of the Columbia Bank where the Tasman Sea and the Pacific Ocean meet. In Maori tradition Cape Reinga is the final departing point for the spirits of the dead on their journey to the underworld domain of Hine-nui-te-po, the goddess of death. The twisted and gnarled vegetation along the coast is where the spirits have desperately attempted to cling to this world.

The lighthouse, constructed in 1941, was the last watched lighthouse to be built in the country.

Dargaville Museum *

Harding Park, Mangawhare, Dargaville (well sign-posted from the town centre)
Open daily 9 a.m. to 4 p.m.
www.dargavillemuseum.co.nz
Entrance fee

Situated on a hill just west of the town with great views over the Northern Wairoa River (New Zealand's longest navigable river), this museum is easily recognised by the two masts of the *Rainbow Warrior* in front of the main building. While the displays focus mainly on local history and in particular maritime history, there are some standout exhibits.

The Maori section holds the largest pre-European waka in the country at 16.2-metres-long and carved by stone tools from a single totara trunk.

The original gum-digger's slab hut reconstructed within the museum is actually listed as an historic building in its own right.

A carving named Poutu Ki Rongomaeroa was found locally but is not in any local carving style and is said to be linked to the mysterious Waitaha people, a Polynesian culture occupying New Zealand before Maori.

Doubtless Bay **

www.doubtlessbay.com

Known to Maori as Rangaunu, this large enclosed bay was first discovered by Kupe who landed at Taipa around 900 AD and encompasses some of the best beaches of the north, including Coopers Beach, Cable Bay, Taipa and Taupo Bay. At the eastern end of the bay is historic Mangonui Harbour, once a thriving whaling station. Sheltering the bay to the west and north is the Karikari Peninsula at the end of which is Matai Bay, without question one of the finest beaches of the north.

Goat Island ***

The reserve is well sign-posted from SH1 at Warkworth.

Established in 1975, Goat Island is New Zealand's first marine reserve, and as such offers some of the best snorkelling in the country. The centre of the reserve is Goat Island and the narrow channel between the island and the beach teems with sea life. Huge snapper, giant crayfish and schools of blue maomao are common. This is a very popular spot in the summer and can get crowded on the weekends. Snorkelling equipment can be hired in Leigh.

Gum Diggers Park *

Heath Road, sign-posted from SH1, 25 km north of Kaitaia
Open daily 9 a.m. to 5.30 p.m.
www.gumdiggerspark.co.nz
Entrance fee

Set on an actual gum field, this park is a fascinating insight into an industry unique to Northland. The kauri gum had a wide range of uses including high-quality varnishes but it was hard won by men working in difficult conditions. The footwear used in the extraction of gum gave rise to the very Kiwi word 'gumboot'. This gum field was based on two extinct kauri forests: the first forest may have declined owing to climate change 150,000 years ago, while the second forest was subjected to a more severe event such as a tsunami about 45,000 years ago. Information boards and reconstructions detail both the kauri gum industry and life on the gum field, and the trees in this park are said to be the oldest preserved timber in the world.

Henderson Bay **

13 km north of Houhora to the Henderson Bay Road turnoff and 6 km to the beach on an unsealed road

If getting away from it all is what you are after, then this pristine sweep of golden sand is the place. This unspoiled beach is popular with local surfers and, apart from a single rubbish bin, there are absolutely no facilities, though there is accommodation nearby.

Hokianga Harbour **

Named by the Polynesian explorer Kupe, this long finger of water stretching far inland has been much favoured by both Maori and European. The magnificent golden sand hills are well worth a visit and are easily reached by water taxi from Opononi wharf (just call Pete, 09 405 8872). The statue of Opo the Dolphin outside the Opononi pub commemorates the friendly dolphin whose antics attracted huge crowds and publicity in 1953 before she met an untimely death trapped between rocks. The small museum inside the Hokianga Visitor Centre at Omapere has an Opo display.

Mangungu Mission House *
Motukiore Road, 3 km from Horeke
Limited summer opening hours
www.historic.org.nz
Entrance fee

Tucked away in the upper reaches of the harbour beyond Rawene is the Mangungu Mission House. Built in 1838–39 on a hill overlooking the harbour, the view from the mission has changed very little from the time when the house was new. Many of the Hokianga chiefs signed the Treaty of Waitangi here in February 1840.

Rawene *

This is New Zealand's third-oldest European settlement and is the access for the ferry to Kohukohu on the northern shore. Among its many old buildings is historic Clendon House built in the 1860s, the home of Captain James Clendon, the first US consul to New Zealand. The house has limited summer opening hours (visit www.historic.org.nz).

Te Ara Manawa Walkway *
Clendon Esplanade on the eastern side of the township

Mangroves are a common feature of shallow northern harbours, but only in the Far North do they grow to the size of small trees. Usually associated with the tropics, the single New Zealand species *Avicennia marina* subspecies *Australiasica* is the southernmost in the world, and in recent years, with the warmer weather, this species has been rapidly expanding its habitat. The short boardwalk complete with information board takes only around 20 minutes, allowing the visitor to walk among these fascinating trees at any tide.

Kai Iwi Lakes **

From Dargaville take SH12 north to Omamari Road and follow this road for 11 km to the lakes.

These three small lakes are basin-type dune lakes formed in consolidated sand with no outlets or inlets, relying entirely on rain to maintain the level of water.

The small beaches have dazzling white sand the consistency of powder, while the water varies from a light aqua to a deep blue where the shallows suddenly drop off into very deep water. This is a very popular spot for swimming and water skiing, with a camping ground and basic facilities available.

Kaitaia — Far North Regional Museum *

South Road (southern end of the shopping centre), Kaitaia
Open Monday to Friday 10 a.m. to 4 p.m., weekends 1 p.m. to 4 p.m.
www.farnorthmuseum.co.nz
Entrance fee

This small local museum has as a special feature the huge anchor of the French ship the *St Jean Baptiste*. While the voyages of Captain Cook are well documented, what is not so well known is that the French explorer Francois de Surville was exploring New Zealand at the same time as Cook and at one stage their ships passed within a few kilometres of each other off North Cape during bad weather in December 1769.

While sheltering in Doubtless Bay, de Surville was forced to cut both his anchors, and these were later recovered by diver and adventurer Kelly Tarlton. The other anchor is in Te Papa, Wellington.

Kawakawa Hundertwasser toilets ***

Whoever had the bright idea to commission the famous Austrian artist Frederick Hundertwasser to design the public toilets at Kawakawa was truly inspired. This small but amazing building has turned this sleepy little junction town into a major tourist attraction and well worth the stop whether you 'have to go' or not. The toilets are located in the centre of the main street.

Kawiti Glow-worm Caves **

5 km south of Kawakawa and 1 km off the main highway at Waiomio
Open daily 9 a.m. to 5 p.m., guided tours only
Phone 09 404 0583 or 09 404 1256
Entrance fee

Located on the historic Kawiti marae, these caves combine history, glow-worms and limestone formations. Discovered in the seventeenth century by Roku, the runaway wife of chief Haumoewarangi, who hid in the caves, they are over 200 m in length, up to 20 m at their highest point and 12 m wide. The famous fighting chief Kawiti, who held the British at Ruapekapeka, is an ancestor of this marae. Entrance to the caves is by guided tour only and includes a short bush walk.

Kerikeri

Collins Brothers Steam Sawmill **

Inlet Road, Kerikeri — sign-posted from Kerikeri Road
Open Monday to Friday 8 a.m. to 4 p.m., closed public holidays
Phone 09 407 9707
www.steamsawmill.co.nz
Entrance fee

Established in 1983, this is not a museum but one of the few commercial steam sawmills in the world. By utilising redundant plant, the Collins brothers, Dave and Mike, use steam to generate electricity and are self-sufficient in fuel by using wood offcuts. Well worth a visit, the mill is open to visitors during operation hours only.

Kerikeri Mission Station ***

Kerikeri Basin
Open daily November to April 10 a.m. to 5 p.m., May to October 10 a.m. to 4 p.m., closed Christmas Day
www.historic.org.nz
Entrance fee

Not one, but two, of New Zealand's oldest buildings sit side by side on the upper reaches of the Kerikeri Inlet, all that is left of the mission founded in 1819 alongside the main pa of the Ngapuhi chief Hongi Hika.

Now known as Kemp House, the original mission building was begun in 1821 for the Butler family and is New Zealand's oldest surviving European building. The Kemp family lived in the house from 1832 through to 1974, when the house and contents were acquired by the Historic Places Trust. Next door is the Stone Store built in 1832 to house mission supplies and wheat from the nearby Te Waimate mission farm. Functioning as a general store, it was acquired by the trust in 1975.

Unfortunately the busy main road cuts through the middle of the Kerikeri Inlet, causing damage to the foundations of the Stone Store and generally detracting from this picturesque and historic place. Plans are afoot for a by-pass road.

Koropito Pa **

Kerikeri Basin

One of the strongholds of the Ngapuhi chief Hongi Hika, this attractive pa site overlooking the river is a short 10-minute walk from the Stone Store. The layout and fortifications of the pa are much clearer here than at many other pa sites, and informative panels make this a worthwhile side trip.

Rewa's Village *

1 Landing Road
Open daily 9.30 a.m. to 4.30 p.m.
Phone 09 407 6454
Entrance fee

Across the bridge is Rewa's Village, an historically accurate reconstruction of a pre-European Maori fishing village/kainga which includes detailed information on traditional Maori life and plant use. Usually adjacent to a fortified pa, a kainga would be sited close to cultivated areas, fishing and hunting grounds, and was where most people lived most of the time, only retreating to the fortified pa in times of uncertainty.

Rainbow Falls **

Here the Kerikeri River drops nearly 30 m, creating a spectacular waterfall. The falls can be accessed by an attractive one-hour walk up the river from the Basin carpark or a five-minute walk from the end of Rainbow Falls Road off Waipapa Road.

Steamboats on the Kerikeri Inlet **

Kerikeri Basin
Phone 09 407 9229
www.steamship.co.nz
Bookings essential

The usual image of a steamboat is a huge paddlewheel multi-deck vessel, so it comes as a surprise to see the tiny SS *Firefly* plying the placid waters of the Kerikeri River. A restored 1882 kauri steamboat, this small vessel would have been ideal to navigate the narrow and often tidal inlets of New Zealand's shores when land travel was almost impossible. Its larger relation, the SS *Eliza Hobson*, is a replica of an earlier wood-fired vessel. A steam and heritage festival is held in November.

Koanga Gardens **

SH1 north of Kaiwaka
Open daily 9 a.m. to 5 p.m.
www.koanga.org.nz

Kay Baxter is a passionate advocate of preserving old varieties of fruit and vegetables in the firm belief that, not only do these fruit and vegetables taste better, but their preservation also helps maintain a broad genetic base. Her collection of plants is incredible, as is her willingness to share both her knowledge and the plants. Koanga Gardens is the outlet for the Koanga Gardens Trust, which for the past 20 years has been collecting and saving heritage vegetables and fruit. Surrounding the shop, which sells seeds and plants, is a vegetable garden and small orchard that varies considerably from season to season. For details of open days and workshops visit the website.

Matakohe — the Kauri Museum ***

Church Road, Matakohe; on SH12, 26 km from SH1 on the road to Dargaville
Open daily November to April 8.30 a.m. to 5.30 p.m., May to October 9 a.m. to 5 p.m., closed Christmas Day
www.kauri-museum.com
Entrance fee

Opened in 1962, originally set up to celebrate 100 years of local European settlement, this large museum now focuses on every aspect of the kauri industry and is one of the country's top visitor attractions. It is not hard to see why.

The museum has the largest display of kauri gum including gum containing fossilised seeds, a spider and a flea trapped aeons ago as the sticky gum oozed from the tree. In the central hall is a massive slab of kauri 22.5 m in length and cut from the heart of a single tree. The collection of kauri furniture is superb, and the display of kauri panelling clearly demonstrates why this beautiful timber was so widely used. A display of machinery, both hand worked and machine driven, includes a vintage 1929 Caterpillar 60, the type of machine that replaced the bullock teams formerly used to haul logs.

And who can resist the unique collection of chainsaws.

The steam sawmill is original and on every Wednesday much of the machinery is in operation.

Matauri Bay **

The long sweep of sandy beach fronting Matauri Bay (30 km north of Kerikeri) is largely undeveloped, and the bay is now best known as the final resting place of the Greenpeace ship the *Rainbow Warrior*, sunk first by French saboteurs in Auckland harbour in 1985. A monument to the ship is on the bluff at the northern end of the bay, while the ship itself lies in the clear waters between the beach and the Cavalli Islands. The *Rainbow Warrior* is now appropriately a natural reef sheltering sea life and a very popular diving spot.

Ninety Mile Beach ***

Why this beach was named Ninety Mile Beach is a bit of a mystery as the beach is closer in length to sixty miles. If accuracy wasn't important, why not One Hundred Mile Beach? Precise distances aside, this magnificent sweeping beach has room enough for everyone. Ahipara Beach at the southern end is the most sheltered part of the beach and safest for swimming, while at the other end the giant Te Paki sand hills have become a firm favourite for sand surfing.

The beach is drivable for a few hours both sides of low tide, but only for the experienced. Check your insurance first.

The annual Snapper Classic fishing competition is held on the beach in February each year for the heaviest snapper caught by surf casting off the beach. It is the biggest and most lucrative fishing competition of its type in New Zealand, attracting entries from all over New Zealand and Australia. Visit www. snapperclassic.co.nz

Puketi Kauri Forest ***

The forest entrance is 13 km along the Puketi Road between Okaihau and Kerikeri.

While other forests contain larger trees, this 20,000-hectare reserve gives the visitor a feel of the great kauri forests of the past. The Manginangina kauri walk is a short 10-minute board loop that passes through a stand of magnificent mature trees, while longer tracks lead much deeper into the forest.

Ruapekapeka Pa *

35 km north of Whangarei on SH1 turn right at Towai into Ruapekapeka Road. The pa site is 4 km down this road, which is unsealed and narrow in places.

This pa was the site of the final battle in the war of the north in 1845. The British, outnumbering the Maori three to one, were confounded by Kawiti's innovative defences, which unlike traditional pa featured underground bunkers and foxholes to protect the defenders from cannon and musket fire. The pa fell only when the Maori, believing the British would not attack on a Sunday, were caught off guard and were forced to abandon it. The outline of the pa is very clear and complemented by good information boards.

The pa site has great views over the surrounding countryside. Note that the carpark is a little way from the site, and the British position is not to be confused with the actual pa, the entrance of which is marked by a fine carved gateway.

Tane Mahuta and friends ***

12 km north of the Visitor Centre and five minutes' walk from the road

Situated in the Waipoua Forest, Tane Mahuta is the world's tallest kauri tree. Named after Tane, the god of the forest, this tree, while still impressive, was not among the giant trees both legendary and recorded in European times.

Just 1 km north of Tane Mahuta is Te Matua Ngahere, the second-tallest tree and much broader in diameter than Tane Mahuta. The girth of Te Matua is 16.5 m, Tane Mahuta 13.8 m and the largest recorded tree, a massive 32 m.

Ten minutes' walk from the Tane Mahuta carpark is the Four Sisters grove. Well worth the extra time, this grove gives the visitor a much better appreciation of the atmosphere of the kauri forest than any single tree.

Te Waimate Mission **

Te Ahu Ahu Road, Waimate North
Open November to April 10 a.m. to 5 p.m. Monday to Saturday
www.historic.org.nz
Entrance fee

Set in attractive grounds, with a broad outlook over very picturesque countryside, this simply furnished mission house was built in 1832 for the Clarke family and originally was surrounded by numerous mission buildings. The adjacent church of St John the Baptist was built in 1871.

Tutukaka Coast and the Poor Knights Islands ***

Lying northeast of Whangarei, Tutukaka is the base for trips to the Poor Knights Islands. Considered one of the top diving spots in the world, the islands are now a marine reserve and are famous for their deep clear waters, underwater caverns and rock formations. Situated between warm tropical and cooler southern currents, the waters surrounding the islands have a spectacular variety of sea life, and boat operators cater for novice snorkellers as well as experienced divers.

North of Tutukaka are the superb beaches of Matapouri, Whale Bay and Sandy Bay.

Waipu

Highland Games **
www.highlandgames.co.nz

Every New Year's Day, Waipu hosts the largest highland games in the southern hemisphere. Held annually since 1871 and attracting visitors both locally and internationally, the games feature Highland dancing, piping, drumming, tossing the caber, hammer throwing and tossing the sheaf.

The House of Memories **
Waipu is just off SH1 and the museum is easy to find in the main street.
Open daily 9.30 a.m. to 4 p.m.
www.waipumuseum.com
Entrance fee

The local museum, known as the House of Memories, commemorates the extraordinary double migration led by the charismatic religious leader Norman McLeod. Leaving Scotland and initially settling in Nova Scotia, Canada, over 900 people further migrated to Australia before finally arriving in the Waipu area in 1853. While most settled there, many families also settled in Leigh, Kauri and Whangarei Heads. The museum building also houses the Waipu Information Centre.

Waipu Caves *

13 km from SH1 — clearly sign-posted at several points between Waipu and Whangarei
(the last 5 km of the road is unsealed and narrow)

This cave system, just a short walk from the road, features limestone formations, stalactites and stalagmites, and is one of New Zealand's best glow-worm caves. A torch is essential as the caves are quite deep and it is necessary to wade through shallow water to see the glow-worms, which are about 100 m to the left from the cave entrance.

Waitangi Treaty Grounds ***

Open daily 9 a.m. to 5 p.m., closed Christmas Day
www.waitangi.net.nz
Entrance fee

While the Treaty House may not compare with grander houses elsewhere, its simple Georgian elegance and superb location give this historic site a presence not found elsewhere. Largely prefabricated in Australia, the house was originally constructed in 1833 as the family home for James Busby, who acted as a British official in the Bay of Islands.

Often described as the 'birthplace of the nation', the Treaty of Waitangi was signed here by many, but by no means all, local Maori chiefs on 6 February 1840, before it travelled around the country. Together with the superb carved meeting house and beautiful grounds, the Treaty House is not to be missed. Authentic Maori cultural shows are held in the evening.

The Treaty House is the centre of Waitangi Day celebrations, attracting large crowds to the day's events and often becoming the focus of vigorous protests over Maori issues.

Whangarei

A.H. Reed Memorial Park *

The reserve is on Whareroa Road, which is off the end of Mill Road.

Bordered by the Hatea River, this park contains several large kauri, some up to 500 years old. Named after pioneer publisher Alfred Reed, the park also contains fine stands of totara and a waterfall. The tracks are well formed, of easy grade and short.

Bream Head/Te Whara **

The track entrance is from the beach access carpark at Ocean Beach, 40 km from Whangarei and 3 km from Urquharts Bay.

Named Te Whara by Maori after Manaia's principal wife, and Bream Head by Captain Cook when he mistook tarakihi for bream, this coastal reserve contains rare flora and fauna including kiwi and kaka. The walk to the top takes around three-and-a-half hours return, and the view from the top encompasses the coastline, both north and south, the harbour and offshore islands. Partway up the track are the remains of a radar station built during the Second World War to survey shipping in the area. In June 1940 the RMS *Niagara* struck a German mine off Bream Head and although no lives were lost, a large amount of gold went down with the ship.

Ocean Beach below the head is a magnificent sweep of sand beach renowned for its surf.

Clapham Clock Museum ***

Town Basin
Open daily 9 a.m. to 5 p.m.
www.claphamsclocks.com
Entrance fee

Not interested in clocks? Think again. This incredible collection is the largest in the southern hemisphere and has over 1200 clocks on display. Begun by Archibald Clapham in 1900 and gifted to the city in 1961, the huge variety of clocks includes long case, cuckoo, mantel, alarm clocks and even wristwatches. Nineteenth-century clocks make up a significant part of the collection and many of the clocks were brought to this country by early settlers, including the intriguing 1820 Ballet Clock. Not confined to clocks, the collection also encompasses clockwork devices such as a 200-year-old dulcimer music box. The oldest dated clock is from 1720, though a clock built by a blacksmith is thought to be much older.

The museum is located in the attractive Town Basin, a collection of cafes and shops alongside the yacht-lined inner harbour.

The Fernery *
At the end of First Avenue or via Cafler Park in Water Street

Located in the heart of Whangarei, the Fernery has a collection of over 80 native ferns housed in a very attractive purpose-built conservatory (watch out for the slippery bricks). The Filmy Fern house is a light-controlled and air-conditioned room designed to provide the perfect conditions for these rare and delicate plants. Alongside the Fernery is a subtropical hothouse and a cactus house.

Mt Manaia **

From the city take Riverside Drive out towards the Whangarei Heads, and the beginning of the track is from the carpark of the Mt Manaia Club, 30 km from the city.

This distinctive mountain (460 m) is easily recognised by the numerous volcanic outcrops that define the peak. In Maori legend the rocky peaks are the figures of the rangatira Manaia, his two daughters and his wife, who were pursued by the chief from whom Manaia stole his wife. All were turned to stone by the god of thunder.

From the top the views are spectacular in all directions. Keep an eye out for kaka parrots in the bush leading up to the peak. The track is well formed and takes around two-and-a-half hours return. The historic school at the base of the mountain was established in 1858 and the pupils were originally taught in Gaelic, a reflection of the strong Scottish background of the early settlers.

Parahaki (Parihaka) Memorial *
Memorial Drive to the peak off Riverside Drive

Towering over the city, this lookout with its war memorial has extensive views over the city, harbour and far to the south and west. Several tracks lead up through bush to the lookout from the city area and all take less than an hour one way. It is a shame that such a viewpoint is so shabby and overgrown.

Smugglers Cove **
The track to the cove begins at the carpark at the very end of Urquharts Bay Road.

Not just a colourful name but an actual smugglers' hideout where crates of whisky were brought ashore and concealed at the bay to avoid Customs. This beautiful white sandy beach, overhung with pohutukawa, is only accessible by a 20-minute walk from Urquharts Bay. On Busby Head overlooking the bay is an ancient pa site, and on the headland on the harbour side are the remains of a gun emplacement built during the Second World War to protect the harbour.

Whangarei Falls *

Kiripaki Road, on the road to Tutukaka

Few cities, big or small, can boast such an appealing waterfall within the city boundaries. The falls drop 25 m into an attractive bush-lined valley, and the pools above and below the falls are ideal for swimming. There is an extensive picnic ground at the top of the falls.

Whangarei Museum and Heritage Park ***

4 km from SH1 on SH14 to Dargaville

Open daily 10 a.m. to 4 p.m.

www.whangareimuseum.co.nz

Entrance fee to museum building and kiwi house

This large and rambling complex has some real gems and is well worth the 4-km drive out from the city. As well as the Clarke Homestead and the museum, there are a kiwi house, old railway stations, a bird recovery centre, observatory, working vintage machinery, and a bush walk.

The Clarke Homestead **

The original heart of the complex, the Clarke Homestead (also called Glorat) was built in 1886 as the family home of Alexander and Mary Clarke. What makes this house unique is that it has never been restored and contains original wallpapers, carpets, wooden Venetian blinds, much of the furniture and old outbuildings. Of special interest is the frieze in the hallway inside the front door. Still vibrantly coloured, the frieze is a pattern of exotic fruit and leaves coming down the wall from the high 14-foot (over 4 m) ceilings.

Jane Mander Study **

Originally a tower on top of the family home, Pukenui, in Hatea Drive, this study is where author Jane Mander, most notable for her books *Allen Adair* and *The Story of a New Zealand River* (on which the film *The Piano* was based), did most of her writing. The Jane Mander Study now stands behind the homestead and contains a small Jane Mander display.

Oruaiti Chapel **

Now standing in the grounds of the Clarke Homestead, this is the smallest church in New Zealand at just 6 m in diameter. Built in 1861, the chapel originally had a thatched roof (later kauri shingles) and is very unusual in that it is octagonally shaped, though why it is this shape no one knows.

Woof Woof the Talking Tui ***

To the right of the museum is the Native Bird Recovery Centre, where all injured birds, native or not, are cared for and 60 per cent of the birds achieve full recovery. As well as having an excellent information display, the centre also houses a small aviary of permanently injured birds, and this is where Woof Woof lives. Wedged in a tree after falling from his nest, this tui permanently lost the use of his wings. Tui are well-known mimics but this bird has a huge repertoire of phrases all sounding exactly like his rescuer Robert Webb. While parrots have a parrot accent, Woof Woof's voice is very much a human one. And the name Woof Woof? No one is quite sure where it came from but in keeping with this bird's personality, it is a name he chose for himself. Guaranteed to delight young and old, a visit to this bird is worth the trip alone.

Women's Cells *

A must for all those *Bad Girls* fans, these two cells, built in 1900, are originally from behind the Whangarei Police Station. While there were just two cells for women, there were eight cells for men.

AUCKLAND

Albert Park ***

Princes Street, City

Up until 1840, the area now comprising Albert Park was the site of the pa Te Horotiu, then in 1845 Albert Barracks was established. During the 1860s defensive walls were constructed when settlers feared invasion from the Waikato (remains of the barrack walls can be seen in the University of Auckland grounds) and in 1879, when threat of invasion had receded, the city took over the area after the army left. Through the 1880s the city set about creating the park, which today still retains its strong Victorian flavour.

During the Second World War the park's ornamental guns were buried, as it was feared they would attract an enemy air attack, and at the same time extensive tunnels and air-raid shelters were constructed under the park. In 1977 two of the guns were uncovered and returned to the park.

Merchant Houses *

North of the main entrance to the park, along Princes Street, are a number of original Victorian houses, now owned and preserved by Auckland City Council. These houses are not open to the public.

Trees **

Albert Park has some notable trees. There are several huge specimens of Moreton Bay Fig (*Ficus macrophylla*), native to Queensland, Australia, whose massive limbs weighing many tonnes extend horizontally from the short trunk, and along Princes Street is a row of Washington palms (*Washingtonia robusta*). Near the flagpole is a single specimen of the rare tree ombu (*Phytolacca dioica*), a native of Argentina and easily recognised by the gnarled spreading root system above ground.

University Clock Tower **

Princes Street, City

The foyer is open to the public

Across from Albert Park in Princes Street is the distinctive University Clock Tower building, completed in 1926. Originally the Arts building for the university, it was designed by American-born architect Roy Lippincott, working as a junior architect for the Melbourne company of Walter Burley Griffin (designer of the Australian federal capital, Canberra). An eclectic mixture of Arts and Craft and Gothic, the building attracted criticism at the time for not being 'English' enough. There is a fine mosaic floor in the foyer.

Alberton **

100 Mt Albert Road, Mt Albert
Open Wednesday to Sunday 10.30 a.m. to 12 noon, 1 p.m to 4.30 p.m., closed Monday, Tuesday, Good Friday and Christmas Day
Entrance fee

Originally built as a farmhouse in 1863 for Allan Kerr Taylor and his wife, Sophie, and later expanded to 18 rooms, Alberton was famous for its garden parties, balls and music, and Sophie Kerr Taylor was a leading advocate of votes for women. The house contains many original features including family furniture and, in some rooms, the original nineteenth-century wallpaper.

Alexandra Park Trotting ***

Corner Greenlane and Manukau Roads, Epsom
www.alexpark.co.nz

Established in 1890, the Auckland Trotting Club has been based at Alexandra Park (then known as Potters Paddock) since 1912. In recent years major improvement of facilities has made a night at the trots a great evening's entertainment. In the restaurant Top of the Park, each table has a magnificent view over the whole race track, while at ground level picnic tables are ideal for an inexpensive summer evening out.

The highlight of the year is Carnival Week in early March culminating in the Auckland Cup (usually the second Friday in March).

All Saints Anglican Church, Howick ***

Corner Selwyn Road and Cook Street, Howick
Koha/donation

Set in a very pretty churchyard surrounded by old headstones, All Saints Church was designed by Frederick Thatcher and built at a cost of 47 pounds, 3 shillings and ninepence. It is even said that Bishop Selwyn himself helped with the actual building. The first service in this, Howick's first European building, was held on 21 November 1847 when the building consisted of only the walls and rafters.

The stained-glass window was presented by Robert McLean and dedicated on 20 December 1891, and a memorial to the children who died in the scarlet fever epidemic of 1851 can be found on the lychgate.

Auckland Art Gallery ★★★

Corner Wellesley Street and Kitchener Street, City
Open daily 10 a.m. to 5 p.m., closed Good Friday and Christmas Day
www.aucklandartgallery.govt.nz

Occupying two buildings adjacent to Albert Park, the Auckland Art Gallery has a collection of over 12,500 works including major collections of Maori, Pacific and New Zealand artists.

Designed in the French Chateau style, the main building was opened in 1887, housing the public library and municipal offices. In February 1888 the gallery was opened, which eventually took over the entire building when the new library was built across the road. Founding donor Sir George Grey presented the library and art gallery with a substantial collection of books, manuscripts and paintings, many of which are very rare. The new gallery on the other side of Lorne Street was opened in 1995 in a building previously occupied by the telephone exchange.

Auckland Domain ★★★

The main entrance to the Domain is in Park Street, Grafton.

Developed around the cone of an extinct volcano, the 75-ha park has strong Maori connections and contains two pa sites, Pukekaroa and Waikohanga. The first Maori king, Potatau Te Wherowhero, is honoured on Pukekaroa by a totara tree enclosed by a fence.

Within the park are a mixture of bush walks, playing fields, formal gardens, an eclectic collection of old statuary and new sculpture and, of course, the museum (see 'Auckland War Memorial Museum'). A couple of small paddocks hidden behind the hospital still contain cattle and are a reminder of the Domain's origin as a farm. Popular with local runners, several of the tracks have acquired curious nicknames, such as the Red Path and the Ho Chi Minh Trail. The building now housing the restaurant was created as the 'ideal New Zealand house' at the 1913–14 Great Industrial Exhibition.

The Domain hosts a wide range of annual events (www.aucklandcity.govt.nz), of which the most popular include Christmas in the Park, Symphony under the Stars and Teddy Bears Picnic.

Christmas in the Park **

Held in early December, this concert has, as the name suggests, a Christmas theme with plenty of opportunities to sing along, culminating in a fireworks display. While the concert is free, proceeds from donations go to charity.

Symphony under the Stars **

This concert in February holds the record for the largest classical music concert in the world, attracting around 200,000 people. Naturally the theme is classical music and a firm favourite, Tchaikovsky's *1812 Overture*, is complete with cannon fire supplied by the New Zealand Army.

Teddy Bears Picnic **

Who can resist the sight of thousands of young children clutching their favourite teddies and taking them on Ted's very own day out? Held in February each year, the picnic features free entertainment, storybook characters and, of course, a bouncy castle.

The Winter Gardens **

These gardens comprise two large glasshouses linked by a formal courtyard and ornamental pond. The houses were completed in 1921, but lack of funds delayed the opening of the complex until 1928. The northern 'cool' house contains temperate plants and has a continual and stunning display of flowering plants, while the southern 'hot' house contains tropical plants including the only fruiting cocoa in the country. Both houses have recently been refurbished, as has the Fernery which was established on the site of an old quarry.

Auckland Harbour Bridge ***

Affectionately known as the 'Coathanger', construction on the bridge began in 1955 and it was opened on 30 May 1959. Constructed by Dorman Long and Cleveland Bridge Engineers, the bridge opened up the area north of the Waitemata Harbour, previously only accessible by ferry or a very long road trip. With a span of 1020 m, the bridge was originally just four lanes, with another four lanes added in 1969, which were quickly nicknamed the 'Nippon Clippons', a reference to their construction by Japanese. Under the bridge, on the north side, the earthworks of Onewa pa are still discernible.

Auckland Marathon and Half Marathon **

www.aucklandmarathon.co.nz

Attracting over 5000 competitors, this is Auckland's largest marathon and has great appeal for runners and walkers as the course, beginning in Devonport, is the only event that crosses the Harbour Bridge.

Auckland Regional Council Botanic Garden **

Hill Road, Manurewa

Daylight saving hours (mid-October to mid-March) 8 a.m. to 8 p.m., non-daylight saving hours (mid-March to mid-October) 8 a.m. to 7 p.m.

www.aucklandbotanicgardens.co.nz

Opened in 1982 on 64 ha in Manurewa, the gardens may lack old-world garden charm but this is more than made up for in the fascinating range of plants not possible in confined older city gardens. The gardens are ideal for a long ramble through a diverse array of over 10,000 plants in 24 collections ranging from formal flower beds (the dahlias are incredible) and rose gardens through to the more exotic South African collection. The hanging flowering baskets in the cafe area have an appeal all of their own, and entrance to the gardens is free. The gardens also host the Ellerslie Flower Show in November each year.

Auckland War Memorial Museum ***

Auckland Domain

Open daily 10 a.m. to 5 p.m., closed Christmas Day

www.aucklandmuseum.com

Koha/donation

One of Auckland's more impressive buildings, this is both a war memorial and a museum, and houses two halls of memory listing the names of all those killed in major twentieth-century conflicts. The hill on which the museum stands is the highest point of the Domain and is known as Pukekawa, or 'hill of bitter tears', though it was also once called Observatory Hill. Opened in 1929 and later expanded, the museum holds a particularly outstanding collection of Maori and Pacific material.

Highlights include:

- The Maori court, which contains one of the finest collections of Maori art in the world including the war canoe Te-Toki-A-Taupiri, the meeting house Hotunui, the enigmatic Kaitaia carving, and a magnificent collection of korowai (cloaks).
- Scars on the Heart, a walk-through exhibition telling both the heroic and tragic stories of New Zealand's involvement in war in a way that is both personal and informative.
- The Discovery Centre, an interactive exhibition for children that never fails to be both entertaining and educational.
- Anzac Day (25 April), when the Cenotaph and consecrated ground in front of the museum is the site of the principal Auckland dawn commemoration of the landing of the Australian and New Zealand troops on Gallipoli Peninsula, attracting a crowd of over 7000.
- The celebration of Matariki, the southern New Year, in June, with special exhibitions and events.

Auckland Zoo ***

Motions Road, Western Springs
Open daily 9.30 a.m. to 5.30 p.m. (closes at 5 p.m. June to August)
www.aucklandzoo.co.nz
Entrance fee

A unique combination of zoological and botanical gardens, Auckland Zoo has over 150 different species in a variety of habitats. As with most modern zoos, animals can be seen in open enclosures rather than in cages, and the highlights of these are Pridelands, Hippo River, Sealion and Penguin Shores (with great underwater viewing of sealions), and the spider monkeys, who on their own island are a hit with both children and adults alike. The zoo runs a number of different events as well as opening on summer evenings.

Avondale Market **

Avondale Racecourse, Ash Street, Avondale

This very popular Sunday market reflects, and caters for, the wide diversity of immigrant cultures in the city. This is not a market of knick-knacks but a serious market where the locals come to do their weekend shopping and the ethnic diversity of the area is reflected in the exotic food available, from live catfish to an amazing array of Asian vegetables.

Bishopscourt **

8 St Stephens Avenue, Parnell

Designed by Frederick Thatcher and built between 1861 and 1863, these beautiful wooden buildings are grouped round a central courtyard. Originally built for Bishop Selwyn, Bishopscourt is still the residence of the Bishop of Auckland and, as such, is not open to the public.

Butterfly Creek *

Tom Pearce Drive, Auckland International Airport
Open daily 9 a.m. to 5.30 p.m. September to March, 9.30 a.m. to 5 p.m. April to August
www.butterflycreek.co.nz
Entrance fee

A favourite with children, this park combines a butterfly house, tropical aquarium (including clown fish), a seahorse tank, birds and farmyard animals. If that is not enough, there are a miniature train that runs through wetlands, the Treasure Island mini-golf course, a playground and a cafe — truly something for everyone.

Cascades Kauri Regional Park ***

The beginning of the track is at the end of Falls Road, which is off Te Henga Road between Scenic Drive and Bethells Beach.

The City of Auckland walk within this park is one of the best places in Auckland to experience the New Zealand bush. After crossing the swingbridge below the carpark, the walk follows the pretty Waitakere Stream, which is lined with tree ferns and nikau palms. A side track leads to the Cascade waterfall, which can be disappointing as the falls are almost entirely hidden within a narrow gorge. A feature of the walk is the kauri trees, including two giants that somehow survived the bushman's axe. The loop walk on the well-formed track takes about an hour.

Chinese Lantern Festival ***

Albert Park, City

www.aucklandcity.govt.nz

This increasingly popular festival in February is the last event of Chinese New Year celebrations and sees Albert Park lit by hundreds of lanterns in classical and contemporary designs. Food stalls, fireworks, fortune telling, crafts, music and dance create a lively family outing for a summer evening.

Civic Theatre **

Corner of Wellesley and Queen Streets, City

Built in less than a year, the Civic opened as a picture theatre in December 1929. The main auditorium is designed to represent an open-air theatre, with eastern arches and a twinkling star-studded ceiling, while the foyer areas are heavily decorated in exotic faux oriental style, which was internationally in vogue at the time.

During the Second World War, a nightclub in the basement level was popular with American troops on R & R in Auckland, attracted no doubt by the dancer Freda Stark who was famous for performing clad only in gold paint.

Completely restored in recent years, the Civic continues to show films and host live shows.

Coast to Coast Walkway **

Begins in Queen Elizabeth Square at the bottom of Queen Street in the city and finishes in Onehunga.

This walk, taking in many of Auckland's best-known landmarks such as Mt Eden and One Tree Hill, also includes a number of lesser-known gardens and parks such as the University of Auckland gardens. The walk is 13 km, takes about four hours, and regular bus services from Onehunga return to the city.

Cornwall Park and One Tree Hill Domain/Maungakiekie ***

The main entrance to the park is off Greenlane Road, Greenlane.

The heart of these two adjacent parks is the extinct volcano of One Tree Hill and the volcanic nature is evident with the very distinct crater to the west of the summit. Known as Maungakiekie (mountain of the kiekie, a native vine), the area was home to a substantial Maori population supported by the rich volcanic soil and terraces; kumara pits and house sites cover the higher slopes of the hill.

The tree after which One Tree Hill is named itself had a turbulent past. Originally, a totara tree (Te Totara I Ahua) stood on the summit and this was cut down in the nineteenth century by a settler, for firewood. A number of pine trees were planted, of which one survived, giving the summit its distinctive look through most of the twentieth century. This tree in turn was fatally damaged by a Maori protester and eventually felled in 2001. Maungakiekie was returned to the ownership of the local iwi Ngati Whatua in 2006.

Sir John Logan Campbell, who named the area One Tree Hill after the totara tree and donated the park to Auckland City, is buried on the summit next to the obelisk.

The park is noted for its mature trees including an avenue of oaks and the olive grove situated above the picturesque cricket ground.

Acacia Cottage *

Originally situated in Shortland Street in the city, this cottage was occupied by John Campbell and his business partner, John Brown, in 1841, and is Auckland's oldest surviving building. Moved to the park in 1920, the house is restored and contains period furniture.

Dacre Cottage/Okura Bush Walkway **

Drive north from the intersection of East Coast Bays Road and Oteha Valley Road; after 4.5 km turn right into Haigh Access Road and the track begins at the end of the road.

Built by the sea captain Ranulf Dacre in the 1850s, this cottage is unusual both in style and construction in that it was built of brick rather than wood. Restored in recent years, the cottage is only accessible on foot (or by water) along the attractive Okura Bush Walkway. The walk from Okura is about 4 hours return and the track is well formed only until about halfway when it becomes rough and muddy. (However, at low tide you can walk along the coast as an alternative to the track.) The first part of the track passes through a magnificent stand of mature bush including an impressive grove of puriri trees.

Devonport Ferry **

The ferries run at frequent intervals from the wharf in front of the Ferry Building at the bottom of Queen Street in the city. Phone Fullers Ferries, 09 367 9111.

The easiest access to Devonport from the city is by ferry and the short 15-minute trip from downtown Auckland will take you to the suburb with its Victorian atmosphere, shops and cafes. From here it is an easy walk to the volcanic cones (Mt Victoria, North Head), Cheltenham Beach (superb swimming at high tide only) and the small but fascinating Navy Museum (see 'Navy Museum').

The National Maritime Museum, across the harbour from Devonport (see 'New Zealand National Maritime Museum'), has an extensive exhibition of the history of ferries on the Waitemata Harbour.

Diwali Festival of Lights **

www.aucklandcity.govt.nz

One of the most important and ancient of Hindu festivals, Diwali (or Deepavali) has become the largest festival of Auckland's substantial Indian community. The lighting of lights and firecrackers symbolises the triumph of knowledge and wisdom over ignorance and greed. Held in the Aotea Square at the end of October (see website), this colourful festival is a celebration of food, dancing, culture and craft. And, of course, no Indian event would be complete without some Bollywood-type dancing.

Eden Gardens **

24 Omana Ave, Epsom (off Mountain Road)
Open daily 9 a.m. to 4.30 p.m.
www.edengarden.co.nz
Entrance fee

Hidden away on the eastern side of Mt Eden are Eden Gardens, a botanical haven established in 1964 in a former quarry. The gardens are reputed to have the broadest (as opposed to largest) collection of camellias, as well an extensive collection of the subtropical vireya rhododendrons, clivias and hibiscus.

Farmers Parade ***

In late November 1947, the first Farmers Santa Parade attracted a crowd of 15,000 and was led by a pipe band and the 'Farmers Girls' marching team. Begun by the founder of Farmers Trading Company, Robert Laidlaw, as a gift to the children of the city, the early parades included children from the city orphanages in buses as part of the parade. Held annually on a Sunday in late November down Queen Street in the city, the parade has been a firm favourite with each generation of Auckland's children, delighting young and old. The parade now attracts over 250,000 spectators.

Farmers Santa *

Almost as big an attraction as the Farmers Parade was the giant Farmers Santa erected each year on the facade of the Farmers Building in Hobson Street in the city with a mechanical finger that beckoned visitors to enter the store. This Santa is now installed each Christmas on the building on the corner of Queen and Victoria Streets in the city.

Glenbrook Railway **

From the Drury turnoff on the Southern Motorway, follow the signs to Waiuku and turn left into Glenbrook Station Road.

Trains operate on Sundays and most public holidays between Labour Weekend and Queen's Birthday. The gates open at 10 a.m. on those days and trains run on the hour from 11 a.m. to 4 p.m.

www.railfan.org.nz

Entrance fee

Opened in 1977, the Glenbrook Vintage Railway uses 10 km of track formerly part of the old Waiuku branch line opened in 1922 and closed in 1967. The open days feature steam train rides on a vintage steam locomotive and carriages, and especially popular with the very young are the Friends of Thomas (the Tank Engine) events.

Grafton Bridge *

Between Symonds Street and Grafton Road, City

Spanning Grafton Gully between Symonds Street and Grafton Road, this bridge, opened in 1910, was, at the time, the longest reinforced concrete arch in the southern hemisphere. At 97 m long and 43 m high, the bridge was often the place from which people leapt to their deaths — though a perspex barrier is now in place to deter jumpers.

Heroic Garden Festival ***

www.heroicgardens.org.nz

Held over two days in February each year, this garden festival features over 20 private gardens of Auckland's gay and lesbian community, most of which are open to public viewing only during this event. First held in 1997, this charity fundraiser includes a wide variety of quality gardens from all over Auckland, from tiny meticulous city apartment arrangements to subtropical park-like gardens. The festival — now considered to be the best display of New Zealand gardening styles — includes popular gardens from the past festivals together with new gardens, so there is always something fresh to see.

Highwic House **

Corner of Gillies Avenue and Mortimer Pass, Newmarket
Open Wednesday to Sunday 10.30 a.m. to 12 noon, 1 p.m. to 4.30 p.m., closed Monday, Tuesday, Good Friday and Christmas Day
Entrance fee

Highwic House is described as one of New Zealand's 'finest timber Gothic houses', with its style taken from an American pattern book popular at the time, *The Architecture of Country Houses* by AJ Downings. Like many early houses, Highwic began modestly and over the years expanded considerably; the original portion was built in 1862 and then extended in 1873. Built by Alfred and Eliza Buckland to house their 21 children, Highwic House remained in the same family until 1978.

Horse racing, Ellerslie Race Course **

Greenlane Road East, Ellerslie

www.ellerslie.co.nz

Auckland's enthusiasm for racing can be detected in the names Newmarket and Epsom given to the areas used for horse racing in the early days of the colony. The first meeting, at what then was known as Epsom Downs, took place on 5 January 1842. By 1849 racing was well established and in 1853 the Auckland Jockey Club was formed, which in turn became the Auckland Racing Club. On 25 and 26 May 1874, the Club held its first races at Ellerslie to celebrate Queen Victoria's birthday.

While a long-standing Auckland tradition is a day at the races on New Year's Day, Auckland Racing Club's glamour event is the three-day [!] Auckland Cup Week held in March when the top horses and jockeys compete for the country's richest horse-racing prizes.

Howick Pioneer Village ***

Bells Road, Lloyd Elsmore Park, Pakuranga

Open daily 10 a.m. to 5 p.m.

www.fencible.org.nz

Entrance fee

Most historic villages tend to be a forlorn collection of old buildings dumped in the middle of nowhere and with no particular purpose. Howick Pioneer Village is the exception as it has very cleverly focused on a theme, the Fencible settlement. Fencibles were soldier/settlers who had served in the British army and who, in return for military duties, were given land by the government as part of their pension. Panmure, Onehunga and Otahuhu were all Fencible settlements strategically placed to protect Auckland from attack from Maori in the Waikato, and invasion by the French who were active in the Pacific at that time.

Howick Pioneer Village is an extensive and very well presented collection of original buildings covering a period from 1840 to 1888, from the very modest raupo hut to the much grander home. Live days are held monthly, each with a unique theme, and are particularly popular. Check the website for details.

There are over 30 buildings including: an early sod cottage used as temporary accommodation on arrival; Puhinui, the largest house in the village, built in 1861; and Bell House, built in 1850/51 near Pakuranga Creek and moved to its present site in 1885. Bell House was the nucleus around which the village was originally established and now functions as a restaurant.

Hulme Court *

350 Parnell Road, Parnell
Not open to the public

Built in 1843 in the Regency style, this is reputed to be Auckland's oldest building on its original site. Later purchased by Colonel Hulme after whom the house is named, it was used as Government House during the 1850s and was also at one time the home of Bishop Selwyn. The bluestone walls have since been plastered over, but the hipped slate roof is original.

Hunua Falls **

From Hunua Village drive north and then turn right into White Road. After 1 km, turn right into Falls Road and the carpark is another 2 km.

Especially impressive after heavy rain, these 28-m falls flow over hard basalt rock, the rim of an ancient volcano. There is a good picnic ground here and the pool at the base of the falls is a popular swimming spot. A short walk over the bridge leads to another viewpoint and to the Cossey Reservoir Walk, a three-hour loop via the reservoir and Cosseys Gorge.

Kaipara Harbour **

Around 1350 AD, after first landing at Kawhia, the waka *Tainui* voyaged north and entered Kaipara Harbour, beginning a long settlement of Maori in the area. In 1772 French explorer Marion du Fresne discovered the entrance but did not enter the harbour and it wasn't until 1836 that the first ships safely negotiated the bar. The entrance to the harbour is wild, with constantly shifting sandbars, an enormous shift in water volume with each tide and a narrow entrance. The harbour was an important waterway, though, with inlets and rivers reaching far inland, and wrecked numerous ships, despite the building of the lighthouse at Pouto on the North Head. While kauri was king, the Kaipara flourished, but after the timber was exhausted the harbour declined into a quiet backwater and in 1947 was closed as a port of entry.

Aucklanders tend to dismiss this huge harbour as a dirty, shallow windswept expanse of water, and certainly, from the land, the harbour appears very tidal and not easily accessible. However, the way to appreciate the harbour is from the sea, and it is from the sea that this great bay gives up it secrets. Kaipara Cruises offers trips on the harbour ranging from a three-hour trip out of Helensville to a three-day cruise that explores the northern reaches of the harbour, and a day trip crosses the harbour from Shelly Beach near Helensville to Pouto on the North Head. Visit www.helensville.co.nz/kewpie_cruises

Karekare Beach ***

Karekare Road, off Piha Road, Waitakere

This is the quintessential west coast beach with towering bush-clad cliffs framing a wild stretch of foaming surf. Made internationally famous as a location for the film *The Piano*, the beach is also the start of a number of popular walking tracks to the north and south. The black sand is coloured by the high iron content from the volcanic rock and this makes it very hot underfoot on a sunny summer's day.

Like all beaches in the area, the surf is very dangerous and all care should be taken when swimming and fishing. Karekare Beach Races are held each year in February, though the date varies to match low tide.

Kelly Tarlton's Antarctic Encounter and Underwater World ***

Tamaki Drive, Orakei
Open daily 9 a.m. to 6 p.m.
www.kellytarltons.co.nz
Entrance fee

Deservedly one of Auckland's and New Zealand's leading tourist attractions, this was the first walk-through tunnel aquarium in the world and the brainchild of adventurer-diver Kelly Tarlton. Substantially expanded and upgraded in recent years, Kelly Tarlton's now includes the Antarctic Encounter featuring gentoo and king penguins. It is one of only three places in the world that breed penguins in captivity, and gentoo penguin chicks can be seen in November and December and king penguin chicks in early March.

The main tank contains over 1500 fish and 60 species including three species of shark, some up to 2 m in length. Other highlights include gigantic crayfish, piranhas, turtles and stingrays. Try and coincide your visit with the feeding times — early afternoon is best.

Not to be missed is the feeding time at Stingray Bay, a giant 350,000-litre open-topped tank that is 2.6 m at its deepest point and constructed of clear acrylic for optimum viewing. This is a great opportunity to get up close and personal with these magnificent and personable animals, the largest of which is over 250 kg (and all still have their stings).

Kumeu Show **

Kumeu Showgrounds, Access Road, Kumeu
www.kumeushowgrounds.co.nz/kumeushow

Held in the second week in March, the Kumeu Show is very much a case of town come to country. Retaining all the traditional aspects of a country agricultural fair, the show has competitions for the best sheep, pigs, goats, horses, poultry and cattle as well as alpacas and llamas. Highland dancing, shearing and wood-chopping events add to the fun along with over 500 trade stalls catering for all tastes, city and country.

Mangere Mountain **

Main entrance at end of Domain Road off Coronation Road, Mangere Bridge

One of the largest and least modified of Auckland's 50 volcanic cones, Mangere is a quiet haven compared to the better-known volcanoes. The rich volcanic soils sustained a large Maori population in pre-European times, growing kumara and taro, with easy access to seafood in Manukau Harbour. Maori land boundaries indicated by low stone walls fan out from the base of the mountain, and kumara pits and house sites are clearly visible inside the crater. Nearby, good examples of lava flows can be seen in Kiwi Esplanade and lava caves in Ambury Park.

Melanesian Mission *

44 Tamaki Drive, Mission Bay

The short-lived Melanesian Mission began life in 1859 with the arrival of 38 Melanesian students on the ship *Southern Cross*. However, after an outbreak of dysentery which killed 14 students, the mission shifted to Norfolk Island in 1864. Of all the mission buildings only the distinctive dining hall, with its volcanic stone walls and shingle roof, remains and appropriately now operates as a restaurant.

MOTAT — Museum of Transport and Technology ***

Great North Road, Western Springs

Open daily 10 a.m. to 5 p.m., closed Christmas Day

www.motat.org.nz

Entrance fee

Considerably improved over the last few years, this museum, first opened in 1964, has an amazing collection of unique machines and vehicles in two parts: MOTAT 1 is the main collection, while MOTAT 2, about 1.5 km away, houses the aviation, railway and military collections.

The heart of the museum is the old pumphouse, which provided water from the nearby Western Springs (now a park behind MOTAT) for a young Auckland City, pumping water to reservoirs in Ponsonby and Khyber Pass. The magnificent Beam pumping engines have been restored to working order and are a sight to see in action on live days (check website for details).

The small aviation exhibition at MOTAT 1 has a replica of Richard Pearse's 1903 aeroplane, and a fascinating display on the enigmatic aviatrix Jean Batten. MOTAT 2 (Motions Road or catch the tram) is worth visiting for its Avro Lancaster Bomber and the world's only Solent Mark IV Flying Boat, and on live days the Rail section is particularly popular.

In addition to an extensive tram collection, MOTAT also runs tram trips on a 1.1-km line from the entrance to the zoo, and among its large vehicle collection is the world's first chilled beer tanker.

Mt Eden/Maungawhau ***

The vehicle entry is off Mt Eden Road, Mt Eden.

One of the most popular viewpoints in Auckland, Mt Eden, or Maungawhau (mountain of the whau tree), is a perfectly formed cone with a very distinctive crater. Apihai Te Kawau included Maungawhau in the 3000 acres he gifted to the Crown to establish the settlement of Auckland. As on so many of Auckland's volcanoes, the evidence of terraces, house sites and kumara pits is very clear. The top becomes very crowded with cars and tour buses, at times, so walking up is often the more pleasant option.

Muriwai gannet colony **

The walkway (30 minutes return) is at the end of Motutara Road, Muriwai.

It will come as a surprise to most people that this gannet colony has been established only in recent times. Early in the twentieth century gannets began establishing nesting sites on Oaia Island, which lies 1.5 km offshore, and then on Motutara Island. In 1979 they established themselves on Otakamiro Point on the mainland. Now, each year from August to April, over 1200 pairs nest here and the proximity of the nesting birds gives the public easy and close access. Fur seals can also be seen on Oaia Island.

Navy Museum ***

Spring Street, Devonport (500 m from the ferry terminal)
Open daily 10 a.m. to 4.30 p.m., closed Good Friday, Christmas Day, Boxing Day

This small museum alongside the naval base at Devonport and established in 1841 is crammed full of great stuff, and though a little hard to find, is well worth the effort, with many highlights.

One display details one of New Zealand's finest naval moments when, in 1939, at the Battle of the River Plate, four ships including two New Zealand ships, the *Achilles* and the *Ajax*, forced the commander of the *Graf Spee* to scuttle his ship outside Montevideo, Uruguay. The deck plate of the *Achilles* is on display.

Nicknamed the 'Lucky Ship', HMS *New Zealand* is reputed to be the only Allied ship to have operated continually throughout the entire First World War. This is attributed to a Maori blessing placed on the ship and honoured by the captain, who wore a piupiu as a cloak into battle. Even though the ship took a direct hit at the Battle of Jutland, the shell failed to explode, and the piece of metal torn from the ship is on display. After the Battle of Scapa Flow, HMS *New Zealand* collided with a ship of the same class, HMS *Australian*. Just which ship caused the collision remains undetermined, but HMS *Australian* needed serious repairs while the *New Zealand* sailed away virtually unscathed.

Just inside the door are two items of special interest. The first is a wooden rum barrel, as, up to 28 February 1990, a daily ration of rum was issued to sailors on New Zealand ships. The second item on the wall is a long fork, looking much like King Neptune's trident but with five prongs. Known as a fizzgig, this implement was used to spear salted meat out of barrels, and was standard issue on New Zealand naval ships until 1956.

New Zealand Fashion Week **

www.nzfashionweek.com

Since 2000, Fashion Week has gone from an industry trade show to an extravaganza of international and local interest in New Zealand's fashion designers. The success of the show is indicative of the meteoric rise of a distinct New Zealand style as local designers move confidently in the tough international market, with Australia as the key market taking over 70 per cent of New Zealand's apparel exports. In the past confined to those in the industry, the week attracted so much interest that the show now features 'Best of Fashion Week' for the general public, focusing on fashion for the coming summer season.

New Zealand National Maritime Museum **

Viaduct Basin, Quay Street, City
Open daily 9 a.m. to 6 p.m. October to April, 9 a.m. to 5 p.m. May to September
www.nzmaritime.org.nz
Entrance fee

Situated on the waterfront in downtown Auckland, this museum houses four themed collections relating to New Zealand's maritime history.

Highlights include:
- A unique collection of small craft and yachts, and in particular KZ1, which stands outside the entrance to the museum.
- The Hawaiki collection of canoes from throughout Polynesia, which focuses on the incredible early Polynesian exploration of the Pacific.
- The Rocking Cabin display, which gives the visitor the unique opportunity of experiencing life aboard an immigrant ship in the 1850s.
- The anchor from the infamous HMS *Bounty* of mutiny fame.
- A wide collection of model ships, as well as the original builder's model of the *Dominion Monarch*. Builder's models were constructed to show the board members what they were getting for their money and were the feature of many shipping company boardrooms.

North Head Historic Reserve ***

Main entrance at end of Takarunga Road, Cheltenham

Formed by an eruption 50,000 years ago, this area attracted Maori with its rich volcanic soil and easy access to seafood, and Maunguika (North Head) was one of three cone pa in the area with the main pa at Takarunga (Mt Victoria).

A pilot station was established as early as 1836, but it wasn't until 1885, with the threat of a Russian attack, that the government constructed three batteries to protect the approaches to Auckland. Most of the tunnels and underground rooms visible today were built at this time, as were the two oldest buildings on the summit, a small stone kitchen and army barracks.

The disappearing gun still intact on the South Battery was one of three placed on North Head in 1886 and is one of the few left in the world. The guns retracted underground after firing, to be reloaded undercover and out of sight of the enemy.

For many years rumours circulated that the tunnels between North Head and Mt Victoria contained the dismantled original Boeing One, though no evidence has yet been found.

Onehunga Blockhouse **

Jellicoe Park, Corner Quadrant Road and Grey Street, Onehunga

This brick blockhouse built in 1860 was one of ten small forts designed to protect Auckland from attacks from the Waikato. Situated on a strategic high point on what was then called Green Hill, the Onehunga Blockhouse has a wide view to the south, as an attack was most likely to come from that direction. A careful inspection of the brick walls reveals a single vertical brick and regular spaces in the exterior walls. These were originally the loopholes from which the muskets were fired.

Subsequently used as the Council Chambers and a school, the building is well preserved and the feature of the very pleasant Jellicoe Park. Two other buildings are now also on the site: Laishley House, built in 1856, was originally situated at 44 Princes Street, Onehunga; and a Fencible house, built in 1859, recognises Onehunga as a Fencible settlement.

Parnell Pool **

Judges Bay Road, Parnell

Originally a tidal swimming pool enclosed by a rock wall, the Parnell Pool is Auckland's only saltwater pool. The building was awarded a Gold Medal in 1858 by the New Zealand Institute of Architects and still features the stylish stone and glass mosaic that graced the front of the building. For some unknown reason the pool is 60 m long, which doesn't match the usual swimming pool lengths of 25, 33 or 50 m. This is a great place for the serious swimmer and for family fun.

Pasifika ***

Western Springs Park, Great North Road, Western Springs

www.aucklandcity.govt.nz

First held in 1993, the Pasifika festival now attracts over 250,000 people and is a major celebration of Pacific Island culture. Groups from all over the Pacific, but in particular those from Samoa, Tonga, Niue, the Cook Islands and the Tokelaus, compete in music and dancing competitions, provide Pacific-influenced food and drink, and sell traditional and contemporary artwork and crafts. The largest festival of its type in the South Pacific, Pasifika is held in March each year.

Piha **

A wild beach with dangerous rips and currents, Piha is also one of New Zealand's top surf beaches. Although board riding was not introduced until 1956 by two Californian lifeguards, a surf life saving club had been long established at the beach. Such is the reputation for rough surf that in 1950 an Australian life saving team, after a competition at Piha, vowed never to compete at the beach again, and to date no Australia team has returned.

In the middle of the beach is the distinctive Lion Rock, and in the bush behind the beach are a number of popular walks including the Nikau Grove and Kitekite Falls walks.

Puhoi **

1 km off SH1 north of Waiwera

In 1863 a small group of settlers from villages near Pilsen in Bohemia settled along the Puhoi River north of Auckland. With help from local Maori, who supported the settlers through their first year, the number of Bohemians eventually numbered around 200 by 1881, and the area still retains a strong Bohemian flavour. A small museum has been set up in the old convent school (the settlers were Roman Catholic), and the church of St Peter and St Paul built in1881, has stained-glass windows featuring local family names such as Schollum, Rauner, Schischka, Wenzlick, Bayer and Straka. The historic Puhoi Pub is a firm local favourite, as is the Puhoi Valley Cheese Factory 3 km up the road from the village. The popular Kiwi slang saying 'Up the boohai', meaning the back of beyond, is said to have been derived from 'Up the Puhoi'. The village is also a popular starting point for kayaking on the Puhoi River.

Rain Forest Express **

Jacobson's Depot, Scenic Drive, 5 km from Titirangi

www.watercare.co.nz

This popular narrow-gauge train ride travels through lush native bush, over nine bridges and through 10 tunnels to a short walk that leads to a view over the Upper Nihotapu dam, part of Auckland's water supply. The wooden Quinn's viaduct is the most substantial of the bridges, and through the tunnels glow-worms and cave weta are visible.

Rainbow's End rollercoaster **

Wiri Station Road, Manukau

Open daily 10 a.m. to 5 p.m. (to 7 p.m. during summer school holidays)

www.rainbowsend.co.nz

Entrance fee

For rollercoaster fans, Rainbow's End has New Zealand's only serious roller-coaster, The Corkscrew, featuring a double screw. For the less adventurous, there are the rollercoaster-like Dragon's Flight and Gold Rush.

Round the Bays ***

www.roundthebays.co.nz

A real Auckland institution, the run/walk was first held in 1972 and attracted 1200 entries. Held annually in early March, the event now has over 40,000 participants and thousands more join in the festivities at the finishing line.

The fun run on a flat 8.4-km course from the city to St Heliers Bay is popular with companies, both big and small, who sponsor staff to enter.

Savage Memorial Park **

Hapimana Street off Tamaki Drive, between Okahu Bay and Mission Bay

Michael Joseph Savage was elected New Zealand's first Labour Prime Minister in 1935 and his government introduced many key aspects of the welfare state. At the time of his death in 1940, over 200,000 Aucklanders lined the streets to watch the funeral procession make its way to his burial site on a bluff called Takaparawha above Tamaki Drive. The memorial consists of an obelisk, formal gardens and a reflecting pool and has wide views over the city and harbour. However, the whereabouts of his remains are a mystery. In the room under the obelisk is the original tomb but recently this was found to be empty. Further investigation has revealed another coffin beneath this tomb but it is not yet known if this in fact contains the body of Michael Joseph Savage.

Sky Tower ***

Victoria Street, City

Open daily Sunday to Thursday 8.30 a.m. to 11 p.m., Friday and Saturday to midnight

www.skytower.co.nz

Entrance fee

Despite all the controversy prior to and during construction, and whether you love it or hate it, the Sky Tower is now as much a part of the Auckland landscape as Rangitoto Island or the Harbour Bridge, and whatever your opinion on its architectural merits, there is no argument that the view from the top is spectacular.

At 328 m, the Sky Tower is the tallest building in the southern hemisphere and the twelfth tallest in the world (taller than Sydney's AMP tower!). The tower took two and a half years to build, contains over 15,000 cu m of concrete and has foundations that go down over 15 m. The mast at the top provides essential telecommunications facilities and houses the antennae for 17 radio stations. The high-speed elevators take only 40 seconds to reach the three public observation levels, all of which have 360-degree views of Auckland.

Snowplanet **

Small Road, Silverdale, off SH1, Silverdale off-ramp

Open daily Monday to Wednesday 10 a.m. to 10 p.m., Thursday and Friday 10 a.m. to 11 p.m., Saturday 9 a.m. to 11 p.m., Sunday 9 a.m. to 10 p.m. (open at 9 a.m. school holidays)

www.snowplanet.co.nz

Entrance fee

New Zealand's only indoor snow slope, Snowplanet has half a metre of real snow and three lifts all set in a chilly alpine temperature of -5 degrees. There are two slopes: a 220-m Superslope for more experienced skiers and snowboarders, and a shorter 60-m learner slope with a gentler gradient. For those who just want to watch, there is a much warmer restaurant and bar with a good view onto the slopes.

St Stephen's Chapel **

Judge Street, Parnell

Tucked away on a bluff above Judges Bay, this picturesque small chapel was built for the signing of the Constitution of the Anglican Church of New Zealand in June 1857. Designed by Fredrick Thatcher, the wooden building was used as Bishop Selwyn's semi-private chapel and today functions as a local church.

Stardome Observatory **

Manukau Road entrance to One Tree Hill Domain, Royal Oak

Opening times varying depending on the time of year, but generally open evenings Wednesday to Saturday and afternoons during the weekend, bookings essential

www.stardome.org.nz

Entrance fee

For those wanting to learn about basic astronomy, the Stardome features an all-sky 360-degree panoramic theatre with over 3500 stars, delivered by special effects projectors. The courtyard telescopes give the visitor an opportunity to see highlights of the night sky for themselves and the Zeiss telescope can be booked for the more serious sky watcher.

Stockade Hill *

Corner Ridge Road and Mellons Bay Road, Howick

A stockade was built on this hill in 1863 and was used for several months during the New Zealand Wars.

While all that remains of the stockade are ditches and earthworks, the views over the Hauraki Gulf are magnificent and well worth the short walk up the hill. A monument to the soldiers from the district now stands in the centre of the stockade.

Symonds Street Cemetery **

Symonds Street, City

Established in 1846 by the Church of England, this cemetery was the principal burial ground for the newly established Auckland. Closed in 1886, the cemetery straddles both sides of Symonds Street and when the motorway was extended, over 4100 graves were removed. The cemetery was divided into different religious denominations as was common at the time, including Presbyterian, Roman Catholic, Anglican and the distinctive Jewish section on the corner of Symonds Street and Karangahape Road.

Many notable people are buried in the cemetery including New Zealand's first Governor, Captain William Hobson, who died on 10 September 1842. His grave is located between Grafton Bridge and the on-ramp to the Southern Motorway.

Tamaki Drive ***

Linking the city with Orakei, Okahu Bay, Mission Bay, Kohimarama and St Heliers, Tamaki Drive provides some of Auckland's finest views and inner city beaches, and the 8-km road is popular with cyclists, runners and walkers as well as motorists. Often very crowded on summer weekends, Tamaki Drive has numerous pohutukawa which are a spectacular sight when flowering in early summer.

The Trevor Moss Davis Memorial Fountain at Mission Bay, built in the 1950s of Sicilian marble, becomes, in summer, a happy de facto swimming pool for the very young.

Tawhitokino Bay ***

From Kawakawa Bay, follow the coast road for 4 km to Waiti Bay.

This little-known bay is a gem on the Firth of Thames coast with a long sandy beach fringed by pohutukawa trees. It is safe for swimming in all tides and has an uninterrupted view of the Coromandel Peninsula. The walk from the carpark to the beach takes around 45 minutes over shore and headland. Plan the walking part of your trip within three hours either side of low tide via the equally pretty Tuturau Bay.

Tepid Baths **

100 Customs Street, City
Open daily Monday to Friday 6 a.m. to 9 p.m., weekends and public holidays 7 a.m. to 7 p.m.
Entrance fee

Saltwater pools until 1974, the Tepid Baths were built in 1914 and were then divided into separate 'male' and 'female' pools. The 'male' pool is now the main 25-m lap pool and the 'female' pool is a shallow pool for younger swimmers.

Although now upgraded with modern facilities, the pool still retains its distinctive Edwardian atmosphere.

V8 Supercar Championship ***

www.v8supercar.co.nz

There are Holden families and Ford families, and every year around April tens of thousands of Holden and Ford fans flock to Pukekohe for New Zealand's number one motorsport event, New Zealand's only round of the Australasian V8 Supercar Championship. Held over three days, powerful V8 cars thunder around the Pukekohe Park Raceway thrilling the crowds with petrol-charged action. However, from 2008 the race will move to a 4-km street circuit in Hamilton.

Waikumete Cemetery **

Great North Road, Glen Eden
Gates are opened at 7.30 a.m. and closed at 6 p.m. (winter) and 8.30 p.m. (summer)

Waikumete Cemetery, at over 100 ha, is the largest cemetery in New Zealand and has been the main Auckland cemetery since 1908 but was used for local burials as early as 1886. A vast rolling landscape of both new and old graves, it has some historic sections notable in their own right:

- Unidentified passengers from the 1979 Air New Zealand Erebus crash are buried in a site near the main entrance marked by a memorial.
- Mausoleums are uncommon in New Zealand cemeteries but Waikumete contains a large number of these, mainly for Dalmatian families from West Auckland, including two fine examples belonging to the Corban and Nobilo winemaking families.
- During the 1918 influenza epidemic, the dead were transported from the city to Waikumete by train and buried in a large unmarked grave now marked by a granite memorial.
- A granite slab marks the Holocaust memorial next to the Hebrew Prayer House, and buried at the base of the memorial is an urn of ashes taken from the Auschwitz Concentration Camp.

Waitakere Dam Railway **

Operates on Sundays at 10 a.m., 11.30 a.m., 1 p.m. and 2.30 p.m., bookings essential
www.waitakeretramline.org.nz

Originally built in the early 1900s to transport construction materials for the new city reservoir in the Waitakere river valley, the 2-ft-gauge tramline runs over 2.5 km through tunnels and over bridges and viaducts to the final stop just below the Waitakere Dam. The scenery includes native bush, glow-worms in a cave, and the rugged landscape of the river valley below.

Waiwera Hot Pools ***

SH1, 46 km north of Auckland
Open daily Sunday to Thursday 9 a.m. to 10 p.m., Friday and Saturday to 10.30 p.m.
www.waiwera.co.nz
Entrance fee

Long known to Maori, Waiwera (wai means water, wera means hot) was also called Te Rata, or The Doctor, in recognition of the healing nature of the water. A hotel was first built in 1875 and from that point on, Waiwera has remained a firm hot springs favourite. While there is a surface hot water spring, the modern pool complex taps water 400 m below the ground to avoid any harmful contamination with surface water.

The pool complex is extensive with something for everyone from private pools, quiet pools to soak in, through to a pool with a giant movie screen and, of course, hydroslides, which are especially fun in the dark. In addition to the hot pools, Waiwera has developed Infinity Spa, which offers a wide range of health and beauty treatments.

Wenderholm Beach ***

SH1, 1 km north of Waiwera

Combining a fine sandy beach, pohutukawa trees, an historic homestead and a bush walk, Wenderholm Regional Park, between the Puhoi and Waiwera rivers, is an ideal family destination for a day out. The open beach is backed by an extensive picnic area with large shady trees often missing from New Zealand beaches.

Wenderholm, meaning 'winter home', was an earlier name of the historic house built around 1857 and now known as Couldrey House. The house is open from 1 p.m. to 4 p.m. on Saturday and Sunday all year round and every afternoon between Boxing Day and Waitangi weekend (with a small entrance fee). Right behind the house a track leads up through a fine stand of native bush to a great viewpoint over the Hauraki Gulf. The walk to the lookout will take around 45 minutes return and around two hours for the Perimeter Track.

Whatipu ***

Take the road through Titirangi to Huia on the northern side of the Manukau Harbour and continue through Huia along a narrow unsealed road to Whatipu.

Standing on the broad windswept sands of the North Head of the Manukau, it is hard to believe that it is less than one hour's drive to downtown Auckland. The crashing surf of the wild and treacherous Manukau bar is in direct contrast to the sheltered bays just inside the harbour entrance, while the rugged volcanic bush-covered slopes of the northern shore are markedly different to the barren sand country to the south. The area was once the terminal for a tramway that ran along the coast extracting kauri from the bush inland to be shipped to Onehunga. At that time the vast sandy swamp between Whatipu and Karekare didn't exist, as this has formed only over the last hundred years. The stark rock, Paritutu, on the harbour mouth may look easy to climb, but be warned, it is very difficult to get back down again. A popular fishing spot, Whatipu is also the beginning of the Gibbons Track, a six-hour loop walk along the cliff tops, returning along the beach.

Woodhill Forest Bike Park ***

SH16, sign-posted 6 km past Kumeu

The pine-covered sand hills of Woodhill Forest are a mountain-bike heaven with scores of all-weather tracks where it is possible to ride for over six hours without repeating any of the trails. The tracks suit all levels from beginners to thrill-seekers and have great names such as Big Mama, Spaghetti (and Tortellini for variation), Cookie Trail and The Python.

HAURAKI GULF

Great Barrier Island ***

The largest and most distant island of the gulf, Great Barrier, or Aotea in Maori, is believed to be the original landing point of the first Polynesian explorers — who named the country Aotearoa, or 'land of the long white cloud', because from sea, the first indication of land is the long low cloud.

Now considered remote, in early times when travel was by sea, the island was readily accessible and has a long history of both Maori and Pakeha occupation. While it is no untouched wilderness, having been ruthlessly stripped of its timber, the island, with a population of around 1000 people, has a relaxed lifestyle, beautiful beaches and some of the best fishing in the country. The western side of the island has several excellent bush-clad harbours, while the east has great beaches. The main settlement is Tryphena in the south of the island (where the ferry terminal is) and while there is no public transport as such, in typical island style, getting around the island is easily arranged. Barrier Airlines, Mountain Air and Island Air all operate flights to the island, and Fullers (two-and-a-half hours one way) and Sealink (four-and-a-half hours one way) operate regular ferry trips there.

Beaches ***

All the good beaches are on the eastern side of the island. Medlands, the closest beach to Tryphena, is a beautiful stretch of white sand and has good surf, while Kaitoke is the longest beach on the island. Two other good beaches are Awana Bay and, in the north, Whangapoua. At the end of Whangapoua beach are the graves of some of the 130 people who lost their lives when the SS *Wairarapa* struck rocks off Miners Head in October 1894.

Fishing ***

The fishing both on and under water around Great Barrier is legendary, particularly for snapper and crayfish, and several operators based on the island provide services to suit.

Kaitoke Hot Springs *

5 km from Whangaparapara on the Whangaparapara Road

A pleasant two-hour return walk to hot springs located in a fork of a stream, the water is quite shallow and it is not easy to get a good warm soak, despite all attempts to dam the stream.

Kauri Dam Walk ★★★

The Kaiaraara track to the dam is about 5 km from Port Fitzroy.

While patches of kauri remain, the island was heavily logged from 1862 through to 1940 and the use of stringer dams to drive the huge logs down to the sea was common. Built by George Murray in 1926, this is the best-preserved kauri dam in the country and is over 9 m wide and 5 m high. The walk is about three-and-a-half hours return and can be linked to the Mt Hobson/Windy Canyon Track making it a full-day tramp.

Palmers Track to Windy Canyon and Mt Hobson/Hirakimata ★★★

Sign-posted from the summit of Whangapoua Hill on Aotea Road between Awana and Okiwi.

A spectacular walk through Windy Canyon to the summit of Mt Hobson/Hirakimata takes around two hours return to the canyon, and four hours return to the top of the mountain, which at 627 m is the highest point on the island. The volcanic nature of the area is particularly evident, with dramatic outcrops and rocky bluffs, as well as the narrow ravine of Windy Canyon itself. From the summit the view of the gulf is exceptional, though be aware that the peak is often shrouded in mist and cloud. The top of the mountain is, oddly enough, also the nesting ground of a rare seabird, the black petrel.

Kawau Island — Mansion House ★★★

Regular daily ferries operate from Sandspit to Kawau.

Open daily 10 a.m. to 3.30 p.m., closed Christmas Day

www.doc@govt.nz

Entrance fee

The original house on Kawau Island was built in 1845 for the manager of the nearby copper mine. In 1862 George Grey (Premier of New Zealand 1877–79) purchased Kawau Island for 3500 pounds and over the years greatly expanded the house, planted exotic trees and stocked the island with an array of animals including monkeys, zebras, kookaburras and wallabies. Many of the trees still exist and there is still a colony of kookaburras on the mainland. The Parma wallaby from Australia is now extinct in that country, and wallabies from the island (where they are a pest) have been shipped home. It is a pity the Australians don't want all their possums back as well.

The 20-metre chimney of the engine room at the copper mine still exists and is about an hour's return walk from Mansion House.

Little Barrier Island/Hauturu ***

Established as a wildlife reserve in 1895, this island has played a pivotal role in the preservation of some of New Zealand's most endangered wildlife. The island is largely virgin bush with only a small portion having ever been cleared. It is now completely predator-free. The forest contains hard beech, a cooler-climate tree that usually occurs much further south, and the nikau palms are a subspecies with broader leaves than their mainland counterparts. Rising to 722 m, Hauturu (meaning 'resting place of the wind') is home to over 300 plant species, birds that are extinct or close to extinction on the mainland (including saddleback, stitchbird, kaka, kakariki, kiwi, black petrel, brown teal, and kokako), 14 species of reptile including skink, gecko and tuatara, several species of weta, and both species of native bat.

Access to the island is restricted, often booked out well in advance, and landing on the island is by permit only. To apply for a permit to visit Little Barrier, phone the Department of Conservation (DoC) Warkworth area office on 09 425 7812.

Motuihe ***

This small inner-gulf island of only 179 hectares has a particularly colourful history and it is a pity that access to the island isn't easier. Long settled by Maori, it was briefly farmed by John Logan Campbell in the early 1840s and then became the quarantine station for Auckland. A small cemetery on the northern end of the island contains the graves of those who didn't make it through quarantine. During the First World War it was a prisoner-of-war camp for Germans captured in Samoa, which was, at the time, a German colony. The island's most famous prisoner was the dashing Count Felix von Luckner, who engineered a daring escape on Christmas Day and, after a long sea chase, was finally captured near the Kermadec Islands and imprisoned in Lyttelton Harbour.

A naval training base during the Second World War, some buildings remain from this period, and more recently the island is undergoing reforestation and pest clearance for its new role as a bird sanctuary. Two fine sandy beaches, one facing west and the other east, together with short walks make this an ideal swimming and picnic spot in any weather. Reubens Water Taxi provides a service from downtown Auckland to Motuihe Island (freephone 0800 111 161).

Motutapu Island *

Motutapu is in direct contrast to its near neighbour Rangitoto, from which it is separated by a mere few metres. While Rangitoto is less than 700 years old and volcanic in origin, Motutapu comprises sedimentary rock reaching back millions of years. The island has a long history of Maori occupation, and while the eruption of Rangitoto destroyed the villages at the time, it also laid down a layer of ash extremely beneficial for cultivation.

Currently the 1500-ha island is undergoing an intense replanting and predator-removal programme. There are a number of tracks over the rolling grassy hills with vistas over the gulf (there is very little native bush on the island). Motutapu is not easily accessible but there is a ferry service to Islington Bay on Rangitoto, then take a short walk across the causeway at Gardiners Gap. Home Bay on the eastern side of the island is a good swimming beach and has a wharf and basic camping ground.

Rangitoto Island ***

The largest and youngest of Auckland's volcanoes, Rangitoto erupted from the sea about 600–700 years ago and was last active only 350 years ago. The island has unusual plant life adapted to the raw lava environment, and in recent years has been cleared of exotic pests such as possums and the brush-tailed wallaby. Many of the roads, stone walls and the swimming pool were built by prison labour in the 1920s and '30s and still remain.

A number of private ferry operators run trips to Rangitoto Wharf and some to Islington Bay Wharf. Check with the Auckland Visitor Centre (phone 09 979 2333) for details of all services. Take care not to miss your ferry back, as there is no overnight accommodation on the island and alternative transport to the mainland is expensive.

Lava caves **

A side track just below the summit (20 minutes return) leads to extensive lava caves, some collapsed and some intact. It is possible to scramble through the caves, and a torch is useful.

McKenzie Bay and lighthouse ***

From the wharf the coastal track (one hour one way) through pohutukawa forest leads to Rangitoto's only sandy beach. The concrete lighthouse was first built in 1882, but it took over 20 years to sort out a dispute between the Auckland Harbour Board and the Marine Department and the lighthouse finally began operation in 1905.

Rangitoto baches **

In the 1920s and '30s Aucklanders built small holiday houses called baches on public land at Rangitoto Wharf, Islington Bay and McKenzie Bay. Most have now been removed but around 30 baches have been kept as examples of the innovative do-it-yourself beach culture of the period.

Rangitoto plant life ***

The flora of Rangitoto has had to adapt to one of the world's harshest environments of barren, dry lava fields. One such tree is the pohutukawa, and the island is home to the largest pohutukawa forest in the world, the honey of which is now internationally renowned for its medicinal properties.

Another plant is the fascinating kidney fern. Usually glossy, wet and very fragile looking, this fern shrivels up like a very dry leaf in the very hot weather, returning to normal only when there is sufficient moisture.

Rangitoto summit ***

A comfortable two-and-a-half hours return, the walk to the summit (259 m) is a steady climb on a well-formed path and leads to a magnificent view over Auckland and the Hauraki Gulf. If you decide to return via McKenzie Bay, keep an eye on the time and make sure you make the last ferry back.

Tiritiri Matangi ***

Tiritiri Matangi is both an inspirational conservation story and the country's most accessible island bird sanctuary, home to some of New Zealand's rarest birds.

Stripped of its native bush, the island was farmed from 1850 to 1970, with only a few coastal remnants remaining on this small, relatively flat island of only 230 ha. In a bold move, the Department of Conservation embarked on a programme not only to replant the island, but also to develop it as an open sanctuary with easy access for the public. Equally importantly it was decided to involve the public in tree planting, and there is hardly an Auckland school child who wasn't involved in the massive operation to plant over a quarter of a million trees between 1984 and 1994. The result has been an overwhelming success and led not only to a haven for endangered birds but also to this island being used as a model for many other such reserves around the country.

Once the predators were removed and some cover established, recovery of birdlife was spectacular and over 70 species of bird have been sighted on the island, of which 11 were relocated here. The birds include takahe, hihi, little spotted kiwi, brown teal, kokako, saddleback, bellbird and kakariki, many of which are very common on the island, especially around the bird-feeding stations.

The island has a variety of short walks and the longest walk will take three to four hours; the terrain is not particularly hilly. Recommended, and costing only a few dollars more, is the short, guided walk from the wharf to the historic lighthouse given by the ranger when arriving on the island. Hobbs Bay, a five-minute walk from the wharf, is the best swimming beach.

There are regular ferries from both downtown Auckland and nearby Sandspit (freephone 0800 888 006).

Waiheke Island **

www.waiheke.co.nz

The most populated and easily accessible of all of the gulf islands and once a haven for those looking for the good natural life, Waiheke is much more cosmopolitan these days with smart cafes and highly regarded wineries. Underneath, though, it still retains its relaxed bach-culture charm. With a population of only 8000, Waiheke is a short 30-minute ferry ride from downtown Auckland and has a good transport system so it is easy to get around.

Onetangi Beach ***

Waiheke's longest beach, Onetangi is a long stretch of pure white sand and is popular with swimmers, kayakers and surfers, but at over 2 km long it is never crowded. A yearly horse race is held on the beach in February and although quite a distance from the wharf, there is a good bus service, so it is easy to get to.

Palm Beach **

This small sandy beach on the northern coast of the island is sheltered from most winds and is particularly safe for swimming.

Stony Batter ★★★

6 km from Onetangi at the end of Man o' War Road

Taking its name from the unusual rocky outcrops formed over eight million years ago, the Second-World-War fortifications are the most extensive in the Auckland area and are a Category 1 Historic Place. While the big guns have gone, nearly everything else is intact and accessible. Stairways, tunnels, living areas and the gun emplacements cover a wide area, and underground some of the concrete looks as fresh as the day it was poured.

The views across the Hauraki Gulf to the east and south are extensive. The Batter is only a 20-minute walk from the end of the road, but getting there can be tricky as there is no public transport.

Whittaker's Musical Experience ★★

Artworks Centre, 2 Korora Road, Oneroa

Open 10 a.m. to 4 p.m. except Tuesday and Friday

www.musical-museum.org

Retired couple Lloyd and Joan Whittaker have New Zealand's largest range of musical instruments, including pianos, guitars, harps, squeeze boxes, accordions and a theatre organ dating back to 1877. In addition to playing around 30 instruments themselves, the couple also host other musicians in regular concerts. Some of the instruments date back hundreds of years and visitors can try their hand at playing them.

Wineries ★★★

In recent years a small number of very good wineries have been established on Waiheke, producing, in particular, some excellent red wines.

Goldwater Estate ★★

18 Causeway Road, Putiki Bay

www.goldwaterwine.com

The first vineyard established on Waiheke in 1978, the Goldwater vineyard on Waiheke is planted in chardonnay, merlot, cabernet sauvignon and cabernet franc.

Stonyridge Vineyard ★★★

80 Onetangi Road, Onetangi

Cellar door open daily 10 a.m. to 5 p.m., guiced tour of cellar, vineyard and olive grove in the weekends at 11.30 a.m.

www.stonyridge.com

Established in the early 1980s, Stonyridge is perhaps the mostly widely recognised label of the Waiheke vineyards, with its reds gaining international recognition. The terrace restaurant overlooking the vineyard is a great place for a long Italian lunch.

Te Motu Vineyard ★★

76 Onetangi Road, Onetangi Valley

Open daily 11 a.m. to 7 p.m.

www.temotu.co.nz

Strong on reds including cabernet merlot, this vineyard also offers whites including sparkling wine, and is open for tastings. The Shed restaurant is open for lunch and evening dining (check website for evening dining hours).

COROMANDEL

Broken Hills **

Take Morrisons Road opposite the Pauanui turnoff on SH25 and after 1 km turn left into Puketui Road and follow to the carpark at the end of this road.

Gold was discovered here in 1893 and a maze of short walks leads to a fascinating array of old mine shafts, battery sites, tunnels, and even a cave that served as the local jail. Most of the walks are less than 30 minutes, except for Water Race and Golden Hills Mine Tracks which, together, form a loop that takes around three hours to complete. This last track takes in the water race and associated tunnels, and the much longer Collins Drive, a 500-m tunnel created, not to find gold, but as a short cut through steep country. A torch is necessary for the Collins Drive and there are some great lookout points from this track as well.

Coromandel Coastal Walkway **

This one-way track can either be accessed from Fletchers Bay 27 km from Colville, or from Stony Bay 9 km north of Port Charles.

The track, well formed and medium- to easy-grade, winds through regenerating bush and has great views over the coastline at the top of the peninsula and out to Great Barrier Island. However, this track links the northern end-points of the roads of both the east and west coasts and although only three hours' walk one way, the trip by road is around 120 km (camping grounds either end). You either have to walk back the way you came or have someone take a car around to meet you. An alternative is Coromandel Discovery who will provide the transport to the beginning of the track from Coromandel town and pick you up at the other end (0800 668 175).

Coromandel Town

Coromandel Gold Stamper Battery ***

410 Buffalo Road (2 km north of the town)
Tours daily but depending on the time of year
Ph 07 866 7933
Entrance fee

Walking into this building is like stepping back in time as the battery has a timeless and hard-working feel that no modern tourist trap can duplicate. One of only three stamper batteries still working in New Zealand, this is the only battery still on its original site and the only six-headed stamper battery left in the world. Set up as a teaching facility as part of the School of Mines, the battery also acted as a public facility processing quartz for local miners, and at first was driven by water but converted to a diesel-driven operation in 1899.

In addition, there is the largest working water wheel in New Zealand and you can try your hand at panning for gold in the creek below.

Across the road is the historic Buffalo Cemetery which takes its name from the HMS *Buffalo*, whose seaman, David Wanks, was killed while loading spars in January 1838 and buried here.

Driving Creek Railway and Potteries ★★★

Driving Creek Road (3 km north of Coromandel town)
Train trips twice daily 10.15 a.m. and 2 p.m.
www.drivingcreekrailway.co.nz
Ph 07 866 8703
Entrance fee

One of the peninsula's most popular visitor attractions, this narrow-gauge railway through rugged bush is the vision of well-known potter Barry Brickell. Although Barry moved to Coromandel in 1961, he acquired the 22-ha block of land only in 1973 with the intention of replanting the land in native trees, establishing a pottery and building a railway to supply the pottery with clay and the kiln with firewood from pine trees on the property.

Over 30 years later the pottery is well established, more than 25,000 trees have been planted and 3 km of track lead up to a lookout point playfully called the Eyeful Tower which has fantastic views over the surrounding countryside.

The railway through rough country is an engineering feat in itself with bridges, tunnels, switchbacks, a double-deck viaduct and even a spiral. During the summer, and especially through January, extra trips are run, but bookings are essential.

Historic Coromandel ★★

While most of the buildings are recent historic lookalikes the town has a number of important buildings dating back to the gold-rush era. While gold was discovered just north of Coromandel by Charles Ring in 1852, it was not easy to mine and it wasn't until much later that technology for extracting it was developed, leading to a boom in Coromandel gold fields that lasted well into the twentieth century. The Information Centre has an excellent leaflet, complete with map, and includes the following important buildings.

Government Buildings and Court House ***
355 Kapanga Road

One of the few Auckland Provincial Government buildings remaining, this administration centre was built in 1873 and now houses the Information Centre.

Coromandel School of Mines Museum **
841 Rings Road

Opened as a teaching facility in 1898 and now the local museum, the school still has geological specimens in their original glass cases along with an extensive collection of historical photographs. Behind the museum is the old jail still with the scorch marks on the floor where a prisoner tried to burn his way out of jail but only succeeded in killing himself.

Ring's House **
2365 Rings Road (not open to the public)

The oldest house on the peninsula, this home was built in 1852 in the Colonial Regency style for Charles Ring who had, two years earlier, discovered gold in the area.

Old Assay House ***
2 Kapanga Road

Built in 1874 for the National Bank this attractive small building is now a commercial premises.

Keltic Fair **
www.kelticfair.co.nz

First held in 1990 as a small local event, this fair on 2 January quickly became one of the peninsula's most popular holiday events. As the name suggests, Celtic tradition is the theme of the fair and, as well as food and craft stalls, there is music all day, and even a 'pacifists battle'. The fair is located in the grounds of the Coromandel Area School.

K2 Cycle Race ***

www.arcevents.co.nz

The race takes its name partly from the 200-km length of the race and also from the township of Kuaotunu which means 'to inspire fear in young animals' which, given the rugged hilly nature of the cycle course, is aptly named.

Not strictly a Coromandel town event, the race, in October each year, begins and ends in a different town and there is a shorter 100-km event as well as the classic 200-km. Billed as New Zealand's toughest one-day cycle race and attracting over 1000 cyclists from all over the country, the course is unrelentingly hilly and not for the faint-hearted.

Seafood **

Coromandel is home to a small fishing fleet, famous green-lipped mussel farms and a popular spot for recreational fishing in the Firth of Thames. A number of outlets in Coromandel sell fresh seafood and in February host the Coromandel Flavours festival focusing on local produce including seafood of every variety.

In June the Kings of the Coromandel Fishing Tournament runs a competition for the largest kingfish with a prize of $90,000 for the biggest fish over 100 pounds. Visit www.kingsofthecoromandel.co.nz

Hahei

Cathedral Cove ***

The access road is well sign-posted from the Hahei shops but parking can be problematic during the busy holiday period.

This beautiful small beach, fringed with pohutukawa trees, is the quintessential Coromandel beach, but is becoming a bit crowded in the height of the holiday season. The two parts of the beach are linked by a sea cave (hence the name Cathedral Cove) and the coastline is now protected as part of the Te-Whanganui-A-Hei Marine Reserve. The beach access is along a well-formed track and takes around 45 minutes each way and there are toilet facilities at the beach itself.

Te Pare Historic Reserve Hahei ***

The track to the pa site begins at the end of Pa Road, or leads up from the southern end of the beach.

Location, location, location! Stronghold of Ngati Hei, who arrived in the area on the waka *Arawa* in 1350, this must be one of the most beautifully situated pa sites in the country. The broad terraces that occupy this rocky headland with the sea on three sides have the most magnificent outlook over Mercury Bay and Hahei Beach. Another pa is clearly visible on the hill behind Te Pare while the rocks below are a popular fishing spot and of course Hahei beach itself is very safe for swimming.

Hot Water Beach **

Take the Hahei/Cooks Beach turnoff 26 km south of Whitianga.

This long sandy beach is attractive in its own right, but a natural hot water spring at the southern end of the beach adds considerably to its appeal. The hot water is easy to locate on the beach just below the rocky bluff, but the crowds that pack in here make the location of the spring impossible to miss. Accessible only two hours either side of low tide, the trick is to find a spot with the right mixture of hot and cold water as the spring can be very hot in places. It is especially entertaining on an incoming tide watching as people frantically reinforce their sand barriers against the rising breakers, eventually to find their pool overwhelmed by the sea.

During the holiday season the thermal area is very crowded but the rest of the beach is relatively undeveloped, and it is easy to find a quiet spot north of the spring. There is a small lagoon ideal for the younger children, but be aware that the surf here can be treacherous and has claimed a number of lives.

Karangahake Gorge Historic Walkway ***

Following the line of the old Paeroa-to-Waihi Railway, this flat well-formed track begins at Crown Hill Road, Karangahake and ends at the Waikino Visitor Centre, a distance of around 7.5 km. The walk includes the ruins of the Victoria Battery, the Crown Hill Battery, a 1-km rail tunnel, the rail bridge over the Ohinemuri River, and of course the rugged gorge itself. A short side detour leads to the Owharoa Falls. The most popular part of the walk is the loop from the Crown Hill Battery through the rail tunnel, over the bridge and returning back to Crown Hill on the other side of the river, taking, in all, less than an hour.

This area was once a flourishing gold-mining town in the late nineteenth and early twentieth centuries with three large batteries, the Woodstock, Crown and Talisman crushing the gold-bearing quartz extracted from mines under Karangahake Mountain. The Victoria Battery at Waikino was the largest in New Zealand with 200 stampers creating a thumping sound that carried for many miles.

There are walks across the river from the Visitor Centre through the mining areas and, from the Waikino end of the track, a steam railway operates between Waikino and Waihi town.

Martha Mine Waihi *

www.marthamine.co.nz

In 1878 gold was discovered at Martha Hill behind what is now Waihi town and work quickly began on establishing a mine. By 1882 a stamper was in operation and the huge Victoria Battery at Waikino was constructed in 1897. The Cornish pumphouse (a short walk from the Waihi Information Centre) was built in 1904 and is often mistaken for the ruins of an old church. Waihi was the centre of a bitter six-month strike in 1912 which resulted in the death of miner Fred Evans, one of only two deaths during industrial disputes in New Zealand.

The Martha mine was finally closed in 1952 and by that time had produced 174,160 kg of gold and 1,193,180 kg of silver.

During the 1980s, with gold prices rising, the Martha mine was reopened, though this time as an open-cast mine and then closed again in mid-2006. There is a viewing platform on the western side of the pit and tours of the closed mine are offered (bookings essential on 07 863 9880). There are also plans to move the Cornish Pumphouse 200 metres from its present site, as it is currently in danger of collapsing into its own shaft (for details on the move visit the website and go to 'updates').

Opoutere Beach ***

The turnoff to Opoutere is 10 km north of Whangamata and the beach access a further 5 km from the turnoff.

If you are wondering what the rest of this coast was like before the baches took over, this is one of the few undeveloped beaches in Coromandel. Access is by a five-minute walk and even in the middle of summer it is not hard to find a quiet spot on this magnificent sweep of sandy beach. The Wharekawa Harbour Sandspit Wildlife Refuge is an important breeding ground for several endangered birds including the New Zealand dotterel, so leave the dog at home and stay out of the roped-off areas during the breeding season.

Opera Point and New Chums Beach **

On the road from Whitianga to Coromandel turn off at Te Rerenga to Whangapoua and the carpark is 5 km on the right just before Whangapoua settlement.

A 15-minute walk follows an old tramway leading through a nikau gully to the small but secluded New Chums Beach (you will get your feet wet at high tide). The flat area behind the beach was the site of Craig's Sawmill, established in 1862, while on the headland above is the fortified Ruakawa pa with the defence trenches clearly visible. It is a bit of a scramble up to the pa but worth the effort as the outlook over the Whangapoua Harbour to Matarangi is extensive and it is very obvious why this point was chosen as a defended site. There is an unformed but reasonably clear track that returns from the headland back along the ridge to the carpark.

Opito Bay and Otama Beach ***

From Kuaotunu take the Black Jack Road to Otama Beach (5 km) and Opito Bay (a further 3 km). Note: the road is narrow, unsealed and winding.

These two beaches are, for so many people, the total Coromandel beach experience. The first beach, Otama, is a long stretch of white sand with only a few houses at the southern end and backed by sand dunes that are now a nature reserve protecting the whole length of the beach from further development. The beach looks out over the Mercury Islands and the best access is from the northern end at the bottom of the Black Jack hill.

Opito Bay is more developed but the access along the beach is easier with several good picnic spots and toilet facilities. At the southern end of the beach is an old fortified pa site with grand views out over small offshore islands and out to the Mercury Islands beyond.

Neither beach has any shops or accommodation though there is a basic camping ground at Otama (water but no toilets).

Papa Aroha Walk *

15 km north of Coromandel on the road to Colville

Just 20 minutes return, this is a fine reserve of coastal bush especially noted for its pohutukawa, but also containing kohekohe and puriri. Alongside the track is Joe's Grave, the final resting place of an unknown sailor found on the shore nearby.

Pauanui **

Most New Zealand coastal settlements have grown from a cluster of self-built baches to busy townships in a haphazard manner and without the benefit of planning or design. Pauanui, however, was built completely from scratch in the early 1970s and, as such, has far better beach access than most New Zealand beaches, as well as excellent cycleways and footpaths. A regular ferry operates between Pauanui and Tairua, a short distance across the Tairua river estuary, but a long way by road. While parts of the town may look a bit like a Lockwood museum, the Waterways area is well known for some of the most extravagant seaside houses in the country.

Right in the centre of the town is a landing strip where light aircraft take off and land just metres above the beach. At the southern end of the beach, Mt Pauanui is a short but steep climb to the top (387 m) and the reward is fantastic views north over Pauanui and Tairua.

Rapaura Water Gardens *

586 Tapu-Coroglen Road, Tapu
Open daily 9 a.m. to 5 p.m.
www.rapaurawatergardens.co.nz
Entrance fee

Established in the early 1960s by Fritz and Josephine Loennig, these gardens are the place to come for quiet relaxation and contemplation. A well-established garden, there is a short walk that links the sculptures and water features set among mature trees and shrubs. In spring, iris, azaleas and rhododendrons are in bloom followed in summer by water lilies, hydrangeas, orchids and begonias. There is also a longer bush walk to a pretty waterfall, 'The Seven Stairs to Heaven', and in summer the cafe is open while accommodation is available all year round.

Shakespeare Cliff and Lonely Bay **

After landing at Cook's Beach (and obviously naming it after himself) in November 1769, Captain James Cook observed the transit of Mercury across the face of the sun from this point, and thereby accurately calculated his longitude and latitude position (hence the name Mercury Bay). Located between Cook's Beach and Flaxmill Bay, the headland has extensive views over the bay and a plaque commemorates Cook's visit and indicates features around the bay. Cook fancied he saw a likeness to an orator reciting Shakespeare outlined in the cliff, and named it after the bard. A steep track leads down to the quiet, pohutukawa-lined Lonely Bay, one of Coromandel's loveliest small beaches.

Square Kauri Walk **

On the Tapu-Coroglen Road 9 km from Tapu

A short 20-minute return walk leads to this huge kauri over 40 m high and more than 1000 years old, and named for the relatively square nature of the trunk.

Tairua **

www.tairua.info

Tairua began life as a timber-milling town shipping out vast quantities of kauri and other native timber from the small port on the Tairua River. Today, visitors are attracted by the fine sweep of surf beach that faces out to Slipper Island and Shoe Island and beyond them, the Aldermen Islands, well known for their excellent fishing. The views from the top of the volcanic peak Paku are dramatic and it is easy to see why this was once a major fortified pa. The Coromandel coast was discovered by Kupe around 950 AD and Maori have long settled here, originally attracted by the now extinct moa.

Thames

Butterfly and Orchid Gardens **

3.5 km north of Thames on SH25

Open daily from 10 a.m. to 4 p.m. (to 3 p.m. in winter)

www.butterfly.co.nz

Entrance fee

Over 400 butterflies from 15 to 25 species make their home in a garden of tropical shrubs and flowering plants. A butterfly has a life span of only two weeks and the garden has to continually breed up to 1000 replacement butterflies per month. The trick to enjoying the visit is to take your time, move slowly and sit for a while and wait for the butterflies to come to you. The relatively restricted opening hours coincide with the time the butterflies are most active and the warm tropical temperature of the butterfly house makes a visit here especially appealing in winter.

Historic Thames **

The largest settlement on the Coromandel, the main street of Thames, Pollen Street, still retains a facade that would be familiar to a visitor from 1900 when the town had a population of 18,000 and over 100 hotels (only four remain). Originally two settlements, Grahamstown in the north and Shortland in the south, Thames flourished in the second half of the nineteenth century in response to the gold mined both locally and on the peninsula. Given its proximity to the mines, Grahamstown dominated early Thames, but after a disastrous flood in 1917, followed by the decline of mining, the retail and service centre of the town moved further south to Shortland. Most of the historic buildings are in Grahamstown and this area contains Thames' four museums. The Information Centre has a leaflet with all the historic buildings and includes a map, ideal for a self-guided walking tour.

Thames Historical Museum *
Corner Pollen and Cochrane Streets
Open daily 1 p.m. to 4 p.m.
Entrance fee

This small museum focusing on local Thames history includes a 1928 movie projector, a collection of Brown's bicycles originally manufactured in the town, and historical items connected with A & G Price Foundry, one of New Zealand's earliest and most important engineering works.

Thames School of Mines and Mineralogical Museum ***
101 Cochrane Street
Open daily 11 a.m. to 3 p.m. (to 4 p.m. from 19 December to 26 February).
Closed Christmas Day and Good Friday
Entrance fee

A superb museum, and of the 30 mining schools established throughout New Zealand, only Thames and Reefton have survived. This complex comprises two parts, the school and the mineral collection. The school, opened in 1886 and closed in 1954, was the largest in the country and the current building has largely survived unaltered, with classrooms looking much as they would have 100 years ago. The Mineralogical Museum was opened in 1900 and has an incredible collection of minerals from both New Zealand and around the world, still in their original Edwardian glass cases.

Thames Museum of Technology *
Bella Street
Open 10 a.m. to 4 p.m.
Entrance fee

This huge pumphouse, built in 1898 for the Anglo-Continental company, was, at the time, the largest deep-level mining pump in the southern hemisphere, and reached a depth of over 300 m. In addition to photographs and a working model of the pump, the museum also displays a range of industrial artifacts.

Goldmine Experience **
Corner SH25 and Moanataiari Road
Open daily 19 December to 26 February 10 a.m. to 4 p.m., rest of the year
10 a.m. to 4 p.m. weekends only
www.goldmine-experience.co.nz
Entrance fee

Established on the famous Golden Crown mine site, the Goldmine Experience has both a working five-head stamper battery and an underground mine. Gold was discovered in the area in August 1867, in what eventually was one of the richest gold strikes in the country, producing over 2,250,000 oz of gold. The site is quite extensive and, in addition to the mine and battery, there is an audio-visual and photographic display, steam-powered machines and even a weta colony. Originally set up by ex-goldminers keen to see the gold-mining heritage of Thames preserved, the Goldmine Experience is still run by volunteers today.

Kauaeranga Valley *

An extensive network of walking tracks leads deep into the heart of the Coromandel hills from this very pretty river valley. It was timber, and not gold, that attracted Europeans to this valley behind Thames and, from 1871 through to 1928, the magnificent kauri forests were milled virtually to extinction. While the scars of the forestry era still remain, the bush has reclaimed much of the land, and the old pack tracks and tramlines now form part of the extensive track system.

Short walks include Model Dam walk (20 minutes return), Nature Walk (30 minutes return), Booms Historical Walk (30 minutes return), Murray's Walk (30 minutes return) and Billygoat Landing Walk (20 minutes return) while the popular track to the Pinnacles is an all-day tramp. Edward's Lookout (one hour return) is popular for abseiling and has views over the valley. Check with the DoC Visitor Centre at the entrance to the valley for up-to-date track and weather information.

Pohutukawa Festival *

www.pohutukawafest.com

Coromandel's official launch into summer, this festival has a range of events all over the peninsula, and is held in November and December to coincide with the flowering of New Zealand's iconic Christmas tree, the pohutukawa. The coast road from Thames to Coromandel is particularly notable for many fine old trees clinging to the cliffs and bluffs above the sea, and any suggestion to widen the narrow winding road is fiercely resisted by locals.

309 Road *

Linking Whitianga and Coromandel town, travelling along this road is a flashback to the early days of travel on the peninsula. Narrow, winding, unsealed, but not too long (42 km), the road wends its way along river valleys and twists up through the rugged Coromandel Range (summit 306 m). Not suitable for large vehicles or nervous drivers.

Just past the summit on the Coromandel side is a kauri grove that survived the bushman's axe and which gives a glimpse of the magnificent forests of the past (30-minute return walk). Half a kilometre down the road from the kauri grove are the Waiau Falls, a small waterfall in the bush with a swimming hole.

Yet further still down the Waiau valley are the fascinating Waiau Waterworks, a one-hectare garden of water-powered sculpture, a water-driven clock, a pedal-powered pump, and, unlike most gardens, this one has plenty of things to play on.

Waihi Beach — Orokawa Bay Walk ***

The track begins at the northern end of Waihi Beach and can be a little tricky to reach right on high tide.

The short 40-minute one-way walk on a well-formed track leads to an untouched white sandy beach with a backdrop of old pohutukawa trees. Just inland from the beach a track leads to the 25-m William Wright Falls, and a further hour north of Orokawa is the even more secluded Homunga Bay. The track to both bays traverses rocky headlands with great views along the coast and out to Mayor Island. For those not wanting to walk, Waihi Beach is an 8-km stretch of sand that goes all the way to Bowentown Heads, the northern entrance to Tauranga harbour.

Waitewheta Tramway Walk *

Turn right into Waitawheta Road 12 km east of Paeroa off SH2 and follow the rather tortuous road signs to the carpark at the end of Franklin Road.

Following an old logging tramway used to extract kauri, this track has a gentle gradient but there are numerous river crossings, the bridges long since gone though the piles still remain. The track leads through a spectacular river gorge with rocky bush-clad bluffs, and near the beginning of the track there are some great swimming holes. The whole track can take up to seven hours return, but as it is a return track the walk can be as long or as short as required.

Wentworth Falls Walk **

Wentworth Valley Road is off SH25, 2 km south of Whangamata.

Dropping down a 50-m rocky bluff Wentworth Falls are reached by an hour one-way walk through attractive native bush. There is a viewing platform overlooking the falls, and a tricky narrow track to the swimming hole at the bottom of the falls. The track continues beyond the platform to a viewpoint at the top of the waterfall.

Whangamata ***

Few beaches can compare to the magnificent sweep of Whangamata's main ocean beach. One of New Zealand's best and most reliable surf beaches, Whangamata has always attracted a large and young crowd over the summer and for those aged between 16 and 24 at least one short summer holiday should be spent at this beach resort. Those in authority have for years tried to suppress the enthusiasms of youth, but each New Year's Eve at Whangamata demonstrates that the spirit of New Zealand hoonism is alive and well and will not be beaten.

While Whangamata is the Coromandel's busiest and most boisterous resort, the beach is extensive, and for those wanting a quieter experience the southern end, around the point from the main beach, will provide just that.

Whangamata Beach Hop **

www.beachhop.co.nz

In a few short years this has quickly become New Zealand's premier Rock 'n Roll festival celebrating the best of the '50s and '60s. Attracting up to 40,000 people, the heart of the Hop is the grand parade of over 1000 classic cars and hot rods taking to the streets of Whangamata. In addition to the cars, there are Rock 'n' Roll bands, dance competitions and all that hair cream and dressing up that makes Rock 'n' Roll such a fun era.

Whitianga Scallop Festival *

www.scallopfestival.co.nz

Whitianga, on the broad sheltered Mercury Bay, is a major port base for both recreational and professional fishers alike. The recently established Scallop Festival has been a big success, not only focusing on scallops (over 35,000 consumed at the 2005 festival) but all the best seafood and local produce the area can offer, along with entertainment, scallop-opening competitions and a seafood auction. Held in August, away from the busy summer season, the festival has an uncrowded, relaxed and friendly atmosphere.

Maori meeting house, Waitangi

Whangarei Heads

Auckland's Round The Bays Fun Run and Walk

Sky Tower, Auckland

The field thunders for home at Ellerslie during Auckland Cup Week

Whangamata Beach Hop

Driving Creek Railway, Coromandel

Ngaruawahia Regatta

Italian Renaissance Garden, Hamilton Gardens

White Island, New Zealand's only active marine volcano

Waimangu Valley, Rotorua

Wainui Beach, Gisborne

Rere Falls, Poverty Bay

New Zealand's oldest prison, Napier

Sarjeant Gallery, Wanganui

New Zealand's last paddle steamer PS *Waimarie* on the Whanganui River

WAIKATO

Cambridge *

www.cambridge.co.nz

Promoting itself as the town of trees and champions, Cambridge is indeed tree-lined and surrounded by notable horse stud farms. Famous horses from the Cambridge area include Sir Tristram, Zabeel and Empire Rose. Trees define Cambridge, and a leaflet of a walking tour of trees is available from the information office.

Armistice in Cambridge *

Unusually Cambridge celebrates Armistice Day as well as the more traditional Anzac Day. The armistice marked the end of the First World War and was signed on the eleventh hour of the eleventh day of the eleventh month of 1918. The town's two-day celebration attracts over 10,000 people and features a wide range of activities including battle re-enactments and one of the largest shows of military vehicles in the country. Cambridge has built a special relationship with the small French town of Les Quesnoy, which was liberated by New Zealand troops at the very end of the First World War.

New Zealand Horse Magic **

Cambridge Thoroughbred Lodge, SH1 Karapiro, 6 km south of Cambridge
Open daily 10 a.m. to 3 p.m.
Phone 07 827 8118
www.cambridgethoroughbredlodge.co.nz

This lodge offers an excellent and friendly introduction to the New Zealand thoroughbred industry. The lodge has 13 different breeds of horse including Lipizzaner, miniature, Kaimanawa and draught horses. The lodge is home to Rough Habit, New Zealand's richest horse with winnings of over $5.2 million, that yet, as a yearling, was considered to have no potential and sold for a mere $1700. These attractive working stables can hold up to 200 horses and the best time to visit is around February/March when visitors have the opportunity to get up close to the horses and foals. Depending on numbers, the lodge holds regular horse shows but it pays to check ahead for these.

The main gate is often shut, but don't be put off; it is closed to keep the horses in, so please close the gate behind you.

Hamilton

Agricultural Field Days ***

www.fieldays.co.nz
Entrance fee

In June each year Mystery Creek, just south of Hamilton, is host to the largest agricultural field days in the southern hemisphere. Packed with displays of every kind of merchandise and information relating to every type of agriculture, this is no mere 'show and tell'. Serious business is conducted here, as well as showcasing new ideas, innovations and inventions. On a lighter side there are sheepdog trials, tractor racing, wood-chopping competitions, motorcross and much more to keep the crowds entertained. Even for those who have no connection with agriculture, a day out here is informative and enjoyable. The field days attract large crowds, making traffic and accommodation problematic, so it pays to plan ahead.

Balloons Over Waikato **

www.balloonsoverwaikato.co.nz

Attracting balloonists from New Zealand and around the world, and over 100,000 spectators, this is the country's leading hot-air balloon festival. Fantastically shaped balloons of all types rise just after sunrise and travel round the region. The Night Glow event with the balloons lit up at night is especially appealing. The festival is held in April each year on Innes Common just to the west of the central city.

The Church of Jesus Christ of the Latter-day Saints (Mormon Temple) *

www.mormon.org

Situated to the west of Hamilton is the largest Mormon church in the southern hemisphere. Particularly prominent at night when the church is floodlit, the area is also famous locally for its Christmas lights. Tours are available from the Visitor Centre.

Hamilton Gardens ***

The gardens are located on SH1 on the eastern side of the river.
Most of the gardens are open all year round. The central theme gardens are open 7.30 a.m. to 6.30 p.m. in the winter and to 8 p.m. in the summer. The Victorian

Flower Garden Display house is open daily 10 a.m. to 4 p.m.
www.hamiltongardens.co.nz

These 50-ha gardens are Hamilton's 'must see' attraction. Superbly situated on the banks of the Waikato River, they are not merely a collection of plants, but focus on plant use, both practical and recreational. The gardens are extensive so, if time is short, the first stop is the Paradise gardens representing major historical garden styles: Japanese Garden of Contemplation, American Modernist Garden, English Flower Garden, Italian Renaissance Garden, Indian Char Bagh Garden, and the Chinese Scholars Garden. Nearby are the kitchen and herb gardens. The rose gardens are particularly extensive, well laid out in rose types and are the trial gardens for new breeds prior to general release.

The gardens hold many special events throughout the year, especially in summer (see the website for details).

It's Astounding! Riff Raff Statue **

Victoria Street, 100 m north of the museum

Richard O'Brien, creator of *The Rocky Horror Picture Show*, worked as a barber on the ground floor of the Embassy Theatre in Hamilton from 1959 to 1964. The inspiration for the show came in part from the B-grade movies and double features shown in the theatre at the time. The theatre, one of Hamilton's oldest, has now been pulled down and the statue of Riff Raff stands in a small square on the site of the theatre.

Waikato Museum of Art and History *

Corner Grantham and Victoria Streets
Open daily 10 a.m. to 4.30 p.m., closed Christmas Day and Boxing Day
www.waikatomuseum.org.nz
Koha/donation

This modern museum is attractively situated on the bank of the river and prides itself on changing exhibitions rather than static displays. The whare waka (canoe house) is outstanding. This large gallery overlooking the river houses the historic Tainui waka *Te Winika*, and on the surrounding walls and roof is a very fine collection of carvings and woven panels.

The museum has a small but comprehensive collection of contemporary art and every year in August hosts one of New Zealand's leading art awards, The Trust Waikato National Contemporary Art Award Exhibition.

Waipa Delta Paddle Boat *

Memorial Park off Memorial Drive (use Bridge Street for best access to Memorial Drive)

www.waipadelta.co.nz

Paddle steamers were not unusual on nineteenth-century New Zealand rivers and shallow waterways. The original paddle steamer, the *Waipa*, was launched on the Waikato in 1876 and later changed its name to the *Delta*. The *Waipa Delta*, built in 1985, is a replica of this early steamer and is a great way to see the Waikato River. For details of sailings, see the website.

About 200 m north of the *Waipa Delta* dock and awaiting restoration is the hulk of the gunboat *Rangiriri*, which patrolled the Waikato River in the 1860s during the New Zealand Wars.

GALWAY COUNTY LIBRARIES

Waikato River *

After years of ignoring the river, the city has, in recent years, realised what an attractive asset it has running through the heart of the city. Now extensive walkways run along the banks of the river, particularly on the western city side. An appealing walk starts at the road/rail bridge in the centre of the city, and heads south along the river bank to the older Victoria Street bridge. After crossing this bridge, turn left into Memorial Park with its formal gardens, war memorial, aviary, children's playground, band rotunda, *Waipa Delta*, hulk of the *Rangiriri*, and Harvard aeroplane. This eventually leads back to the first bridge.

The walk takes less than an hour, and a short stretch, just before the end, is along streets, as not all of the river bank is accessible to the public.

Huntly — Waikato Coalfields Museum *

26 Harlock Place

Open daily 10 a.m. to 4 p.m., closed Good Friday, Christmas Day, Boxing Day, New Year's Day

www.coal.net.nz

Entrance fee

This small but comprehensive museum is housed in the local mine manager's house originally built in 1890 for William Tattley of the Taupiri Coal Mine. One of the few industrial museums in the country, its displays include an extensive collection of photographs, a recreated mine tunnel, and the interior rooms of a typical miner's cottage of the 1930s.

Kawhia ***

This large tidal harbour has a long and important Maori history beginning with the arrival of two important waka, *Tainui* and *Aotea*. The harbour was named by Turi, the captain of the *Aotea*. Now a quiet backwater that is as yet unspoilt by modern development, Kawhia has a relaxed, unhurried atmosphere that is in direct contrast to busy Raglan to the north and a world away from the east coast beaches such as Whangamata and Ohope Beach.

Kai Fest **

This annual festival of Maori food and culture is held in Omimiti Park on the weekend closest to Waitangi Day and attracts over 10,000 people. As well as traditional food such as hangi, puha, paua, kanga wai and mussels, there are also Maori craft, art, kapahaka and music.

Racing whale boats ***

In the small museum in the same building as the Information Office is a racing whale boat built of kauri in the 1880s, the only craft of its kind in New Zealand. Longer and narrower than actual whale boats, these were popular racing boats in the nineteenth century. Now, on New Year's Day, crews from communities around the harbour race replicas of whale boats, competing for the appropriately named Whale Boat Racing Cup, in the only race of this type in the country.

Sacred pohutukawa tree **

Just along the beach from the marae, this tree, Tangi Te Korowhiti, marks the spot where the Tainui waka tied up. The tree is tapu and should be treated with respect.

Tainui waka **

Kawhia is the final resting place of the Tainui waka, which is behind the historic Anaukitirangi marae, marked by two stones one at either end of the waka and over 20 m apart. Hoturoa, the captain of the *Tainui*, is featured on the tekoteko (the figure at the top of the front gable) of the meeting house.

Te Puia Springs hot water beach *

Accessible for two hours either side of low tide are hot water springs that are situated directly out from the main track to the beach from the carpark. This beach is exposed to the westerly wind so bring a substantial digging tool to make a protective wall around your very own hot pool in the sand.

Lake Karapiro *

www.lakekarapiro.co.nz

Located just 8 km west of Cambridge, this lake was created by the construction of the Karapiro Dam in 1947 and has become one of New Zealand's leading freshwater sports venues. While an attractive picnic and swimming venue in its own right, Lake Karapiro hosts top-rated water-based events virtually every weekend through the summer, including rowing, powerboat racing, waka ama, waterskiing, dragon boat racing and canoeing.

Madonna Falls *

25 km south of Te Kuiti on SH4

New Zealand has very few roadside shrines but these sacred falls known as Whaea o te Rere are an exception. A special contraption has been set up making it easier to collect the water which is said to have healing powers.

Matamata

Firth Tower Estate Museum **

Tower Road 4 km east of Matamata

Open daily 10 a.m. to 4 p.m.

www.matamata-info.co.nz/firthtower

Entrance fee

Josiah Clifton Firth liked towers and they were highly fashionable in the late nineteenth century. His house on the slopes of Mt Eden featured a substantial tower and on his 10,000-ha Matamata Estate he decided to build a tower in the innovative building material, concrete. Essentially a massive folly, the tower has the appearance of a defensive fortification, with walls 46 cm thick and loopholes for rifles. In fact the area faced no military threat when the tower was begun in 1880. The 20-m tower offers good views over the local countryside.

The museum is very well presented and has excellent displays of local history, both in the tower and in the other historical buildings moved onto the site.

Hobbiton *

Daily guided tours only
www.hobbitontours.com

With the international success of Peter Jackson's *The Lord of the Rings*, Matamata is one of the very few places where the sets have survived. A nearby farm was the location of Hobbiton in the film and the landowner now conducts tours of what little remains of the set. These are daily guided tours only and take approximately two hours. Tours can be booked at either the Matamata Information Centre or direct.

Mercer *

Tucked away in what is left of Mercer's shabby main street is the gun turret of the HMS *Pioneer*, a gunboat used by British forces against Maori in the New Zealand Wars of the early 1860s. The vessel was built in 1863 and wrecked on the Manukau bar in 1866. The turret, complete with gun loopholes, is all that is left of the gunboat and is now a war memorial.

Miranda Shorebird Centre ***

283 East Coast Road, Miranda, Firth of Thames
www.miranda-shorebird.org.nz

Miranda on the coast of the Firth of Thames is recognised by the Ramsar Convention as a wetland of international significance. Each year thousands of birds from the Arctic tundra, as well as New Zealand breeding shorebirds, converge on these rich tidal feeding grounds. At high tide, the birds are found on the shell banks and at low tide, out feeding on the mudflats.

There are wading birds all year round, but large flocks of bar-tailed godwits (7000–10,000) arrive about September — having flown 11,000 km from Siberia non-stop — and stay through to March. Other common birds are wrybill plover, New Zealand dotterel, variable oystercatcher, black-billed gull, pied stilt, curlew and sharp-tailed sandpiper, red-necked stint, eastern curlew, banded dotterel and ruddy turnstone.

Mokau and whitebaiting **

Mokau River is one of the most prolific whitebaiting rivers on the west coast of the North Island. The young of the smelt family, whitebait come to the river between mid-August and mid-November, and with the fish come the whitebaiters to their favourite places along the river, with their time-honoured fishing techniques. Most famously, whitebait is made into fritters.

The river was once an important link inland for both Maori and Pakeha. River trips can still be made on the *Cygnet* (visit www.mokaurivercruises.co.nz), a small vessel originally built to collect cream from upriver farms and take the cans to the dairy factory right by the river. The factory, long since closed, still exists.

Mokau is the home of the author June Opie, whose book *Over My Dead Body*, telling of her battle with polio, sold over 100,000 copies in New Zealand and became an international bestseller. There is a June Opie display at the local Tainui Museum (open daily 10 a.m. to 4 p.m.).

Opposite the museum in the middle of the main street is a German mine found in the area in December 1942, though why the Germans wanted to mine the Mokau River mouth is anyone's guess. Quite possibly something was lost in translation.

Mt Pirongia **

The track begins at the carpark at the end of Corcoran Road, which is off Te Pahu Road.

Dominating the skyline of the western Waikato is the extinct volcanic cone of Mt Pirongia (959 m). A stronghold of the wily Patupaiarehe (fairy people), this mountain is surprisingly rugged, and the original bush is an unusual mixture of cooler- and warmer-climate plants. The track to the summit is a slog, but a good alternative is the much easier walk to Ruapane and Tirohanga, not much lower than the peak. From the carpark the track is a gradual climb, some of it through fine taraire forest. Not far from Ruapane the track becomes steeper before arriving at the well-defined rocky outcrop giving fantastic views back over the lush Waikato. Beyond Ruapane the track leads to another rocky outcrop, called Tirohanga, with even better views. About three hours return.

Ngaruawahia

Ngaruawahia Regatta **

Turangawaewae marae, River Road

Entrance fee

Held on the Saturday nearest St Patrick's Day (figure that one out!) at the Turangawaewae marae at Ngaruawahia, this is a great opportunity to experience Maori culture first hand. The highlight of the day is the waka racing on the river, which includes waka hurdling and the famous 'Chase the bride' race. Local and visiting kapahaka groups perform on a barge anchored in the river throughout the day, and Maori food and craft are readily available. Delicious watermelon is at its best and ideal for what is usually a very hot day. There is no access to the marae complex for visitors.

Turangawaewae marae ***

River Road

Not open to the public

The official home of the Maori King, this beautifully carved complex was created from a gorse-covered wasteland in the 1930s by the energetic and charismatic Princess Te Puea. The marae is not open to the public.

Otorohanga Kiwi House Native Bird Park **

Well sign-posted from the main road, the park is situated in Alex Telfer Drive.

Open daily 9 a.m. to 4.30 p.m., closed Christmas Day

www.kiwihouse.org.nz

Entrance fee

One of the earliest and largest breeding programmes for kiwi, this native bird park is still one of the best places to see kiwi. The park prides itself on rotating several pairs of kiwi each day so the visitor is guaranteed to see these nocturnal birds on the move. Set in attractive native bush, the park has a wide range of other native birds as well as tuatara and geckos.

Paeroa

The Big Lemon and Paeroa Bottle **

In the beginning was the Big Bottle, long before the Big Carrot, the Big Crayfish, or the Big Trout. Just to be confusing, Paeroa now has two big bottles, but the original bottle erected in 1969 is on the southern end of the town by the Ohinemuru River bridge.

Lemon and Paeroa, more commonly just L&P, was created in 1904 using water from a local spring and was originally known by the reverse name Paeroa and Lemon. The promotional phrase 'World famous in New Zealand since ages ago' has now become part of everyday New Zealand language.

Battle of the Streets *

Entrance fee

Originally conceived by locals wanting to put Paeroa on the map, this race held in February each year is now one of New Zealand's leading motorcycle races and attracts thousands of people. The local streets are turned into the famous 'Hacksaw' circuit and thunder to the sound of the country's most powerful motorbikes. Contact the Paeroa Promotions Trust for more information: 07 862 8000.

Pureora Forest ***

The Barryville Road turnoff is 56 km from Te Kuiti and 20 km from Mangakino on SH30. The Visitor Centre is a further 3 km down Barryville Road.

This magnificent forest was saved from the axe by protesters who, in 1978, perched themselves on platforms in the trees. Logging was finally halted in the early 1980s and the area is currently a mixture of forest park and commercial forest, giving some interesting contrasts between pristine native bush and clear-felled pine forest. It is also worth noting that the roads in the forest are a combination of forestry and narrow metalled roads, some little better than tracks and rough in parts.

Buried Forest *

The turnoff to the Buried Forest is 2 km from the Visitor Centre on the Barryville Road.

The Taupo eruption over 1800 years ago flattened and buried the forest existing at the time under ash. Part of this forest was accidentally uncovered in the 1970s and the ancient logs can be seen along this short track. Though this is not exactly riveting viewing, the logs are only a short detour off the road and not too much out of the way.

Centre of the North Island *

2 km on from the track to Mt Pureora, turn right into Waimanoa Road. The entrance to the track is a further 3 km along this road.

A short track leads to a plaque marking the geographical centre of the North Island, set among attractive bush. An added bonus is a gigantic rimu tree right next to the plaque.

Mapara Scenic Reserve **

Travel 26 km south of Te Kuiti on SH4 and turn left into Kopaki Road. The reserve is off Mapara South Road, which is 2 km down Kopaki Road.

One of the last strongholds of the rare kokako, this reserve is the most accessible for those who want to hear or see this elusive attractive bird whose song is so distinct.

The track in the reserve leads through the territories of several birds so the chance of hearing these birds is very high but you will need to be very patient to actually see one. The best chance is two hours after dawn, so you just have to get up early, especially in summer. Allow around one hour for the loop track, lots more if you are a serious birdwatcher.

Mt Pureora **

From the Visitor Centre turn right into Link Road. Travel a further 10 km and look out for a carpark on the left-hand side of the road. The Link Track to the top is opposite the carpark.

While not a distinct peak, the round peak of Mt Pureora at over 1100 m has amazing views over the central North Island including Lake Taupo.

The Link Track is gradual and well formed and takes around two-and-a-half hours return. Leading up through beautiful forest, much of it moss- and lichen-covered like some hobgoblin forest, the vegetation close to the summit suddenly turns subalpine and includes tussock. In bad weather the summit can be very exposed.

Poukani — the biggest totara tree in the whole wide world! **

The entrance to the track is 10 km from the Barryville Road turnoff towards Mangakino.

Called Poukani, this giant tree, over 42 m tall, is very impressive and ought to attract more visitors than it does. The second- and third-largest totara trees are in nearby Pureora Forest. The walk to the tree takes about one hour return.

Totara Walk **

The beginning of the walk is just 200 m from the Visitor Centre.

The short flat walk takes less than 30 minutes but contains some magnificent trees such as totara, maire, rimu and tawa. The height of some of these trees has to be seen to be believed — they are huge.

Putaruru Timber Museum *

SH1, 2 km south of Putaruru
Open daily 9 a.m. to 4 p.m.
Phone 07 883 7621
Entrance fee

In such a country originally abundant with timber, the early logging industry made a massive contribution to the development of colonial New Zealand. This is the only museum wholly dedicated to the timber industry and is on the site of the original Tuck and Watkins sawmill, while right next door was the pine nursery established in 1926 for New Zealand Perpetual Forests. The original timber mill is now the main museum building. The displays are extensive, covering every aspect of timber and related industries and include an impressive collection of chainsaws, a wood-chopping display and a display of local wildlife. The items are not that well labelled and, clearly, the museum could do with a good injection of cash, but for those interested in industrial heritage, well worth the stop.

Raglan and surfing ***

www.raglan.net.nz, www.raglansurf.co.nz

Situated on the wild coast 50 km west of Hamilton, Raglan is known worldwide for its left-hand breaks. In reality there are four surfing areas — Wainui Beach, Manu Bay, Whale Bay, and the Indicators — of which Manu and Whale produce the best left-hand breaks. Raglan is also very reliable, with good waves most of the time and is therefore host to a number of national and international surf competitions. Serious surfers should visit www.raglansurf.co.nz

The township has good cafes, and nearby Mt Karioi and Bridal Veil Falls are popular local attractions.

Rangiriri battle site **

SH1, 1 km north of Rangiriri township

The invasion of the Waikato began in October 1863, and initially the Maori heavily fortified their defences at Meremere, which included cannon (but no cannonballs). The British decided that a full attack on Meremere would meet with high casualties and bypassed the pa using water transport. The Maori abandoned Meremere and re-established themselves at Rangiriri.

On 20 November, 1500 British troops attacked Rangiriri including bombarding it from gunboats on the river. However, the Maori defences held and British casualties on the first day (over 130) far outnumbered the defenders'. In confused negotiations on the second day, General Cameron took the pa and the Maori defenders moved south. The final battle of this campaign was at Orakau, east of Kihikihi.

Rangiriri Cemetery *

The cemetery is in the nearby Rangiriri township and contains the graves, neatly laid out in rows, of the soldiers killed storming the pa. The officers, however, were buried in the Symonds Street cemetery in Auckland. The Maori dead were buried in a mass grave but later removed.

Taupiri Mountain **

Taupiri is the sacred mountain of the Tainui people and on the lower slopes of the mountain are the main burial grounds of the iwi. There is a track to the top of the 288-m peak and the views are fantastic, especially on a clear winter's day when snow-covered Mt Ruapehu is clearly visible. The beginning of the track is to the left of the small marae, which is accessed by the metal road on the north side of the bridge. Use the carpark by the river, as the carpark by the marae is for the marae only. Needless to say, the track is steep and rough in parts, but well worth the effort, taking at most one-and-a-half hours return.

Te Aroha **

www.tearoha-info.co.nz

Once a flourishing spa town, Te Aroha has in recent years successfully renovated its Edwardian Domain. Modern hot pools (open 10 a.m. to 10 p.m.) with family appeal complement the historic buildings including the 1898 Cadman Bath House, which now houses the local museum, and the renovated No. 2 Bath House. Restored tearooms and boarding houses complete the picture. The 'Day in the Domain' festival is held each year in March.

Mokena soda spring geyser *

At the back of the Domain is the only hot soda water geyser in the world. Erupting every 40 minutes to a height of around 4 m, the soda water is reputed to have medicinal values.

Mt Te Aroha *

The track to the top of the mountain begins at the rear of the Domain by the Mokena geyser and is approximately two-and-a-half hours one way.

The views from the top of the 952-m mountain are spectacular over both sides of the Kaimai Range. The track is well marked but does require a reasonable degree of fitness.

Wairere Falls **

The track to the falls starts at the end of Goodwin Road off Te Aroha-Okauia Road about 20 km south of the town.

Set in attractive native bush, these spectacular falls drop in two stages over the Okauia Fault. The walk to the lower lookout takes around 45 minutes and to the top of the falls a further 45 minutes. In very strong westerly weather the water is blown forcibly upwards at the top of the falls.

Te Awamutu Museum ***

135 Roche Street
Open Monday to Friday 10 a.m. to 4 p.m., weekends and public holidays 10 a.m. to 1 p.m.
www.tamuseum.org.nz
Koha/donation

This small but professionally curated museum has two outstanding exhibits. The first is the highly unusual and incredibly stylish carving of Uenuku, a god who appears as a rainbow and whose spirit was brought to this country on the Tainui canoe in the form of a stone. Believed to have been carved around 1400, Uenuku is distinctly eastern Polynesian in style and is a very rare carving from this period. A great taonga (treasure) of the Tainui people, the Uenuku carving has an exceptionally powerful life force and should be treated with the utmost respect.

The second is the Finn exhibition. Te Awamutu is the home of Tim and Neil Finn, legendary New Zealand musicians of Split Enz and Crowded House fame. While the exhibit is a little thin on material, it is still worth a visit.

Te Kuiti — Tokanganui-a-noho meeting house **

Southern end of Rora Street
Not open to the public

This magnificent carved building is one of the most important meeting houses of Ngati Maniapoto. Built in 1873 using carvers from the Bay of Plenty, it was presented to the local people by Te Kooti in recognition of the sanctuary given to him and his followers.

Waitomo

Collectively known as the Waitomo Caves, this area in fact has three separate cave systems open to the public — the Glow-worm Caves, Aranui, and Ruakuri — as well as a number of other attractions in this fascinating limestone country.

For the more adventurous, several companies offer exciting options both below and above ground, including blackwater rafting, abseiling and guided caving.

Aranui Caves **

www.waitomocaves.co.nz
Open daily 9 a.m. to 5 p.m.
Entrance fee

These are located 3 km west of the Glow-worm Caves. The formations here are more spectacular although without glow-worms, with multi-coloured stalactites, some of which are huge (one is 6 m long and estimated to weigh 2.5 tonnes). Formations include the Butcher Shop, Aladdin's Cave, the Temple of Peace, and Cathedral Majestic.

The Glow-worm Caves ★★★

www.waitomocaves.co.nz
Open daily 9 a.m. to 5 p.m.
Entrance fee

The best known and most spectacular (and the most crowded) are the Glow-worm Caves. The tour begins with a walk through a number of limestone formations including the Cathedral, the Banquet Chamber, the Pipe Organ, and the Catacombs. However, the highlight of the trip is a silent boat journey through the amazing glow-worm grotto lit only by thousands of tiny pinpricks of light. The glow-worm is the laval stage of the tiny insect *Arachnocampa luminosa*, which gives off light to attract food. While glow-worms are common throughout New Zealand, it is here that the combination of glow-worms in such great numbers and the boat trip in the dark makes Waitomo such a special place.

Mangapohue natural bridge ★★

26 km from Waitomo on Te Anga Road

Just a short distance from the road (10 minutes) are two natural arches one on top of the other, cut through limestone by the Mangapohue Stream. The walk to the arches is through an attractive gorge, which at night has glow-worms. A torch is necessary if a night walk is planned.

Marakopa Falls ★★

31 km from Waitomo on Te Anga Road

The Marakopa River cascades 30 m creating a spectacular waterfall. Only a short 15-minute walk from the road, this waterfall together with the Mangapohue natural bridge, which is on the same road, is worth the detour.

Ruakuri ★★

www.ruakuri.co.nz
Open daily, closed Christmas Day
Entrance fee

Ruakuri, meaning 'den of wild dogs', was first discovered by Maori 400–500 years ago. Reopened in 2005, this cave has 1.5 km of twisting limestone passageways, hidden waterfalls and fascinating cave formations.

Ruakuri Walkway ★★★

2 km from the Waitomo Glow-worm Caves next to the entry to Aranui Cave

The short 30-minute walk along the Waitomo River is crammed with fantastic limestone outcrops, caves, and a huge natural tunnel. The unspoilt bush features luxurious growth, in particular ferns, mosses and lichens. The area has glow-worms at night but don't forget your torch. The track is well formed and clear even if the signage is a bit confusing. If you do nothing else in this area, make sure you include this walk in your itinerary.

BAY OF PLENTY

Maketu *

Maketu is the original landing place of the Arawa waka, and is still today part of Arawa territory of Ngati Whakaue. From the hill, the views are extensive looking to the north over the lagoon and beaches as far as Mt Maunganui. The historic Maketu marae, with its superb carved house Whakaue, was built in 1928 and lies alongside the lagoon. Maketu is also home to the famous Maketu Pie, of which the smoked fish pie is one of the most popular choices.

Mayor Island ***

This unique island is well worth the two-and-a-half-hour boat trip from Mt Maunganui. In pre-European times the island supported a significant Maori population which traded in obsidian, a rare volcanic glass that was a highly valued commodity in a stone-age culture. Several major pa sites are still visible. With the coming of iron tools the island population fell substantially, and as the island was unsuitable for farming it has been virtually untouched for over 200 years. The island is an extinct volcano and the distinct crater has two small lakes, making it reminiscent of a James Bond movie set. Indeed at one stage the New Zealand Navy considered digging a short canal to one of the lakes to build a secret offshore harbour. The crater also contains a superb pohutukawa forest, and recent clearance of pests has led to a recovery of native birdlife including bellbirds. Regular boat trips run to the island in summer (www.blueoceancharters.co.nz).

Mt Maunganui ***

Sand, sun, surf and sophistication, 'the Mount' is as close as New Zealand gets to a beach resort. Situated on a peninsula, the Mount is bounded on the east by one of New Zealand's best surf beaches, to the west by a sheltered harbour, and to the north by the magnificent dormant volcano Mauao.

The surf beach is one of the country's best and host to numerous sports events, including surfing, beach volleyball and surf life saving, and, while the main beach can get a bit busy in summer, it is not hard to find a quieter spot on the extensive sands stretching towards Papamoa and beyond. Pilot Bay on the harbour side is a sandy, sheltered beach more suited to families with small children. It is also the base of New Zealand's most popular Half Ironman competition held every year in early January.

The legend of Mauao (meaning trapped by the dawn) is a moving story of a mountain determined to drown himself rather than gaze forever on his lost love, who instead found himself trapped by the dawn's light on the edge of the sea (and in case you have forgotten, mountains can only move at night).

There is a 3-km walk around the base of the Mount and numerous tracks up to the 232-m summit.

And when the outdoor activities get too much, at the foot of the Mount are hot saltwater pools, catering for both energetic youngsters and those wanting to relax.

Ohiwa Oyster Farm *

111 Wainui Road, 1 km south of Ohope

Established in 1967 as part of a government initiative to encourage aquaculture, this farm is the most southern fishery to grow Pacific oysters. The main beds can be viewed from the road and a small shop sells both raw and cooked oysters.

Ohope Beach and Ohiwa Harbour *

Ohope Beach, just over the hill from Whakatane, has over 11 km of superb sandy surf beach, though in recent years it has lost its small seaside village charm and now has the feel of a very large retirement village. Nearby Ohiwa Harbour is very tidal, with over 70 per cent of the seabed exposed at low tide, and is one of the most important refuges for wading and migratory birds including the godwit, which flies non-stop from the Arctic each spring. There are reserves for birdwatching on both sides of the harbour entrance.

Opotiki

Hiona St Stephens Church ***
Church Street

The church is not always open and a key can be obtained from either the museum across the road or the church op shop next door.

Throughout the 1860s Maori resistance to the pressures of European settlement grew, and many backed the new religious and political movement Hauhauism, led by charismatic leader Te Kooti. The Reverend Volkner, a missionary based at Hiona, regularly reported to the authorities the movement of Hauhau in the area and was, not surprisingly, regarded by Maori as a government spy. After visiting Auckland, Volkner insisted on returning to the area despite warnings that he was in danger. In March 1865 he was killed by Hauhau in the church in a very grisly manner. However, Maori versions contend that Volkner was hanged as a government spy and that the manner of his death was much exaggerated by settlers keen to have government troops stationed in the district.

In reaction to Volkner's death, the government sent forces to the Opotiki area, where fighting continued off and on until the final surrender of Te Kooti at Waiotahi in 1889. Volkner is buried at the back of the church.

Hukutaia Domain/Burial Tree **

From the town, turn left into Woodlands Road just over the Waioeka River bridge and the reserve is 7 km down the road.

This small reserve of low rainforest was established in 1918 primarily to protect Taketakerau, an ancient puriri tree. The tree was used by the local Upokorehe hapu to conceal the bones of the notable dead from desecration by enemies, though after the tree was damaged the remains were buried elsewhere. Thought to be over 2000 years old, this huge tree is highly tapu.

From 1933 to 1970 local amateur botanist Norman Potts travelled throughout New Zealand to gather plants and thereby created one of the most extensive collections of native trees and shrubs in the country. His work was continued by Marc Heginbotham from 1970 to 1990.

The Motu Challenge **

www.motuchallenge.co.nz

Recognised as one of New Zealand's leading multi-sport events, the Motu Challenge is a demanding race through native-bush-covered hills and valleys and down the Waioeka River. Attracting almost 1000 entrants, the race is in four stages: 65-km mountain bike, 17-km run, 52-km cycle racing, and finally a 27-km kayak, 8-km road cycle and 3-km race to the finish. Held in October each year, the race begins and ends in Opotiki.

Swim with the dolphins ***

The unpolluted waters of the East Coast of New Zealand offer the unique opportunity of viewing and swimming with these magnificent, intelligent and friendly sea mammals. Whales are also frequent visitors to this coast. Tour operators out of Whakatane and the Mount offer a wide range of tours including snorkelling and diving as well as swimming with the dolphins.

Tauranga

The Elms Mission House ***
Mission Street

Open Wednesday, Saturday, Sunday, public holidays 2 p.m. to 4 p.m.

www.theelms.org.nz

Entrance fee

Superbly sited on a bluff above the harbour, the Mission House was built in 1847 and is regarded as New Zealand's finest Georgian building. Unlike other missions, which were prefabricated elsewhere, this house was built of kauri on the Te Papa site. The house is virtually unaltered, including the beautiful curved staircase to the dormer bedrooms. The house contains some of the original furniture including a 'campaign' table from the 1820s, which is designed to come apart and be transported from place to place.

What also makes this mission special is that many of the mission outbuildings are still on site. The tiny freestanding library built in 1839 was the first permanent building at Te Papa mission, and still contains 1000 of the original books. Easily missed in the extensive grounds are the belfry dating from 1843 and a fencible cottage originally from Onehunga.

The entrance to the mission is from behind the house, although the most attractive view of the house is from the other side. The mission building has very short opening hours, which is unfortunate for this is a particularly attractive historic place. The grounds are open all the time.

Historic Village *
17th Avenue West

Previously the ill-fated Tauranga Museum, this village is a curious mixture of replica and original buildings that hasn't quite yet found its new purpose. Part retail, part community centre and part museum, it nevertheless contains some worthwhile gems. To the right of the 'village' church is a collection of original headstones from a military cemetery of soldiers who died in the New Zealand Wars of the 1860s. The church itself was built by the chief Taiaho Ngatai, who was converted to Christianity by Anglican missionaries and had this chapel built on tribal land at Matapihi. Near the church is historic Okorore, a house built in 1844 by John Faulkner and originally in Beach Road.

Montana Jazz Festival **
The Strand

Whoa! Where did that come from? Within a few short years The Strand on Tauranga's waterfront has been transformed into one of the best cafe strips in New Zealand. Over 30 restaurants pack in side by side offering every sort of cuisine, and live music creates a buzz that competes with Ponsonby Road, Oxford Terrace or Courtenay Place. Throw in a warm summer's evening and there is no better place to be.

The Strand and other central streets are closed off to traffic for the annual jazz and blues festival, attracting thousands of people to Tauranga with top blues and jazz acts. Held on the Saturday and Sunday of Easter, this is New Zealand's longest-running jazz festival.

Whakatane

Fishing **

The Eastern Bay of Plenty is famed for superb fishing in uncrowded waters. While the range of fish to be caught is wide, including snapper, kingfish, terakihi, trevally and marlin, the area is particularly notable for catches of yellow-fin tuna which run from early December through to April (though this is unpredictable).

Numerous boat operators in the area cater for all levels of experience for fishing and diving, and the One Base Tuna Tournament held in January attracts a large field of contestants (www.wsfc.co.nz).

Nga Tapuwae O Toi Track **
The Whakatane entrance to the track can be accessed by a set of concrete steps behind Pohaturoa Rock.

This 18-km circular track links Whakatane with Ohope Beach. The most popular part of the walkway, though, is the Kohi Point Track which follows the coastline from Whakatane to Ohope and takes around three hours one way. A short side trip leads to the ancient pa site Kapu-te-rangi established by the early Polynesian navigator Toi around 900 years ago, and is believed to be one of the oldest pa sites in the country though very little remains. Taumata

Kahawai pa on Kohi Point is much more impressive and Otarawairere Bay is a great place for a swim and a picnic, though at high tide the track between Kohi Point and the bay is impassable, so check the tide times first.

Toi's Challenge is a popular but demanding race held in November on the walkway and can be completed as a run or walk either as an individual or a two-person team.

River Walk **

Toroa, the captain of the famous waka *Mataatua*, was given instructions by his father Irakawa before leaving Hawaiki to look for three distinct landmarks that would mark the place to settle. These landmarks are still visible 800 years later within the central business area of Whakatane and linked by a walk. Maps are available from the Information Centre by the river.

The first landmark is Muriwai's Cave (partially collapsed) where Irakawa's daughter lived. It was highly tapu until 1963, when the tapu was lifted. The second is Wairere Falls, and while not so spectacular it is nonetheless attractive as a waterfall right in the middle of town. And finally, Pohaturoa Rock contains a highly tapu cave where tohunga performed sacred ceremonies.

Wairaka Statue *

The first settler in the area, arriving over 1000 years ago, was Tiwakawaka, a grandson of Maui, the legendary explorer and discoverer of Aotearoa. Further settlers arrived later with the famed voyager Toi, who established himself at Kapu-te-rangi above Whakatane, which is one of the oldest pa sites in the country. Two hundred years later the waka *Mataatua*, captained by Toroa, arrived and moored in the estuary of the river. The men climbed up to Kapu-te-rangi, leaving the women and children behind on the *Mataatua*. A swift outgoing tide put the waka in danger of being carried out to sea but, in a breach of tradition, Toroa's daughter Wairaka saved the day by picking up a paddle and exclaiming 'E! Kia Whakatane au i ahau' (let me act like a man), and, with the other women, brought the waka back to safety.

This action is the origin of the name of both the river and the town, and a statue commemorating Wairaka overlooks the entrance to the river.

Whirinaki Forest **

Famed for huge trees, rare birdlife and pristine waterways, the 55,000-ha Whirinaki Forest lies between the wild and mysterious Urewera National Park and the pine trees of Kaingaroa, the largest planted forest in the world. In the 1980s Whirinaki, like Pureora, was a major conservation battleground with the forest finally being saved from the axe, but leaving side by side the oddly contrasting landscapes of untouched native bush and commercial pine forests. Matai, kahikatea, miro, totara and rimu grow to a magnificent size in the forest, and support such birdlife as kaka, kereru and the endangered whio, or blue duck.

There are a number of short walks near Minginui, but for a full appreciation of the forest the longer walks along the Whirinaki River are recommended. The forest is also popular with hunters after red deer and wild pigs.

White Island ***

White Island is one of New Zealand's most active volcanoes and New Zealand's only marine volcano, with approximately one third of the mountain above sea level. The volcano is unusual in that the water in the crater is derived from rainwater and condensed steam, as the volcano is actually sealed from the surrounding sea water, with the vent below sea level. The steam from the crater is sometimes visible from the mainland depending on the level of water in the lake.

Known to Maori as Whakaari (to be made visible) and named White by Captain Cook in 1769, it was purchased by a Danish sea captain, Philip Tapsell, in the late 1830s. In 1913 a Canadian company, The White Island Sulphur Co. of Vancouver, set up on the island to extract sulphur, but this ended in disaster in 1914 when a lahar killed all the men working there and destroyed the buildings. The ruins visible today are the remains of a factory built in 1923 and closed in 1933.

White Island is one of the world's most accessible marine volcanoes, and a boat tour to the island includes a two-hour walk right inside the crater, where visitors are issued with a hard hat and a gas mask. Eruptions are frequent on the island, the last major one in 2000, although the volcano is unlikely to erupt without warning and no eruptions have occurred while visitors have been on the island. Visit www.whiteisland.co.nz for more information.

There is also the option of taking a helicopter to the island, locally or from Rotorua.

White Island diving **

A combination of the warm Auckland current and the proximity of the volcano makes the waters around White Island several degrees warmer than the surrounding ocean. This attracts a wide variety of species of fish, including subtropical species only found much further north, and in huge numbers to this one location. Diving is amongst an aquatic volcanic landscape and, in addition, the water's clarity allows for visibility up to 30 m, making this a great spot to go diving (www.divewhite.co.nz).

Whitewater rafting ***

The eastern Bay of Plenty is well known for some of the finest whitewater rafting in New Zealand through unspoilt scenery on the Rangitaiki, Wairoa, Kaituna and Motu rivers. The Rangitaiki River has three sections of difficulty, suiting the beginner through to the more adventurous. For the very keen looking for excitement, the untamed Motu River will hold a great appeal, offering trips from one to four days. Visit www.wetnwildrafting.co.nz for more information.

ROTORUA

Agrodome **

Western Road, Ngongotaha

From the city centre, take SH5 towards Hamilton, at 9.5 km turn right into Western Road and the Agrodome is 500 m on the right.

Open daily 8.30 a.m. to 5 p.m., sheep shows 9.30 a.m., 11 a.m., 2.30 p.m.

www.agrodome.co.nz

Entrance fee

While the complex is part of a 160-ha sheep and cattle farm, it is the sheep show for which the Agrodome is justifiably famous. This humorous and informative performance includes 19 breeds of sheep, sheep shearing, working dogs and lamb feeding. What makes this show more appealing is that the showmen are local farmers who take time from their farms to run the show and have a natural Kiwi approach to their audience.

Opening the business in 1971, Godfrey Bowen (world-famous sheep shearer) and George Harford, a local farmer, were joined in 1972 by Godfrey's brother Ivan, who was five times the world champion sheep shearer.

Adjoining the farm is the Adventure Park, which includes bungy, freefall extreme and the famous Zorb, a steep downhill run inside a transparent 3.2-m globe.

Blue and Green Lakes **

On the Tarawera Road, the Blue Lake is 8 km from Te Ngae turnoff. The Green lake is nearby.

These two water-filled volcanic craters are obviously named for their colours and are known respectively in Maori as Tikitapu and Rotokakahi. On the northern shore of the Blue Lake is a sandy beach and a boat ramp adjoining a large picnic area. A further 2 km on is a lookout point on a narrow ridge between the lakes, from which the colours of the two lakes can be compared. From this carpark a 5-km track circumnavigates the Blue Lake and takes approximately one-and-a-half hours. Access to the Green Lake is restricted to members of local iwi.

At nearby Lake Okareka, Boyes Beach on Millar Road is a popular swimming spot.

Blue Baths ★★★

Government Gardens, next to the Rotorua Museum

Open Monday to Friday 10 a.m. to 7 p.m., Saturday and Sunday 10 a.m. to 8 p.m.

www.bluebaths.co.nz

Entrance fee

This pool opened in 1933 and was designed in the Spanish mission style by architect John Mair. The baths were considered in their day the height of sophisticated and elegant bathing, and unusual for the time in that women and men swam together.

For years the Blue Baths were one of Rotorua's great attractions and widely acknowledged as one of the country's finest art deco buildings. But the years took their toll and the baths were closed in 1982. Left to decay, the baths were at one stage up for demolition. However, in a joint project between the council and the developer, the baths were restored and reopened in December 1999. While the facilities and museum part of the baths are very attractive, the single open-air public pool is rather small and plain and access is by a side door rather than the main entrance.

Government Bath House ★★★

Government Gardens

This striking building was originally opened in 1908 and was the government's first venture into actively encouraging tourism, particularly after the drop-off in visitors after the Tarawera eruption destroyed the Pink and White Terraces. Promoted as a spa where people could 'take the waters' for medicinal purposes, the Bath House at its peak catered for over 70,000 baths per year as well as other special treatments such as mud baths, electric therapy and massage. Over the years the fad for spa treatment faded and eventually the Bath House was closed. At one stage the building was a popular local nightclub.

In 1969 the South Wing was reopened to house the Rotorua Museum and in 1977 the Rotorua Art Gallery opened in the North Wing.

Government Gardens ★★★

These superb gardens were established on land gifted by Ngati Whakaue 'for the benefit of the people of the world'. Developed into formal gardens at the end of the nineteenth century, the area now features the striking Government Bath House, the Blue Baths and the Polynesian Spa. The park contains formal gardens, historical sites and hot water springs and is linked through to the lakefront park. The thermal areas on the lake edge are unpredictable and visitors should always stay on the marked paths.

The distinctive arch marking the entrance at the eastern end of Arawa Street was built of totara to celebrate the visit of the Duke and Duchess of Cornwall in 1901. It originally stood on the intersection of Hinemoa and Fenton Streets.

The lawn bowls and croquet grounds in front of the Bath House create a unique genteel picture and are complemented by the beautifully restored 1903 Edwardian tea pavilion overlooking the bowling green.

Hell's Gates/Tikitere **

Travel east from Rotorua on SH30 and after 12 km turn right towards Whakatane. Hell's Gates is 4 km on the left.

Open daily 8.30 a.m. to 8.30 p.m., guided tours 9.30 a.m., 1.30 p.m., 3.30 p.m.

www.hellsgate.co.nz

Considered to be the most active of the Rotorua thermal areas, Hell's Gates has the largest active mud volcano-iti (a very small volcano) and a hot waterfall. This reserve is of great importance to the Ngati Rangiteaorere tribe, who have lived in this area for more than 700 years, and is the only one that is Maori-owned. All the guides at Hell's Gates are of Te Arawa descent, and the guided tours are free. As well as the thermal area there are cooking pools and a Maori carver on site (Monday to Friday only) who can even help you create your own carving.

In addition to the thermal area there are hot mineral pools and a spa complex, which offers a bath of mud from the site said to be good for the skin.

Hinehopu/Hongi's Track **

At the eastern end of Lake Rotoiti, turn off SH33 into Tamatea Street and continue for 500 m to the carpark where the track begins. Very limited car parking at the Lake Rotoehu end.

This well-formed track through attractive bush links Lakes Rotoiti and Rotoehu and takes around two hours return. The highlight is the famous matai tree under which, as a baby, Hinehopu was hidden from enemies by her mother. It was also under this tree that she met her husband Pikiao, and many of the Ngati Pikiao iwi trace their lineage directly back to this couple.

It was also along this track that Ngapuhi warriors, led by Hongi Hika, launched their attack on Rotorua by dragging their waka along the track from Rotoehu to Rotoiti.

Jambalaya Festival ***

www.jambalaya.co.nz

This three-day Easter festival fuses Brazilian and Cuban music and dance with a distinctive Pacific beat and is one of Rotorua's most popular events. The festival is packed with workshops, shows and dance parties and culminates in a Carnival Parade in the central city which prides itself on having 'no boring bits, no vehicles and no advertising'.

Kerosine Creek *

Kerosine Creek Road is on the right just past Rainbow Mountain Reserve. The hot stream is 2 km down this unsealed forestry road.

A popular swimming hole with locals, Kerosine Creek is a hot water stream heated by the water of the creek passing over hot rocks. The temperature of the water varies considerably and you need to move up and down the creek to find a spot to suit. Particularly popular is the hot waterfall, great for a neck and back massage.

Note that this is a public reserve and as there is no knowing what might go in the water upstream, it is best not to put your head underwater. Also it is relatively isolated and in recent years there have been considerable problems with cars being broken into.

Kuirau Park *

Corner Ranolf and Lake Roads

This public park highlights the extent of geothermal activity in the Rotorua area. In the northern part of the park hot springs are tucked in among the trees and bushes, while steam and gas rises from grates in the street, creating an odd contrast to the quiet flower beds and children's playground at the southern end. The park has experienced small eruptions in recent years and is particularly active in wet weather.

Lake Rotorua **

Covering over 80 sq km, Lake Rotorua is the second-largest lake in the North Island. Formed from the collapsed crater of a large volcano, the last eruption was about 140,000 years ago, and the whole depression left behind is now known as the Rotorua Caldera. Mokoia Island in the centre of the lake is a rhyolite dome of volcanic rock and Rotorua City is situated on the southwest shore of the lake.

Lake Tarawera ***

This large lake of beautiful clear water, renowned for its trout fishing, lies at the foot of Mt Tarawera and was substantially altered by the 1886 eruption. Nine days prior to the eruption a mysterious waka was seen on the lake by a party of tourists returning by boat from the Terraces but as the waka approached the boat it suddenly disappeared. Believed by many to be a waka wairua (spirit canoe) warning of approaching doom, it is said that a reappearance of the waka will signal the next eruption.

The access point at Tarawera Landing has a small sandy beach and boat ramp (2 km past the Buried Village). To the right of the carpark is a short walk to the Wairoa Stream, the outlet for the Green Lake, and to the left another short walk leads to Maori rock drawings. From here the launch MV *Reremoana* (www. purerotorua.com) takes visitors to the foot of the mountain at Te Ariki and to Hot Water Beach.

For the more active, the Eastern Okataina Walkway follows the shore of Lake Okataina to Humphries Bay on Lake Tarawera. This attractive walk through native bush is well formed and takes around three-and-a-half hours one way. The track begins from the carpark at the end of Okataina Road.

The Luge ***

Fairy Springs Road
Open 9 a.m. to 8 p.m. summer, and to 6 p.m. winter
www.skylineskyrides.co.nz
Entrance fee (some restrictions apply and riders must be older than six years)

This is great fun and one of the most popular (and expensive) attractions in the Rotorua area. The small ride-on karts have a unique braking and steering system that makes them fully controllable, going as fast or as slow as the rider wants. Three separate sealed tracks wind down the hillside and riders return to the top via a chairlift. To use the Luge you must first travel to the top via the Skyline Gondola, a 900-metre cable ride that ends 487 m up Mt Ngongotaha with broad views over the city and lake.

Mokoia Island **

Occupied by the Te Arawa iwi for over 700 years, Mokoia Island was prized as a strategic defensive site and a rich fertile area to grow the valuable kumara. Of particular fame is the great love story of Hinemoa and Tutanekai. Hinemoa, forbidden by her family to marry the handsome warrior Tutanekai, swam at night from the shores of the lake to the island guided only by the sound of Tutanekai's flute (now in the Rotorua Museum). On reaching the island Hinemoa warmed herself in a hot pool now known, not surprisingly, as Hinemoa's Pool. In recent years the island was considered too isolated and the last residents left in 1953.

Now famed as a bird sanctuary, Mokoia Island is an excellent place to see rare birds such as the saddleback, stitchbird, brown teal and North Island weka. In addition to the conservation area, historic areas include the site of Tutanekai's whare, Hinemoa's Pool (which the visitor can swim in) and an ancient stone carving of the kumara god.

A number of tour operators based on the lake run boat trips to the island (www.mokoia-island.com).

Mt Tarawera ***

Lying 24 km south of Rotorua, this mountain is a series of rhyolite domes, and was split down the middle by the basaltic eruption of 1886 which created a spectacular 6-km rift. The two main peaks are Tarawera and Wahanga, and at 1110 m the top of the mountain is definitely subalpine.

In the early hours of 10 June 1886, Rotorua experienced a series of small earthquakes, followed at 1.30 a.m. by an explosion and a large quake. At 2.30 a.m. three peaks had erupted and at 3.30 a.m. Lake Rotomahana blew out, covering a huge area in ash and volcanic debris. Heard as far away as Wellington and Auckland, the eruption was at first mistaken by some to be an attack by Russian warships. The eruption buried several nearby villages, including Te Wairoa, destroyed the famous Pink and White Terraces and killed at least 150 people. Rather than the more familiar circular crater usually associated with volcanoes, the crater at Tarawera is a gigantic raw rip along the whole length of the mountain, and is particularly impressive from the air. Many lakes surrounding the mountain were drastically altered, including Lake Rotomahana which originally was only one quarter of the size of the present lake.

The mountain is now private property and access can only be gained through tours operated by Mt Tarawera Ltd (www.mt-tarawera.co.nz).

Ohinemutu Village and St Faiths Church ★★★

One of the most important Ngati Whakaue settlements, Ohinemutu has been the heart of Maori Rotorua for hundreds of years. Overlooking the lake is St Faith's Church, built in 1910 with Tudor-style overtones and an interior decorated with fine weaving and paintings. Of special note is the window showing Christ as a Maori chief and placed in such a way that he appears to be walking on the waters of Lake Rotorua. Services on Sunday are held in English and Maori. Behind the church are the graves of returned soldiers, buried above ground as the area is too hot for underground burials.

Ohinemutu also has the beautifully carved meeting house Tama Te Kapua on Te Papiouru marae. The meeting house is named after the captain of the Arawa waka, who brought the ancestors of the Arawa iwi to Aotearoa around 1350 AD.

Ohinemutu is a contemporary Maori community, not a tourist attraction, and while the local people welcome visitors, every respect should be shown to both people and places.

Polynesian Spa ★★★

Hinemoa Street
Open daily 6.30 a.m. to 11 p.m.
www.polynesianspa.co.nz

The modern-day spa is situated on the site of the Priest Pool, which became famous in 1878 when the waters of the spring were reputed to have cured the arthritis of Catholic priest Father Mahoney. In 1882 the Pavilion Bath House was opened, later to be replaced by the Ward Baths in 1931, which in turn became the Polynesian Pool in 1972.

There are two types of water used at the spa — acidic and alkaline. The Radium and Priest Pools are acidic and are noted for their therapeutic effect on arthritis, rheumatism and general muscular aches. As the pools are drawn directly from springs below, the water clarity and properties vary constantly.

The water for the main pool, Family Spa, and Lake Spa Retreat is sourced from the nearby Rachel Pool (just behind the Blue Baths) and is more alkaline and softer and is temperature controlled by the addition of cold water.

The location of these pools on the lakefront adds to the attraction, as does the fact that there are separate adult and family areas. Many pools, including the Retreat, overlook the lake edge and Sulphur Point with its birdlife, steaming hot pools and view out to Mokoia Island.

Pukaki ***

Second floor, Rotorua District Council Buildings — entrance at the end of Haupapa Street
Open 8.30 a.m. to 4.30 p.m.

Pukaki, one of the most important Te Arawa carved figures and featured on the 20-cent coin, is not in a museum but in a glass gallery in the council buildings where he presides over the central city.

Born in Tutanekai's pa on Mokoia Island around 1700, Pukaki led his Ngati Whakaue iwi through a period of major tribal conflict with Tuhourangi to the south, eventually forcing their opponents back to Tarawera and allowing Ngati Whakaue to occupy Ohinemutu.

Created in 1836 from a single piece of totara by the master carver Te Taupua, the carving commemorates the conquest of Pukeroa-Oruawhata. It was originally a gateway to the pa at Ohinemutu, but the lower part of the gateway was removed in the 1850s and Pukaki then stood next to the meeting house Tama Te Kapua. The carving shows Pukaki holding his sons, Wharengaro and Rangitakuku, and below is his wife, Ngapuia.

Rainbow Springs Nature Park **

Fairy Springs Road
Open 8 a.m. to 9 p.m. winter, and to 11 p.m. summer
www.rainbowsprings.co.nz
Entrance fee

There are two parts to this complex: the Kiwi Encounter and the Rainbow Springs. The springs have their origin on the extinct volcano, Ngongotaha, which has no established streams to drain rainfall. The water is gradually filtered through the porous volcanic soil and emerges cool and crystal clear at the spring. Each day over two million litres of fresh water rise out of the ground, creating the perfect environment for trout to flourish. Viewed both in the pools and through a glass-sided pool, the fish include rainbow, brown, and tiger trout as well as brook char. Set in attractive bush with native birds, tuatara, geckos and skinks, the 1 km of walking track in the nature park is now open at night, lit by a unique multicoloured lighting system.

Opened in 2004, Kiwi Encounter is a unique opportunity to see kiwi conservation in action. As well as the nocturnal kiwi house, visitors can see the hatchery and young chicks in the nursery and, if the timing is right, actually see a kiwi hatch. This is an innovative joint operation with the Department of Conservation and over 100 eggs are hatched here each season with the birds eventually released in the wild. Kiwi Encounter is by guided tour only, strictly limited to groups of 15 people, so bookings are essential.

Redwood Grove — Whakarewarewa Forest **

Main entrance to the grove is from the Visitor Centre off Tarawera Road about 500 m from the Te Ngae/Tarawera intersection.

Gates to the carpark open 5.30 a.m. to 8.30 p.m.

Hugely popular with runners, mountain bikers and walkers, the highlight of this forest is the extensive grove of huge redwood trees planted as part of early forestry experiments, though there are also extensive areas of Douglas fir and larch. The actual Whakarewarewa Forest stretches from Rotorua City right through to the Blue and Green Lakes and is a complex maze of tracks that can take from 30 minutes to all day. There is excellent signage and maps are available at the Visitor Centre.

Rotorua Marathon ***

Held for over 40 years, this is New Zealand's most popular marathon attracting large numbers of runners to Rotorua each autumn. The course is a lap round the lake and is regarded by runners as both demanding and scenic. There is a hilly section about midpoint of the northern side of the lake and a taxing long straight stretch into the city past the airport to the finish. Visit www.rotoruamarathon.co.nz

Rotorua Museum of Art and History/Te Whare Taonga O Te Arawa ***

Government Gardens

Open October to March 9 a.m. to 8 p.m., April to September 9 a.m. to 5 p.m., closed Christmas Day, guided tours 9.30 a.m., 11 a.m., 1 p.m., 2.30 p.m., 4 p.m.

www.rotoruanz.com/rotorua.museum

Entrance fee

It is not hard to see why this fantastic small museum has won numerous awards for excellence, and visitors to the city should include this on their itinerary, preferably as their first stop. The museum is divided into four parts.

Take the Cure looks at the Bath House and Rotorua as a spa town, and includes actual therapy rooms where the most bizarre of treatments took place under the name of baineology (the scientific treatment of disorders by water). Don't miss a visit to the basement area under the building featuring four original 1908 mud baths.

The Spiritual World of the Te Arawa display contains taonga (treasures) of the local iwi, Te Arawa. Among the many fine exhibits is the flute with which Tutanekai guided Hinemoa to Mokoia Island, an exquisitely carved window featuring the dreaded bird woman Hatupatu, and a photographic display of Te Arawa rangatira.

Tarawera — Te Maunga Tapu tells the story of the Tarawera eruption and the geology of the Rotorua area.

Ake! Ake! is the moving story of B Company of the 28th Maori Battalion who lost over 600 men in battles in Greece, Crete, North Africa and Italy from 1940 to 1945. 'Ka maumahara to tatou ki ratou — We will remember them.'

Don't miss the short film *Rotorua Stories*, but remember to hold on to your seat! The guided tours are recommended and both the tours and the films are included in the entrance fee.

Te Puia ***

Hemo Road, Whakarewarewa

Open October to March 8 a.m. to 6 p.m., April to September 8 a.m. to 5 p.m.

www.tepuia.com

Entrance fee

It is hard to go past Te Puia as a combination of geothermal action and Maori cultural experience. However, its very popularity means that it is often crowded, and while Pohutu is both the largest and most active geyser in the area (reaching heights of up to 30 m), other geothermal areas offer more variety. As well as the geyser, there are pools of boiling mud and scalding hot water throughout the thermal valley.

At the entrance to Te Puia on the Rotowhio marae are some examples of very fine carving including the wharenui Te Aronui a Rua, a waka taua. and a pataka. To the left of Te Aronui a Rua is an older carved house, and alongside that Te Rito, the weaving school. Cultural performances are held in the wharenui at midday and in the evening.

The entrance to the geothermal area is through a superb gateway carved in 1909 and depicting the lovers Hinemoa and Tutanekai.

Established in 1973 to preserve traditional craft and based at Te Puia, the New Zealand Maori Arts and Crafts Institute has produced some of the finest carvers and weavers in the country. Visitors to the institute have a first-hand opportunity to see carvers and weavers at work. Craft produced onsite is also for sale.

Te Wairoa — the Buried Village **

From the city centre travel 3 km east on Te Ngae Road and turn right at the roundabout into Tarawera Road. The Buried Village is 12 km on the right just before Lake Tarawera.
Open November to March 8.30 a.m. to 5.30 p.m., April to October 9 a.m. to 4.30 p.m., guided tours 11 a.m., 1.30 p.m., 3 p.m.
www.buriedvillage.co.nz
Entrance fee

In the early hours of 10 June 1886, Tarawera erupted without warning in the greatest volcanic eruption in New Zealand's recorded history. Te Wairoa and three other villages were destroyed, as were the famous Pink and White Terraces, then considered one of the eight wonders of the world. Rotorua was covered in ash and the land surrounding the mountain was devastated, killing over 150 people.

At Te Wairoa, the area has been cleared of ash and debris to expose the remains of the village and the famous Rotomahana Hotel which catered for visitors travelling to the Terraces. A guided tour is recommended and all the guides are direct descendants of the Tuhourangi people who lived at Te Wairoa before the eruption.

As well as the ruins of the village, there is an excellent small museum (included in the entrance fee) giving both a geological and human background to the eruption and which is better than many public museums.

Trout Fishing ***

The Rotorua area is famous for trout fishing and of the 16 lakes there, 11 are considered fishable as are numerous streams around the area. The key fishing lakes are Rotorua, Okataina, Rotoma, Rotoiti and Tarawera. The main fish stock is rainbow trout, though there are also brown, brook and tiger trout.

Related to the Pacific salmon, rainbow trout (*Oncorhyncus mykiss*) were introduced into New Zealand in 1883 from California and in their seagoing form are known as steelhead trout. They can grow up to 5 kg and have a preference for cool water with plenty of oxygen present.

There are numerous local trout-fishing guides (many based in sports shops), all with their own secret spots and favourite techniques.

Wai-o-Tapu ***

27 km south of Rotorua on SH5

Open daily 8.30 a.m. to 5.30 p.m.

www.geyserland.co.nz

Entrance fee

Wai-o-Tapu has been active for over 150,000 years and has the most surface geothermal activity in the area. As well as hot mud pools and boiling springs, the park has several unique features. As you enter the park there are a series of very deep craters (some up to 20 m deep), at the bottom of which is furiously boiling muddy water that gives a very vivid impression of looking deep into the raw earth. The huge Primose Terrace is a 1.5-ha sinter terrace that has developed slowly over the past 700 years and is the largest such terrace in New Zealand. Stealing the show are the coloured pools (these vary considerably with the conditions), including the multicoloured Artist's Palette, the Champagne Pool and the amazingly bright green Devil's Bath. The Lady Knox Geyser (named after Lady Constance Knox, the daughter of Lord Ranfurly, then Governor-General) erupts to a height of up to 20 m each day at 10.15 a.m. (with a bit of assistance) but is not in the main part of the park, so allow 20 minutes' travel from the ticket office. The nearby huge Mud Pool is well worth the short detour and is free to enter.

The reserve is only accessible on foot but the tracks are very well maintained and unobtrusive and walks take between 30 and 75 minutes.

Waikiti Valley Thermal Pools *

Take SH5 27 km south to the Wai-o-Tapu turnoff. The valley is 6 km from SH5 down the road
directly opposite the turnoff.
Open daily 10 a.m. to 10 p.m., closed Christmas Day
www.hotpools.co.nz

Tucked away in a quiet side valley, this mineral pool consists of a large family pool,
a small soaking pool and private spas, and is fed by the impressive hot spring Te
Manaroa. Accessed by a short walkway from the pool complex, this large spring
fringed by mosses and ferns pulsates scalding hot water down a steaming narrow
river past the pools. The swimming pool cools the soft calcite-laden water by a
series of somewhat home-built cascades, more a testament to Kiwi ingenuity
than to refined engineering. The complex has facilities for camper vans and is a
very pleasant place to spend an evening, especially on a cold winter's night when
the steaming hot river is particularly impressive.

Waimangu Volcanic Valley ***

From Rotorua travel 14 km south on SH5, then turn left (clearly sign-posted) and the valley is
6 km along this road.
Open daily 8.30 a.m., last admission 3.45 p.m. (4.45 p.m. January)
www.waimangu.com
Entrance fee

The thermal activity in the Waimangu Valley is a direct result of the 1886 Tarawera
eruption, and is the newest geothermal system in the world (prior to 1886 there
was no activity in the valley). Lake Rotomahana exploded to 20 times its original
size and seven craters erupted in the area that now makes up the Waimangu
Volcanic Valley. The valley is extensive and has several walks downhill through
native bush linking the various thermal activities, and finally leading down to
Lake Rotomahana. There is an option of a lake cruise and a bus to return to the
Visitor Centre. The valley is the site of the world's largest recorded geyser, which
was active between 1901 and 1904 and threw hot water, rocks and sand to an
unbelievable height of 400 m. In 1917 a huge explosion created the Frying Pan
Lake, the world's largest hot water spring, killing two people.

Waimangu Valley is also a scenic reserve and wildlife refuge and has won a
number of New Zealand eco-tourism awards.

Whakarewarewa — the Thermal Village *

Tryon Street, Whakarewarewa
Open daily 8.30 a.m. to 5 p.m. with regular guided tours, cultural performances
11.15 a.m. and 2 p.m. daily
www.whakarewarewa.com
Entrance fee

A Maori village has been established on the northern edge of the Whakarewarewa thermal area for well over 200 years, and it is this area that now comprises the Thermal Village, separate from the actual main geothermal area now known as Te Puia.

The village is an actual Maori community with a geothermal background and is an opportunity to observe daily life, albeit with a strong tourist bent. The meeting house, Wahiao, is particularly impressive, and don't miss the tiny Catholic Church of the Immaculate Conception built in 1904 and surrounded by tombs built above ground, the ground being too hot for burials.

Xterra **

www.xterranz.com

Held in April each year, this popular multi-sport event for individuals and teams is a 1-km swim, a 30-km mountain bike race and an 11-km trail run all off-road and through some of Rotorua's most stunning forest scenery. As well as the main Xterra event, there are running and mountain bike options, all held on the same day. All the events are based around the attractive (but cold for swimmers) Blue Lake.

GISBORNE & EAST CAPE

East Cape Highway 35, Opotiki to Gisborne ***

Usually treated as one entity, the East Cape is, in reality, two distinct regions. From Opotiki to Cape Runaway the road hugs the rugged Bay of Plenty coast, weaving in and out of sandy bays and small rocky coves. The climate is wetter, the landscape is more forested. The iwi here is Whanau-a-Apanui. In contrast, the southeastern side of the cape is drier, more barren and the road is mainly inland, touching the coast occasionally. The beaches are wider, more sheltered, and sandy. This is home to the Ngati Porou iwi.

A notable feature of the East Cape is the numerous marae, often with historic carved meeting houses (wharenui). Meeting houses are not tourist attractions or public halls, but a living representation of the ancestors of local people. You should no more walk on to a marae than walk uninvited into someone's house. Please seek permission before entering a marae.

Accommodation and facilities in general are limited on the cape, so it pays to plan ahead, even in the off-season.

The following highlights are based on travelling from Opotiki to Gisborne.

Motu River **

The wild rugged river is one of the last untouched rivers in the country as it winds its way through bush-covered hills from the foothills of the Urewera country to the sea. Jet-boat trips up the river are available.

Raukokore — Christ Church ***

This extremely photogenic Anglican church sits on a flat promontory jutting out to sea. In the graveyard behind are the graves of Eruera and Amira Stirling, two notable twentieth-century Maori leaders.

Waihau *

Famous for its excellent fishing, this small settlement has a substantial boat ramp and good facilities.

Te Araroa — the largest pohutukawa in the world **

This huge tree known as Te Waha O Rerehou is over 20 m high and 40 m at its widest point and is located on the beach at Te Araroa by the school.

Reputed to be over 600 years old, it is also tapu so do not climb on the tree.

Te Araroa is also the birthplace of Sir Apirana Ngata, one of the most influential Maori leaders of the twentieth century, who, in particular, encouraged the revival of Maori art, craft and tradition at a time when it was at a very low ebb.

East Cape Lighthouse **

20 km from Te Araroa on a metal road

Now located on the easternmost point of mainland New Zealand, this lighthouse was originally built in 1900 on nearby East Island after ignoring local Maori advice that the island was tapu. After endless problems with access (four men were drowned building the lighthouse) and continuing landslides and earthquakes, the lighthouse was dismantled and moved to its present position in 1922.

There is a one-hour-return walk to the lighthouse from the carpark, which is steep in places and includes a long flight of steps.

St Mary's Church ***

SH35, Tikitiki
Koha/donation

This small church situated below the fortified pa site, Pukemarie, is without a doubt one of the finest carved churches in the country. Constructed in 1924 under the encouragement of Sir Apirana Ngata, the church is a memorial to Ngati Porou soldiers who died in the First World War. Ngata was keen to revive dying arts and craft, so local weavers and carvers were employed in creating the fine interior, while the carved pulpit was a gift from the Te Arawa iwi of Rotorua.

Waipiro Bay **

Around 1900, Waipiro Bay was the largest settlement on the East Coast, shipping out sheep, cattle and timber, and it was here that Robert Kerridge opened his first picture theatre in 1923. Now a ghost town, the centre of the settlement is the Iritekura marae with its fine meeting house carved in the traditional Ngati Porou style by master carver Pine Taiapa.

Tokomaru Bay ***

This is a magnificent sweep of sandy beach with plenty of room for everyone. At the northern end of the bay are the freezing works and shipping offices and stores, surprisingly large buildings for this small community, but now in ruins.

Anaura Bay ***

Considered to be one of the finest beaches on the East Coast, Anaura Bay is a great swimming, fishing and diving spot. This bay was Cook's second landing place in New Zealand, though bad weather prevented him from provisioning his ship and after two days, on the advice of local Maori, he sailed south to Tolaga Bay.

Anaura Bay Walkway begins at the north end of the unsealed road and takes around two hours return. The walk traverses one of the few fragments of coastal forest on the East Cape and there are fine views back along the bay and towards Motuoroi Island.

Tolaga Bay **

This is the most substantial settlement on the East Coast with dramatic cliffs flanking a wide bay with a fine sandy beach. At the southern end of the bay is the famous Tolaga Bay Wharf, reputed to be the longest in the southern hemisphere. Over 600 m in length, the wharf was completed in 1929 and is currently undergoing restoration.

Cook's Cove Walkway begins near the wharf and takes around two-and-a-half hours return. The well-formed track is mainly through manuka and farmland and leads to the small cove where Cook anchored for a week in October 1769 to replenish supplies.

Whangara Beach*

Made famous by Witi Ihimaera's novel *The Whale Rider* and the film of the same name, the centre of this small community is the meeting house crowned by the famous ancestor Paikea riding a whale.

Eastwoodhill Arboretum ***

2392 Wharekopae Road, Ngatapa — 35 km from Gisborne
From Gisborne take SH2 south. At the large roundabout just over the Waipaoa River turn right
and after 50 m turn left, then follow the signs.
Open 9 a.m. to 5 p.m., closed Good Friday and Christmas Day
www.eastwoodhill.org.nz
Entrance fee

Billed as 'the largest collection of northern hemisphere trees in the southern hemisphere', Eastwoodhill has over 4000 exotic trees and shrubs set out over 150 ha. The arboretum is the life work of William Cook, who started planting trees when he returned to his farm after the First World War, inspired by the gardens he saw in Britain. Over the next half-century until his death in 1967, William sourced trees from all over the world, estimated to have cost him over 55,000 pounds. The one-hectare Homestead Garden is recognised as a Garden of National Significance, and numerous tracks throughout Eastwoodhill allow the visitor to spend any time from a 30-minute walk to half a day. From the highest point, Mt Hikurangi is visible on a clear day.

Every time of the year has something special: autumn is the most popular time to visit, when the trees are changing colour, but spring has a great show of daffodils.

Gisborne City

Beaches (in order of distance from the city)

Waikanae and Midway Beach *
Stretching for miles from the Turanganui River to the Waipaoa River mouth, this great uncrowded beach is within walking distance of downtown. Both Waikanae and Midway have patrolled swimming in summer, unlike some of the beaches further north. However, after easterly storms this beach can turn ugly with piles of driftwood washed down the Waipaoa River.

Wainui Beach **
5 km east of Gisborne

Famous for its surf, this long sandy beach has waves to suit everyone from the apprentice surfer to the very experienced.

Makorori Beach ***

10 km north of Gisborne

The pick of the beaches north of Gisborne and almost undeveloped, there are numerous points to access this golden sandy beach from the road.

Tatapouri *

13 km north of Gisborne

Tatapouri has a short stretch of sandy beach but an excellent boat ramp for those going fishing or diving.

Pouawa **

19 km north of Gisborne

The last sandy and easily accessible beach north of Gisborne, Pouawa has good surf in an easterly swell.

Captain Cook statues ***

Gisborne has two Cook statues: one on Kaiti Hill and the other at the mouth of the Turanganui River near Waikanae Beach.

The bronze statue on Kaiti Hill was erected in 1969 to mark the bicentennial of Cook's landing and was cast from a marble statue purchased in Italy in the late nineteenth century in the belief that it was Captain Cook. In fact, the uniform is Italian and not British, and the facial features bear no resemblance to Cook. Just who this is no one knows, but this Italian now has his place in Gisborne folklore.

Next to the faux Cook is a pohutukawa planted by the late Princess Diana in 1983.

Cook's Memorial *

Kaiti Beach Road

It is appropriate that Cook's first landing place in New Zealand was also the landing place of the seagoing waka, *Horouta* and *Te Ikaroa-a-Rauru*, around 1350. At first glace this grand memorial seems at odds with the piles of logs and ships of the port but in reality the port continues a seafaring tradition stretching back nearly 800 years.

Cook's first landing in New Zealand on 9 October 1769 was also his least successful. Misunderstandings with local Maori led to bloodshed, and three days later Cook left and, unfortunately, named this prosperous area Poverty Bay, '… as it afforded us not one thing we wanted'.

Gisborne Airport *

Is it a plane? Is it a train? Gisborne Airport is the only airport in New Zealand, and surely one of the few in the world, where a railway line cuts right across the runway. It is probably just as well that the line is not that busy, and, for those who really want to know, the planes give way to the trains.

Kaiti Hill Lookout ***

Originally the site of the historic Titirangi Pa (named after a mountain in Hawaiki), the views from here look south across Poverty Bay to Young Nick's Head and as far south as the Mahia Peninsula. For those who want to walk to the lookout, tracks start opposite the Cook Memorial in Kaiti Beach Road.

Poho-O-Rawiri ***

Queen's Drive at the foot of Kaiti Hill

Reputed to be the largest carved meeting house in the country, this magnificent wharenui was opened in 1930, though many of the carvings were in fact carved by Arawa craftsmen in Rotorua. The tekoteko figure is the revered ancestor Rawiri Te Eke Tu A Terangi.

Rhythm and Vines **

www.rhythmandvines.co.nz

Within a few short years this concert, held outdoors in the Waiohika Vineyard, has become one of New Zealand's most popular New Year's concerts. The music lineup focuses on the best New Zealand musical talent in an 18-hour event that sees in the New Year and continues well into the small hours.

Tairawhiti Museum ***

Stout Street

Open weekdays 10 a.m. to 4 p.m., weekends and public holidays 1.30 p.m. to 4 p.m.

www.tairawhitimuseum.org.nz

Koha/donation

This superb museum won the inaugural Supreme Tourism Award and focuses heavily on both ancient and contemporary history and the art of the Tairawhiti area. As expected in an area so rich in Maori history, the museum has an outstanding collection of taonga (treasures) from local iwi and a permanent exhibition on Company C (men from the region) of the famous Second World War Maori (28) Battalion. Locals and visitors alike will also enjoy the exhibition that compares photographs from 1890 to 1910 with current photographs of the same places.

Te Moana Star of Canada Maritime Museum **

This museum-within-a-museum exhibition is the wheelhouse and captain's cabin of the ship *The Star of Canada*, which ran aground on rocks on the Gisborne foreshore in June 1912. Local jeweller William Good purchased the wheelhouse and placed it on an empty section next to his house in Childers Road. In 1983 the *Star* was left to the city of Gisborne and moved to its present location. This section of the museum houses numerous exhibits related to maritime history and the sea in general, and not to be missed is the amazing collection of old surfboards.

Toihoukura Visual Maori Arts and Design **

Cobden Street
Open Monday to Friday 8.30 a.m. to 5 p.m.
Phone 0508 765 983

This institution grew out of marae restoration projects in the East Cape area during the 1970s and '80s. Under the guidance of influential contemporary Maori artist Sandy Adsett, the school was established in 1993 and is now recognised as one of the most important schools of Maori art and design showcasing innovative art in a wide range of contemporary and traditional mediums and styles.

While not a regular gallery, Toihoukura usually has art permanently on display and often has exhibitions, so it is worthwhile calling by, or check by phoning 0508 765 983.

Grey's Hill Lookout *

Take the Back Ormond Road from Gisborne and after 5 km turn right into Waimata Valley Road. The lookout is 2 km down this road but is not well sign-posted.

From this lookout there are broad panoramic views over the plains, out to Young Nick's Head and west into the wild hill country inland from Gisborne.

Manutuke **

14 km south of Gisborne on SH2

Manutuke has two important nineteenth-century meeting houses, Te Mana-ki-Turanga and Te Poho Rukupo, both carved in the Turanga style under the influence of local chief Raharuhi Rukupo. Te Mana-ki-Turanga was built in 1883 and features carvings of the separation of Rangi and Papa, and Maui hauling his fish from the sea. Te Poho Rukupo, built in 1887 to honour Rukupo, originally stood near his grave but was moved to the present site in 1913.

Manutuke was also home to one of the most impressive meeting houses in the country, Te Hau-ki-Turanga. Built in 1842 the meeting house was dismantled and moved to Wellington in 1867 and is now in Te Papa Museum of New Zealand.

Matawhero Church **

6 km from Gisborne on SH2 towards Napier

This simple wooden church was built in 1866 and was the only building in the Matawhero district spared by Te Kooti in his raid on the district in 1868.

Millton Vineyard *

118 Papatu Road

Open Labour Weekend to Easter, Monday to Saturday 10 a.m. to 5 p.m., January seven days a week

www.millton.co.nz

Established in early 1984, Millton Vineyard was New Zealand's first commercial certified organic winegrower and prides itself on producing top-quality, internationally recognised wines using bio-dynamic techniques. The vineyard is favoured by locals as a picnic spot, in the vineyard's pleasant gardens.

Morere Hot Springs and Nature Reserve **

SH2, north of Nuhaka.

Open daily 10 a.m. to 5 p.m. and 9 p.m. in summer. Closed 24 and 25 December

www.morerehotsprings.com

Entrance fee

These hot springs are set in the Morere Nature Reserve, halfway between Gisborne and Wairoa, which has a number of tracks ranging from 30 minutes to three hours. It is particularly famous for the luxurious growth of its nikau palms. The springs are especially unusual in that the mineral water is actually ancient sea water, even though Morere is situated inland from the ocean. There are a number of pools indoors and out, for both families and those wanting a more relaxed soak. The mineral pools are reputed to have therapeutic value, though the water temperature is more warm than hot. The small spa-like pools known as the Nikau Pools are oddly made of stainless steel, giving the feeling of soaking in a large kitchen sink.

Rere Falls **

Ngatapa, 13 km beyond Eastwoodhill Arboretum

Here the Wharekopae River tumbles down an escarpment to form a broad, though not particularly high, waterfall. A very popular swimming hole in summer, the falls area also has a large grassed picnic area.

Te Urewera National Park — Lake Waikaremoana ***

This large lake, formed only 2000 years ago by a massive landslide across the Waitakeheke River, lies at the heart of the rugged Te Urewera National Park. The lake is over 240 m deep and has deep bays that reach far into rugged bush-covered terrain. Over 600 native plants have been recorded in the area, and the bush is mostly untouched. Te Urewera is also the land of the Tuhoe people, known as the 'Children of the Mist', fiercely independent and the last Maori iwi to be influenced by Europeans.

Giant Rata/Tawa Walk **

The loop track is just off the Ngamoko Track 2 km from the Visitor Centre on the road to Wairoa.

This loop takes around 30 minutes return, and features mature tawa that can grow up to 25 m. They also have an attractive open canopy, giving a light green feel to the usually dense New Zealand bush. A short detour leads to a massive rata with a convoluted and twisted trunk, believed to be over 1000 years old.

Hinerau Track/Aniwaniwa Falls *

Track begins from the carpark of the Aniwaniwa Visitor Centre

This short walk through beech forest (30 minutes return) leads to three cascades known as the Aniwaniwa Falls, together over 40 m high. There is also a viewpoint over the lake and Panekiri Bluff.

Lake Waikareiti Track *

The track begins 200 m from the Visitor Centre.

About one hour each way this moderate-grade walk leads through red and silver beech to Lake Waikareiti, which is free from introduced aquatic plants and is known for its remarkable water clarity.

Lake Waikaremoana Great Walk **

The walkway follows the shores of Lake Waikaremoana for most of its 46 km. It is by no means flat but is within the reach of a moderately fit tramper who is prepared for a three- to four-day trip. The weather in the area is very changeable and can be cold and wet even in summer, and it is not unusual to have snow in winter. This tramp is becoming increasingly popular, so it is necessary to book huts and campsites well ahead in the busy season. However, as an alternative, a water taxi is available for those who wish to shorten their trip or even do sections of the walk as a day trip. Visit www. lakewaikaremoana.co.nz for more information.

Papakorito Falls *

1.2 km from the Aniwaniwa Visitor Centre down Aniwaniwa Road

Only a few minutes' walk from the carpark along a grassed track, this attractive waterfall tumbles 20 m over rocky outcrops into the pool below.

Whatapo Bay ***

The track to the bay is 5.5 km from the Visitor Centre on the road to Wairoa.

One of the best sandy beaches with excellent views over the lake, Whatapo Bay is an easy 10-minute walk from the road.

TAUPO & THE CENTRAL NORTH ISLAND

Aratiatia Rapids **

From the junction of SH5 and SH1, take the road to Rotorua. After 3 km turn left into Aratiatia
Road and the rapids are 2 km down this road.
Release times are 10 a.m., 12 noon, 2 p.m. all year round and a further release at
4 p.m. 1 October to 31 March

The first and smallest hydro station on the Waikato River, the building of the dam
severely reduced the flow of water down the Aratiatia Rapids to a mere trickle.
However, water is now released through the dam floodgates for 30 minutes several
times a day. For the best experience it pays to arrive just before the release times.
Most people tend to watch from the bridge but there is an excellent viewpoint
just downstream, accessed by a short track to the left just over the bridge.

There is also good fishing in the lake, and further downstream the Ngawapurua
Rapids are a popular spot for experienced kayakers.

Army Museum Waiouru ***

SH1
Open 9 a.m. to 4.30 p.m.
www.armymuseum.co.nz
Entrance fee

This is undoubtedly one of New Zealand's finest museums and has a wide appeal
regardless of interest in things military. Purpose built, the fort-like museum,
complete with moat, stands in open tussock country, and while comprehensive, it
is small enough to comfortably manage in one visit. The detailed and informative
displays follow the campaigns of the New Zealand Army from colonial times,
through to a captured Soviet ZPU-1 heavy machine-gun used as an anti-aircraft
weapon in Afghanistan.

At the centre of the museum is Roimata Pounamu, a ceremonial area featuring
a wall of over 400 greenstone tiles down which runs water representing a wall of
tears. In this area is a plinth through which a database of every person from all
New Zealand forces who died in the course of duty can be accessed. There is an
excellent Gallipoli display, a reconstructed First-World-War trench complete with
rats, and an exhibition covering Greece, Crete, North Africa and Italy, where a
large number of New Zealand forces served in the Second World War.

All the machinery throughout the museum is in working order, including a
Second-World-War Sherman tank.

Don't drive past this museum!

Orakei Korako Cave and Thermal Park ***

Open 8 a.m. to 5 p.m.

www.orakeikorako.co.nz

Entrance fee

This particularly active and unpredictable thermal area consists of three large broad silica terraces containing geysers, boiling springs and mud pools. The terraces, formed by an earthquake in 131 AD, are covered with brightly coloured hot-water algae and multi-hued silica deposits created by aeons of hot water cascading over the rocky base. Above the terraces is the Ruatapu Cave, at the bottom of which is the warm Waiwhakaata Pool (pool of mirrors), where visitors can make a wish that will come true provided they have their left hand in the water and tell no one what they have wished for. In the cave is a small but moving memorial plaque to Adama and Witaiana Mikaere, both killed in Libya in 1941, aged 22 and 19 years.

With the fewest visitors of all the thermal areas, this one is the least crowded and feels the most natural. Accessed by a short boat trip across the Waikato River, the area is relatively compact and with 2.5 km of good tracks and boardwalks is easily managed by most people.

Raurimu Spiral *

Spiral Lookout, SH1, Raurimu, south of Taumarunui

This famous spiral solved an early engineering problem in the construction of the main trunk railway from Auckland to Wellington. By the use of horseshoe curves, loops and tunnels, the line climbed over 130 m within the short distance of 2 km. In reality it is hard to see the spiral except from the air. The lookout has a distant view of parts of the track but even that is not easy to see unless there is a train on the track. However, the homemade model, in the 'No. 8 wire, do it yourself' tradition, in front of the lookout is a Kiwiana gem.

Taupo

AC Baths *

Spa Road

This large modern pool complex uses thermal water for the main swimming pools and mineral water for the private pools. There are indoor and outdoor lap pools and family pools, smaller pools for quiet relaxation as well as private mineral pools. Part of the large family pool is set aside for 'bombing', and is particularly popular with younger males. 'AC' stands for the Armed Constabulary, who originally built a pool in 1886 on the site of a hot spring.

Craters of the Moon *

From Taupo take SH1 north for 6 km, then turn left into Karapiti Road. The carpark is 1.7 km down this road.

Koha/donation

The Craters of the Moon is one the most recent and most active thermal fields in the area and is constantly changing. The most common thermal activity is steam vents, though there is one major crater of furiously boiling mud or water depending on the water levels. The area is open, with intriguing low-growing plants that have adapted to the inhospitable environment.

To avoid disappointment it is best to approach the Craters of the Moon as an interesting walk rather than a major geothermal experience.

Huka Falls ***

Well sign-posted 2 km north of Taupo off SH1

The sheer volume of beautiful bright clear water that gushes through the narrow gap more than makes up for the modest size of these falls. Over 200,000 litres per second roar over the 3-m falls with a fury that is truly impressive.

Huka Falls Walkway **

From SH1 turn into Spa Road, after 1.5 km turn left into Country Avenue and the track starts at the carpark at the end of this road.

An excellent way to visit the Huka Falls as an alternative to driving, this well-formed track is generally flat all the way to the falls and takes about 60 minutes one way. At the beginning of the track is a hot spring on the edge of the river and, nearing the falls, you will hear them well before you see them. For the more energetic, a further track continues on to the Aratiatia Rapids, another two hours' walk downstream.

Taupo Hot Springs Spa *

On the road to Napier, 1 km on the left from SH1

Open daily 7.30 a.m. to 9 p.m.

www.taupohotsprings.com

Set in the pretty bush-lined Onekeneke Valley, these pools tap into a mineral hot spring reputed to be good for the skin and the relief of arthritis. The pool also offers beauty therapy and massage treatments. As well as the large mineral pool and smaller soaking pools, there are a family pool, a hydroslide and children's playground.

Taupo Museum *

Story Place, off Tongariro Street (SH1) behind the Information Centre
Open daily 10.30 a.m. to 4.30 p.m., closed Good Friday and Christmas Day
www.taupomuseum.co.nz
Entrance fee

The museum has the very cleverly recreated Ora — Garden of Well-being, the New Zealand garden that won the gold medal at the 2004 Chelsea Flower Show. The garden has strong central North Island connections, with thermal themes inspired by Orakei Korako as well as original artwork by Lyonel Grant and technical input from Richard Taylor of the Academy Award-winning Weta Workshops.

Another highlight is what has become known as the 'Reid Carvings', a highly unusual meeting house carved in a mix of Arawa and Tuwharetoa styles. The house was created for Lucy Reid (who later donated the carvings to the people of Taupo) by her uncle Tene Waitere in the 1920s. Tene is recognised as an exceptional carver famous for the gateway and the meeting house at Whakarewarewa. Unlike most carved houses, this one is not based round an ancestor, though it does follow traditional lines in its structure.

Taupo sports events

Taupo is home to a number of major sports events that pack out the town's accommodation and eateries, so it pays to plan well ahead.

Great Lake Relay ***

www.relay.co.nz

First held in 1994, this relay race in February each year now has around 8000 competitors walking or running in teams of 10 to 18, the 18-leg distances ranging from 5.2 km to 14.4 km.

Levene Half Marathon *

www.taupohalfmarathon.org.nz

Billed as the largest half-marathon in the country, the course starts in the town centre and follows SH1 south, then loops back along the lake to town again. The course is almost flat and is a combination of road, footpath, track and some farmland. It is usually run in August.

New Zealand Ironman ***

www.ironman.co.nz

The only Ironman event in New Zealand and held on the first weekend in March, this gruelling race attracts nearly 1000 entrants who swim 3.5 km, cycle 180 km and then finish off with a full marathon of 42 km.

Wattyl Lake Taupo Cycle Challenge ***

www.cyclechallenge.org.nz

Attracting up to 10,000 cyclists, the Challenge was first held in 1977 and is New Zealand's largest cycling event. Billed as a non-competitive ride (yeah right!), the event is 160 km around Lake Taupo and has six entry types: Solo, Relay, Enduro (twice round), Super Enduro (three times round), the Classic Race for elite cyclists, and a 5-km ride for the very young. The Challenge is held annually in November, and the atmosphere and local support make it a great ride to enter.

Tongariro National Park ***

Gifted to the people of New Zealand in 1887 by paramount chief Te Heuheu Tukino IV on behalf of the people of Tuwharetoa, the park contains the three volcanic peaks of Ruapehu, Ngauruhoe and Tongariro. These active volcanoes erupt periodically, the last major event being the eruption of Ruapehu in 1995/96. Surrounding the mountains are wide-open fields of golden tussock, pristine streams, herb fields and untouched rainforest interwoven with the stark volcanic landscape of lava and ash. In Maori legend a number of mountains originally occupied the area, but in a fierce battle for the love of the beautiful Pihanga (a smaller mountain to the northeast), Tongariro drove his rivals, including Taranaki and Tauhara, from the area.

There are numerous tracks and walks throughout the park, many based round or near the Whakapapa village on the northern slopes of the mountain. The park is also home to two skifields, Turoa and Whakapapa.

Skiing Mt Ruapehu ★★★

www.mtruapehu.com

There is nothing quite like skiing a live volcano and no one will forget the photos of the 1995 eruption of skiers literally stopped in their tracks, turning and watching the explosion from the mountain's crater. Odds are there was some very fast downhill skiing that day!

Mt Ruapehu has two distinct ski areas, Whakapapa on the northwest of the mountain and Turoa on the southwest, each accessed from different sides of the mountain. Whakapapa is the largest developed ski area in the country, with 30 groomed trails and with slopes to suit beginners through to the very experienced. Turoa is reached by a 17-km road from Ohakune and, while smaller than Whakapapa, is considered to have New Zealand's best terrain park.

Ruapehu is very exposed to every weather from every direction. On a clear day the views are spectacular over Lake Taupo to the north and Taranaki to the west, but bad weather can strike quickly and severely, so skiers should come well prepared.

Taranaki Falls ★★

Starts in Ngauruhoe Place behind the Chateau in Whakapapa Village, Tongariro National Park

The well-formed loop track takes around two hours return and traverses beech forest, subalpine herb fields and open tussockland with excellent views of Ruapehu and Ngauruhoe. The waterfall is a single 20-m drop through a narrow gap over the edge of a lava flow.

Tongariro Crossing ★★★

Universally described as 'the best one-day walk in the world', the Tongariro Crossing traverses the most dramatic volcanic landscape in New Zealand. The vistas are superb, and the atmosphere is like a visit to the beginning of time. It will come as no surprise that parts of *The Lord of the Rings* were filmed here.

The trip is usually started at the Mangatepopo end with a steady climb up the steep Mangatepopo bluff on to the southern crater. If a side trip up Ngauruhoe is planned it is from this point, and while the scree slope is solid-going upwards, it is a quick trip down and the view from the crater is magnificent. From the south crater the climb is up and over the rim of the active Red Crater, along the rim of the central crater and then a long way downhill via the Ketetahi Hut. If you are planning a two-day trip, a good alternative with far fewer people (the Ketetahi Hut is usually packed in summer), is to take the Waihonunu track from the north side of the Red Crater, down the raw and rugged lava valley and stay overnight in either the Oturere or Waihonunu huts and then exit the park on SH1.

Transport can be arranged from Taupo, Turangi and National Park. The weather is notoriously fickle, and even in the height of summer the mountain top can be very exposed to freezing rain and wind, so good weatherproof and warm clothing is essential.

Tongariro National Trout Centre **

SH1, 4 km north of Turangi
Open daily 10 a.m. to 4 p.m. 1 December to 30 April, 10 a.m. to 3 p.m. 1 May to 30 November
Koha/donation

Trout in the Taupo area are sustained by wild trout spawning in the rivers and lakes, and while they usually spend some part of their life at sea, in this area, Lake Taupo acts as a substitute ocean. The hatchery is a safeguard should a natural disaster seriously affect the trout numbers in the area. The complex raises trout from eggs and at all times of the year there are usually trout in some growth stage on show. The Visitor Centre has excellent displays on all aspects of the trout fishery including a fascinating collection of rods and flies. The hatchery is set in attractive native bush with well-formed paths and leads down to the Tongariro River.

Tongariro River — Turangi ***

Regarded as one of the best stretches of trout water in the world, the Tongariro River has hosted the rich and famous, including royalty (this was one of the late Queen Mother's favourite fishing spots), but at the same time is accessible to the everyday fisherperson. While rainbow trout predominate, brown trout are also caught in this very attractive fast-flowing river. There is a lengthy track along the eastern side of the river giving access to a large number of excellent fishing spots, and the Turangi Information Centre has a free and comprehensive map of the river. Several local fishing shops hire fishing gear and local guided trips are also available. A specific licence is required to fish in the Taupo Fishing District. These are available from fishing shops and the Information Centres. A licence to fish on Lake Rotoaira is only available from the Turangi Information Centre.

Wairakei

Volcanic Activity Centre *

Karetoto Road, off Huka Falls Road

www.volcanoes.co.nz

Entrance fee

For those interested in the geology and origin of New Zealand's volcanic regions, this exhibition offers excellent comprehensive and accessible information along with a film presentation of the 1995/96 Mt Ruapehu eruptions and a simulation of the 1987 Edgecumbe earthquake. The Centre was originally set up by the Geological and Nuclear Sciences Institute, which is next door.

Wairakei Steamfields ***

2 km on the right from the junction of SH1 and SH5; poorly sign-posted and not to be confused with the Wairakei Thermal Valley.

Open 6.30 a.m. to 5.30 p.m. March to September, 6.30 a.m. to 6.30 p.m. October to February

The drive to the lookout leads through and under the fascinating maze of pipes and streams that are the Wairakei Geothermal Power Development. The pipes tap into vents of subterranean superheated steam, which is then fed into the geothermal power station down by the river. The lookout provides an excellent overview of the whole field though there is a complete lack of information provided.

Wairakei Terraces *

2 km on the right travelling towards Taupo from the junction of SH1 and SH5

Open daily 9 a.m. to 5 p.m.

www.wairakeiterraces.co.nz

Entrance fee

The well-presented, reconstructed Maori village and thermal area here are owned and staffed by the local Tuwharetoa iwi. In addition to the village they have recreated miniature silica terraces similar to the famous Pink and White

Terraces which are surprisingly attractive. The furiously boiling geyser at the top of the terrace is particularly impressive and has been created by tapping into excess hot water from the steamfield. Also on offer in the evening, and limited to 80 people, is an introduction to Maori culture, a hangi and a concert. The animal park in the middle, with alpacas and deer, sits oddly with the rest of the complex, but does appeal to children.

TARANAKI

Cape Egmont Lighthouse *

From New Plymouth drive 45 km south on SH45. Just south of Pungarehu turn right into Cape Road. The lighthouse is 5 km at the end of this road.

This lighthouse was built in cast-iron sections in 1864 in London and originally erected on Mana Island north of Wellington. In 1887 it was dismantled and rebuilt at Cape Egmont where it stands today. It was converted to electricity in the late 1950s and automated in 1986. The cape is not the most westerly point in the North Island; that distinction belongs to Cape Maria van Diemen in the Far North.

Forgotten World Highway *

This highway (SH43) runs between Stratford and Taumarunui and is rich both in natural and human history. Not a fast road, the highway is 155 km long of which a short section is still unsealed, and the trip takes around three hours.

Moki Tunnel *

Known as the Hobbits Hole long before *The Lord of the Rings* films were even made, this 180-m single-lane road tunnel was built in 1936.

Mt Damper Falls *

10 km past Whangamomona and just past the Moki Tunnel, turn left towards Ohau. The falls are about 20 minutes down this road.

These 85-m falls on the Tongaporutu River are the highest falls in the North Island and are a 20-minute walk from the road on a badly formed track.

Whangamomona *

Established in 1895, this historic village is now famous for its January Republic Day festival, which attracts thousands of people to the township. The festival was first held in 1989 and declared the Whangamomona area a republic (complete with its own passport) as a protest against regional government boundary changes that took the district out of Taranaki.

Hawera

Elvis Presley Room *

51 Argyle Street

Visiting by appointment only

Phone/fax 06 278 7624, mobile 027 498 2942

Koha/donation

Kevin Wasley is a long-time Elvis fan and has created in his garage his very own collection dedicated to 'The King', containing over 5000 recordings as well as souvenirs and memorabilia. Kevin has been to Elvis's home Gracelands no less than 17 times. Highlights of his collection are a 1968 autographed Christmas album, original concert tickets and a scarf from a 1974 Memphis concert.

This is a private collection and viewing is strictly by appointment only.

Hawera water tower *

55 High Street

Open Monday to Friday 8.30 a.m. to 5 p.m., weekends and public holidays 10 a.m. to 2 p.m., closed Christmas Day

Entrance fee

In 1884, 1895 and 1912, fires in Hawera burnt down significant parts of the business area and this water tower was built in response to demands from insurance companies that the town improve its ability to fight fires. Completed in January 1914, the 54.2-m tower has fine views over the surrounding countryside. Access is gained from the Information Office.

Tawhiti Museum ***

401 Ohangai Road, well sign-posted from both Normanby (north) and Hawera (south)

Open September to May, Friday, Saturday, Sunday, Monday 10 a.m. to 4 p.m., January every day 10 a.m. to 4 p.m.

Phone 0800 921 921

www.tawhitimuseum.co.nz

Entrance fee

In 1975 Nigel and Teresa Ogle bought the old Tawhiti cheese factory and eventually turned it into one of New Zealand's best private museums. Combining both miniature and life-sized models, the displays are meticulous in their detail and guaranteed to fascinate both young and old. The diorama of a Maori raiding party comprises hundreds of tiny figures, painstaking in their detail. While the museum focuses on South Taranaki history, the appeal of this museum is much broader than that. Don't miss the working reconstruction of a waterwheel, the vintage tractor collection, and the special display on Chinese settler and entrepreneur Chow Chong (Chau Tseung), who developed a fungi export business that gave local farmers a much-needed source of cash during difficult times.

Inglewood — Fun Ho! National Toy Museum **

Rata Street

Open Monday to Friday 9 a.m. to 5 p.m., weekends 10 a.m. to 4 p.m.

www.funho.com

Entrance fee

In 1935 Fun Ho! began making toys for the New Zealand market and at its peak the factory in Inglewood employed nearly 200 workers. Production finally ceased in 1987 but Barry Young, a former employee, acquired much of the old plant and casts and opened the Fun Ho! museum in 1990. Originally made of lead, the toys have been made from aluminium since 1941, and today over 100 toys are still handmade using the sand-casting technique from the original casts, many dating back over 60 years. The toys are made on the premises and the process can be viewed by the public. Firm favourites are still tractors, trucks and fire engines. The toys are simple and robust and now Richard Jordon still makes new toys and repairs old ones up to 60 years old. The Fun Ho! museum comprises a collection of all the Fun Ho! toys (over 3000 models), old plant and photos from the original factory, the current workshop and a shop selling over 100 toys made from the original casts.

New Plymouth

The Bowl of Brooklands **

Adjoins Pukekura Park

In 1934 Brooklands, a family farm, was bequested to the people of New Plymouth, and together with neighbouring Pukekura Park now forms a parkland of over 50 ha. This open-air theatre set among the water and trees has long been part of New Plymouth's musical life. In the 1950s and '60s huge theatrical productions (including *Hinemoa and Tutanekai* in 1966) for the Festival of the Pines drew large audiences. Today New Plymouth attracts major international acts way beyond what would be expected in a small, relatively isolated city. WOMAD (World Of Music And Dance) makes the Bowl of Brooklands its New Zealand home every two years.

Coastal Walkway *

This 7-km walk leads from Port Taranaki through the city centre to Lake Rotomanu and the mouth of the Waiwhakaiho River, though it can be accessed at any point. Included in this walk are Paritutu Rock, Fitzroy Beach and, by the city centre, Len Lye's famous kinetic sculpture, the Wind Wand.

The Festival of Light **

Each summer between mid-December and mid-February, Pukekura Park is transformed into a fairyland of lights. The festival attracts huge crowds of locals and visitors with its live music and other entertainment, and in the neighbouring Bowl of Brooklands, top local and international acts are also part of the festival.

Govett-Brewster Art Gallery **

Queen Street
Open daily 10.30 a.m. to 5 p.m.
www.govettbrewster.org.nz
Koha/donation

In 1962 Monica Brewster bequeathed to the New Plymouth City Council 50,000 pounds to create a trust to set up a gallery named the Govett-Brewster Art Gallery (combining both her maiden name, Govett, and her married name).

Now one of the finest contemporary art institutions in the country, the gallery is dedicated to showing exhibitions that are both intellectually challenging, exciting and cutting edge. This is no collection of modern paintings, but a mixture of contemporary art expression in the broadest possible terms. A special feature is a collection by the artist and kinetic sculptor Len Lye, who left a significant part of his work to the gallery.

Paritutu and Sugar Loaf Islands *

The track begins off Centennial Drive near the port.

Paritutu (154 m), like the offshore islands, is a volcanic plug — cooled magma that has hardened in a volcanic tube following an eruption over 1.7 million years ago. The rock is also an old fortified pa site. The climb to the top takes around 30–40 minutes return and is graded hard, but the view over the port and city is great. The offshore islands, Moturoa and Whareumu, are part of a marine reserve and local boat charters run trips there from the nearby port.

Puke Ariki Museum ***

1 Ariki Street

Open Monday, Tuesday, Thursday, Friday 9 a.m. to 6 p.m., Wednesday to 9 p.m., weekends 9 a.m. to 5 p.m., closed Christmas Day

www.pukeariki.com

Koha/donation

Set on a small rise in the heart of the city, this stunning modern museum is a real credit to the city. Not too large to be overwhelming the displays cover the natural and human history of Taranaki. The Maori gallery upstairs contains a good collection of carvings in the distinct local style, while the Taranaki Life exhibition on the ground floor covers every aspect of historical and contemporary life.

Highlights include:

- a Maori cloak, unique in that it is the only cloak made entirely of dogskin
- a fine collection of paepae para (lintels) in the distinctive local Taranaki style
- the head of Ferdinand the Bull, Taranaki's rugby mascot since the late 1950s, and named after the bull in the children's book *Ferdinand the Bull*, who would rather smell flowers than fight
- a Swanndri display. In 1913 local Taranaki tailor William Taylor registered the name Swanndri for a showerproof bushman's shirt. Made in limited quantities until 1952, when new techniques allowed much greater production, the Swanndri became hugely popular during the 1950s and '60s.
- the historic Richmond Cottage built of volcanic stone, located next to the museum (and with limited opening hours).

Pukekura Park ★★★

The main entrance to the park is at the top of Liardet Street.

www.newplymouthnz.com

One of the finest public parks in New Zealand, Pukekura Park opened in 1876 as the Recreational Ground, on land that had previously been a swampy valley. In 1908 the park changed its name to Pukekura and in 1934 an adjoining farm, Brooklands, was added, creating a parkland of 52 ha. The central lake, with its distinctive red bridge, and with Taranaki in the background, has been a popular feature of pictorial calendars for decades. Scenes from *The Last Samurai* were filmed on the cricket ground at the main entrance to the park, with the cricket pavilion recreated as a Japanese building. The unique Fernery opened in 1928 and comprises four distinct houses, the first of which has over 100 New Zealand ferns suited to cool, wet conditions.

Oakura — Koru pa ★

From Oakura turn left into Wairau Road. The pa is 4 km down this road and is well sign-posted.

Koru pa is situated on some of the oldest inhabited land in New Zealand, dating from around 1000 AD and occupied until 1826 when invading Waikato forced Taranaki tribes further south. Situated on a loop of the Oakura River, the pa is highly unusual as stone is used on the outer facings of the defensive ditches. This is especially obvious on the upper terraces. The outline of the pa is very clear, in particular the deep kumara pits, ditches and terraces. The pa has an unusual feel in that it is bush covered though there is an excellent view of the river below from the top terrace. Some theorists claim that the use of stone indicates a much older culture stretching back thousands rather than hundreds of years. While the pa site is well maintained, the access is an unformed track across farmland.

Opunake Beach ★

Opunake Beach lies in a broad cove below the town and is open to strong westerly swells that make the beach one of New Zealand's top surf destinations. A recently built artificial reef has ensured even better waves. Situated on SH45 (now known as the Surf Highway), Opunake is just one of Taranaki's famed surf beaches and in virtually every weather a good swell will be running somewhere in the province.

Parihaka International Peace Festival **

Parihaka marae, off SH45

www.parihaka.com

This biennial festival celebrates the remarkable actions of the people of Parihaka who in 1881 met armed forces with peaceful action and courteous resistance. The protest against continued land sales led to the mass arrest of the men, including the leaders Te Whiti and Tohu, and a five-year military occupation of the pa. Although the protest eventually failed, the actions at Parihaka and the leaders Tohu and Te Whiti have come to symbolise the fight for indigenous rights through passive resistance. A plough used by the Parihaka men to remove survey pegs is held in the Puke Ariki Museum. The peace festival at Parahaki features music, craft, workshops and food.

Patea

Aotea monument **

Egmont Street (SH3)

The memorial to the Aotea waka is one of New Zealand's best-known works of folk art. Built of concrete in 1933, the monument commemorates the settlement of the district in the fourteenth century by Turi and his wife Rongorongo. The waka actually landed at Kawhia and Turi and his hapu travelled overland to the river previously described to him by the explorer Kupe. Paepae in the Park is an annual festival celebrating Waitangi Day (6 February) set in the park behind the monument and attracting top musical acts and large crowds.

Patea Museum *

127 Egmont Street

Open Tuesday to Saturday 10 a.m. to 3 p.m., closed public holidays

Phone 06 273 8354

Koha/donation

Diagonally across from the Aotea monument is a small museum housed in Patea's oldest building (1869). More like a cluttered antique shop, this museum will appeal to those who enjoy an enthusiastic and eclectic style of collection rather than the sparse modern style. There are fine collections of local Maori art, a small display about Dalvanius and the Patea Maori Club (famous for their hit 'Poi-E'), a collection of cream cans, horse-drawn ploughs, light switches and light bulbs, and a series of murals by Oriwa Haddon painted on pinex panels (originally from a local pub) to celebrate the centenary of the European settlement of the district.

About 200 m further down the road in an old shop is a freezing works display. For years the freezing works was the town's main employer and when the works closed in the early 1980s, the townspeople, with virtually no other employment, were devastated. This display, viewed through the windows, tells part of that story and how this gutsy little town refused to die.

Pukeiti ***

From the city, take Carrington Street which then becomes Carrington Road. The gardens are at 2290 Carrington Road, 25 km from the city.
Open daily September to March 9 a.m. to 5 p.m., April to August 10 a.m. to 3 p.m.
www.pukeiti.org.nz
Entrance fee

In a province well endowed with great gardens, Pukeiti is world-renowned for its collection of over 2000 rhododendrons. Situated at an altitude of 400 m on the foothills of Mt Taranaki, the cool, wet climate and rich volcanic soil is ideal for growing rhododendrons and related plants. Founded in 1951, the gardens now cover 25 of the 350 ha owned by the trust. The rhododendron festival in October/ November coincides with the peak flowering period and attracts a large influx of visitors. However, different types of rhododendrons flower from July through to March, and the popular large-leaf varieties flower through August and September. Over the summer period the large vireya rhododendron collection is in flower, as is the extensive hydrangea collection. Of special note is the flowering of the giant Himalayan lily, which has a short flowering period around Christmas.

Mount Taranaki ***

Sitting at the heart of the Taranaki province and rising to 2518 m, this mountain is almost the perfect volcanic cone and it is little wonder that local people just love their mountain. The volcano is currently dormant and last erupted only 250 years ago.

In Maori legend Taranaki was forced to flee the central North Island after losing a battle with Tongariro over the love of the beautiful Pihanga. The valley he carved out as he fled was filled with his tears and became the Whanganui River.

Snow-covered in winter, the mountain is ringed by the luxurious bush of Egmont National Park, established in 1881 and now covering 33,000 ha. Named Egmont by Captain Cook, the mountain officially carries both names, while the national park retains the name Egmont.

The climb to the top is hard work and takes around eight to nine hours return. The weather is notoriously fickle so anyone attempting the climb should be very well prepared for alpine conditions, even in summer. The most popular route is from the North Egmont Visitor Centre and good local guides are also available.

If climbing the mountain is not an option, there are bush and alpine walks ranging from 15 minutes to two hours from the North Egmont Visitor Centre, and bush walks around the picturesque Dawson Falls area on the southwest side of the mountain. Visit www.doc.govt.nz for more information.

The Round the Mountain cycle race in January is a popular event that circumnavigates the mountain. First held in 1911, this 150-km race attracts a large field of over 4000 cyclists (www.roundthemountain.co.nz).

Taranaki Rhododendron and Garden Festival ***

www.rhodo.co.nz

With an equable climate and fine volcanic soil, Taranaki has more than its share of the country's finest gardens and of the 24 gardens of 'national significance', eight are to be found in this province.

In October/November each year Taranaki hosts one of New Zealand's leading garden events, the Taranaki Rhododendron and Garden Festival. The heart of the festival is the rhododendron collection at Pukeiti, but over 40 gardens are open to the public, ranging in type from coastal and subtropical to alpine. Although some of the gardens are open all year round, most are only open during the festival or by appointment.

Other notable gardens in Taranaki are Hollard Gardens (Kaponga), Tikorangi (the Jury Garden), Te Kainga Marire, Woodleigh, Ngamamaku, Te Popo, and Tupare.

Waitara

Manukorihi pa *

North Street, 1 km east of the town centre

Not open to the public

Built in 1936 as a tribute to Sir Maui Pomare, the impressive carved meeting house Te Ikaroa-a-Maui sits above the Waitara River across from the town. Along with Sir Peter Buck and Sir Apirana Ngata, Maui Pomare had a long and influential parliamentary career and did much to reverse the fortunes of Maori who in 1900 were at their lowest ebb. Pomare died suddenly in Los Angeles in 1930 and his ashes are buried beneath the statue in front of the meeting house. The meeting house and carved gateway are clearly visible from the road.

Pukerangiora pa *

Coming from New Plymouth turn right into Waitara Road about 2 km before the turnoff to Waitara. The pa is 8 km on the left down Waitara Road.

A major pa on a high bluff overlooking the Waitara River with wide views back to the coast, Pukerangiora saw bitter fighting during the Musket War period in the 1820s and '30s. At one stage the pa fell to invaders, forcing many of the defenders to try and escape by leaping from the cliffs above the river. During the New Zealand Wars of the 1860s, the pa was the centre of a campaign led by the elderly Major General Pratt who adopted slow siege tactics, including a series of redoubts and a long sap which is still clearly visible. Pratt's technique, described as 'a mile a month', drew criticism from the colonists and one report said 'The war in Taranaki maintains its peaceful course'. The pa eventually fell to the General.

The site is not well maintained and the signage minimal and confusing, but don't be put off by that. The main carpark is about 200 m past the first sign and is easy to miss. The military sap to the pa is behind the trees to the left of the first sign. The road from the turnoff is also sign-posted with the location of the redoubts built as part of the attack on the pa.

WANGANUI

Whanganui River Road **

Beginning at Upokongaro and finishing in Raetihi, the 91-km road built in 1935 covers some of New Zealand's most fascinating back country as it follows the course of the Whanganui River for much of its length. Many of the names of the settlements along the river are of biblical origin — Hiruharama (Jerusalem), Atene (Athens), Koriniti (Corinth) — though quite how Ranana (London) crept in is anyone's guess. This is not a road that can be hurried as it is narrow and winding and a long stretch is still unsealed with few facilities. What's more, the locals drive fast and are disinclined to give way.

Jerusalem/Hiruharama **

Once a thriving settlement, Jerusalem is set in a bend of the river above which sits the pretty church of Hatu Hohepa (St Joseph), one of New Zealand's most photographed churches. The convent next to the church was the home of Mother Aubert (1835–1926), who came from France and established the order of The Sisters of Compassion in 1892. Mother Aubert was well known in the district for her charitable work and use of native plants for medicinal purposes. James K. Baxter, the acclaimed poet, established a short-lived commune settlement in 1969, and *Jerusalem Sonnets* and *Jerusalem Daybook* were written there.

Just downriver is Moutoa Island, site of the historic battle of 1864 when upriver supporters of the anti-British Hauhau were defeated by their lower-river opponents.

Kawana Flour Mill **

9 km south of Jerusalem

In 1854 Governor (Kawana) Grey presented the Poutama people with the machinery to build a flour mill. The mill operated until 1913, then fell into disrepair until in recent years when it was faithfully restored. The mill contains the original millstones and upstairs the walls are lined with historic photographs and an excellent diagram showing how the mill operated. The cottage next to the mill was moved to the site from its original position across the road.

Koriniti ★★★

Koha/donation

This beautiful historic marae features three carved meeting houses, Poutama (1888), Te Waherehere (1845) and Hikurangi Wharerata (1975). The marae is open to visitors except when a function is being held.

Pipiriki ★★

The stretch of the river above Pipiriki, which is not accessible by road, is considered to be the most attractive part of the Whanganui as it meanders through the Whanganui National Park. Once a busy river port. it is now the base for tramping, jet boating, kayaking and other adventure trips along the river and for access to the Bridge To Nowhere.

Wanganui

Cook's Garden ★

St Hill Street

The gardens are actually an athletic stadium made famous when Peter Snell ran New Zealand's first sub-four-minute mile in 1962. The viewpoint over the stadium is marked by an old wooden fire-tower with bells dated 1874, and on the street below the tower is Wanganui's fine wooden opera house, built in 1899.

Durie Hill elevator and tower ★★★

The tunnel to the elevator is opposite the City Bridge at the end of Victoria Street.
Open Monday to Friday 7.30 a.m. to 6 p.m., Saturday 9 a.m. to 5 p.m., Sundays and public holidays 10 a.m. to 5 p.m.
Entrance fee to elevator

Across the river from the city is the distinctive 33.5-m tower atop Durie Hill. Built in 1919 to promote easy access to the hill suburb, this is the only public underground elevator in New Zealand. The elevator exits at the bottom of the tower. From the top, views include not only the city and environs, but also, on a fine day, Taranaki and Mt Ruapehu.

Sarjeant Gallery **

Queen's Garden

Open daily 10.30 a.m. to 4.30 p.m., Anzac Day 1 p.m. to 4.30 p.m., closed
Christmas Day and Good Friday

www.sarjeant.org.nz

Koha/donation

This very stylish art gallery was built with the aid of a bequest from local
businessman Harry Sarjeant, and opened by Prime Minister William Massey
in September 1919. The building is clad in Oamaru stone, and a special
feature is the use of natural light, especially from the beautiful 13-m-high
central dome. The gallery was one of the first to collect photography as a
fine art medium, and has significant collections of the works of Edith Collier,
Philip Trusttum, Gretchen Albrecht and Lawrence Aberhart.

The gallery is in the centre of Queen's Park, in which are also situated the
library, museum and War Memorial Hall, the latter awarded the New Zealand
Institute of Architects Gold Medal in 1961. Originally a pa site, the park was
also the site of the Rutland Stockade built to defend the fledgling settlement.

Waimarie paddle steamer **

1a Taupo Quay

Daily cruises November to May, weekend cruises May to November, no cruises
August

Phone 06 347 1863

www.wanganui.org.nz/riverboats

Built in 1899 as a kitset in London, the *Waimarie* (originally named *Aotea*) was
one of a fleet of 12 riverboats owned by Alexander Hatrick, that worked the
river between the coast and Taumarunui. In 1935 the Whanganui River Road
was opened, leading to a slump in river traffic, and the *Waimarie* was finally
taken out of service in 1949. Rescued from the mud in 1993, she was back on
the river in 2001 and now is New Zealand's only authentic coal-fired paddle
steamer, and runs regular cruises up the river to Upokongaro.

Whanganui Regional Museum ★★★

Watt Street, adjacent to Queen's Park

Open daily 10 a.m. to 4.30 p.m.

www.wanganui-museum.org.nz

Koha/donation

This is one of the best regional museums and while it focuses on the Wanganui distinct and in particular the river, it contains some of the country's most important artefacts and is not too big to be overwhelming.

Not to be missed is Lindauer Gallery, the largest collection of Lindauer paintings in the country with around 20 paintings on display at any one time. Sir Walter Butler commissioned Gottfried Lindauer to paint portraits of rangatira for a London exhibition. After the exhibition the paintings returned to New Zealand and many have been displayed at the museum since 1928.

Upstairs in the natural history collection is one of the most important collections of moa bones, with a number of complete skeletons of several species widely ranging in size from giant to hen size.

In the central hall is the magnificent waka taua (war canoe) *Te Mata*. Over 22 m in length, this waka was built before 1810 from a single totara log and took part in several battles, with the musket holes to show for it.

MANAWATU, RANGITIKEI & KAPITI

Feilding Saleyards **

Manchester Street
Guided tour Fridays 11 a.m.
Phone 06 323 3318
www.feilding.co.nz
Small charge

Saleyards, where sheep and cattle are sold, are a vital ingredient of the rural economy, but for those not directly involved in agriculture, the operation of a saleyard can be plain confusing. However, in enterprising Feilding, which has one of New Zealand's largest saleyards (around 15,000 sheep and 1400 cattle are sold each week), a tour is available, with local farmers acting as guides. This personable and friendly tour will unlock the mysteries of how a saleyard works. Sale days are every Friday, the tour is at 11 a.m. and bookings are essential. Wear sensible shoes and bring a rainproof jacket.

Foxton

De Molen Windmill ***

Open daily 10 a.m. to 4 p.m.
www.windmill.org.nz
Entrance fee

Finding a full-sized seventeenth-century Dutch windmill with arms whirring in the wind in the main street of a small New Zealand town is a sight not to be missed. The brainchild of Dutch immigrant Jan Langen, this working windmill was built from actual Dutch plans (with only small adaptations to the New Zealand building code) and the working machinery was imported from the Netherlands. The windmill operates during opening hours (except in very high winds) and actually processes New Zealand wheat into flour, which can be purchased at the shop on the ground floor of the mill. Well worth the short detour off SH1, and for those of Dutch origin be prepared for a big lump in your throat.

Foxton Beach — Manawatu Estuary *

Considered one of the most important wading bird habitats on the west coast of the North Island, the Manawatu River mouth attracts a wide range of Arctic breeding birds including bar-tailed godwits, red knots, sandpipers, golden plovers and curlews. Important birds that breed at the estuary are the royal spoonbill and the wrybill (an unusual bird with a beak that curves sideways). The beach/river mouth area is 7 km from the town.

Foxton Flax Stripping Museum **

The museum is behind the windmill.
Open daily 1 p.m. to 3 p.m., closed Christmas Day, Good Friday and Anzac Day
Phone 06 363 7095
Entrance fee

Flax was an important industry in colonial New Zealand and in the heyday of the flax industry the stretch of the Manawatu River between Foxton and Palmerston North supported 70 flax mills; Foxton alone had eight in 1912. Flax fibre has long been superseded by imported and synthetic yarns, and this museum now houses the only working stripping and scutching machines in the country. Every bit as interesting as the machinery is the man in charge, Gordon Burr. Known locally as Mr Chatterbox, Gordon has worked all his life in the flax industry and what he doesn't know about flax isn't worth knowing. Whether you are interested in flax or not, Gordon's enthusiasm and charm will make this one of the best working museum experiences in the country. And don't forget to buy a cake of flax soap.

Trolley Bus and Doll Collection *

55 Main Street
Open Tuesday to Sunday 10 a.m. to 5 p.m.
Phone 06 363 6656
Entrance fee

Enthusiastic husband-and-wife team Christina and Ian Little between them collect dolls and trolley buses. Ian has the largest private collection of trolley buses in the world, with 14 from Auckland, Wellington, Christchurch and Dunedin (only Wellington still uses trolley buses). His interest in trolley buses began in 1949 when as a boy he stood on the wharf with his father watching the new Dunedin trolley buses being unloaded from a ship, one of which he later purchased in 1966 for one pound. Opened to the public in 1986, the buses are in working order and rides are available along the 4 km of overhead wire set up in Foxton streets.

While Ian collected buses, Christina set about making and collecting dolls. The highlights include a French wax doll 160 years old, a collection of Princess Diana dolls dressed in Diana's most famous frocks, and a kewpie doll collection, the oldest of which dates from 1910.

Kapiti

Kapiti Island **

One of New Zealand's most important bird sanctuaries, Kapiti Island lies 5 km off the coast, is 1965 ha in area, and its highest point, Tuteremoana, is 520 m. Occupied by Maori around 1150 AD, Kapiti originally was part of the territory of Rangitane, ancestor of the Rangitane iwi of the Manawatu. In 1822 the island was occupied by Te Rauparaha, driven south from Kawhia, and it was from this island base that the great fighting chief launched his devastating attacks on the South Island.

Now an important nature sanctuary, the island is home to many rare birds including the little spotted kiwi (extinct on the mainland), weka, kaka, tieke (saddleback) and hihi (stitchbird). It is reasonably accessible, though visitor numbers are regulated, and you must obtain a visitor's permit from the Department of Conservation first. Email kapiti.island@doc.govt.nz for more information.

Paraparaumu Golf Course ***

376 Kapiti Road, Paraparaumu

Private club but visitors are welcome, though it is essential to book at least a week ahead.

www.paraparaumubeachgolfclub.org.nz

Ranked as one of the top 100 golf courses in the world, the club was originally established in 1929 but the redesign of the course in 1949, by Australian Open Champion Alex Russell, quickly established Paraparaumu as one of the country's leading golf courses. Over the years the course has hosted numerous national and international tournaments and international champions, including Tiger Woods who played in the New Zealand Open in 2000.

Southward Museum — Paraparaumu ***

Otaihanga Road just off SH1

Open daily 9 a.m. to 4 p.m.

www.southward.org.nz

Entrance fee

Sir Len Southward started collecting cars in 1956 after a long association with the motor industry, and this museum is by far the most outstanding such collection in New Zealand. Opened in 1979 the museum has over 250 vehicles with around half that number on display at any one time. As well as vintage and veteran cars there are motorcycles, aircraft, fire engines, stationary engines, traction engines and motoring memorabilia.

Highlights include:

- 1895 Benz Veto
- 1912 Phanomobile
- 1920 Stanley Steam Car
- 1927 Bugatti T38
- 1941 NSU Kettekbrakt
- 1950 Gangster Cadillac
- 1955 Gullwing Mercedes-Benz
- 1972 Treka Utility Van
- 1982 Taipan Sports Car.

Wellington Tramway Museum **

Queen Elizabeth Park, Mackays Crossing entrance, SH1, Paekakariki

Open 11 a.m. to 4 p.m. weekends and public holidays, closed Christmas Day

www.wellingtontrams.org.nz

Entrance fee

Established in 1964 when the last of the tramlines in Wellington City were being closed. The operational trams are all from Wellington and built between 1905 and 1952. The 2 km of track take the visitor from the museum buildings to the beach where there are picnic facilities, walking tracks and views to Kapiti Island and across Cook Strait. During the Second World War the area was a major American base for soldiers on leave from the Pacific.

Ohakea Museum *

Ohakea Air Force Base, SH1 between Sanson and Bulls
Open daily 9.30 a.m. to 4.30 p.m.
Ph 06 351 5020
www.airforcemuseum.co.nz
Entrance fee

The small museum at Ohakea Base is dedicated to the history of the New
Zealand Air Force and in particular the squadrons based at Ohakea. There is a
fine collection of aeroplane engines including a cutaway of a Rolls-Royce Avon
Mk 1, and a Harvard stripped of its outer covering giving the visitor a clear view
into the cockpit and engine.

The cafe, which can be accessed separately from the museum, overlooks the
runway, the only place in the southern hemisphere where the public can view
a military airbase. A Skymaster and Skyhawk are on view directly in front of
the cafe.

Shannon — Owlcatraz **

SH57
Open daily 10 a.m. to 3 p.m., guided tours
www.owlcatraz.co.nz
Entrance fee

The ruru, or morepork, is still a common bird in the New Zealand bush (as well
as some urban areas), and while its haunting call is familiar to most people, this
creature of the night is very rarely seen. Owlcatraz is an opportunity to see this
small owl up close in a special nocturnal aviary built to enable visitors to meet
Owl Capone, Owle Macpherson and Owlvis Presley. Owlcatraz has other animals
and birds, such as the North Island weka, as well as a purpose-built glow-worm
cave. All tours are guided.

Palmerston North

Hoffman Kiln *

615 Featherston Street

Listed by the Historic Places Trust as one of the country's 10 most important
industrial sites, the Hoffman Kiln is unmarked and sadly neglected.

This type of kiln was developed in Germany in the 1850s, though the Palmerston North kiln is an updated version of the original design. Designed to be fired continuously with each chamber being loaded, heated and unloaded one after the other, the kiln produced 9000 bricks per day.

While most firings were around six weeks, the longest continuous firing for this kiln was three months. Coal was fed into the chamber through small holes in the kiln by men working under the corrugated-iron roof structure.

New Zealand Rugby Museum **

87 Cuba Street

Open Monday to Saturday 10 a.m. to noon, 1.30 p.m. to 4 p.m., Sunday 1.30 p.m. to 4 p.m.

www.rugbymuseum.co.nz

Entrance fee

Crammed full of every conceivable type of rugby memorabilia, this small museum is well worth a visit even if your interest in rugby is only marginal, while rugby fans should plan to spend a few hours here. The collection has both New Zealand and international material and the wall of New Zealand and international rugby jerseys will help those who have trouble sorting out which colour belongs to what team. And what is a stuffed kiwi doing in a rugby museum? On the 1924/25 tour of Britain the New Zealand team took along a stuffed kiwi in a glass case to give to the first team that beat them, but being undefeated the kiwi came back home. Typifying the wide range of material held here is a broken shield used by protesters against the 1981 Springbok tour.

Savage Crescent *

Savage Crescent can be accessed off either Park Street or College Street, both of which run off Fitzherbert Avenue.

The first Labour Government under Michael Joseph Savage aggressively developed state housing throughout the country, but Savage Crescent is unique in that the whole development is still original. Developed from 1939 to 1946, the crescent is a mixture of housing designs from this period, with some of the houses being quite different in style from those typically associated with state housing.

A walk round the entire crescent will take less than an hour.

Te Manawa *

396–398 Main Street

Open daily 10 a.m. to 5 p.m.

www.temanawa.co.nz

Koha/donation, and entrance fee for the Mind section

This museum is divided into three parts: Life (History), Art, and Mind (Science). The style of this museum is 'less is more' and unfortunately the displays are so thin on the ground that the feel is more of a lighting showroom than a museum. Despite that, the Science area has a great interactive section popular with children (especially the Crazy House), and the Life section has some very impressive palisade carvings from the Puketotara pa, and part of a meeting house created by the master carver Hokowhitu MacGregor.

Sanson Rugby Grandstand *

On SH1, 500 m south of the Sanson-Palmerston North intersection

This iconic grandstand is symbolic of the enthusiasm of grassroots rugby that has made such a small nation a major international player in this sport. With a sign proudly proclaiming Manawatu Rugby, the stand is simply built of corrugated iron and overlooks a single field maintained by grazing sheep rather than a ride-on mower.

Rangitikei

Taihape — Gumboot Day ***

Held annually on Easter Tuesday, Gumboot Day was established in 1985, inspired by the popular Fred Dagg/John Clarke 'The Gumboot Song' and the need to give the old railway town of Taihape a distinctive festival. The event includes gumboot races, gumboot decorating and of course the annual attempt on the world gumboot-throwing record. The New Zealand record is 38.66 m for men and 24.92 m for women, though sadly the world records for both men (63.98 m) and women (40.87 m) are held by people from Finland. The word gumboot is peculiar to New Zealand having arisen out of the rubber boots used by gum diggers in Northland.

Rangitikei River ★★★

The Rangitikei River is considered to be one of the best whitewater rafting rivers in the country with dramatic scenery as well as wild water. Kayaking, fishing and jet boating are also popular and these activities can be arranged from either Mangaweka or Taihape. Mokai Gravity Canyon just south of Taihape (www.gravitycanyon.co.nz) boasts the highest bungy jump in the North Island as well as other extreme adventures. The Information Centre in Hautapu Street (SH1) Taihape has details of the many activities in the area. Visit www.rangitikei.co.nz

Stormy Point Lookout, Rangitikei ★★

On SH54, 15 km from SH1 turnoff 6 km north of Hunterville

While there a number of good viewpoints overlooking Rangitikei, by far the most spectacular view is from Stormy Point. Of particular interest are the broad river terraces considered to be one of the best preserved sequences of river terraces in the world and each formed during a period of climatic cooling, the oldest of which is 350,000 years.

Te Apiti and Tararua Wind Farms ★★

These two wind farms located north and south of the Manawatu Gorge are the largest such farms in the southern hemisphere. With the hills rising to 1500 m and exposed to the prevailing westerly winds, the farms take advantage of being located in one of the windiest places in the country. The windmills are of Danish design, which is most appropriate in a district settled by Scandinavian immigrants (in nearby Dannevirke and Norsewood east of the Tararua Range).

Tokomaru Steam Engine Museum ★★

SH57, 18 km from Palmerston North

Open Monday to Saturday 9 a.m. to 3.30 p.m., Sunday 10.30 a.m. to 3.30 p.m., closed Christmas Day and Good Friday

www.tokomarusteam.com

Entrance fee

While the collection has a working steam locomotive (with over 1 km of track and the old Tokomaru Station), this museum is dedicated to the industrial and agricultural use of steam in all its amazing variations. The private collection of

Colin and Esma Stevenson, the machinery has been collected from all over New Zealand and is a mixture of imported and locally made plant.

Highlights include:
- 1869 steam engine (New Zealand's oldest) used for hauling ships to the Wellington dry dock
- 1897 Aveling and Porter portable steam engine
- 1929 Marshall Tandem Steam Roller complete with steam-assisted steering (early power steering).

In the extensive workshop area (which is not always open to the public) is a metal press rescued from a factory in nearby Palmerston North. However, the press originated in Germany where, during the Second World War, it manufactured parts for the Luftwaffe, and it still bears the very visible scars where it was hit several times by Typhoon fighters.

Visitors beware: do not call Colin and Esma steam enthusiasts, as they insist on being described as steam preservationists.

See the website for 'Steam Up' days.

Waitarere Beach Shipwreck *

Waitarere Beach, 7 km from the turnoff on SH1 north of Levin

In 1879 the sailing ship the *Hydrabad* was wrecked on Waitarere Beach. Unable to be salvaged, much of the ship was stripped of its more valuable items leaving the hulk to slowly decay. Alternating between being exposed and being entirely covered in sand, the wreck is high on the beach, a short walk south of the carpark.

HAWKE'S BAY

British Car Museum **

63 East Road, Haumoana, on the road to Cape Kidnappers
Opening hours are when Ian Hope is there, which is most days between 10 a.m. and
4 p.m. but ring ahead on 027 231 3916 just to make sure.
Entrance fee

This place is special, but come with the expectation of an experience rather than
a collection of pristine showroom cars. In 1998 Ian Hope moved his growing
collection of cars into an unused packing house and now has over 300 vehicles
of British origin including over 30 Morris Minors and 40 Vauxhalls. Cars are
jammed in everywhere and in every sort of condition, though Ian claims 80 per
cent are in working order. The oldest car is a 1931 Austin 7, and the rarest a
1958 Vanguard Sportsman. In addition to the cars there are old petrol pumps, car
manuals, number plates, car badges and old road signs.

Cape Kidnappers **

The striking cliffs of this cape at the southern extremity of Hawke Bay are also
home to over 2000 breeding pairs of gannets. The colony at the cape is the most
accessible and largest mainland gannet colony in the world, as gannets usually
nest on islands. The birds arrive at the beginning of August and leave by the end
of April, and the best time to see chicks is in December and January.

The walk to the cape is around five to six hours return and runs along the
coast all the way from Clifton. However, at high tide, parts of the track are
impassable and it is essential to check tide times before you set out. If walking
isn't an option, there are several tour operators running vehicular trips to the
cape (www.hawkesbaynz.com).

Cape Kidnappers Golf Course **

www.capekidnappers.com

This 18-hole course, designed by American Tom Doak, is built above the dramatic
cliffs of Cape Kidnappers, so has spectacular sea views as well as providing a
great golfing experience. Cape Kidnappers was named Course of the Year in
2004 by *Travel and Leisure Golf*, and was ranked 27th in *World Golf* magazine's Top
100 Golf Courses in the World 2005.

Hastings

New Zealand Horse of the Year Show **

www.hoy.co.nz

This show was conceived in 1953 and now has a permanent home in the Hawke's Bay Showgrounds. It covers four disciplines including show jumping, dressage, harness and eventing. An extensive trade show complements the events which attract horse lovers from all over the country.

Rush Munroe Ice Cream Garden *

704 Heretaunga Street West

Frederick Rush Munroe established his Ice Cream Garden in 1931 to sell his handmade ice creams, taking advantage of the fresh fruit in the Hawke's Bay region. While the gardens are now on the shabby side, the ice cream is superb and is still made to original recipes with no artificial flavouring or additives, and using only real fruit and natural ingredients.

Spanish mission Hastings **

The people of Hastings have always seemed slightly put out that Napier received more attention than Hastings did in regard to the 1931 earthquake. Even the recent name change from Napier Earthquake to Hawke's Bay Earthquake was on the insistence that the quake damaged much more than just Napier. This was true, but Napier was doubly devastated by the fire that followed when the water system failed. Hastings, however, was able to contain any fires immediately.

With all that said, Hastings, like other towns in the region, suffered major damage and, like Napier, was rebuilt in the style of the day. In the case of Hastings, though, the style was more Spanish mission than art deco. Hastings has, in the Westermans Department Store (1932), one of the finest period buildings in the province, unique in the fact that not only the facade has been preserved but also the glass shop front, the interior oak panelling and even some of the original signage. The building now houses the Hastings Information Centre, from which visitors can obtain a self-guide leaflet for a walking tour of Spanish mission Hastings.

Splash Planet *

Grove Road

Open daily October to March 10 a.m. to 6 p.m., closed Christmas Day

www.splashplanet.co.nz

This water theme park has over 12 different pools, rides and slides in a six-hectare recreation area with something to appeal to all ages. Attractions include Master Blaster, Sky Castle Screamer, Never-ending River, Pirate Fortress, Formula One racing cars, bumper boats, mini-golf and beach volleyball. The best place for the family on a hot summer's day.

Hawke's Bay wineries ***

The Hawke's Bay climate with its hot dry summers combined with excellent grape-growing soils produces some of the best wines in the world. Of all the grape-growing areas in New Zealand, Hawke's Bay grows the widest range of varieties, including pinot noir, merlot, syrah, chardonnay, sauvignon blanc, riesling and pinot gris. There are over 30 wineries in the Hawke's Bay area, all with their own style, ranging from large sophisticated affairs with top-of-the-range restaurants to more homely or historic vineyards where a picnic among the vines is more the order of the day.

Brookfields Vineyards **

Brookfield Road, Meeanee, Napier

Cellar door open daily 10.30 a.m. to 4.30 p.m., closed Good Friday and Christmas Day

www.brookfieldsvineyards.co.nz

This friendly family owned and operated vineyard was originally established in 1937, and, as well as producing award-winning wines, has a special ambience all of its own. There is outdoor lunchtime dining and a very atmospheric evening restaurant. One of the closest wineries to Napier city, it is easily accessible by cycle, car or taxi.

Craggy Range Vineyards **

253 Waimarama Road, Havelock North

Cellar door open daily 10 a.m. to 5 p.m.

www.craggyrange.com

Set in Tukituki Valley, this large stylish winery produces single-vineyard wines with no blending, though grapes are sourced from other areas. The renowned Terrôir restaurant was named by *Wine International* UK in their Top 13 Winery Restaurants in the World.

Mission Estate Winery ***

198 Church Road, Taradale

Cellar door open Monday to Saturday 9 a.m. to 5 p.m., Sunday 10 a.m. to 4.30 p.m.

www.missionestate.co.nz

New Zealand's oldest winery, Mission Estate was originally established in nearby Meeanee in 1851 primarily to produce altar wine. Superbly situated with broad views over Napier, the winery is housed in the beautifully restored seminary building originally constructed in the early twentieth century. In addition to the stylish restaurant overlooking the gardens, the Mission provides free wine-tasting and conducts tours of the historic building.

Mission Estate concerts **

Begun in 1993 with a performance by Dame Kiri Te Kanawa, the Mission concerts quickly became Hawke's Bay's premier musical event, and tickets often sell out even before the performer is announced. Held in the natural amphitheatre in the vineyard, acts have included Shirley Bassey, Beach Boys, Doobie Brothers, Rod Stewart and Ray Charles. There is limited seating, with most of the crowd picnicking on the slopes above the stage.

Ngatarawa Wines **

305 Ngatarawa Road, Bridge Pa, Hastings

Cellar door open daily Labour Weekend to Easter 10 a.m. to 5 p.m., rest of the year 11 a.m. to 4 p.m.

www.ngatarawa.co.nz

Ngatarawa cellars are housed in historic racing stables that were built in 1890. The wines are produced by Alwyn and Brian Corban, whose family has been making wine since 1902, initially in the West Auckland region and at

Ngatarawa for over 25 years. In addition to cellar sales, visitors can picnic under the trees in the vineyard.

Sileni Estates **

2016 Maraekakaho Road, Bridge Pa, Hastings

Cellar door open daily 10 a.m. to 5 p.m.

www.sileni.co.nz

Internationally recognised for its stylish modern architecture, Sileni offers a first-class restaurant, wine-tasting, a vineyard tour, and one of the country's best gourmet stores, which stocks an amazing selection of cheeses as well as locally made olive oils.

Te Awa Winery ***

2375 State Highway 50, Hastings

Cellar door open daily 9 a.m. to 5 p.m.

www.teawa.com

Established in 1992 on Gimblett Gravels, Te Awa not only takes pride in being a single-estate vineyard, with a strong tradition of red wine, but also offers first-class dining in an attractive restaurant set amongst the vines.

Trinity Hill Winery ***

2396 State Highway 50, Hastings

Cellar door open daily Labour Weekend to Easter 10 a.m. to 5 p.m., rest of the year 11 a.m. to 4 p.m.

www.trinityhill.com

Located in the famous Gimblett Gravels vine-growing area, this vineyard produces wine from 16 different varieties, more than any other vineyard in New Zealand. The handsome modern winery built in 1997 was designed by Auckland architect Richard Priest and was honoured in 2002 as a 'stand-out' building by the New Zealand Institute of Architects. In addition to cellar sales and tastings, the cellar is a venue for exhibitions of contemporary New Zealand art, and behind the winery is an extensive picnic area (platters are also available).

Kahungunu meeting house **

300 m from the roundabout on SH2, Nuhaka

The central ancestor of this magnificent meeting house is Kahungunu, after which the iwi of Hawke's Bay and Wairarapa take their name. Built as a war memorial after the Second World War, the traditional style of this house contrasts with the modern and more colourful meeting house Tane Nui A Rangi 2 km north of Nuhaka.

Lake Tutira **

SH2, 44 km north of Napier

This popular swimming and picnic spot was originally part of the Tutira Station owned by farmer and author Herbert Guthrie-Smith. Guthrie-Smith early on recognised the need for conservation of native plants and birds, and in 1921 published his massive book, *Tutira: the story of a New Zealand sheep station*, based on years of painstaking observation and note-taking. The picnic area at the southern end of the lake was the site of the station's woolshed and is now the beginning of several tracks in the Tutira Country Park. The walks include the Lake Waikopiro Loop Track, a 30-minute circular walk round this small lake adjoining Tutira, and the three-hour tramp to Table Mountain Trig with spectacular views both inland and over Hawke Bay.

Mahia Peninsula *

From Nuhaka on SH2, turn left at the roundabout and travel 40 km to Mahia.

Jutting out into the Pacific, the wild and barren Mahia Peninsula separates Poverty Bay from Hawke Bay and is a popular fishing, diving and surfing area. The north side of the peninsula is characterised by small rocky bays and has a good boat-launching ramp, while on the southern side the wide sweep of Opoutama Beach is a favourite swimming and surfing spot, though Blacks Beach further south has the best surf. The Mangawhio Lagoon is an important wetland reserve and, for the more energetic, there is a two-hour walk through the Mahia Peninsula Scenic Reserve, a rare remnant of coastland forest in this bare landscape.

Mohaka Viaduct and River *

The white cliffs above the Mohaka River are a spectacular backdrop to the massive Mohaka Viaduct. The highest railway viaduct in New Zealand at 97 m, the 270-metre-long viaduct was opened in 1937 and is of steel girder construction. The river is popular for kayaking and whitewater rafting.

Napier

Art deco Napier ***

On 3 February 1931 a massive earthquake hit the Hawke's Bay region, causing widespread damage from Wairoa in the north to Dannevirke in the south, killing 258 people and devastating the small cities of Hastings and Napier. Napier city suffered particularly badly when fire broke out in the central business area following the quake. Large sections of Bluff Hill collapsed and the surrounding lagoons all but disappeared when the land rose over two metres. The city, however, was rebuilt in what was then the most fashionable of styles — art deco, Spanish mission and stripped classic — and as all the new buildings had to be built in concrete and to low level, the resulting effect is surprisingly uniform and appealing.

A good starting point for exploring art deco Napier is the Art Deco Shop in Tennyson Street, which offers guided walking tours, a self-guiding booklet, and books, gifts and souvenirs (www.artdeconapier.com).

Art deco weekend ***

www.artdeconapier.com

One of Hawke's Bay's most popular events, this celebration of the 1930s lifestyle is held over a three-day period on the third weekend in February and has been running for over 20 years. Over 80 events ranging from picnics and themed dinners through to jazz concerts and vintage car displays culminate in a huge street parade through Napier on the Saturday. The province is packed out so you need to plan ahead, and dressing up in the 1930s style is essential.

Bluff Hill Lookout *

Situated in Bluff Hill Domain above the port of Napier, the lookout point has fine views from Mahia in the north to Cape Kidnappers to the south. The views over the city and plains are limited.

Clive Square *

This small square is notable for its formal flower beds, huge Moreton Bay fig tree and immensely tall Washingtonia palms. Set out as a garden in 1884, the square became the temporary Napier shopping centre after the 1931 earthquake and was affectionately known as 'Tin Town'.

Hawke's Bay Museum ***

Marine Parade
Open Monday to Friday 10 a.m. to 4.30 p.m., weekends and public holidays 11 a.m. to 4 p.m.
www.hawkesbaymuseum.co.nz
Entrance fee

This excellent museum achieves that fine balance between entertainment and information that is often lacking in contemporary museum displays.

On entering the Nga Tukemata section of the museum, the visitor is greeted by a superb group of four brothers carved locally in the early twentieth century with their names written across their chests. Among the numerous treasures are fish hooks carved in the distinctive Ngati Kahungunu style where birds are carved into the bone and adzes are adorned with spirals — again a style peculiar to the East Coast.

As expected, there is a comprehensive display on the earthquake and, even more informative, an excellent display on just what is art deco style. 'Dinosaurs — only in Hawke's Bay' tells the story of amateur fossil hunter Joan Wiffen who discovered the bone of a land dinosaur in 1975. At the time, experts believed that New Zealand had had only marine dinosaurs.

Marine Parade ***

Built on rubble from the 1931 earthquake, the reserve on Marine Parade embodies an earlier age when promenading by the sea was a popular recreational activity. A few years ago this area was particularly tired-looking but recent improvements have restored it to its former glory and now formal gardens link the various attractions such as the Sound Shell, swimming pool and skating rink. In particular, new paths and cycleways along the length of the foreshore have proved especially popular with locals and visitors alike. Unfortunately the beach along the waterfront is not very attractive for swimming, being both dangerous and mainly shingle.

Highlights along the Parade from north to south are as follows.

Ocean Spa Pool **

Open Monday to Saturday 6 a.m. to 10 p.m., Sundays and public holidays 8 a.m. to 10 p.m.

This is a great outdoor swimming complex overlooking the sea complete with a heated lap pool, spa and family pools as well as a steam room, sauna and cafe.

Pania of the Reef ***

In Aotearoa's very own Little Mermaid story, Pania left her sea people to be with her human, land-dwelling lover Karitoke. However, her desire to see her family became too strong and on visiting them for the very last time, her family trapped her in a cave below the sea where Pania became a reef with her arms forever reaching out for Karitoke. When the statue of Pania on the waterfront was recently stolen, the overwhelming affection of the local people for the statue was evident and she was soon restored, with great ceremony and relief, to her rightful position.

The Colonnade ***

This Italianate structure was built as a memorial to the earthquake victims and features the bell from the HMS *Veronica*, which was anchored at Napier at the time of the earthquake and whose seamen were vital in the rescue efforts immediately following the quake.

The Sound Shell **

This art deco stage was built in the 1930s and is a popular spot for performances of all types, especially during the art deco weekend.

National Aquarium of New Zealand ***

Open every day 26 December to 31 January 9 a.m. to 7 p.m., rest of the year 9 a.m. to 5 p.m.

www.nationalaquarium.co.nz

Entrance fee

Much further down the Parade but worth the walk, this superb aquarium has the largest collection of marine and freshwater fish in the country. The aquarium is in two parts: the first part is a tour through different parts of the world, while the second part has a tunnel through a huge fish tank giving an excellent 'underwater' view of the fish. The scary animals are all here: crocodiles, sharks and piranha, along with the vegetarian cousin of the piranha, the gentle paku. As well as fish, the complex has a walk-through kiwi house and reptiles including the tuatara.

Napier Botanical Gardens **

Spencer Street, off Chaucer Road South

Tucked away in a gully on Bluff Hill, these gardens were established as early as 1855 and contain a number of very large specimen trees as well as formal flower beds, ponds and an attractive stream running through the middle. The steep paths lead up to an old cemetery established at the same time as the gardens which includes the graves of early missionaries William Colenso and Bishop William Williams. The well-maintained gardens are a good place to start a walk on Bluff Hill, and are only let down by the barren, shabby bird aviaries near the lower entrance to the gardens.

Napier Prison **

55 Coote Road

Daily tours 9.30 a.m., 3 p.m.

www.napierprison.com

Entrance fee

Opened in 1862 with 25 men and 24 women, the inmates included lunatics, alcoholics, children and dispossessed Maori and a regime that included hard labour in the quarry opposite (now the Centennial Gardens). The current building is still largely in original condition and includes the solitary confinement cells, the hanging yard with a public gallery, a small graveyard, and cells complete with original bunks.

Finally closed in 1993, the prison is now a popular backpackers complete with regular ghost sightings! Tours are conducted daily. The prison was also the setting for the reality television show *Redemption Hill*.

Ocean Beach ***

25 km west of Havelock North

In contrast to the shingle beaches of Hawke Bay, Ocean Beach is a huge sweep of golden sand that stretches for miles. Although very popular in the summer months, it is largely undeveloped and never crowded.

Onga Onga **

Just off SH50, 18 km west of Waipawa, Central Hawke's Bay

This small township has 11 registered historic buildings and is well worth the detour. Many of the buildings such as the old butcher's shop and school are tiny. Several buildings have been shifted to an historic park next to the Department of Conservation office, including a back-country hut. Even the public toilets are housed in the old police cells.

Southern Hawke's Bay

Bindalsfaering *

Coronation Street, Norsewood, 100 m north of the Pioneer Museum

A bindalsfaering is a type of Norwegian fishing boat, looking for all the world much like a mini Viking ship. This one was presented to Norsewood by the Norwegian government on the occasion of the centenary of the settlement of the district.

Dannevirke Gallery of History *

14 Gordon Street, Dannevirke
Open Monday to Friday 9.30 a.m. to 4 p.m.

Dannevirke, meaning Danes work, is named after a fortification in Schleswig (now part of Germany) and, like Norsewood, was settled by Scandinavians but, in this case, mainly Danes. The local museum, known as the Gallery of History, has a wide range of artefacts from the early settlement of the town and naturally has a special appeal to Danish visitors. Particularly fascinating is the somewhat creepy 'Danish Hair Embroidery'. This piece celebrates the marriage of Brendt and Lisbet Johannsen and was delicately embroidered in human hair in 1886. In a glass case is the sad sight of a fine pair of huia, shot in 1889 in the Pohangina Valley and believed to be the last pair in the area.

Dave's Den *

363 High Street (SH2), Dannevirke
Open most days, roughly 10 a.m. to 4 p.m.
Phone 06 374 8432
Entrance fee

The meticulous collection of over 8000 model cars began while David Pawson was on holiday in Norfolk Island in 1981. Mainly Matchbox, Lledo, Dinky and Trax, the collection is arranged in series order, many with their original boxes alongside.

Norsewood Pioneer Museum *

Corner Coronation Street and Thor Street, Upper Norsewood
Open daily 8.30 a.m. to 4.30 p.m., closed Good Friday, Anzac morning and Christmas Day
Entrance fee

On 15 September 1872 two ships carrying Scandinavian immigrants landed at Napier. They were the *Hovding* from Christiania (now Oslo) and the *Ballarat* from London, and their passengers were Norwegian and Danish families sponsored by the New Zealand government and destined to develop the rugged southern Hawke's Bay. Initially 19 families settled in Norsewood and Dannevirke, and over the years many more Norwegians, Danes and Swedes joined them.

The museum is spread over a number of buildings and contains a wide range of items reflecting a colonial heritage with a strong Scandinavian flavour. Among the items are a nineteenth-century Royal Copenhagen porcelain communion jug used in the local Lutheran Church, as well as the pulpit from the Dannevirke Lutheran Church. In the garage display is the fascinating Scandi wagon, an early horse-drawn cart used locally and of distinctive Scandinavian design.

The nearby Norsewood cemetery is believed to be the largest Scandinavian cemetery in Australasia, and mainly contains the graves of Norwegian settlers.

Te Mata Peak ***

Te Mata Peak Road, Havelock North

The rugged barren peak of Te Mata, rising 399 m above the Tukituki Valley, offers the most spectacular view in every direction, from Mahia to the north through to Ruapehu on a particularly fine day. For those who prefer to walk, there are numerous tracks beginning at the carpark entrance to the peak and, for those even more adventurous, there is a mountain-bike-only track from just below the peak.

Wairoa

Giant Puka, Waiata Reserve *
SH2, 4 km north of Wairoa

The size of the puka tree will come as a surprise to those who consider this tree suitable for the small city garden. Believed to be the largest puka tree in New Zealand and standing 10 m tall, this broad multi-branched tree has much smaller leaves in the mature form than the more familiar wide leaves of the young tree. The track to the tree is not well marked and is overgrown, but the reserve is very small and it is impossible to get lost. After crossing the stile, follow the fenceline up the hill to some steps which lead to an indistinct track. The puka is not marked but it is right next to the dilapidated picnic table.

Maori Film Festival **

This recently established festival, held in October, is unique in New Zealand as the only festival to feature films both in Maori and about Maori. The festival attracts film buffs to the town from all over the country including many of the stars, directors and producers. The heart of the festival is the Gaiety Theatre on Marine Parade, restored and reopened in the mid-1990s. Originally built in 1928, it collapsed in the 1931 earthquake, was rebuilt and then closed in the late 1960s like so many local picture theatres.

Portland Lighthouse *
On the south bank of the river next to the Wairoa River bridge

Built of kauri in 1878, the lighthouse originally stood on Portland Island off the coast of the Mahia Peninsula. When the lighthouse closed in 1958, it was moved to its present position on Marine Parade to save it from demolition. The lighthouse is the start of the Riverside Heritage Walk along what used to be a bustling river port.

Diagonally across from the lighthouse is the famous Oslers Bakery. A family business since 1902, this bakery has won numerous awards including New Zealand Baker of the Year 2005, Best Cake Baker 2005, and New Zealand Supreme Pie Maker 2002.

WAIRARAPA

Castlepoint **

Known for safe swimming, surf and fishing, the setting of Castlepoint is dramatic with a lighthouse atop the raw cliff face of Castle Rock overlooking the coastal settlement. The lighthouse is one of New Zealand's most stylish, with a slender taper from 5 m at its base to 3 m at the top. Built in 1912, and automated in only 1988, the lighthouse can be seen 30 km out to sea.

Castlepoint is also famous for it beach races, which have been held annually in March since 1872. The races apply the sweepstake form of betting where punters place their bets and are then allocated horse numbers after the tote has closed.

Cobblestone's — Wairarapa Early Settlers Museum **

169 Main Street, Greytown
Open Monday to Saturday 9 a.m. to 4.30 p.m., Sunday 10 a.m. to 4.30 p.m.
Entrance fee

The heart of this complex is the Huntwell Stables, built in 1857 to service the fortnightly mail run from Greytown to Wellington. The small wooden stables are complemented by the original cobblestone floor and yard, while next to the stables is a fine 1858 woolshed. In addition, there is a single-roomed school, a cottage made of hand-pitsawn timber and the attractive Wesleyan Church with its tall windows and plain austere interior.

Fell Locomotive Museum ***

SH2, Featherston (middle of the main street)
Open daily 10 a.m. to 4 p.m., closed Anzac morning and Christmas Day
www.featherstoncounty.com
Entrance fee

Housing the only remaining Fell engine in the world, this smart small museum tells the marvellous story of the famous Rimutaka Incline and John Fell's ingenious system designed to tackle that most difficult terrain. In addition to locomotive H199, the museum contains the only piece of the original track, the Fell brake van built in Petone in 1898, a great display of photographs, as well as an audiovisual presentation of original archive film. A small pit allows the visitor to look under the Fell engine, and a model of the Incline gives a graphic picture of the rugged terrain the railway line traversed.

Holdsworth Tararua walks **

On SH2 south of Masterton, at 1 km south of the Waingawa River bridge, turn right into Norfolk Road and travel a further 16 km to the parking area.

Tucked in the foothills of the Tararua Range alongside the Atiwhakatu Stream, Holdsworth is the starting point for numerous walks ranging from five minutes to five hours. From here a walk to the Holdsworth lookout takes one hour return, while longer walks for more experienced trampers lead deep into the heart of the rugged Tararua mountains. The camping area set in a glade by the river is particularly attractive.

Masterton

Balloon Fiesta *

www.nzballoons.co.nz

Held annually in March, this five-day event attracts over 15,000 people to Henley Park. The balloons launch each morning at dawn and the fiesta culminates in Night Glow, an evening event featuring the tethered illuminated balloons, fireworks and music.

Golden Shears ***

www.goldenshears.co.nz

A three-day event that attracts both national and international competitors to Masterton for New Zealand's premier shearing event, including a trans-Tasman test. Established in 1960, Golden Shears quickly became a major event on the national calendar, especially when televised during the 1960s and 1970s. As well as shearing, other events include wool classing and wool handling, and there is also a 'wool triathlon', a combination of all three disciplines. The main events are held on the Saturday, which is always the first Saturday in March.

Queen Elizabeth Park cricket oval ***

Established in 1877, the attractive Queen Elizabeth Park along the Waipoua River contains a real gem, the loveliest cricket ground in the country in the most traditional English style. The beautifully kept cricket green is surrounded by mature European trees (not a native tree in sight), with a tiny Victorian grandstand built in 1895 and alongside, an Edwardian band rotunda built to celebrate the coronation of Edward VII in 1902.

In addition to the cricket oval, the gardens, named to commemorate the visit of the young Queen Elizabeth in 1954, have attractive formal gardens, aviaries, a miniature railway, a children's playground, a swing bridge over the river, and, across the road, a modern swimming pool complex.

Shear Discovery **

12 Dixon Street
Open daily 10 a.m. to 4 p.m.
www.sheardiscovery.co.nz
Entrance fee

At first glance it is hard to believe that the tidy building housing the museum, Shear Discovery, is actually two historic shearing sheds, Glendonald (built 1903) and Wilton (built 1900). Masterton folk were originally horrified at the sight of two dilapidated old woolsheds being dumped in the centre of town right across from their splendid Queen Elizabeth Park, but the museum now does the town real credit. It is the only museum in the country dedicated entirely to the history of the wool industry, and the well-presented exhibitions of every aspect of this very Kiwi industry include the Trethewey statue 'Shearing a Ram' (commissioned in 1925 for the Great Empire Exhibition in London), a range of historic shearing gear and the Golden Shears Hall of Champions.

Martinborough Fairs **

www.martinboroughfair.org.nz

Established in the late 1970s as an outlet for local craftspeople, the two fairs, held in February and March, attract enormous crowds from Wellington and the southern North Island. The heart of the fairs is The Square, from which radiate streets in the shape of the Union Jack, designed by immigrant John Martin in 1879. The international names of many of the streets — New York, Venice, Panama, Cork, Suez — are places he visited.

Martinborough wineries ***

In 1979 the Department of Scientific and Industrial Research (DSIR) identified the Martinborough area as having climate and soil types similar to Burgundy, and by the early 1980s four vineyards were established: Ata Rangi, Chifney, Dry

River, and Martinborough. Now Martinborough produces some of New Zealand's finest and internationally acclaimed premium wines. The wine-growing area is small and compact (with a couple of exceptions) and within a short distance of the town. Cycle tours are popular and several places in town hire bikes. However, be aware that many of the vineyards have very restricted opening hours, so, if you have a favourite vineyard, it pays to check ahead to see if they are open. Toast Martinborough, a celebration of local wine and food (with several good olive growers in the district), is held each year on the third Sunday in March. The following vineyards are open all or most of the year.

Alana Estate *

Puruatanga Road

Cellar door open daily 10.30 a.m. to 5 p.m.

www.alana.co.nz

Set on the edge of the famous Martinborough Terrace, this new and still somewhat stark vineyard offers excellent food and wine tastings, and unlike many local vineyards is open all year round.

Coney Wines ***

Dry River Road, 6 km from Martinborough on Jellicoe Street

Cellar door open Friday to Sunday 11 a.m. to 5 p.m., closed August and September

www.coneywines.co.nz

Owner-operators Margaret and Tim Coney pride themselves on combining good food and wine in this new vineyard in the Dry River area. The stylish cafe, in the Mediterranean courtyard style, offers lunch and has wide views over the Wairarapa plain to the Tararua mountains.

Martinborough Vineyard *

Princess Street

Cellar door open daily 11 a.m. to 3 p.m.

www.martinborough-vineyard.co.nz

One of the four original vineyards in the area, it is now one of the largest and also one of the closest to town, specialising in pinot noir.

Murdoch James ★★★

Take Jellicoe Street towards Lake Ferry and at 6 km turn left into Dry River Road and continue a further 3 km to the winery.

Cellar door open November to March daily, except Wednesdays, 11 a.m. to 5.30 p.m.; April to October open Friday to Monday, 12 noon to 3 p.m

www.MurdochJames.co.nz

This family vineyard was established in 1986 on a north-facing terrace overlooking Dry River and specialises mainly in reds. The winery offers tastings, tours, a stylish cafe (good food and views, open for lunch only), and a picnic area by a small lake among the trees and vines.

Palliser Estate Wines ★

Kitchener Street

Open daily 10.30 a.m. to 4 p.m. (to 6 p.m. on weekends in summer)

www.palliser.co.nz

Close to Martinborough, this is the first vineyard when entering the town from the north, and like most vineyards in the area specialises in pinot noir, chardonnay, pinot gris and riesling.

Te Kairanga Wines ★★

Martins Road

Cellar door open 10 a.m. to 5 p.m., wine tours Saturday and Sunday at 2 p.m.

www.tkwine.co.nz

The heart of this vineyard is the pretty 130-year-old workers' cottage set among the vines where visitors can taste the wines and picnic on the grass under the trees.

Tirohana Estate ★★★

Puruatanga Road

Open daily 9 a.m. to 6 p.m., closed Anzac morning, Good Friday and Christmas Day

www.tirohanaestate.com

This small, very friendly, family owned and operated boutique winery was established in 1988. The winery has very pleasant gardens and a terrace with tables and chairs for picnics.

Papawai marae, Greytown **

From Main Street, turn into Papawai Road and the marae is 2.5 km on the right.

Under the leadership of Tamahau Mahupuka, this marae played a major role in the Kotahitanga (Maori Parliament) movement in the late nineteenth century and early twentieth century and was the focus of many key meetings to address important Maori issues. The house, Hikurangi, was opened in 1888 and the lively Maori newspaper *Te Puke ki Hikurangi* was published here from 1897 to 1913.

Of particular note are the unique tekoteko, carved figures representing ancestors, on the palisading surrounding the marae. Usually these face outwards to protect the pa, but at Papawai they face inwards, representing peace between Maori and Pakeha.

Paua Shell, factory and shop *

54 Kent Street, Carterton

Shop open daily 9 a.m. to 5 p.m., factory open Monday to Friday 9 a.m. to 5 p.m.

www.pauashell.co.nz

Until recently paua (abalone) was a very lowly regarded material used only for the tackiest of souvenirs. Now the iridescent qualities of the shell have been rightfully rediscovered, and paua jewellery is particularly highly prized. At the Paua Shell, visitors to a small factory behind the large shop can see the raw paua shell being crafted into a range of objects.

Pukaha, Mt Bruce ***

SH2, 30 km north of Masterton

Open daily 9 a.m. to 4.30 p.m., closed Christmas Day

www.mtbruce.org.nz

Entrance fee (guided walks are extra)

This 1000-ha reserve is a remnant of the dense forest that once covered this area known as the Seventy Mile Bush and almost totally cleared at the end of the nineteenth century. Now an important bird sanctuary, this National Wildlife Centre also has breeding programmes for threatened species, in particular kokako, hihi, kiwi, kaka and the Campbell Island teal, while the wider reserve is home to kaka, kiwi and kokako.

Currently the public can access only the area along the Bruce Stream, along well-formed, wheelchair-friendly paths that link a number of aviaries containing rare native birds and a nocturnal kiwi house. The bush is especially handsome and the trees are well labelled. The walk takes around one hour. A viewing deck off the cafe overlooks the takahe enclosure. It is worth trying to time a visit to the eel feeding at 1.30 p.m. and the kaka feeding at 3 p.m.

Putangirua Pinnacles **

12 km southeast on the Cape Palliser Road from the junction of Lake Ferry Road

This walk on a good track takes about one-and-a-half hours return and leads to the fascinating 'badlands' formations featuring gravel pinnacles, or hoodoos. Over many thousands of years the Putangirua Stream has eroded the loose gravel soils to form a series of deep gullies including tall, pillar-like hoodoos. These pillars are topped by rock, which sheds rain and prevents the soft gravels from eroding, creating high fluted formations. There is a picnic area and camping ground at the entrance to the walk.

The wild nature of the southern coastline has it own special beauty, though in southerly weather it is very exposed.

Ruakokopatuna Caves *

Take Jellicoe Street from Martinborough for 6 km and then turn left into Dry River Road. After 9 km, turn into Blue Back Road and the caves are 3 km down this unsealed road.
Koha/donation

These cool caves and the stream are a pleasant, if modest, adventure on a hot summer's day. The caves follow an underground stream through limestone rock and have a sprinkling of glow-worms. The track is unformed and you will get your feet wet.

Stonehenge Aotearoa *

Take Park Road out of Carterton and follow the signs.
Guided tours for the public on weekends only, bookings essential
www.astronomynz.org.nz

This full-scale model of Stonehenge, opened in 2005, is built on a hill overlooking the plains and has been adapted to function in the southern hemisphere. More than just a replica, Stonehenge Aotearoa also details ancient and modern methods of astronomy, time and navigation including early Polynesian celestial seafaring abilities.

Tauherenikau horse racing **

wairarapa.racing@xtra.co.nz

This popular country track is famous for the casual atmosphere of its summer race meets (January 2) where picnics and barbecues under the massive totara and kahikatea trees are the order of the day. Races have been held here since 1871 on a track that, at the time, was noted as 'a very dangerous piece of ground to ride over owing to the number of holes thrown up during the earthquake of 1855'.

The elegant grandstand burnt down in 1955 during a race and, despite urgent calls of 'Fire!', patrons were reluctant to evacuate the grandstand until the race was finished. The historic ticket office and members stand still remain.

Especially popular for Wellingtonians is to travel to the race meet by train, the atmosphere on the return journey becoming particularly festive after patrons have enjoyed some time at the legendary local pub known as 'The Tin Hut'.

Tui Brewery, Mangatainoka, 'Yeah right' *

Impossible to miss, SH2, 24 km south of Palmerston North
Open daily 10 a.m. to 4 p.m., tours 10.30 a.m. and 1.30 p.m. Monday to Friday, bookings essential
www.tui.co.nz

The Tui Brewery comes as a surprise in the wide-open spaces of northern Wairarapa and southern Hawke's Bay. The seven-storey brewery was originally established by Henry Wagstaff in 1889 to take advantage of the clean waters of the Mangatainoka Stream and is in complete contrast to the empty landscape around it. In recent years Tui beer moved from being a regional brand to a major player in the market with its innovative 'Yeah right' billboard campaign. While 'Yeah right', indicating disbelief, has always been part of New Zealand English, this advertising campaign for Tui beer moved the saying into mainstream slang. The tour of the brewery includes beer tastings.

Army Museum, Waiouru

Korea display, Army Museum, Waiouru

Peter Janssen

Te Apiti Wind Farm, Manawatu

Civic Square, Wellington

Wither Hills Vineyard, Marlborough

Mussel-opening competition

Whale watching, Kaikoura

Maruia Springs

Anatini, Waitaki Valley

World Busker Festival, Christchurch

Hector's dolphins, Akaroa Harbour

Wheels Week, Ashburton

WELLINGTON

Archives New Zealand/Treaty of Waitangi ***

10 Mulgrave Street, Thorndon
Open Monday to Friday 9 a.m. to 5 p.m., Saturday 9 a.m. to 1 p.m.
www.archives.govt.nz

Archives New Zealand holds some of the country's key founding documents and the most important of these is the only copy of the Treaty of Waitangi. What will come as a surprise to most people is that the document is much longer than the rather battered and ragged first page that is usually shown. After the Northern chiefs signed the Treaty at Waitangi on 6 February 1840, the document travelled the length of Aotearoa to be signed by chiefs at various locations (though many refused to sign). Laid out in date order of signature, the remaining pages are in much better condition than the first page signed at Waitangi.

The Constitution Room is light and temperature-controlled and protected by a massive vault-like door. Also on display is New Zealand's earliest document — the 1835 Declaration of Independence of Northern Chiefs all in Maori, the elaborate Charter of 1840 that constituted New Zealand as a separate colony, and part of the massive petition to government in 1893 that led to New Zealand being the first country in the world to grant voting rights to women.

In addition to the documents on permanent display, Archives New Zealand also has two rooms with excellent temporary exhibitions.

Bolton Street Cemetery **

Established in 1840 to service the tiny settlement, this was Wellington's main cemetery until 1892 (though burials continued until 1967) and, as was usual practice at the time, was segregated by religion into Anglican, Jewish and Public areas. The tall column near the rose gardens is the Seddon Memorial. Richard Seddon was a monumental figure in early New Zealand politics, introducing important social legislation during his periods as Premier and then Prime Minister from 1893 to 1906. During his term as Premier, in 1893 New Zealand passed legislation allowing women to vote, a move Seddon actually opposed but had to accept as the process begun by his predecessor John Ballance, was well under way. Seddon, who died in office during a sea voyage from Sydney to Wellington in June 1906, is buried here along with his wife and daughter, and there is a memorial to his son killed in action in 1918.

Just metres down the hill is the grave of Harry Holland, first leader of the Labour Party from 1919 to 1933. The gravestone, curiously that of a naked man, was unveiled by the first Labour Prime Minister Michael Savage in 1937.

In 1967, despite strong opposition, the Wellington motorway cut through the heart of the cemetery and over 3600 graves were disinterred and reburied in a mass grave. An excellent display of the history of the cemetery is in the replica chapel.

Botanic Gardens ***

Main entrance Tinakori Road, Thorndon. Top entrance from the Cable Car.

www.wbg.co.nz

Begonia House open daily 10 a.m. to 4 p.m. May to August, 10 a.m. to 5 p.m. September to April

The hilly nature of Wellington has led to the creation of a unique botanical garden with little hidden valleys and winding paths linking various parts. Although 12 acres were set aside as a reserve as early as 1844, the garden was not formally established until 1868. Many existing trees date from this early period, planted to ascertain the economic potential of imported species in the southern climate. In 1871 the gardens were considerably expanded by the addition of a further 54 acres of remaining bush.

The formal garden, at the Tinakori Road entrance, is famous for its spectacular spring displays of tulips and has a sound shell which hosts small concerts in summer. The ever-popular duck pond with the fattest, best-fed birds in the country, is overhung by large cedars planted in 1874. A Garden of National Significance, this was also the first public garden to be classified as an historic area by the New Zealand Historic Places Trust.

A short uphill walk from the main entrance leads to the formal beds of the Lady Norwood Rose garden, opened in 1953 and named after the wife of Wellington Mayor Sir Charles Norwood. Containing over 100 formal rose beds, each bed has a different cultivar. The Begonia House, in addition to the usual collection of tropical and flowering plants, features the giant water lily *Victoria amazonica* best seen in the summer months. The Visitor Centre is located in the middle of the garden, in the appropriately named Tree House, below which are the garden's older buildings, including the original stables.

Brooklyn Wind Turbine ***

Ashton Fitchett Drive, Poll Hill, Brooklyn

Built as part of a research project in 1993, this was New Zealand's first wind turbine, and still generates enough power to supply 60 to 80 homes. To say the site is windy is an understatement, and the turbine is remotely controlled to adjust to the demanding conditions. Standing at 31.5 m high and with blades 13.5 m long, this turbine is a midget compared to the giants in the Manawatu. An added bonus is the exceptional views from Poll Hill.

The suburb of Brooklyn was named after the borough of New York City to which it bears absolutely no resemblance, though it also has a Central Park, and many of the streets are named after US Presidents.

Carter Observatory and Planetarium — National Observatory of Aotearoa **

Botanical Gardens, Upland Road. Easiest city access is via the Cable Car and then a two-minute walk.
November to April, Sunday to Tuesday 10 a.m. to 5 p.m., Wednesday to Saturday 10 a.m. to late
May to October, Sunday to Thursday 11 a.m. to 4 p.m., Friday to Saturday 11 a.m. to late
www.carterobservatory.org
Entrance fee

Perched above the city beside the Meteorological Office, the Observatory offers a Planetarium show (not weather dependent), a detailed tour of the stars and constellations of the southern sky and telescope viewing of the moon and planets (weather dependent). What is unique about the observatory is that it also offers daytime solar viewing (the sun needs to be shining) with a telescope fitted with a special filter lens allowing close-up viewing of the intriguing surface of the sun, with the opportunity to see sunspots and even solar flares.

The Carter Observatory, named after its original benefactor Brian Carter (of Carterton fame), features a rare 1867 nine-and-three-quarter-inch telescope (replaced with a modern lens) built by the famous instrument maker Thomas Cook (not the same as the travel company Thomas Cook). The nearby historic Dominion Observatory built in 1907 is now defunct.

City Gallery Wellington **

Civic Square
Open daily 10 a.m. to 5 p.m.
www.citygallery.org.nz
Koha/donation

This lively gallery focuses on contemporary art expression through a wide range of ever-changing exhibitions. The building, Wellington's old public library, was built in 1939 in the stripped classical deco style, and makes a unique and appropriate space for the innovative art displays.

City to Sea Walkway **

Wellington is a walker's paradise with hundreds of interlinking paths and tracks connecting suburbs, parks and beaches. This popular and well-signed 12-km walk starts from the Bolton Street Memorial Park (cemetery) in the city, and ends in Island Bay where you can catch a No. 1 bus back to town. The walk includes the Botanic Gardens, Aro Valley, Central Park and on through a number of south Wellington parks with spectacular views from Tawatawa ridge near Island Bay. The walk will take five to six hours.

Civic Square ***

New Zealand's finest public square is a relatively recent creation and is a testament to the vision of Wellington city administrators over the past 25 years. The sheltered space bounded on three sides by the two Town Halls, old and new, the Public Library, and the City Gallery is open to the waterfront on the eastern side, and linked to it by the City to Sea Bridge. This is no ordinary bridge but a fantasy walk through fountains and works of art including sculptures by the renowned Ngati Porou artist Paratene Matchitt. The fabulous nikau palm sculptures featured on the library and the surrounding area are the work of local architect Ian Athfield.

The Colonial Cottage Museum *

68 Nairn Street
Open daily 10 a.m. to 4 p.m. Boxing Day to Easter Monday. Rest of the year 12 noon to 4 p.m. Closed Christmas Day and Good Friday
Entrance fee

Most historic houses tend to be large and grand but this, Wellington's oldest building, is a small family home where William and Catherine Wallis raised their 10 children. Built in 1858, the house remained in the Wallis family until 1985, and both the garden and the house have been restored to reflect everyday life for ordinary New Zealanders in the second half of the nineteenth century.

Courtenay Place *

For years the poor end of town, Courtenay Place is now New Zealand's liveliest entertainment strip and Wellington boasts more bars, cafes and restaurants per head of population than New York City (over 350 and rising). Many of these are packed into Courtenay Place and surrounding streets along with the Embassy Theatre (which hosted the premieres of *The Lord of the Rings* films), the historic St James Theatre, The Opera House, the Paramount Theatre (Wellington's oldest surviving picture theatre) and, for live theatre, Downstage Theatre and BATS Theatre. Day or night, this area is buzzing.

Cuba Street Bucket Fountain **

Originally called the Water Mobile, this fountain was part of the redevelopment of Cuba Street in the late 1960s when the tramlines were removed. Designed by architects Burren and Keen and erected in 1969, the fountain works a simple bucket system which, in theory, should merely fill and empty on a regular basis. In reality, however, the whole thing works erratically, with the water sometimes missing the buckets altogether, or the buckets tipping when partially full or swinging completely upside down, often splashing passers-by. This gives the fountain enormous appeal as it is so unpredictable, and it is immensely enjoyable just to sit, watch and wait.

While most of Wellington has embraced a modern future, Cuba Street has somehow clung on to its seedy past and, in many respects, is not a whole lot different to the time when opium dens operated in Haining Street in the 1920s, or when Wellington's most well-known transvestite ran Carmen's Coffee Lounge during the 1960s. The area, still, is an eclectic mix of budget hotels, snazzy cafes, offbeat shops, and the occasional strip joint. The street is named after an immigrant ship, not the country, and in February every second year holds the very popular and lively Cuba Street Carnival.

Government Buildings **

Lambton Quay

Reputed to be one of the largest wooden buildings in the world, the woodwork is designed to mimic stone, at the time considered to be a much more desirable building material than humble wood. Completed in 1876 in the Italian Renaissance style, the buildings housed the Government Departments of the day and were substantially extended in 1907. Sitting on reclaimed land, early photographs show the building practically surrounded by water on three sides. Now occupied by Victoria University, most people only view the building's exterior, but parts of the interior are open to the public and hold some real surprises. To the left through the main entrance (and part of the DoC office), is a display giving a glimpse into the construction techniques, while just beyond that is a recreation of a typical clerical office during the Seddon Government. Further down the hall the old vault is open for view, and then a magnificent wooden staircase leads upstairs to the 1890s Cabinet Room, also open to the public. Along the hallways are numerous historic photographs of early Wellington buildings, people and events.

Hutt Valley

The Dowse **
Laings Road, Lower Hutt
www.dowse.org.nz

This gallery has long been at the cutting edge of innovative exhibitions and events that, whatever the theme, were exciting and challenging. At the time of writing, the Dowse was closed and undergoing major redevelopment with a new building designed by Athfield Architects. Due to reopen in early 2007, check the website for updates, as this gallery has, in the past been well worth the trip to Lower Hutt.

Christ Church **
Eastern Hutt Road, Taita
www.christ-church.org.nz

Sitting rather forlornly in an industrial area between a busy road and a railway line, this Category One historic building is the oldest church in the Wellington area. The first service was held in the church on 1 January 1854 and served what was then the local farming community. The timber church is built of pitsawn heart totara timber and was beautifully restored after being seriously damaged in a fire lit by an arsonist in 1989. The original entrance to the church was from the western side through the cemetery.

Eastern Bays **

From Point Howard to Robinson Bay, a series of picturesque bay settlements cling to the coastline between the sea and the steep bush-clad hills. Protected from the worst of the southerly winds, and frost free by proximity to the sea, the bush here is particularly luxuriant with massive tree ferns and nikau palms.

On a fine day in summer the beaches are a popular destination for Wellingtonians, with easy access across the harbour by ferry to Days Bay (it is a flat cycle ride all the way from the city as well). Days Bay is also the setting of one of Katherine Mansfield's most famous short stories, *At the Bay.*

Most of the bush above the bays is part of the East Harbour Regional Park which contains some excellent short walks, in particular, the Butterfly Creek area behind Eastbourne.

Hutt River Trail **

Running nearly 30 km from the Hikoikoi Reserve in Petone to Birchville in Upper Hutt, this flat trail is a dream for cycling, walking and running, as well as giving great access to the Hutt River for kayaking, swimming and fishing (there are good trout to be had in this river). For those less keen on physical activities, the trail gives easy access to quiet picnic spots on both sides of the river.

The scene in *The Lord of the Rings* films, where the Fellowship travelled down the river Anduin, was filmed on the Hutt River between Moonshine Bridge and Poet's Park in Upper Hutt, with the Elven boats being launched from Poet's Park.

Kaitoke Regional Park **

Waterworks Road, Kaitoke, Upper Hutt

In 1939 large areas of virgin bush were purchased for the local water-supply catchment area and, today, half of Wellington's water is still drawn from the Hutt River from within the park. Now covering 2860 ha, the park has some of the finest untouched bush in the Wellington region, with magnificent stands of old rimu, rata and beech. Kaitoke Park is well serviced by an excellent network of tracks, and was also the site of Rivendell in *The Lord of the Rings* films, the location of which is the junction of the Pakuratahi and Hutt rivers.

Pencarrow Coastal Trail ***

From Eastbourne following Muritai Road along the coast to the end, which is also known as Burdans Gate

This coastal walk encompasses some of Wellington's wildest seascape, being wide open to the worst that the southerly weather can bring, but that very wildness is also its greatest appeal. There are great views of the harbour, and on clear days across to the South Island and the Kaikoura mountains, snow-capped in winter; views enhanced by a short but steep climb up to the old lighthouse. The entrance to Wellington Harbour was even more treacherous in the days of sail than it is today, and from as early as 1842, lights to guide shipping were established here. However, it wasn't until 1 January 1859 that New Zealand's first lighthouse cast its light across the harbour entrance and this, in turn, was replaced by the lower lighthouse in 1906 still operational today. During the *Wahine* foundering in the storm of 1968 many of the survivors and bodies were washed up along this bleak stretch of coast.

While this track follows the coast from the road end right round to the Wainuiomata River mouth (three hours one way) most people only go as far as the lighthouse, a much more manageable one-and-a-half-hour one-way walk. The track is also very popular with mountain bikers.

Petone Museum *

The Esplanade, Petone (end of Buick Street)
Open Tuesday to Friday 12 noon to 4 p.m , weekends and public holidays 1 p.m. to 5 p.m. Closed Christmas Day
www.petonesettlers.org.nz
Koha/donation

This tiny museum covers, in addition to the settlement of the area, the important manufacturing industries that made this part of the Hutt Valley one of New Zealand's most important industrial areas. Displays include the General Motors Plant, Wellington Woollen Mills, Colgate Palmolive and the Railway Workshops. The James Turkington mural in the foyer was originally executed in 1940 and has recently been restored. In recent years Petone has undergone a revival as a place to live, and the very long main thoroughfare, Jackson Street, is now a popular destination for both its shopping and cafes. The historic Petone Police Station built in 1908 is also in Jackson Street.

Rimutaka Trig *

The track off the road is 250 m below the Rimutaka summit on the western side.

This short, one-hour-return, but steep track leads through subalpine vegetation up to the Rimutaka trig (725 m) with broad views over the Wairarapa plain, but be aware that the summit is very exposed and can be exceptionally windy.

Rimutaka Rail Trail ***

The western access is the Kaitoke Loop Road while, in the east, it is the Cross Creek Road.

The 18-km trail takes four to five hours one way and follows what was the old Wellington-Wairarapa railway line prior to the opening of the 8.8-km Rimutaka tunnel in 1955. The tunnel spelt the end of the famous Rimutaka Incline which used the unique three-track Fell system to climb the steep grades. Today the track follows the disused section of the railway through old tunnels, historic bridges and, of course, the Incline itself.

Wallaceville Blockhouse *

It is very strange that the local authorities should completely ignore this blockhouse, when the area has few other historic buildings. The original two-storey building complete with musket loopholes was built in 1860 for hostilities that never eventuated and is one of very few wooden blockhouses to survive. Now a sport clubrooms, the building has no signage or any indication of its intriguing history.

Tutukiwi Orchid House *

Riddiford Park, corner Laings Road and Mytle Street, Lower Hutt
Open daily 10 a.m. to 3.45 p.m.

This small greenhouse tucked away in Lower Hutt holds a surprising range of orchids, both multi-flowered and single-stemmed. Some are housed in small glass display boxes at eye height allowing for close examination of these colourful exotic blooms.

Johnsonville Line — Wellington Rail **

www.tranzmetro.co.nz

Of all the cities in New Zealand Wellington has the most extensive and most patronised rail network, linking the northern districts with the central station. For the visitor, the most scenic line is out to Johnsonville which takes just 21 minutes one way weaving up steep-sided valleys and through no fewer than seven tunnels.

The grand station at Wellington, built in the Classical tradition with massive Doric columns, was opened in 1937. It is believed that the huge entrance foyer, in the beaux-arts style, was modelled on Pennsylvania Station in New York. Now looking decidedly shabby, the station was, at the time, the largest public building in New Zealand, and employed in its construction the latest earthquake-protection technology available at the time.

Karori Wildlife Sanctuary ***

Waiapu Road, Karori
Open daily from 10 a.m. to 5 p.m. (last entry 4 p.m.). Closed Christmas Day
www.sanctuary.org.nz
Entrance fee

Only 2 km from the city, this 250-ha forest was originally Wellington city's water reservoir catchment and had been closed to the public for over 120 years. In the early 1990s Forest and Bird members developed a plan to create an urban sanctuary for native flora and fauna, and from this emerged a charitable trust, the Karori Wildlife Sanctuary (so don't grizzle about paying an entrance fee).

A key element to the success of the sanctuary has been the 8.6 km of predator-proof fencing (a world first) followed by the eradication of predators within the fenced area. Only recently opened to the public, the park has been a resounding success and is now home to numerous native birds including saddleback, weka, brown teal, tomtit, kaka, whitehead and the little spotted kiwi as well as tuatara (best seen on summer afternoons). While the fence keeps the pests out, it doesn't keep the birds in, and many a bird leaves never to be seen again.

The tracks and trails are easily accessible and suitable for all levels of fitness and you can even take a boat trip on the lower lake. For an additional fee experienced guides take two-hour tours and, for something different, a night tour is also available (see the website for details).

And there's more! The sanctuary even has an old gold mine, the Morning Star Mine, now home to glow-worms and cave wetas. By the lake is the Governor's boatshed and the much-photographed historic valve tower, while further up the valley, the upper dam is a rare example of a gravity arch dam and was built in 1908.

Katherine Mansfield Birthplace ***

25 Tinakori Road, Thorndon
Open Tuesday to Sunday 10 a.m. to 4 p.m. Closed Christmas Day and Good Friday
www.katherinemansfield.com
Entrance fee

The surprising thing about this house is that Katherine Mansfield never had good memories of the place, describing it as 'that dark little cubby hole', and yet the house regularly occurs in her writings, especially her short stories. Katherine was born there in 1888 and lived there until 1893 when the family moved to Karori. Eventually, at the age of 19, she left Wellington for Europe. In 1923, at Fontainebleau, France she died of tuberculosis. Now recognised as one of New Zealand's greatest short story writers, her original home has been immaculately restored to reflect a typical lower-middle-class family home of the late Victorian period. With its dark stained wood, heavy drapes and furniture, and over-decorative wallpapers, the house has a somewhat overbearing and melancholic feel. A useful handout relates each room of the house to Mansfield's writing, while the main bedroom has a detailed display of her life. For those not familiar with Katherine Mansfield's writing or life an excellent range of books is available for purchase.

Kathmandu Crazyman Multi-sport Race *

www.crazyman.co.nz

This popular 68-km multi-sport event, held in May each year, includes all the best elements of Wellington's rugged landscape and attracts well over 500 competitors, both individually and in teams. The race begins with a 12-km kayak from Petone to Eastbourne, followed by an 18-km beach and bush run and finishing with a 38-km mountain bike back to Petone. A duathlon option is available for non-kayakers.

Krupp Gun *

Located next to the old Dominion Observatory, this is the only surviving example of 190 such guns manufactured by F. Krupp in Essen, Germany in 1907. The gun was captured by the Wellington Regiment near La Vacquerie in northeastern France in 1918. The site of the gun is the old Botanic Garden Battery, established in 1894 as part of the city's defences during the 'Russian Scare', at a time when Russia was actively expanding into the Pacific.

Makara Walkway **

Leave the swimming gear at home. Makara Beach is definitely not the place for a dip, but is an exposed bay open to the wild waters of Cook Strait. Summer or winter it is a place of solitude, though it wasn't always as barren as it is today. Several Maori pa sites in the area are testament to the richness of both sea and forest and even Captain Cook remarked on the din of the dawn chorus of birdsong from the coast, even though he was almost a kilometre offshore. The loop begins at the southern end of the beach and includes Second World War gun emplacements, a Ngati Ira pa site and spectacular views over Cook Strait. The loop takes three hours or one hour return to the gun emplacements. The coastline is rocky, so good footwear is necessary and wild weather is a bonus.

Makara Peak Mountain-bike Park **

Main entrance South Karori Road
www.makarapeak.org.nz

A mud-splattered heaven for mountain bikers, this bike-only park has six tracks of varying grades from the easy Koru track for first-timers through to Vertigo, a hard-core track for skilled riders. Makara Peak, the high point, rises to 412 m. In all, there are 8 km of 4WD track and 24 km of custom-built single track. If you don't have a bike you can hire one from Mud Cycles just down the road at 338 Karori Road (www.mudbikes.co.nz).

Matiu/Somes Island ***

Located in the heart of Wellington Harbour, this 25-ha island has a long history of human occupation and is now an important nature sanctuary free from predators. Named Matiu by the legendary explorer Kupe, who discovered the harbour around 1000 AD, Maori long occupied the island, mainly as a refuge, as the island lacked permanent fresh water. Purchased by the New Zealand Company and renamed Somes Island after the deputy governor of the Company, Joseph Somes, the island was used as a quarantine station from 1872 for both people and animals.

During both world wars the island was a detention centre for alien residents and a source of much grief to Wellington's Italian community and German and Austrian refugees during the Second World War. There are still the remains of gun emplacements from the Second World War. Several bird species, as well as tuatara, have been reintroduced to the island. There are a number of good walking tracks on the island and East by West stop there on their cross-harbour ferry route (www.eastbywest.co.nz; phone 04 499 1282).

Mt Victoria Lookout ***

Road access signed from the northern end of Oriental Bay

The most accessible of Wellington's numerous hills, Mt Victoria rises 196 m above Evans Bay, to the east, and Port Nicholson, to the west, and has fantastic views over the city, Cook Strait, Hutt Valley and the Tararua mountains. Known to Maori as Tangi Te Keo, the hill is named after the legendary taniwha, Whataitai, whose soul, in the shape of a bird, flew to this point to mourn the death of the taniwha.

The strange pyramid-type monument is dedicated to American explorer Rear-Admiral Richard Evelyn Byrd, an ardent supporter of the Antarctic Treaty protecting 'the white continent of peace'. Included in the monument are rocks from the Koettlitz Glacier and Ross Island in the Antarctic.

Other equally impressive viewpoints in the Wellington region are Mt Kaukau (445 m), Hawkins Hill (495 m) and Tinakori Hill (303 m).

Museum of New Zealand Te Papa Tongarewa ***

Cable Street
Open daily 10 a.m. to 6 p.m., Thursday until 9 p.m.
www.tepapa.govt.nz
Koha/donation (charge for special exhibitions)

Opened in 1998, the museum, known to most New Zealanders as just 'Te Papa', attracted over two million visitors in its first year and has remained a popular attraction to locals and visitors alike. Innovative displays, spectacular exhibitions, and 'hands on' child-friendly exhibits have kept Te Papa lively and relevant as an institution. Covering five floors, the layout is not straight forward with many of the exhibitions subtly blending into one another. Good navigation skills are required. Unfortunately, the superb collection of New Zealand art is not well displayed.

That said, Te Papa is jammed full of New Zealand treasures. The Maori collection is superb, including the very fine Rongowhakaata meeting house Te Hau-ki-Turanga. Built of totara in the early 1840s by master carver Raharuhi Rukupo, it is one of the earliest wharenui built with steel tools. In direct contrast is Rongomaraeroa, the marae created by Cliff Whiting with its amazing ultra-modern wharenui, Te Hono Ki Hawaiki, designed to encompass all the people of Aotearoa and embraced by the net of Maui taming the sun.

The John Britten V1000 motorcycle, 1992, is one of only 10 machines made, and the collection of contemporary women's shoes is to be envied.

Tucked away behind the Treaty of Waitangi exhibition is the superb Hawaiian cloak given to Captain James Cook. At first it appears to be hidden in the dark, but the exhibit is cleverly light-controlled and after a few moments the intricate yellow-and-red feather cloak and helmet are revealed.

Just outside the entrance is a short flight of steps leading down to an amazing view of the foundations and, in particular, the innovative earthquake protection pioneered by New Zealander Dr Bill Robinson.

While the museum is large, there are plenty of spaces to sit and take a quiet break.

Museum of Wellington City and Sea **

Queens Wharf, Jervois Quay
Open daily 10 a.m. to 5 p.m. Closed Christmas Day
www.museumofwellington.co.nz
Koha/donation

Located in the historic Bond Store (built 1892), this excellent museum is often overlooked, in a city well endowed with galleries and museums. Entry to and from the museum is through a recreation of the original 1890s Bond Store. The *Wahine* Disaster section includes a 12-minute film, as well as memorabilia from the *Wahine*. And don't skip the 1920's boardroom of the Wellington Harbour Board with its beautiful wooden panelling and grand courtroom-like layout.

National War Memorial and the Tomb of the Unknown Warrior **

Buckle Street

Open daily 10.30 a.m. to 4.30 p.m. Monday to Saturday, 12 noon to 4.30 p.m. Sunday

www.nationalwarmemorial.govt.nz

Built in two stages, the National War Memorial is dedicated to those who lost their lives in conflicts from the South African Wars through to the Vietnam War. The Carillon and Foyer were constructed in 1932, while, cut into the hill behind, is the Hall of Memories opened in 1964, a sombre space subtly and stylishly decorated. In front of the War Memorial is The Tomb of the Unknown Warrior plainly constructed of bronze and stone and simply inscribed. All that is known of this man is that he died on the Western Front during the First World War where New Zealand suffered over 12,000 fatalities.

The Carillon plays most days at 12 noon and in front of the building is a small statue modelled on the famous Gallipoli painting 'Simpson and His Donkey'.

New Zealand Academy of Fine Arts **

1 Queens Wharf (opposite the Museum of Wellington City and Sea)

Open daily 10 a.m. to 5 p.m.

www.nzafa.com

Founded in 1882, the Academy promotes the very best of New Zealand art by both new and established artists. Professionally displayed in a modern and well-lit gallery, most of the art on show is for sale.

New Zealand Cricket Museum ***

Rugby Street (southern side of Basin Reserve)

Open daily 10.30 a.m. to 3.30 p.m. November to April (and all day on match days) and 10.30 a.m. to 3.30 p.m. weekends only May to October

www.nzcricket.co.nz

Entrance fee

This fascinating compact museum holds a surprising array of cricket memorabilia and will appeal to all sports fans, not just cricket enthusiasts. Housed under the old members grandstand built in 1920, historic items and photos are professionally combined with good text to create entertaining and informative displays on this ancient and often confusing game.

Highlights include: the Addington bat, the third-oldest bat in the world dating from 1743 and looking more like a hockey stick than a modern cricket bat, the retired Plunket Shield, Dennis Lillee's famous aluminium bat, and a ball cleverly made of cork and parcel-string in Stalag 180 Prison Camp during the Second World War. Special displays cover cricket greats such as Richard Hadlee, Bert Sutcliffe, Martin Crowe, Clarrie Grimmet and even Donald Bradman. The entrance, off the busy roundabout that is the Basin Reserve, is not that easy to find, but make the effort, because this museum is worth it. There is a small carpark just inside the gate.

New Zealand Parliament House of Representatives ***

The first capital of New Zealand was at Russell in the Bay of Islands for a period of only nine months before moving to Auckland in 1841. Moving yet further south to Wellington in 1865, the shift reflects the change in population and rising importance of the South Island at the time during the gold-rush period. Parliament met in the old Wellington Provincial Government buildings until they were destroyed in a dramatic fire in 1907. Rebuilding began in 1912 with Parliament finally meeting in the new building in 1918 after construction was interrupted by the First World War. Due to a lack of funds, the southern wing was never built, leaving the existing building curiously lopsided. Typically Edwardian neo-classical in style, the main building is in direct contrast to the Victorian Gothic General Assembly Library next door, built in 1899.

Originally New Zealand had two chambers, a lower house, The House of Representatives, and an upper house, The Legislative Council whose members were selected by the government of the day for seven years. Abolished in 1951, the non-elected Upper House was, no doubt, a serious irritant to a government elected every three years. While New Zealand now has a mixed proportional representation electoral system, the heart of the New Zealand style of government is very much British in origin.

The Beehive (the source of much comment and the origin of many jokes) was designed by British architect Sir Basil Spence and completed in 1981 and now houses parliamentary offices and the main banquet hall.

While the House is in session in Parliament House, the gallery above the main debating chamber is open to the public, though daily tours lasting around an hour, and free of charge, are the most convenient way for a visitor to see the building. All visitors must go through airport-type security checks.

Old Saint Paul's — and other Thorndon Churches ***

Mulgrave Street, Thorndon

www.oldstpaul.co.nz

Open daily 10 a.m.to 5 p.m. Closed Good Friday and Christmas Day

Koha/donation

Designed by Reverend Frederick Thatcher in the Early English Gothic style (Thatcher also designed numerous early New Zealand churches), the church is entirely built of native timber with totara beams, kauri sarking, and matai floors (though the pulpit carved in 1893 is of oak). The first service was held in 1864 and, virtually unaltered since construction, the building is one of the most pleasantly proportioned buildings in New Zealand with an especially warm and inviting interior. However, the church narrowly escaped demolition when the new and larger church opened in 1954, but considerable support finally saved the church from destruction and led instead to its restoration.

The newer Wellington Cathedral of St Paul, one street over in Molesworth Street, is very different and, in the tradition of many cathedrals, it took years to complete. Although designed in 1937, the Second World War delayed construction and the main building was completed in only 1964, with the tower added in 1982. While the huge concrete building has the hollow feel of a massive tomb, around the walls are some interesting historical pieces. It is worth trying to catch a time when the organ is playing as the acoustics are very impressive.

Next door to the Anglican cathedral in Hill Street is the Catholic Cathedral of the Sacred Heart built in 1901 and designed in the Roman basilica style by FW Petre, better known for his massive Catholic churches in Christchurch, Timaru, Waimate, Dunedin and Invercargill.

Oriental Bay **

A small popular inner-city beach, Oriental Bay is lined with stately Norfolk pines and high-rise apartment buildings and, facing north, attracts a crowd on a sunny day. Like so many of Wellington place-names, the bay takes its name from an immigrant ship, which is totally appropriate considering the sandy beach is the result of ballast being dumped in the harbour from early sailing ships. Offshore is the Carter Fountain that operates only when the wind is blowing in the right direction (or preferably not blowing at all). The old band rotunda on the sea wall is now a restaurant. The Freyberg Pool at the city end of the bay is a popular indoor spot for those not keen to brave the elements.

Otari-Wilton Bush's Native Botanic Garden and Forest Reserve ***

Wilton Road, Wilton (No. 14 bus)

Open from sunrise to sunset, Information Centre open daily 9 a.m. to 4 p.m.

www.owb.co.nz

A 'must' for anyone interested in New Zealand plants as these are the country's only public gardens dedicated exclusively to native plants. Established in 1926 as the Otari Open-Air Plant Museum, the first director was pioneer botanist Dr Leonard Cockayne who was instrumental in collecting and classifying many native plants.

The gardens are beautifully laid out and easily accessible with the dramatic Canopy Walkway linking the two cultivated parts of the gardens. To the left of the information centre are the older gardens with impressive collections of hebe, flax, coprosma and threatened species (among others), while the fernery and alpine gardens in the themed area are equally worth visiting. The Nature Walk loop which covers both gardens and an attractive section of bush between the two, takes around 40 minutes, though it does have a steep section with steps. Beyond the Kaiwharawhara stream are several loop walks through original bush areas that can take up to one hour.

Porirua

Colonial Knob *

Main access by the Elsdon Camp in Rahia Street (off Prosser Street)

At 465 m, Colonial Knob is the highest point in Wellington's western hills with views south to the Kaikoura mountains in the South Island and as far north as Mt Taranaki. The well-formed track through regenerating bush takes around two-and-a-half hours return.

New Zealand Police Museum **

Papakowhai Road, Porirua

Open Wednesday to Sunday 10 a.m. to 4 p.m. Closed public holidays

www.police.govt.nz

Entrance fee

Established in 1908 and moved to Porirua Police College in 1996, this small museum has displays that combine memorabilia and photographs to illustrate some of New Zealand's most fascinating criminal and social history.

There is nothing gratuitous here, nor has the museum shied away from the controversial.

The material is wide-ranging, from one of Stanley Graham's guns, through to a real still seized at Canvastown near Blenheim in 1949. Special exhibits cover the *Wahine* disaster, the Erebus crash, the 1981 Springbok tour, the sinking of the *Rainbow Warrior* and an opium den raid in Haining Street, Wellington, in the 1920s.

For the kids (and some adults) there is a box with dress-up clothes,and while the adults browse through the museum, children are kept busy with their very own Junior Detective Mystery which takes around 30 to 40 minutes.

Pataka **

Corner Norrie and Parumoana Streets, Porirua

Open daily 10 a.m. to 4.30 p.m. Monday to Saturday, 11 a.m. to 4.30 p.m. Sunday

www.pataka.org.nz

Rather than create yet another local museum, Porirua City Council have cleverly opted for a more innovative approach and have linked a number of galleries to create an exceptional and original art space. Melody Farm is an eclectic mix of music machines from jukeboxes through to pianolas, radios and early television sets, while the Heritage section covers local history. What makes Pataka special are the fabulous temporary exhibitions that are usually themed and are inclusive of a wide range of art forms (check out their excellent website for the latest information). The galleries also highlight the very best of contemporary Pacific- and Maori-inspired art and are well worth the short detour off SH1.

Titahi Bay *

A popular seaside resort for Wellingtonians in the 1920s and '30s, Titahi Bay is one of the best surf beaches north of Wellington. Long a Maori stronghold, Te Pa O Kapo is an old pa site to the north of the bay (north end of Terrace Road) while, in European times, the bay was home to three whaling stations in the 1820s and '30s, hunting whales migrating through the relatively narrow channel of Cook Strait. This was also the point where the telegraph and telephone cables across Cook Strait came ashore, and the old cable house still exists (now a private home). Mana Island Lookout (south end of Terrace Road) has great views over the strait and to the plateau-like Mana Island, first visited by Kupe around 1000 AD and now an offshore wildlife sanctuary.

Second World War American Buildings *

Porirua has two of the very few buildings left from the substantial American presence in the Wellington area during the Second World War. What was the officers' mess is now the Titahi Bay Public Library, and the soldiers' Recreational Centre in Whitehouse Road is now the Porirua Little Theatre. To the north, in Queen Elizabeth Park in Paekakariki, are information boards relating to the large American camp in that area.

Seatoun **

It was at Seatoun that the Polynesian explorer Kupe first landed at Wellington Harbour around 1000 AD and named the area Te Turanga o Kupe, 'the great standing place of Kupe'.

Located on the eastern side of the Miramar Peninsula (once an island), Seatoun has the two best city beaches, Scorching Bay and Worser Bay. While the southerly is Wellington's wildest wind, the blustery northerly is more common, and these two sandy beaches are protected from the north wind and are safe for swimming, though the water is usually fairly cold.

On the corner of Forbes and Munro Streets is the *Wahine* Memorial. At 6 a.m. on 10 April 1968, during a cyclonic storm with winds up to 200 kph, the inter-island ferry *Wahine* was driven onto Barrett Reef at the entrance to the harbour. It eventually capsized and sank around 1.30 p.m. with the loss of 51 lives. Many of the survivors were washed ashore along this coast and, today, the anchor of the *Wahine* is part of the memorial.

Sevens Rugby Wellington ***

Westpac Stadium (The Cake Tin)
www.westpactruststadium.co.nz

Held in February each year, the AXA New Zealand International Sevens attracts over 30,000 supporters who pack the city for a two-day tournament of Sevens Rugby. Serious early planning is necessary as both tickets and accommodation are booked out well in advance of the games.

The Westpac Stadium, affectionately and accurately named The Cake Tin, was completed in 1999 and holds a crowd of almost 35,000, of which 24,000 are under cover. Easily accessible by public transport and within walking distance from the central city, this stadium is one of the best in the country. Outside of events, tours of the stadium can be arranged via the website.

Thistle Inn ***

Mulgrave Street, Thorndon

Built in 1840, this cosy pub still sits on its original site on a small bluff above what was once the shoreline, and legend has it that boats and waka conveniently pulled up on the beach below the Thistle so the occupants could enjoy a beer. The earthquake of 1855, and numerous foreshore reclamations, have now left the pub some distance from the sea. Restored in recent years, the warm wooden interior, complete with historic photographs, maps and plans and an old beer cellar, is a great place to finish a walking tour of Wellington.

Tinakori Road Houses **

Thorndon

Thorndon is one of Wellington's oldest suburbs and, despite the motorway cutting through the heart of the area, a number of fascinating houses still line Tinakori Road (these are private and not open to the public). From 296 to 306 Tinakori Road, six narrow wooden houses, one-room wide, rise three to four storeys above the road. Number 306 has a shop at street level which was once the local butcher's shop. Built in 1903, several of these houses have corrugated-iron cladding on their sides, a very common feature on many old Wellington buildings. The use of corrugated iron was primarily one of economy as it was light, inexpensive and easy to use, though it also acted as fire protection for Wellington's closely packed buildings. The grand frontage, coupled with the more modest sides and back, led to the comment 'Queen Anne at the front, meat safe at the back'.

Diagonally across from these tall houses is the Shepherds Arms Tavern. Built in 1870, it has undergone numerous style changes since. Next to the tavern, narrow Ascot Street leads to a tiny cottage at number 30 which, unbelievably, housed a school run by Granny Cooper between 1867 and 1888. The oldest house in Tinakori Road, built in the 1860s, is at number 251, while the official Prime Minister's residence, Premier House, is at number 260.

Wellington Airport ***

This airport, with its busy single runway (1936 m), is the top place in the country to watch aeroplanes taking off and landing. For a close-up, comfortable view, the main terminal has massive windows overlooking the runway and is complete with comfy chairs, food and drink, but for a full view of the runway the best spot is in Wexford Road, just off Calabar Road, on the northeastern corner of the airport. The wilder the weather, the more interesting the experience, especially in a turbulent northerly wind.

Wellington Cable Car ***

280 Lambton Quay
Operating hours 7 a.m. to 10 p.m. Monday to Friday, 9 a.m. to 10 p.m. weekends and public holidays

Opened in February 1902 to provide access to the new suburb of Kelburn, the cable car is one of Wellington's great icons. The short ride from Lambton Quay to the top rises 122 m, and a viewing platform has great views over the city. It is an excellent point from which to visit the Carter Observatory, and to walk down through the Botanic Gardens. The small Wellington Cable Car Museum has a beautifully presented history of the cable car, including two perfectly restored Grip Cars built in 1901 and 1905, and the original winding-room machinery, also restored to working order. The museum is open daily 9.30 a.m. to 5 p.m. (www.cablecarmuseum.co.nz).

Wellington's South Coast **

If you are lucky enough to be in Wellington in a southerly gale, head off to the south coast which takes the full force of the wind and sea driving in directly from the Southern Ocean. In a storm, huge seas pound the rocky coast stripped of any substantial vegetation and waves often come over the road. While the wild weather can close the road at the southern end of the runway at Wellington airport, planes usually keep flying! At Lyall Bay, Wellington's best surf beach, hardy surfers take advantage of the conditions regardless of the season. Offshore the inter-island ferries lurch through the white-capped swells, though in these conditions the view from the shore is definitely to be recommended. This coast is home to blue penguins which cross the road at dusk to roost in the bushy cliffs or under houses, not popular with the home owners who are kept awake at night by the nocturnal squawks of these noisy birds.

Wellington Waterfront ***

For years the Wellington waterfront was relatively neglected, severed from the city by busy Jervois Quay. However, in recent times, imaginative redevelopment has made the waterfront from Te Papa to the ferry terminal one of Wellington's liveliest spots, especially on a fine day. The City to Sea Bridge from Civic Square gives easy access to the waterfront where you can go for a walk or a run, skateboard or rollerblade, hire a kayak, watch early-morning rowers work out on the harbour, go fishing, catch a harbour ferry to Petone or Days Bay or just sit and daydream in the sun looking out over Wellington's splendid harbour. This is one of Wellington's many special places.

Wellington Zoo *

200 Daniell Street, Newtown

Open daily 9.30 a.m. to 5 p.m. Closed Christmas Day

www.wellingtonzoo.com

Entrance fee

Wellington is New Zealand's oldest zoo, established in 1906 with a single lion called King Dick (after Richard Seddon) from the Bostok and Wombwell Circus. For a brief time located in the Botanic Gardens, the zoo moved to Newtown where today it has over 500 animals covering 105 species. In addition to lions, tigers and giraffes there are also tuatara and a kiwi house and the zoo runs a popular school holiday programme.

WOW World of WearableArt Awards Show ***

www.worldofwearableart.com

Conceived in Nelson in 1987, this extraordinary show eventually outgrew Nelson and moved to Wellington in 2005. More theatre than fashion, the phrase 'impossible to describe' usually attributed to this show is so apt. Nothing, least of all words, can convey the live drama and spectacle of this amazing show. If a visit to the show is impossible then the WOW Museum is equally jaw-dropping (www. worldofwearableart.com). Held in September/October each year for a period of two weeks, the tickets for the show go on sale in March with the best seats selling out very quickly.

Wrights Hill *

Wrights Hill Road, off Campbell Street, Karori

www.whfrs.org.nz

Rising to 358 m, Wrights Hill has spectacular views over both the city and harbour as well as over Cook Strait to the Marlborough Sounds and south to the Kaikoura mountains. The hill has impressive fortifications built in 1942 to provide the city with long-range protection from possible Japanese attack. Ironically, the guns were cut up for scrap and sold to the Japanese in the 1960s.

South Island

MARLBOROUGH

Classic Fighters Marlborough **

www.classicfighters.co.nz

Held at Easter every second year (odd numbers, that is 2001, 2003, 2005), this airshow based at Omaka airfield focuses on older military aircraft, including rare First World War models, though the show also includes land-based military vehicles such as tanks. Quickly becoming one of the country's most popular airshows, it complements the Aviation Heritage Centre, also based at Omaka.

Edwin Fox Maritime Heritage Project *

Dunbar Wharf, Picton

Built in Calcutta in 1853 of hard Burmese teak, the *Edwin Fox* is of typical East Indiaman design and construction, and just one of two surviving New Zealand immigrant ships (the other is the *Star of India* in San Diego). The ship's first voyage to New Zealand was 20 years later in 1873, arriving in Lyttelton carrying 140 passengers. In the intervening years the ship carried cargo and passengers, including transporting convicts to Australia.

Through the early part of the twentieth century the ship was gradually stripped down and used as a coal hulk and today is only partially restored. Constantly billed as the ninth-oldest ship in the world, one is left wondering where (and what) the other eight older ships are.

Havelock Mussel Festival **

www.musselfestival.havelocknz.com

Within just two years, this festival focusing on the area's famous mussel farms has become one of the region's most popular events. Held on the third weekend in March, the festival presents every conceivable mussel-based dish and the fastest-mussel-opening competition, for which the world record is held by local, Then Dinh, who opened 100 mussels in two minutes and 38 seconds.

Makana Confections Chocolate Factory *

Corner Rapaura and O'Dwyer Roads
Open daily 9 a.m. to 5.30 p.m.
www.makana.co.nz

Located in the heart of wine country, this chocolate factory with free chocolate samples makes a welcome diversion from wine tasting. Large windows in the shop open on to the chocolate-making area where the visitor can see all the production stages of these delicious handmade chocolates.

Marlborough Sounds ***

www.marlborough.co.nz

For most people the experience of the Sounds is limited to the ferry trip from Picton to Wellington but this does not do justice to the hidden attractions of the area. A complex system of drowned valleys, fingers of bush-clad land and islands reach well out into Cook Strait, creating a myriad of bays and coves perfect for boating, kayaking, tramping, fishing (blue cod is the prized fish in this area) and just getting away from it all. Captain Cook used the Sounds extensively as a base during his visits to New Zealand. Water is the natural highway and much of the Sounds is only accessible by sea.

The Sounds fall into two general areas, the first focused on Queen Charlotte Sound, accessed from Picton, and the second on Pelorus/Kenepuru Sounds, accessed from Havelock. Both towns have boat operators offering everything from boat hire to day trips for pleasure, fishing or access to accommodation.

Queen Charlotte Drive **

Linking Picton with Havelock (en route to Nelson), the winding 40-km road may be slow, but it is certainly picturesque. There are great views out over Queen Charlotte and Mapua Sounds and the short walkway at Cullen's Lookout, 3 km from Havelock, is well worth the stop.

Queen Charlotte Track ***

www.qctrack.co.nz

This 71-km track essentially follows the ridge between Queen Charlotte and Kenepuru Sounds and includes numerous bays and coastal bush. The track is not particularly steep (the highest point is around 400 m) and is well formed, and most sections can be undertaken by anyone who is well prepared and moderately fit. While the entire track can be completed in three to five days (the most preferred route is north to south, from Ship's Cove to Anakiwa), easy water access allows walkers to do shorter stretches depending on their timetable, using Picton as a base. Parts of the track are also available to mountain bikes.

Marlborough Vineyards ***

Without a doubt the most extensive wine-growing region in New Zealand and, for wine lovers, the area with the most vineyards open to visitors all year round. It was sauvignon blanc wines from Marlborough that catapulted New Zealand wines onto the world stage, and it is still the wine that is distinctly New Zealand in flavour, and for which New Zealand is best known. Sauvignon blanc wine accounts for over 70 per cent of the wine produced in this area, though most vineyards produce a number of other varietals. The wine-growing area is compact and easy to access and bike tours are popular. The handsome open landscape, with the Wither Hills to the south and the Richmond Range to the north, complements the hot dry summers for which the region is famous. If you go to no other wine area in New Zealand, make time for this one.

The famous Marlborough Wine and Food Festival held in February each year combines wine, food and entertainment, and showcases over 200 wines from 40 vineyards (www.wine-marlborough-festival.co.nz).

Allan Scott Wines ***

Jacksons Road, Blenheim

Cellar door open daily 9 a.m. to 5 p.m.

www.allanscott.com

One of Marlborough's most popular vineyards, Allan Scott offers wine tastings of their well-known range of wines, and indoor/outdoor dining complete with a fresh herb garden used by the kitchen. And if you are looking for a change from wine, across the road, Josh Scott brews Moa Beer in a microbrewery that is open for tastings during the summer months.

Clifford Bay Estate *

Rapaura Road

Cellar door open daily 10 a.m. to 4.30 p.m.

www.cliffordbay.co.nz

In addition to wine tasting, Clifford Bay has an indoor/outdoor restaurant in a very pleasant Tuscan-style courtyard.

Cloudy Bay Vineyards **

Jacksons Road

Cellar door open daily 10 a.m. to 4.30 p.m., closed Good Friday
and Christmas Day

www.cloudybay.co.nz

Cloudy Bay is one of the most internationally recognised New Zealand wine labels and probably the one label that established sauvignon blanc as a leading New World wine on the global wine stage. The vineyard is open for tastings and often has limited-release wines available.

Drylands *

Hammerichs Road, Rapaura

Cellar door open daily 10 a.m. to 5 p.m.

www.drylands.co.nz

Established in the early 1980s, this vineyard is best known internationally for its sauvignon blanc under the Monkey Bay label, and offers wine tasting of their diverse range of wines.

Forrest Estate **

Blicks Road, Renwick

Cellar door open daily 10 a.m. to 4 p.m.

www.forrest.co.nz

Modern sculptures set in a large expansive garden line the drive into Forrest Estate, which produces a wide range of both red and white wines from their vineyards in Marlborough and Hawke's Bay. A great spot for combining wine tasting and a picnic lunch.

The estate also hosts the popular Grape Ride, a 102-km cycle tour held annually in April (www.graperide.com).

Framingham Wine Company **

Conders Bend Road

Cellar door open daily 11 a.m. to 4 p.m.

www.framingham.co.nz

Well known for their rieslings and aromatics, the entrance to this long-established vineyard is through a formal rose-laden courtyard garden. A visit to Framingham's atmospheric underground cellar is a must.

Grove Mill **

Waihopai Valley Road

Cellar door open daily 11 a.m. to 5 p.m.

www.grovemill.co.nz

In addition to wine tasting, Grove Mill has a unique 'Grape Library' where in autumn it is possible to taste the grapes from which different varieties of wine are made and compare the taste of the grape to the finished wine. The vineyard has a pleasant picnic area alongside a restored wetland planted with over 4000 native plants, some of which are labelled to assist with identification.

Highfield Estate *

Brookby Road, Omaka Valley

Cellar Door open daily 10 a.m. to 5 p.m.

www.highfield.co.nz

Built in the distinct faux 'bella Tuscany' style, Highfield is set on Brookby ridge above the Wairau Valley, with wide views from the viewing tower over the plain and the Richmond Range. The restaurant has a very pleasant terrace area and a petanque court.

Hunter's Wines **

Rapaura Road

Open Monday to Saturday 9.30 a.m. to 4.30 p.m., Sunday 10 a.m. to 4 p.m.

www.hunters.co.nz

In addition to the usual wine tasting, Hunter's vineyard offers the visitor an attractive garden setting complete with outdoor sculptures, a fine dining restaurant, olive oil grown on the estate, a picnic area and an 'artist in residence'. The vineyard specialises in chardonnay, gewürztraminer, and a sparkling wine under the Meremere label.

Montana Brancott Winery **

Main South Road (SH1), Blenheim

Cellar door open daily 9 a.m. to 5 p.m., tours on the hour from 10 a.m. to 3 p.m.

www.montanawines.co.nz

Montana was the first winery to set up in Marlborough, in 1976, and is one of the few wineries to offer cellar and vineyard tours, as well as wine tasting, an aroma wheel, cafe, children's playground and an extensive range of wines and wine accessories for sale.

If you are really tight on time, this winery on the main highway is the most accessible of Marlborough wineries and well set up for visitors.

Mud House Wines Co. *

197 Rapaura Road
Open daily 10 a.m. to 5.30 p.m.
www.mudhousevillage.co.nz

This busy complex not only has Mud House wines available to taste but also links a number of outlets, including Prenzel's for olive oil tastings, a cafe and the Quilter's Barn.

Spy Valley Wines ***

Waihopai Valley Road
Cellar door open daily 10 a.m. to 4 p.m. mid-October to May, Monday to Friday June to mid-October
www.spyvalleywine.co.nz

Taking its name from the nearby satellite-monitoring site, this family-owned vineyard is known for its cool-climate grape growing and specialises in sauvignon blanc and aromatics. Opened in 2003, this smart modern winery features an award-winning tasting room designed by New Zealand architects Wraight and Associates.

Saint Clair Estate **

Corner Rapaura and Selmes Roads
Cellar door open daily 9 a.m. to 5 p.m., closed Good Friday, Anzac Day morning, Christmas Day and Boxing Day
www.stclair.co.nz

This friendly vineyard offers wine tastings, a relaxed atmosphere with a cafe, a petanque court, and plenty of space for kids to run around. Right next door is Traditional Country Preserves, which has tastings of their huge range of preserves, jams, chutneys, sauces and pickles, all made on the premises.

Wither Hills Vineyard ***

211 New Renwick Road
Cellar door open daily 10 a.m. to 4.30 p.m.
www.witherhills.co.nz

Without a doubt, Wither Hills is one of the country's most stylish vineyards and is worth visiting for its architecture as well as its wines. Winemaker Brent Marris had a strong influence on the building design, which combines the functionality of a working vineyard with a form that blends into the distinct Marlborough environment. The winery offers wine tasting of vintages as well as varieties, a restaurant, and a splendid view over the Wairau Valley from the top of the building.

Pelorus Bridge walks **

SH6, 18 km west of Havelock

The walks around the Pelorus Bridge at the junction of the Pelorus and Rai rivers give access to some of the best mature forest in the Marlborough region. In addition to black, red, hard and silver beech there are miro, tawa, totara and kahikatea, and birdlife includes bellbirds, tui, kereru as well as the occasional kaka and kakariki. Short walks of less than 30 minutes include the Totara, Tawa and Circle walks, while the Trig K Circuit (417 m high) is a four-hour-return loop track.

Rai Valley Cottage *

1.5 km north of Rai Valley village (SH6) on the road to Tennyson Inlet
Open at all times. Interior is visible through glass panels.

Once a common type of house construction, very few totara slab cottages have survived beyond the nineteenth century. The cottage was built in 1881, with the totara slabs cut on site and fixed with hand-forged nails; the fireplace is constructed of local river stones and the roof of wooden shingles. It is hard to imagine that such a small and basic cottage housed the Turner family of six until 1909 as well as provided food for passing travellers.

River Queen Blenheim *

Riverside Park, Blenheim
Freephone 0800 266 322

While the Opawa River doesn't quite cut it with the Nile or the Amazon, this riverboat experience offers lunch and dinner cruises on a gentle and pleasant tributary of the Wairau River. What the paddle steamer trip lacks in grandeur, the trip more than compensates for with live commentary, evening spotlighting of eels and trout in the crystal-clear water and a sizzling hot plate on which to cook your own meat.

Riverlands Cob Cottage *

SH1, Blenheim

This cottage was built prior to 1860 of a mud and tussock mix with wooden shingles — the use of cob reflects the lack of accessible timber on the Wairau Plain. The cottage was restored in the early 1960s, and the tiny rooms, complete with colonial furniture, can be viewed through glass panels.

Whites Bay ***

The coast of Cloudy Bay is not known for its beaches but, tucked away on the road to Port Underwood, there are a number of very pretty bays including Whites Bay. The bay is named after a black American slave, Black Jack White, who jumped ship in 1828 in Port Underwood and then settled in the area. The small sandy bushclad bay is in direct contrast to the dry open country south of the Wairau River and has a number of short walks — Pukatea Walk (10 minutes), Black Jack/ Loop Track (one hour 30 minutes) and the Rarangi Bay Track (one hour one way) — as well as the all-day tramp to Mt Robertson (1036 m).

Pukatea pa is located on the southwest corner of the bay and the Treaty of Waitangi was signed just north of here on Horahora Kakahu Island. The first Cook Strait telegraph cable was hauled ashore here in 1886, linking the South Island to Lyall Bay in Wellington, and the telegraphists' building, prefabricated in Australia and housing staff from 1867 to 1873, is still on site today.

Wither Hills Farm Park **

Situated on the boundary south of Blenheim and accessed at several points from Blenheim, Wither Hills Farm Park offers a wide range of walking and mountain bike tracks. The open, tawny, tussock country has great views over the town, Wairau Plain and Cloudy Bay. The park entrance on Taylors Pass Road gives access to the shorter Forest Hills, Rotary Lookout, Lower Farm, Short Loop and Stockyard tracks and the mountain bike park.

NELSON

Cable Bay Walkway *

This shingle beach was the exit point for the first international telegraph cable from New Zealand to Sydney, laid in 1876. Prior to this event the bay was known as Rotukura. The walkway runs from the left of the beach up through farmland, bush remnants and pine forest to the Glen. There are terrific views over Tasman Bay, the Bank Boulder and the northwest Nelson mountains. Unless you organise a shuttle, the trip will take around five hours return.

Nearby Happy Valley Adventures offers a wide range of outdoor action ranging from four-wheel motorbikes to the adrenalin-pumping Skywire, a sort of larger-than-life flying fox. Happy Valley also contains the country's largest matai tree, which is 2000 years old, and stands over 40 m tall. Visit www.happyvalleyadventures.co.nz

Kaiteriteri ***

12 km north of Motueka

A small sheltered bay with golden sand, Kaiteriteri has long been one of the most popular beaches in the Nelson region. Tree-topped headlands protect the bay from most winds and frame stunning views across Tasman Bay.

Kawatiri Railway Walkway ***

Junction SH6 and SH63

In 1929 the Nelson/Inangahua railway reached Gowan Bridge, but despite public pressure to complete the project, the line was never completed. The eventual closure of the line in 1955 was accompanied by vigorous protest by local women who staged a sit-in on the line, including Sonja Davies who went on to become a well-known trade union activist and Labour Member of Parliament. The Kawatiri walk (30 minutes return) through beech forest begins at the old Junction railway station (the platform is still there), and includes the Pikomanu railway tunnel and bridge over the Hope River.

Nelson including Stoke and Richmond

Botanic Reserve *
Over the footbridge at the end of Hardy Street, Nelson

The first game of rugby in New Zealand was played on this field on 14 May 1870 between Nelson Football Club (Town) and Nelson College. The Nelson Football Club originally played an odd mix of soccer and Victorian (Australian) rules football, but in 1870 changed its name to The Nelson Rugby Club, thereby becoming the first rugby club in the country. At that stage, rugby was played by teams of 20, and points could only be scored by kicking goals. However, to kick a goal, the ball had to be touched down first, which then gave that team the right to 'try' for a goal. For the record, Town beat College two goals to nil.

The Boulder Bank **
Boulder Bank Drive off SH6, 7 km north of Nelson

At first glance, it is hard to believe that such a prominent breakwater is natural. Over 13 km in length, the bank has been formed from large granodiorite boulders moved southwest from MacKay Bluff during northerly storms, and is one of the very few examples of its type in the world. The bank originally extended to Haulashore Island but in 1906 a cutting was made giving better access to the harbour. The lighthouse was originally cast in Bath, England, shipped to New Zealand in sections, and reassembled in 1861 to begin working in August 1862.

The bank is made up of loose stones and is not easy walking.

Broadgreen House ***
276 Nayland Road, Stoke
Open daily 10.30 a.m. to 4.30 p.m., closed Good Friday and Christmas Day
Entrance fee

Built in 1855 of cob construction, Broadgreen House is typical of a comfortable home of the mid-Victorian period. What makes this place special is the original condition of the house, as it had been owned by only two families prior to being purchased by the city in 1965. Some rooms still retain Victorian wallpaper, but the highlight of the house is the original kitchen. And what a kitchen! It has every conceivable Victorian gadget for cooking, including an open hearth and a coal range, a separate bread oven and a dairy. It still retains the smart original red and black tiles.

The cellar under the house is the hole from which the mud for the cob walls was extracted, and upstairs the costume room has a collection of original nineteenth-century attire.

Centre of New Zealand *

This popular walk begins from the Botanic Reserve and leads up a short but steep hill to a great viewpoint over the city and beyond (around 30 minutes return). Contrary to local belief it is not the geographical centre of New Zealand but a convenient hill used by an early surveyor, John Browning, who was charged by the government to link up previous surveys. To extend the walk, return via the Matai Valley.

Founders Heritage Park *

87 Atawhai Drive, Nelson
Open daily 10 a.m. to 4.30 p.m., closed Good Friday and Christmas Day
www.founderspark.co.nz
Entrance fee

This park has a curious mixture of heritage and replica buildings, some of which are used for historic displays while others function as businesses. There is everything from a steam railway and a Bristol freighter through to a collection of bottled ships, old buses and even chainsaws. The replica windmill at the entrance is hard to miss and Founders Organic Brewery in the middle of the park, complete with cafe, is a popular destination.

The Grampians **

The Grampians are hills directly south of the city topped by communications towers, and views from the platform at the top are reward enough for the trek up the hill. The walk begins from the corner of Trafalgar Street South and Van Diemen Street behind the historic Fairfield House and takes up to 90 minutes return.

Höglund Art Glass **

Landowne Road, Richmond
Open daily 9 a.m. to 5 p.m., closed Good Friday, Christmas Day and Boxing Day
www.nelson.hoglund.co.nz

Ola Höglund and Marie Simberg-Höglund moved to New Zealand from Sweden in 1982 and established Höglund Art Glass International Glass Centre, which now includes an extensive glass-blowing studio, a glass museum, and a glass gallery and store. Their work is internationally recognised and highly sought after by collectors.

The glass gallery is impressive with each colourful and individually designed piece carefully displayed in a purpose-built showcase. The backlighting in the showcase is especially designed to show the clarity of the glass and the vivid colours at their best. A guided tour of the glass-blowing area is also available.

Isel House and Park **

Isel Park, Stoke
House open daily 11 a.m. to 4 p.m.
Koha/donation

Isel House was built around 1850 by Thomas Marsden, who arrived from Derbyshire with his wife, Mary, in 1842. Originally on a farm of 376 ha, it was Thomas who planted many of the trees in the park, a number of them the oldest of their type in the country. The stone front to the house was added in the 1880s by Thomas' son James. Now reduced to a 6-ha park, the woodland garden is particularly attractive in spring when the bulbs, perennials, azaleas and rhododendrons are in bloom.

McCashins (Mac's) Brewery *

660 Main Road, Stoke
Open Tuesday to Saturday 10 a.m. to 5 p.m.
www.macs.co.nz

Opened in 1981, Mac's Brewery led the revolution in introducing New Zealanders to naturally brewed beer, spawning a whole generation of locally brewed beer and making Mac's beers a household name, which is appropriate considering that Nelson is the only hop-growing region in New Zealand. The brewery at Stoke (originally an old cider brewery) offers tours and beer tastings.

MacMillans Hand Thrown Ceramics **

92 Bateup Road, Richmond
Open daily Monday to Friday 9 a.m. to 4 p.m., Saturday and Sunday 10 a.m. to 4 p.m. (5 p.m. in summer)

Nelson has long been famous for its pottery, and is still home to numerous potters, many internationally recognised for their craft. The Nelson information centre has a special brochure on local potters' studios. MacMillans specialises in durable, highly coloured tableware, but also offers visitors an opportunity to create something of their own. They provide bisque ware (undecorated pottery) that can then be individually decorated by hand, and which is then fired, packed and posted to the creator. Beginners can also try their hand at creating their own pottery and very few leave without successfully producing something.

Nelson Provincial Museum Pupuri Taonga O Te Tai Ao *

Corner Hardy and Trafalgar Streets, Nelson

Open Monday to Friday 9 a.m. to 5 p.m., weekends and public holidays 10 a.m. to 4.30 p.m., closed Christmas Day

Koha/donation

Now located in the heart of the city, this modern museum focuses on Nelson's provincial history. Excellent displays tell, in sequence, the natural history of the region, the story of early Maori inhabitants, followed by the colonial history and the importance of local industries including pottery. The museum has a unique database of historical photos that can be accessed by the public through a terminal within the museum.

South Street Cottages **

South Street, Nelson

This short cul-de-sac in the central city is highly unusual in that the whole street is virtually unaltered since the workers' cottages were built in the 1860s. Several of the cottages are available as accommodation. Elliot Street, just north of the city centre, is a similarly preserved street, though in this case the houses are mainly from the period 1910 to the 1930s.

Tahunanui Beach ***

Much of the shoreline near Nelson is very tidal so the city is fortunate to have such an attractive stretch of sandy beach within the city boundaries, especially given the warm sunny nature of Nelson's summers. Very popular as a holiday destination, the beach is very safe for swimming and has all the attractions of a city beach such as skateboard park, mini golf, tennis courts, a hydroslide and plenty of accommodation.

Waimea Estates Winery **

Appleby Highway, Hope

Cellar door open daily 11 a.m. to 5 p.m. September to March, Wednesday to Sunday 11 a.m. to 4 p.m. April to August

www.waimeaestates.co.nz

The awarding-winning Waimea Estates wines focus on sauvignon blanc and pinot, but also include chardonnay, riesling and cabernet/merlot. Close to both Hoglund Art Glass and MacMillan Hand Thrown Ceramics, this vineyard, in addition to wine tasting, has a very attractive indoor/outdoor cafe set among the vineyards with live music every Sunday, and on Saturday during summer.

WOW World of WearableArt and Classic Car Museum ***

95 Quarantine Road, Nelson

Open daily 10 a.m. to 5 p.m.

www.wowcars.co.nz

'Wow' is the right description for this place! Unique in New Zealand, this collection is imaginative and inspiring, and even if you are not remotely interested in either cars or wearable art you will not fail to be impressed. The WearableArt show was first held in Nelson in 1987 and quickly became hugely successful, so much so that eventually it outgrew Nelson and was moved to Wellington. This collection holds the supreme winners from each year and displays a range of costumes in a spectacular and theatrical fashion.

Alongside the WearableArt Gallery is the Classic Car Gallery, which, like its fashion counterpart, is no mere collection, combining high standards of excellence with style and humour.

Even better is that the entire contents of both displays change every six months so there is no reason to refrain from coming back and back and back for more. The building housing the displays was originally the Honda Assembly Plant, now transformed into an imaginative modern museum complete with cafe, a very smart shop and local artists' work for sale.

Nelson Lakes ***

www.nelsonlakesnationalpark.co.nz

Formed during the last ice age, both Lake Rotoiti and Lake Rotoroa are the result of glacier action in the mountains of the upper Buller River. Reaching into the heart of the most northern section of the Southern Alps, the lakes give access to both lower forest, mainly consisting of silver and red beech, and true alpine terrain, which is snow-covered in winter. The birdlife in the 102,000-ha forest is prolific and includes bellbirds, robins and kaka.

The DoC information centre at St Arnaud at Lake Rotoiti has excellent displays on the natural environment, and up-to-date information on walks and tramping in the area. While Lake Rotoroa is larger and deeper, Lake Rotoiti is more accessible and has a wider range of facilities. There is good fishing in both lakes (mainly brown trout) and hunting in the surrounding area for red deer, chamois and pig.

Water taxis operate on both lakes, which are a convenient way to access more remote parts of the lakes or to shorten longer tramps, and a lake cruise operates on Lake Rotoiti.

Kerr Bay at St Arnaud on Lake Rotoiti is the starting point for several good short walks including the Bellbird (15 minutes), Honeydew (45 minutes), Loop (45 minutes) and Peninsula (90 minutes). The circuit track around Lake Rotoiti takes around six hours but can be shortened by water taxi, and the more demanding Mt Roberts track takes five hours and is accessible 1 km west of St Arnaud on SH6.

Tophouse ***

9 km from St Arnaud, Nelson Lakes

www.tophouse.co.nz

The original Tophouse was built in 1846 on the road from Nelson to the lakes, and takes its name from its position at the top of the Wairau, Motueka and Buller rivers, though the licence for the hotel dates back even further to 1844. A series of similar guesthouses through the mountains were built to provide basic food and lodgings for travellers between Nelson, Marlborough and Canterbury.

The current building (a Category 1 Historic Building) was built of cob construction in 1881 (both external and internal walls), and there is an exposed section in the hallway that shows the method of building with cob.

Now offering accommodation in the original hotel and also in cottages, Tophouse has a homely feel, even down to the resident ghost. Sidney (never Sid!) was a tinker who died in the hotel after being thrown from his horse-drawn cart. Previously Sidney used to shake guests awake during the night, but was persuaded to stop alarming visitors after a stern lecture and a promise of Red Leicester cheese at Christmas.

GOLDEN BAY

Abel Tasman National Park ***

www.doc.govt.nz

Abel Tasman is New Zealand's smallest national park at just over 22,000 hectares and in recent years has gained a reputation as being one of the most crowded parks during December through to February. At the same time, the combination of lush bush, spectacular coastline, clear water and stunning sandy beaches make this park hard to resist. The description of 'golden' for the sandy beaches in the park does not do the colour justice, though Golden Bay takes its name not from the colour of the sand but from early gold strikes. An area around Tonga Island was created a marine reserve in 1993.

The park is named after Dutch explorer Abel Janszoon Tasman, who arrived off the coast near Wainui in December 1642 with two ships, the *Heemskerck* and the *Zeehaen*. Unfortunately the stay was both short and unpleasant, when his sailors clashed with local Maori resulting in the death of four of his sailors. Naming the area Moordenaars (Murderers) Bay and the country Staten Landt (later changed by a Dutch cartographer to New Zealand), Tasman never set foot on land and departed from the country in early January.

The two main access points to the park are at Marahau at the southern end, and Totaranui (via Takaka) in the heart of the park.

Abel Tasman Coastal Walk ***

One of the DoC Great Walks, this track is 51 km long, is mainly easy walking, has some of the best coastal scenery in the country and links a series of stunningly beautiful beaches. Unfortunately it is also one of the most popular, and by New Zealand standards crowded in the busy summer months. If crowds bother you, don't be put off doing this walk — just plan a trip outside the mid-December to mid-March period, though even then you are unlikely to have the track to yourself. Parts of the track are only accessible during low tide, so a bit of planning around tides is necessary.

Part of the attraction of the track is that it can be reached by water taxi from Marahau and Kaiteriteri, so you can do all or just parts of the track, though if you plan to stay in the huts you must book ahead.

Kayaking the Abel Tasman Park coastline ***

The sheltered bays, bush-lined coves, clear, unpolluted water and sandy beaches combined with a benign climate make kayaking one of this region's most popular pastimes. Kayak hire companies operate from Takaka and Pohara in the north of the park, and from Marahau and Kaiteriteri in the south, with pick-up and drop-off points as arranged. You can do as little or as much as you want.

Marahau ***

17 km north of Motueka

Not a very attractive beach in its own right, Marahau, just north of Kaiteriteri, is the southern entrance to the Coastal Walk and a good starting point for those wanting to do just part of the track as a day trip. The walk begins at the carpark by the cafe at the northern end of Marahau township. Tinline and Coquille bays are one hour one way, Appletree Bay one-and a-half hours, Stillwell two hours, and Akerstan two-and-a-half hours. Stillwell and Akerstan bays are not accessible at high tide.

Several water taxi companies operate from Marahau and Kaiteriteri for those just wanting to either do one-way trips or access the beaches without the walking.

Totaranui Beach ***

30 km east of Takaka, the road is unsealed, narrow and winding beyond Wainui Inlet.

A broad sandy beach the colour of burnt gold in the heart of the Abel Tasman National Park, the beach is a popular end point for many on the Coastal Walk, but it is also a starting point for several good short walks, both north and south of the beach. Going north, it takes an hour to reach Anapai Bay, two hours to Mutton Cove, and three hours to the lighthouse and seal colony at Separation Point (via Anapai Bay and Mutton Cove). Going south, Skinner Point takes 15 minutes, Goat Bay 20 minutes and Waiharakeke Bay 45 minutes.

The camping ground at the beach is huge and there is also a boat ramp at the northern end of the beach.

Cape Farewell ***

An irresistible combination of the wild West Coast and the gentle reaches of Golden Bay sheltered by the broad sweep of Farewell Spit, this area has in many ways the best of everything New Zealand has to offer. There is an excellent information centre at Puponga (closed June to August) for up-to-date walk information and from which tours out on the Spit can be booked. It is also a safe base to park cars while exploring several close walks. Nearby Puponga Point is an ancient pa site.

Cape Farewell Walk *

This walk through farmland takes less than 30 minutes return and has a great view over the area.

Farewell Spit ***

Over 30 km in length, Farewell Spit is one of the longest recurved sand spits in the world. The delicate ecosystem of the area is home to a rich variety of birdlife (with over 90 species recorded), including migratory birds such as godwits and red knots that arrive in their tens of thousands in the spring and feed in the shallow waters of Golden Bay. The very shallow water is also a death trap for whales and the bay is the site of regular strandings, mainly by pilot whales.

At the end of the spit are an old lighthouse and a gannet colony. In order to preserve the environment, access to the spit is limited to two tour operators, Farewell Spit Eco Tours (www.FarewellSpit.com) and Farewell Spit Nature Experience (www.farewell-spit.co.nz).

Farewell Spit beach walk *

This loop walk following both the 'inside' beach (Golden Bay) and the 'outside' beach (Tasman Sea) is as far as you can go on the part of the spit that is accessible to the public and can take up to four hours return.

Fossil Point **

Beginning from the same point as the Farewell Spit beach walk, this loop takes just over an hour return and leads to fossils clearly visible in the mudstone. Little blue penguins and fur seals are also common.

Pillar Point Lighthouse ***

The lighthouse is rather ordinary but the views are extensive and on a clear day extend as far as Mt Taranaki in the North Island. Around one hour return.

Wharariki Beach ***

A short 45-minute-return walk leads to this beach that has all the drama of West Coast beaches, in direct contrast to gentle Golden Bay. The cliffs and the natural arch of Archway Islands are spectacular, keep an eye out for fur seals.

Grove Scenic Reserve ★★★

On the road from Takaka township to Pohara Beach, sign-posted from Clifton

The small bush reserve hides a fantasy storybook forest with paths that weave through weathered limestone rocks and around old rata trees. After a short walk through the mystical treescape, the path leads to a narrow cleft in the rock to a lookout point high above the plain over Golden Bay. The loop track takes about 30 minutes.

Paynes Ford ★★★

3 km south of Takaka near Paynes Ford Bridge

An easy track leading to spectacular limestone bluffs that are a rock climber's heaven. Mainly used for sport climbing, the area can only be described as challenging, with route names that say it all, such as Goodbye Cream Poofters, Stairway of the Gods, Bored on the Rings, Body Nazis, Rat up a Drainpipe and You're either Dead or You're Not.

Pohara and Ligar Bay ★★

These two beautiful sandy beaches are both safe for swimming and only a short drive from Takaka. The road between the two beaches cuts through a natural limestone arch and the nearby cliffs are popular for abseiling.

Takaka Hill Road ★★★

Long a barrier between Tasman Bay and Golden Bay, the Takaka Hill road, though winding and slow, is now sealed and not at all a difficult drive. Spectacular views and a fascinating geology make the hill a destination in itself. The following are highlights travelling from Motueka to Takaka.

Riwaka Resurgence ★

While the name 'resurgence' hints at gushing waters, the reality is a somewhat quieter affair. From a pleasant picnic area, a short walk follows the Riwaka Stream through mature bush to the base of a cliff from where crystal-clear waters emerge from under Takaka Hill, after flowing underground for 4 km. The cave is popular with divers, who can penetrate the stream underground for up to 800 m, reaching a giant chamber with limestone formations.

Hawkes Lookout **

A short 10-minute walk leads to a marble outcrop high above the Riwaka Valley with dramatic views over Tasman Bay towards Nelson.

Cave Lookout *

As well as fine views east over Tasman Bay, the nearby Ngarua caves feature limestone formations, and a complete moa skeleton in one of the caves. Marble quarried from the area was used in the building of Nelson Cathedral and both the old Parliament Buildings and the Beehive.

Harwood Hole ***

From SH60 turn into Canaan Road and follow this unsealed narrow road for 10 km to the carpark at the end. From the carpark, the walk to the hole is around 90 minutes return.

Harwood Hole is a dramatic tomo over 170 m deep and is the deepest vertical cave shaft in the country. There are no viewing platforms so it is hard to get a good feel of just how deep it is, nor is there any fencing, so don't fall in! The hole wasn't properly explored until December 1958, and the following month, Starlight Cave, which leads from the bottom of the hole, was also discovered. Cavers regularly use the hole, so don't be tempted to throw rocks into the shaft.

Takaka Hill Loop Walk *

Sign-posted on the southern side of the summit

This three-hour loop track winds through typical terrain for the area, with rock formations of karst and marble, and beech forest together with lime-loving plants unique to the area. The giant carnivorous *Powelliphanta* snail is also found in this region. The area is very exposed in bad weather and hidden tomos are common off the track.

Harwood Lookout **

A two-minute walk from the road, the lookout has great views over Takaka, Golden Bay as far as Farewell Spit, and west to the Lockett and Devil ranges. Information boards detailing the geology and ecology of the region make the stop even more worthwhile.

Waikoropupu (Pupu) Springs ***

Take SH60 4 km west of Takaka and after crossing the Takaka River turn left and continue for a further 2.5 km.

Reputed to be the clearest spring water in the world, the springs are not a great gushing mass of water but more a gentle upwelling through eight interconnected vents in the main pool discharging up to 14,000 litres per second at a constant temperature of 11.7 degrees. Surprisingly the water is a mixture of salt and fresh water as the huge underground water system encompassing an area twice the size of Lake Rotorua extends out under the sea. A nifty underwater mirror system at the viewing platform allows a peek at life below the surface.

The reserve in which the springs are located contains some fine old totara and rimu trees, the remains of gold diggings from the late nineteenth century, and a surprising number of native birds.

Wainui Falls **

From Takaka take the road to Totaranui and at Wainui Inlet turn right into the sign-posted road that leads to the falls.

The track to the falls crosses the Wainui River by way of a suspension bridge and leads through lush native bush to the 20-m falls, which are particularly impressive after heavy rain. The return trip takes little more than an hour.

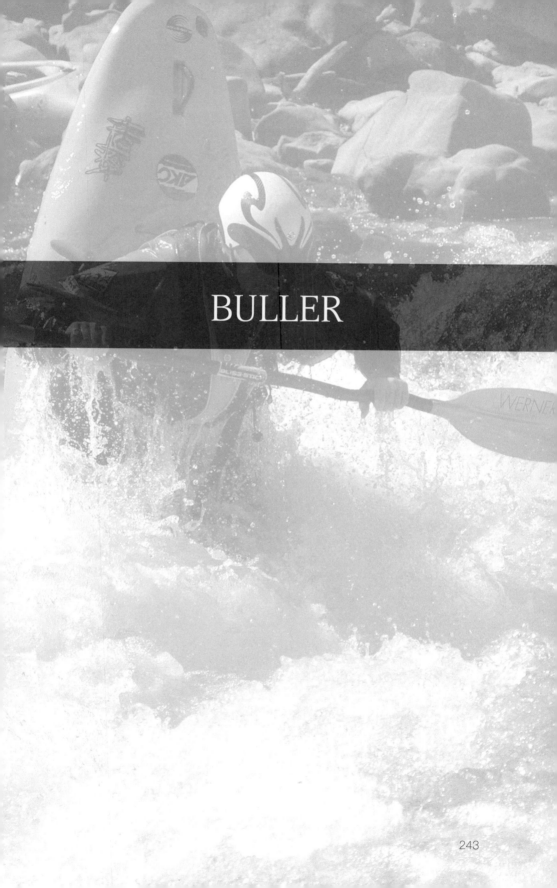

BULLER

Charleston

Constant and Joyce Bay Walk **

Constant and Joyce Bay are sign-posted from SH6, Charleston

This is a short 40-minute walk with great sea views, coastal rock formation, and, if you are lucky, a pod of Hector's dolphins cruising past.

Mitchell's Gully Gold Mine **

SH6, 22 km south of Westport

Open daily 9 a.m. to 4 p.m.

Entrance fee

This is not a mock-up but was an actually working mine from 1866 to 1914 and again from 1977 to 1998. A bushy trail follows a tramline through short tunnels and past old gold workings (bring a torch to explore mine shafts). There is a water-driven stamper battery, and you can try your hand at panning for gold as well. Mitchell's Gully was just one of the many gold mines in the Charleston area, extracting gold washed down from the Alps over thousands of years and mixed in with beach sand.

When gold was discovered in August 1866, the area boomed and by October of that year the population had risen to 1200, and by 1869 to almost 20,000. The town supported 80 hotels, three breweries and even a casino, 'Casino De Venice'. Robert Hannah opened his first shoe shop in Charleston (now the Hannah's chain of shoe stores) and when the postmaster was moved from Wellington to Charleston it was considered a promotion!

Underworld Adventures ***

SH6, Charleston

Tours are daily all year round, more frequent in summer

www.caverafting.com

One of the most popular and successful eco-tour operators on the West Coast, Underworld Adventures was begun by two cavers in 1987, the same year Paparoa National Park was established. Underworld Adventures offers four types of experience, based around the Nile River canyon and cave system in the national park, varying from mild to adventurous in this fascinating limestone and untouched bush country. These range from an open train ride along the Nile River Canyon, through to underwater rafting, glow-worm cave walks, and a full-on caving experience. Bookings are essential.

Charming Creek Walkway ***

At Ngakawau, north of Westport, turn into Tylers Road just before the bridge over the Ngakawau River.

One of the best short walks in the country, this walk mingles superb natural scenery such as the Mangatini Falls and the Ngakawau Gorge with the more appealing manmade features such as old railway tunnels and a swingbridge. The bush is luxuriant, and at the base of the falls is the rare daisy *Clemisia morganii*, found only in the Ngakawau Gorge (most Clemisia are alpine plants). Glow-worms can be found in the tunnels and some of the railway cuttings.

Following the old Charming Creek railway used to extract coal, it takes around three-and-a-half hours to do the whole walk one way (you will need to organise return transport), but around two hours return from Ngakawau to the Mangatini Falls, the more scenic part of the walk.

Denniston and the Incline ***

25 km north of Westport

Only a handful of houses now remain of the bustling coalmining village of Denniston, famous for its spectacular Incline and, in more recent years, for the historical novel *Denniston Rose* by Jenny Patrick, New Zealand's answer to Catherine Cookson.

Opened in 1879 to carry coal from the Rochfort Plateau down to Conn's Creek, the Incline dropped 518 m in just over 1610 m. The system is a simple arrangement, with the down-wagons counterbalancing the up-load. Until the road was built in 1900 the Incline was the only way in and out of Denniston, and it carried people, furniture and all manner of goods as well as coal. In 1887 the population of Denniston was 500 which supported three hotels and eventually peaked at 1500 in 1911. The isolation, improved road transport and the bleak soil-less landscape slowly led to a decline in the town, and finally the Incline itself closed in August 1967.

At the time it was constructed, locals called it the 'Eighth Wonder of the World' and today the Institute of Professional Engineers recognises the Incline as one of New Zealand's outstanding engineering feats. Much still remains of the working gear, and a walking track following the old bridle track weaves its way from Conn's Creek to the top of the Incline. At the top are information panels and the substantial remains of many of the buildings. The huge brake drum, as well as an original wagon displayed at the actual angle (45 degrees) of the Incline, can be seen in the Coaltown Museum in Westport.

Inangahua Museum *

Inangahua Landing
Open daily except Saturdays 10 a.m. to 3 p.m. September to May
Koha/donation

On 24 May 1968 at 5.24 a.m. an earthquake measuring 7.1 on the Richter scale hit Inangahua. While only three people died in the quake, damage to the area was compounded by continual strong aftershocks for the next four weeks, 15 of which registered over 5 on the Richter scale. This small museum has an extensive display of news clippings and photographs of the quake as well as historical information of the surrounding district.

The museum is located in the old Inangahua Hall, which in itself is worth a visit. A typical small rural hall, it was built in the early 1930s and was the venue for local events, concerts and dances. Largely in original condition, the plain timber building has a varnished wooden interior, a small stage accommodated in a corrugated-iron extension, and a kitchen for preparing suppers.

Karamea

Fenian Track *

From Market Cross drive 5 km up the Oparara Loop Road and turn right at the limeworks into Fenian Road to the start of the track.

This track was originally a goldminers' trail to the workings further inland and takes its name from the many Irish nationalists, called Fenians, who worked as miners in the area.

The walk to the Cavern Creek caves takes around three hours return and parts of the track are very rough. You will need a torch for the 100-m Tunnel Cave. There is a great view over the Oparara River from Maloneys Bluff, a rocky overhang that will also give shelter from rain. For those wanting a longer walk, the track continues on to Adams Flat where there is a replica of a typical goldminer's hut.

Heaphy Track ***

One of New Zealand's Great Walks, this 82-km track traverses the heart of the Kahurangi National Park and offers a great range of landscapes from the tussock-clad Gouland Downs Crossing through to the lush subtropical forest complete with nikau palms at the Karamea end of the walk. While the track is well formed and not difficult, there are some long stretches and accommodation in the huts is on a first come, first served basis, so be prepared to camp, especially during the summer months.

The northern end of the track begins up Aorere Valley from Collingwood while the southern end is from the Kohaihai River 15 km north of Karamea. Several operators provide return transport from either end, a 460-km trip by road.

If walking the whole track is not an option, there are several shorter trips along the coastal part of the track from the Karamea end. The Nikau Walk takes around 40 minutes and, as the name suggests, the feature of this walk is the lush nikau palms. The walk to Scott's Beach is a 90-minute return trip through coastal bush to a beautiful beach and great views from a lookout point.

K-Road Mountain Bike Track **

Old logging tracks in the Oparara Valley have been transformed into a 27-km-return-trip mountain bike and walking track, graded easy to medium and with great views along the way.

Lake Hanlon **

20 km south of Karamea

Just 30 minutes return, this well-formed track leads to the small bush-fringed lake, with a good chance of seeing the curious and cheeky weka.

Oparara Basin ***

From Karamea drive north for 10 km, then turn right into McCallums Mill Road and follow the unsealed, narrow road for a further 15 km.

The carpark is the starting point for a number of shorter walks in the magnificent virgin bush and fascinating limestone landscapes of the Oparara River valley. The birdlife in the area is prolific, with the chance of spotting the rare blue duck that makes its home on swift-flowing rivers. Guided walks to the area are available, as are kayak trips. Visit www.karameainfo.co.nz.

Oparara Arch Walk ***

It is a 45-minute-return walk to the largest of the three arches in the area. The Oparara Arch over the Oparara River is over 40 m high and over 200 m long, and is reputed to be the largest natural arch in New Zealand.

Moria Gate Arch ★★★

This is not as large as the Oparara Arch but more picturesque. The walk to the Moria Gate Arch is 60 minutes return.

Crazy Paving and Box Canyon Caves ★★

The carpark for these caves is 2 km beyond the Oparara Arches carpark. Torches are necessary.

The Crazy Paving Cave is a short walk through bush and is notable for the unusual floor patterns, which give the cave its name. Further along is the larger and more open Box Canyon Cave, with short limestone passages and fossils. Both caves are home to New Zealand's only cave spider.

Lower Buller Gorge ★★

Between Inangahua and Westport, the Buller River narrows considerably, cutting through the Paparoa range to the south, and the Mt William range to the north, before reaching the sea. The road through the gorge winds along the river between steep bush-covered bluffs, and at one point, at Hawks Crag, the road is one way only. Attempts to widen the gorge have been resisted by locals, who value the character of the gorge over the ability to drive faster. There are jet-boating and rafting options available through the gorge.

Lyell ★★★

SH6 south of Murchison

When gold was discovered in Lyell Creek in 1862, a township quickly sprang up and by 1873 included a school, post office, church and six hotels. Nothing of the town now remains and the bush has returned, a perfect illustration of the biblical quote 'men go and come, but the earth abides'. Excellent information boards feature photographs showing the town in the late nineteenth century, and the spooky Gothic cemetery, a short walk through the bush, is well worth a visit. Under old trees, decaying headstones with rusting wrought-iron railings are laid out on a hillside, and with dead leaves crunching underfoot, the cemetery has the feel of the quintessential horror movie set graveyard.

Just south of Lyell is the historic Iron Bridge (built 1890), towering over 30 m above the Buller River on massive stone pylons.

Maruia Falls **

11 km on SH65 from the junction with SH6 west of Murchison

The most significant remaining feature of the 1929 Murchison earthquake, the falls were created by a 1-m drop in the bed of the Maruia River. The rushing water has since eroded the river bed further so the falls are now much higher than in 1929, and a popular drop for more adventurous kayakers.

Murchison **

In recent years Murchison has cleverly reinvented itself from a decaying goldmine town to 'Kayak Central'. The nearby rivers — Buller, Matakitaki, Maruia, Matiri and Mangles — offer something for every kayaker from novice to champion. There is also good fishing (mainly brown trout, but rainbows in the Maruia), hunting, and walking in the area. Murchison is the ideal place from which to access the very rugged bush-clad Upper Buller Gorge. The friendly people at the information centre can help with any details. Contact murchinfo@xtra.co.nz

Buller Festival **

Held in March each year, this three-day festival runs rafting and kayaking competitions at all levels of the sport. Visit www.rivers.co.nz

Murchison Museum **

60 Fairfax Street

Open daily 10 a.m. to 4 p.m.

Koha/donation

On 17 June 1929 at 10.15 a.m. an earthquake measuring 7.8 on the Richter scale struck the northwest of the South Island. Centred on the Lyell Range west of the township of Murchison, the quake killed 17 people and caused damage as far away as Nelson and Greymouth, much of the destruction coming from slips, and floods created by the slips.

The local museum in the old Post Office (built 1911) has a large display of photographs and newspaper clippings from the quake. Frequent volunteers at the museum are three sisters, Doris, Gerty and Jessie, who all survived the quake, though Jessie, now in her nineties, is easing back on the volunteer work. Young girls at the time of the quake, Gerty helped her younger sister Doris out from under the rubble of their home just south of Murchison.

In addition to earthquake memorabilia, the museum has the local telephone exchange, still in its original site, and school dental equipment, and next door in a separate building are tools, farm equipment and horse-drawn vehicles.

New Zealand Kayak School **

www.nzkayakschool.com

Professional, friendly staff run a range of courses from October to March for beginners through to rodeo experts, including courses on river safety and one just for women. In addition, the school can create a course for individual or group needs and also hires out gear and provides accommodation.

Six Mile Walk **

Turn off SH60 into Fairfax Street (where the museum is) and continue down the Matakitaki Valley for 10 km.

This easy walk, that takes just over an hour, features New Zealand's oldest hydro power station, commissioned in 1922 and operating until 1975. The well-formed track starts at the power house and follows the water race along the Matakitaki River to the intake weir.

Skyline Walk *

On SH6, 1 km south of the town

A steep 90-minute-return walk through forest leads to a great lookout point over the town of Murchison and three rivers, the Buller, Matiri and Matakitaki.

Punakaiki ***

A stunning combination of sea, beautiful bush and dramatic rock formations, Punakaiki is more than just the Pancake Rocks and Blowhole. There are a number of excellent short walks, good accommodation and cafes, and the road along the coast is spectacular in its own right.

Fox River Caves **

SH6, 12 km north of Punakaiki

The track, an old gold trail, follows the bush-lined northern bank of the Fox River to a limestone cave complete with stalactites and stalagmites. The walk takes two hours return plus whatever time you spend in the caves, and you will need good sturdy footwear (as it can be rocky and slippery in parts) and a torch to explore the caves.

Pancake Rocks and Blowhole ★★★

SH6, Punakaiki

Yes, it can be crowded and yes, you have seen it on a thousand calendars, but when a heavy swell is running this place is spectacular. The unusual layered-limestone rock formations have been formed over millions of years, and in more recent times shaped into the Pancake Rocks seen today. The short well-formed path wends its way above bluffs, sea caves and arches, and narrow fissures in the rock that act as blowholes, best at high tide or in rough weather.

Truman Track ★★★

SH6, 2 km north of Pancake Rocks

Not to be missed, this short 30-minute-return track leads through mature forest of matai, rimu and rata to a short coastal strip of flax and then down to a small sandy cove (which is not safe for swimming). There are dramatic views along the coast and at low tide it is possible to explore the sea caves and the rocky shore. Blue penguins nest here from August to February and the best viewing times are around dawn and dusk.

Reefton

Blacks Point Museum ★★

Franklin Street, Blacks Point

Open October to April, Monday to Friday 9 a.m. to 12 noon and 1 p.m. to 4 p.m., Saturday and Sunday 1 p.m. to 4 p.m.

Entrance fee

The highlight of this goldmining museum is the working stamper, the water-driven machine that crushed the quartz in order to extract the gold. It is significant in that so few working stampers have survived. Stampers often worked 24 hours a day, and in some areas where a number of stampers were operating the noise was constant and overwhelming, only being relieved at midnight on Saturday through to midnight on Sunday, as Sunday was the only day they didn't operate.

Reefton School of Mines *

Shiel Street

Entry is by arrangement with the Reefton Information Centre

www.reefton.co.nz

Entrance fee

Opened in 1886 and not closed until 1970, the School of Mines has a great mineral collection sourced both locally and from around the world, original mining equipment and a collection of technical books.

Reefton, nicknamed Quartzopolis, flourished in the early 1870s and, in keeping with its boomtown image, was the first town in New Zealand to have electric street lighting — just a few years behind New York. Driven by gold-obsessed speculators, investment in local mining companies reached such inflated prices that the market finally overheated and crashed in 1883, causing many companies to fail. There is a short walk around the town with excellent information boards.

Waiuta *

Take SH7 north towards Reefton and 3 km north of Ikamatua, turn right to Waiuta and follow this road for 17 km (only partly sealed).

Though very little remains, Waiuta has a special place in the hearts of West Coasters. The site of the Coast's last great goldrush, in 1905, it was also the richest and most productive of the area's goldmines, with around half of all the gold mined on the West Coast coming from this one mine. In 1939 the mine had a workforce of 250 and the town a population of over 600, but in 1951 the shaft collapsed and overnight the town was abandoned. Over the years, houses, buildings and anything worthwhile were scavenged so that today only six original buildings remain.

Westport

Buller Marathon and Half Marathon **

www.bullermarathon.org.nz

Held in February each year, this is one of the South Island's most popular runs and both the full and half marathon follow the scenic Buller Gorge and finish in the town. The event attracts thousands of entrants so accommodation in the area is at a premium.

Buller River Mouth **

From the west end of Palmerston Street, turn right into Gladstone Street and then left into Derby Street, and finally left into Coates Street, which leads to the beach and breakwater.

The Buller River is confined between two breakwaters on its final stretch to the sea and with a heavy swell running, the river mouth is a place of great drama, especially if a fishing boat or coal barge is navigating the bar. There is easy access out to the end of the breakwater on the north side and the views along the coast are superb. Rare Hector's dolphins are often seen in the area and if you are lucky to strike stormy weather, this is a great spot to while away the hours.

Cape Foulwind and Seal Colony Walkway ***

From Westport take the Cape Foulwind Road for 10 km and then turn into Tauranga Bay Road and drive a further 5 km to the carpark.

From the Tauranga Bay carpark the seal colony is only a 20-minute-return walk to viewing platforms overlooking the colony with excellent sea views along the way. The best time to see seal pups is between December and March, though there are seals all year round. The entire walk takes one and a half hours one way to the Cape Foulwind end of the track, passing the Cape Foulwind lighthouse. A heavy swell makes this walk even more dramatic.

Carters Beach **

6 km west of Westport

The only safe swimming beach on the entire West Coast, Carters is a broad north-facing beach. In addition to accommodation, there is a golf course and it is very close to the airport. Tauranga Bay, just to the south, is considered a better surfing beach.

Coaltown Museum **

Upper Queen Street (why 'Upper' is a bit of a mystery, as the town is flat)
Open January and February 8.30 a.m. to 5 p.m., rest of the year 9 a.m. to 4.30 p.m.
Entrance fee

If you are planning to spend any amount of time in the Buller region, this great little museum is an excellent place to start. Housed in the old brewery that operated from 1880 until 1969, the displays cover every aspect of the history of the Buller district, including gold and coal mining, timber, aviation, shipping, transport, brewing, natural history, earthquakes and disasters, and even a collection of hospital artefacts. The displays are well labelled and comprehensive, backed by an extensive collection of historic photographs and original film footage.

WESTLAND

Arahura and Taramakau road and rail bridges **

Combination rail and road bridges were once very common throughout New Zealand when bridge building was expensive and cars relatively scarce, but few survive today.

Often narrow (some had passing bays in the middle), and with loose timber that rattled beneath the cars, crossing them was, for some drivers, quite nerve-wracking. Just north of Hokitika are two such bridges over the Arahura and Taramakau rivers. The Arahura bridge is the older of the two, built in 1887, and plans are now in place for a new road bridge, so enjoy the road/rail bridge experience while you can.

Barrytown Knifemaking ***

SH6, Barrytown, 1 km south of the All Nations Hotel
Open Tuesday, Wednesday, Friday, Saturday and Sunday, bookings essential
www.barrytownknifemaking.com

With no previous experience, you can turn a piece of metal into a professionally made knife in just one day. From forging through to grinding and polishing, Steven Martin's expert guidance takes absolute beginners through the process of making a knife to your own design, a unique experience. In addition to making the knife, there is the opportunity to learn axe throwing, gold panning and, at the end of the day, taste Steven's very special brew, 'White Lightning'.

Brunner Mine Industrial Site **

10 km from Greymouth via either SH7 or the Taylorville Blackball Road

A suspension bridge built in 1876 links the north and south sections of one of New Zealand's earliest and most important industrial sites, and the scene of the Brunner Mine disaster.

Coal was discovered in the area in the 1840s by Thomas Brunner but it wasn't until 1864 that the first mining began in the area, eventually leading to eight mines working in the immediate area. In 1896 an explosion deep underground in the Brunner Mine killed 65 miners (New Zealand's worst mine disaster), and a memorial with the names of the dead stands on the north side of the river.

The mines eventually closed in 1942 and the Brunner walk (50 minutes) leads through the substantial remains on both sides of the river, including the impressive Tyneside Chimney and beehive coke ovens.

Gillespies Beach *

20 km west of Fox Glacier township, the road is narrow, winding and unsealed for half the length.

Once a thriving but short-lived goldmining settlement, only a few cribs remain at Gillespies Beach, and walks in this area can be as short or as long as you like. There is an historic cemetery nearby. The walk to the lagoon is two hours return, to the pack track tunnel three hours return, and to the fur seal colony four hours return (there are more seals during the winter months).

Glaciers ***

New Zealand is the only place in the world where glaciers reach such low levels within 20 km of the sea. Both glaciers have their own characteristics: Fox is set in a dramatic steep-sided glacial valley, while Franz Josef is more easily viewed from a distance and lies in a bush-clad valley. After years of retreating, both glaciers are currently advancing. From a short distance, the glaciers can appear grubby and a bit disappointing, but once at the face of the glacier, the creaking and groaning of the slowly grinding blue-green ice is awe-inspiring.

Short walks lead to the terminals of both glaciers and guided walks are available on the glaciers themselves. There are numerous walks, both short and long, in the area (including a glow-worm walk at Fox), and the DoC office in Franz Josef is the best place to find out about these, and to check weather updates and track conditions.

There is plenty of accommodation and cafes at both Fox and Franz Josef — the latter is the larger township, though accommodation is at a premium in the busy summer months.

Fox Glacier ***

Larger and longer than Franz Josef, the raw ice-shorn valley is dramatic evidence of the power of moving ice. It is worthwhile taking the short 45-minute walk to the terminal just to appreciate the sheer power and force of this river of ice. The Maori name, Te Moeka o Tuawe, is connected to the legend of Ka Roimata O Hine Hukatere (Franz Josef) in that this glacier is the final resting place (moeka) of Tuawa, who died while exploring the area with his lover, Hinehukatere.

Franz Josef Glacier ***

The northern of the two glaciers, named in 1865 after Franz Josef, Emperor of Austria, by the explorer Julius von Haast, is steeper and faster moving than Fox and is more easily photographed. The Maori name is Ka Roimata O Hine Hukatere, or the tears of Hinehukatere. According to legend Hinehukatere and her lover, Tuawe, were exploring the area when Tuawe was swept away by an avalanche and killed. The copious tears shed by Hinehukatere froze and formed the glacier.

Roberts Point Track — Franz Josef **

This demanding tramp is five hours return from the Glacier Access Road and leads to Roberts Point, with spectacular views over the glacier and mountains. This is a tramp, not a walk, and you need to be fit and prepared for changeable weather — check with the DoC office first regarding weather and track conditions.

Greymouth

Grey River Bar **

One of the world's most difficult ports, the Grey River mouth is exposed to sudden floods, a constantly shifting sandbar and ocean swells generated by thousands of kilometres of exposed Southern Ocean weather. Two breakwaters, one each side of the river, were constructed to harness the flow of the river to scour the channel, and today the southern breakwater is a great spot to watch fishing boats navigate the wild waters of the bar as they enter the river port.

History House Museum *

Greeson Street
Open Monday to Friday 10 a.m. to 4 p.m. and weekends in the summer
www.history-house.co.nz
Entrance fee

Formerly the Grey County Council Chambers, this has a great collection of historic photographs. One room is entirely dedicated to West Coast hotels (at one time numbering over 300), and another room to rugby league, while other collections focus on coal, gold and the port. A video presentation of boats crossing the dramatic Grey River bar is particularly popular.

Monteith's Brewery **

Open daily 8.30 a.m. to 4.30 p.m., tours 10 a.m., 11.30 a.m., 2 p.m. Monday to Friday, 11.30 a.m., 2 p.m. Saturday and Sunday

www.monteiths.co.nz

A few years ago when it was announced that Monteith's beer was to be brewed in Auckland, the outcry was unprecedented, and not just from West Coasters anxious about losing a local industry, but from all round the country, including Auckland. It was clear that Monteith's fans wanted their beer to be brewed on the West Coast and nowhere else.

The Monteith family began the Phoenix Brewery in Reefton in 1868 and later merged with smaller breweries to form the Westland Brewing Company, later to evolve into Monteith's Brewing Company. Today the beer is still brewed by open vat fermentation and uses coal-fired boilers. The tour of the brewery includes beer tastings.

On Yer Bike! **

SH6, 5 km north of Greymouth

Open daily 8.30 a.m. to 5 p.m.

www.onyerbike.co.nz

The West Coast is famous for its rain, and with rain comes mud, and plenty of it, which is just perfect for what is claimed to be 'New Zealand's muddiest off-road adventure'.

The tracks are a mixture of mud, water, narrow bush trails and puddles the size of small lakes. The motorbikes can be operated by those 12 years and older, with passenger options for the younger children. Protective clothing can be hired but don't come in your best gear; it is guaranteed you will get muddy.

On Yer Bike! also includes a huge model of the mining town of Waiuta, a town near Reefton that was the site of one of the West Coast's last gold-rushes.

Haast Pass road from Haast to Wanaka ***

Covering a distance of 145 km, the road through the Haast Pass crosses the lowest of the passes through the Southern Alps at 563 m and follows an ancient Maori trail called Tiora Patea (the way is clear) used to access pounamu on the West Coast. Gold prospector Charles Cameron was the first European to use the pass in 1863, followed a few weeks later by the explorer Julius von Haast, after whom the pass was named.

The pass was used extensively as the most direct route from Dunedin to the West Coast gold fields and later as a cattle trail, but work on the road did not begin until 1929 and reached Wanaka only in 1960. The road is now sealed and rarely blocked by snow, and goes through the heart of Mt Aspiring National Park. Haast township, originally a workers' camp for the Ministry of Works, has very limited accommodation and facilities. The following are ordered north to south.

Clarke Bluff **

Here the Landsborough and Clarke rivers join the Haast, creating a classic braided river downstream from the junction.

Roaring Billy ***

A dramatic cascade of water tumbling over rocks into the Haast River, this is the wettest part of the road with rain falling on an average of 180 days a year and with an annual fall of over 5500 mm. A short track leads to a viewpoint across the river.

Pleasant Flat **

Both a picnic and camping ground, a short loop walk leads to a great view of Mt Hooker.

Thunder Creek Falls ***

It is a short five-minute walk to where the Haast River plunges 30 m through huge boulders.

Gates of Haast Gorge **

Here the road crosses the boulder-filled Haast River with unstable walls of fragmenting schist rock that occasionally blocks the road.

Fantail Creek Falls ***

Although easily seen from the road, it is worth the short five-minute walk for a closer view of this pretty fan-shaped waterfall.

Blue Pools **

This is an attractive 30-minute-return walk through beech forest to a viewing platform over the Makarora River.

Makarora **

Once densely forested in beech, matai, kahikatea and miro, Makarora grew as a timber-milling centre supplying the Otago gold fields. Now noted for its fishing, there is also a 20-minute walk through remnant forest.

The Neck **

Both lakes Hawea and Wanaka were formed by glaciers, which left just a narrow strip of land separating the two lakes. North of the Neck the road follows Lake Wanaka, while south of this point the road is along the shoreline of Lake Hawea.

Harihari — Guy Menzies Park **

SH6, Harihari

At 1 a.m. on 7 January 1931, 21-year-old Guy Menzies left Sydney in his biplane to cross the Tasman Sea with every intention of landing at Blenheim. Nearly 12 hours later, and driven off course in bad weather, Menzies crash-landed upside down in the glamorous-sounding La Fontaine Swamp, which he had mistaken for level ground. A replica hangar alongside the main road houses a reconstruction of his Avro Avian biplane, *Southern Cross Junior*, and historic photographs.

Hokitika

Bonz 'n' Stonz ***

16 Hamilton Street

www.bonz-n-stonz.co.nz

Bonz 'n' Stonz offers visitors the unique experience of creating their own pounamu creation (bone and paua options also available). After choosing a piece of pounamu, a master carver guides you through choosing a design and then working the stone into your own taonga, or treasure, a process that can take several days.

Driftwood and Sand Beach Sculpture **

www.hokitika.org

The beach front at Hokitika is as wild as any stretch on the West Coast, and littered with all size and manner of driftwood. In typical inventive Hokitika style, the town has turned this to an advantage by hosting in January a unique event where creative types are invited to build sculptures from materials only found on the beach. The resulting creations range from fantastical through to amusing and stylish.

Eco World **

64 Tancred Street

Open daily 9 a.m. to 5 p.m.

Entrance fee

The two main attractions here are the kiwi and the giant eels, in addition to tuatara and native fish. Eco World is part of a kiwi breeding programme, with the birds being hatched in captivity and then spending some time here as young birds before being released into the wild. The eels on their own are worth a visit. The large central tank holds both long- and short-fin eels, some up to 60 kg. They are very long-lived, with an average age of 150 years, and the oldest on display is estimated at 220 years old. Eco World allows visitors to feed the eels, so try and time your visit with the summer feeding times of 10 a.m., 12 noon and 3 p.m. — it really is an amazing experience.

Greenstone/Pounamu ***

In Maori legend there were originally two stones, Poutini (greenstone), belonging to Ngahue, and Whaiapu, which belonged to Hine-tua-hoanga. Jealous of Ngahue's stone, Hine-tua-hoanga drove Ngahue out of Hawaiki to Aotearoa on the waka *Tahirirangi*, where Ngahue hid his greenstone near Arahura. Still hidden under the protection of a taniwha, also named Poutini, occasionally small pieces of the stone break off and are washed down the river.

The importance of pounamu within Maori culture cannot be over-estimated; the very name of the South Island, Te Wai Pounamu, directly relates to this stone. Only found on the West Coast, pounamu in pre-European times was highly valued for both ornamentation and for weapons, and in particular, patu, or handheld clubs. (Pounamu keeps a good edge, and patu usually had individual names.) Traditionally pounamu is given as a gift, and is not acquired for oneself.

The Arahura River near Hokitika is the primary source of New Zealand pounamu (greenstone or jade), and there are several outlets in the town where pounamu is sold and visitors can see it being carved into a variety of objects. However, be aware that much of the greenstone sold in this country is from Canada and China, and if you are keen to purchase pounamu, specifically ask if the stone came from New Zealand. Even 'New Zealand made' can disguise the fact that the stone came from elsewhere and was only carved in New Zealand.

There are four main types of pounamu found in New Zealand, each with different names and properties: inganga (pearly, grey-green colour, often translucent); kahurangi (very rare, translucent, light green and flawless); kakotea (dark green, streaky with black spots); and kawakawa (dark green).

Wildfoods Festival ***

www.wildfoods.co.nz

Forget about the fancy food and wine festivals, this is New Zealand's best food festival, with great food and an atmosphere hard to beat.

Held on the second weekend in March, the first Wildfoods Festival in 1990 was a modest affair attracting a crowd of 1800. Now attracting up to 20,000 people and winning numerous tourism awards, the festival combines bush tucker and good music and still retains its small-town feel. While the media focus is on the exotic foods such as huhu grubs, deepfried fish eyes or whisky-marinated duck's tongue, the majority of food stalls provide much more palatable fare such as gorse flower scones, ostrich pie, West Coast whitebait, homemade sausages and much more. Music is provided by several bands, including the famous Kokatahi Band, and in the fine West Coast tradition over 300 50-litre kegs of Monteith's Beer are drunk.

Needless to say, accommodation is stretched, but there are plenty of camping facilities, and the town's natural hospitality always comes to the fore.

Hokitika Gorge ***

From Hokitika take the road out towards Kokatahi and Kowhitirangi and then follow the signs to the gorge.

This short 20-minute walk to the stunning limestone gorge, accessed by a swingbridge over the Hokitika River, is well worth the effort. The water is a vivid turquoise colour, overhung by mature native trees. The upper reaches of the Hokitika are popular with kayakers, while the wild streams further inland attract the very experienced.

Knights Point **

Named after a surveyor's dog, Knights Point was the last section of the West Coast road to be completed, and was opened by Prime Minister Keith Holyoake in November 1965, finally linking Otago with Westland. Now a popular resting spot, there are magnificent coastal views from the point.

Kumara Races **

www.riccartonpark.co.nz

One of New Zealand's most popular country race meetings, the festive Kumara Races attract around 15,000 people to this normally quiet West Coast town. Races were first held at Kumara in December 1887, but moved to a January meeting in the 1940s. The major race, the Kumara Golden Nugget, still has as its winning prize an actual gold nugget.

Though now upgraded, in the past the track was notorious in that the back straight was obscured by tall manuka growing inside the track, and punters had to wait for the horses to emerge before they could tell whose nag was leading. Oddly, the Kumara Races were the country's first race meet to be totally smokefree both inside and out.

Lake Brunner **

Inland from Greymouth, this large tree-fringed lake is popular for boating, fishing (brown trout) and swimming and has a number of attractive short walks. From Moana, the main settlement on the northern side of the lake, and the Maori name for the lake, it is possible to hire boats and canoes. The TranzAlpine stops here, and a few hours at Lake Brunner on a good day has a good deal more appeal than Greymouth, the terminal of the TranzAlpine.

Iveagh Bay ***

This appealing bay 10 km south of Moana has kahikatea forest growing right down to the water's edge. If time is an issue, a pleasant walk of less than half an hour is to take the main Ara O Te Iringa track for a little way, then turn down to the lake and return along the shore. A longer walk (three hours return) leads to a lookout point partway up Mt Te Kinga, while a return trip to the summit (1204 m), with magnificent views over Lake Brunner, the Arnold River Valley and the mountains, will take eight hours return.

Rakaitane Walk, Moana **

Follow Ahau Street down to the carpark.

A short half-hour walk from the outlet of the Arnold River from Lake Brunner, the track crosses the river via a substantial swingbridge and leads through mixed podocarp forest with great views of the mountains across the lake.

Lake Ianthe **

SH6, 22 km south of Ross

This is a beautiful small lake ideal for boating, trout fishing and swimming, and where there is also a picnic and camping area. At the southern end of the lake a short boardwalk leads to a giant matai tree.

Lake Kaniere **

Much smaller than Lake Brunner and 195 m deep, Kaniere is 18 km inland from Hokitika and lies between Mt Graham (828 m) and Tuhua (1124 m), and has an almost completely bush-fringed shoreline. Popular for boating and canoeing, the lake also has brown and rainbow trout, though the nearby rivers and streams offer better fishing prospects. There is a short 15-minute walk through kahikatea forest from the Sunny Bight picnic area, and for those looking for a longer stretch, the Lake Kaniere Walkway is a three-to-four-hour one-way walk from the same picnic area, following the western lake edge through lush native bush to Lawyers Delight Beach.

The Dorothy Falls are a two-minute walk from the road on the eastern side of the lake.

Lake Mahinapua **

10 km south of Hokitika

The placid waters of this small lake are particularly appealing to those wanting a gentle kayaking experience on a pretty bush-enclosed waterway. While most launch from the main picnic area, another option is to kayak up the Mahinapua Creek, which enters the Hokitika River just below the bridge south of the town. The creek is slow moving, lined with native trees and flax, and passes under the historic Mahinapua Creek rail bridge built in 1905 and closed in 1980.

From the main picnic area are several short flat walks including the Bellbird Walk (20 minutes), Swimmers Bush Walk (30 minutes) and the Jum Michael Walk (30 minutes). In the same area are the remains of the Lake Mahinapua steamer, built in Hokitika in 1883 to provide transport for those travelling between Hokitika and Ross.

The longer Lake Mahinapua Walkway (two hours one way) begins opposite the famous Mahinapua pub just north of the picnic area.

Lake Mapourika ***

10 km north of Franz Josef on SH6

This largest of the South Westland lakes, Mapourika is easily accessed from the road, and is excellent for swimming, fishing (trout and salmon) and kayaking. There is a good picnic and camping area at the north end of the lake by MacDonalds Creek.

Lake Matheson ***

5 km west of Fox Glacier township

Possibly the most photographed lake in New Zealand, Lake Matheson is famous for the mirror image of Cook, Tasman and La Perouse mountains reflected in the waters of the lake. The easy flat walk takes around 90 minutes for the full loop through kahikatea and rimu forest, and the best time for photographing the reflection is early morning before the wind gets up and ruffles the water.

Known as a 'kettle lake', Matheson was formed by a large section of ice left behind when Fox Glacier retreated from its last advance around 14,000 years ago and the depression created by the melting ice filled with water.

Okarito

Okarito Trig Walk ★★★

Beginning on the southern end of the Strand in Okarito, 250 m past the memorial, the one-and-a-half-hour walk to the trig is rewarded by spectacular views of Westland National Park.

Pakihi Walk ★★

This short walk (30 minutes return) on the road to Okarito leads through Pakihi Swamp to a platform with expansive views over the forest, sea and mountains.

Three Mile Lagoon Track ★★

Access is the same as the Okarito Trig Walk and is around three hours return, slightly shorter if returning along the coast, though this option is determined by the tides (tides tables are very thoughtfully provided at the beginning of the track). The track follows an historic pack trail over the Kohuamarua Bluff and through forest to the lagoon and then on to the beach.

White Heron/Kotuku colony ★★★

The Okarito area is the home of two rare birds, the Okarito brown kiwi, now identified as a separate species, and the kotuku, or white heron — this being the only New Zealand breeding colony.

The elegant kotuku, *Egretta alba modesta*, is found throughout the South Pacific, Australia and Asia but rare in New Zealand, giving rise to a traditional Maori proverb, 'He kotuku rerenga tahi', a kotuku of a single flight, referring to a once-in-a-lifetime event. The kotuku is the bird featured on the two-dollar coin.

In the Okarito area, the actually breeding colony of around 80 birds is on the Waitangiroto River, just north of the birds' main feeding ground on the Okarito Lagoon. While the birds congregate at the breeding ground between August and March, they feed on the lagoon all year round. An added bonus is that Okarito is also the home of the magnificent royal spoonbill heron.

Visitors wanting to see kotuku have two options. The breeding ground can only be accessed by tours operated between October and March by White Heron Tours (www.whiteherontours.co.nz) based in Whataroa. Another option is to see the birds feeding on the Okarito Lagoon either by kayak through Okarito Nature Tours (www.okarito.co.nz) based at Okarito (morning is best, regardless of tide), or by boat operated by Okarito Wetland Experience (www.explorerfranzjosef.com) based at Franz Josef Glacier.

In addition to the birdlife, Okarito is famous for whitebaiting, is the home of the award-winning author Keri Hulme, and has a number of good nature walks. Kiwi are often heard and occasionally seen on the road at night.

Ross ***

www.ross.org.nz

As in Hokitika, gold was discovered at Ross in 1864 and, within a year, the population had reached 3000. The largest gold nugget, named the Honourable Roddy Nugget (after the Minister of Mines, Roderick McKenzie) was found in Jones Creek in 1909 and weighed over 3 kg. Gold continues to be extracted at Ross — the opencast mine behind the information centre closed only in 2004, and new mining operations are opening up closer to the sea.

The 60-minute Water Race Walkway is highly recommended and starts from the information centre (which also offers guided walks). Beginning at the restored miner's cottage and old Ross jail, the walk continues up Jones Creek, taking in old mine workings, the cemetery and an old miner's hut. You can also try your hand at gold panning in Jones Creek, the very waterway in which the Honourable Roddy was found. Pans are available for hire from the friendly information centre, and panning is best just after heavy rain. While you can drive up past the information centre, the road is very narrow, parking is limited and it is very difficult to turn around. If walking isn't for you, then the bar at the 140-year-old Empire Hotel may be a more appealing way to experience historic Ross.

Speight's Coast-to-Coast Multi-sport Race ***

www.coasttocoast.co.nz

Now in its 25th year, this is New Zealand's best-known multi-sport event, traversing the South Island from Kumara Beach on the Tasman Sea to Sumner Beach on the Pacific. Held in February each year, competitors cycle 140 km (three stages of 55 km, 15 km and 70 km), run 36 km mostly through the mountains, and kayak 67 km down the Waimakariri River, including the gorge. This gruelling event can be completed either in two days (individuals or two-person teams) or in one day, which is for individuals only.

NORTH CANTERBUY
& KAIKOURA

Hanmer Springs **

Constantly wrongly pronounced as 'Hamner', this busy resort is set in a high country basin with extensive accommodation and facilities, and is popular with Christchurch people looking for a weekend away. While the hot springs are the obvious attraction, the area is also famous for its forest walks, good mountain bike trails, adventure sport and in winter, the Hanmer Springs Ski area on Mt St Patrick just 45 minutes away.

Hanmer Springs Thermal Pools ***

Open daily 10 a.m. to 9 p.m.

www.hanmersprings.co.nz

Entrance fee

This huge complex has something for everyone and has twice won the Best Visitor Attraction Award, in 2004 and 2005. There are nine open-air thermal pools, three sulphur pools and four private pools, including hydroslides, quiet rock pools, and even a cooler lap pool for the serious swimmer. In addition to the well-patrolled pools, there are a sauna and steam room, picnic area, cafe and bar. For those looking for a special treat, the spa also offers massage, facials, pedicures and a range of other beauty treatments.

The colder the weather the more appealing the hot pool experience, and if you are very lucky you might strike snow.

Hanmer Forest Walks **

While the area has a mixture of exotic and native forest, it is the imported trees that are the main attraction in the Hanmer area. The forest, originally established in 1903 using prison labour, has extensive planting of Douglas fir and *pinus radiata* for timber production while a number of other species were planted for beautification purposes or to test their suitability for timber.

The forest area is very close to the village and includes a wide range of good walks, especially attractive in autumn when the deciduous trees are changing colour in the cool mountain climate. Short walks include Woodland Walk (45 minutes return), Conical Hill Lookout (one hour return), Majuba Walk (one hour return), Forest Walk (one hour return), and Dog Stream Track (one-and-a-half hours return). Longer walks include Chatterton River Track (two and half hours return), Waterfall Track (three hours return), and, for the very energetic, Mt Isobel Track (five hours return). The information office has up-to-date information on all the walks, and if you have time for only one walk, Conical Hill is the pick, and if the uphill climb is not for you then the Woodland Walk would be.

Kaikoura ***

The physical location of Kaikoura is nothing short of spectacular. Within a short distance of the coast the rugged Kaikoura mountains rise to nearly 3000 metres and off shore the seabed drops steeply into the Hikurangi Trench, also known as the Kaikoura Canyon. The mountains are some of the most recent in New Zealand, formed less than 200,000 years ago during a period of rapid uplift. In recent years the town has flourished, with the advent of whale watching, outgrowing the small town centre sheltered beneath the peninsula and spreading northwards in a rather unattractive manner.

Crayfish ***

One of the local delicacies is crayfish (a spiny lobster-like sea creature without the claws), and renowned for its very sweet and delicate taste. Prolific along these rocky shores, the area actually takes it name from the crayfish — *kai* to eat, *koura* crayfish, though this is much shortened from the original name, Te Ahi kai koura a Tama ki ti Rangi (the fire used to cook crayfish for the chief Tama). Available at most restaurants — though usually at a fairly steep price — crayfish are also available at roadside stalls — usually at half the price and just as tasty.

Fyffe House **

62 Avoca Street, Kaikoura

Open daily November to May 10 a.m. to 6 p.m., June to October 10 a.m. to 4 p.m.

Entrance fee

Built on a site that had been occupied by Maori for 700 years, Fyffe House was originally a two-room cottage built by Captain Robert Fyfe, who established his whaling station, Waiopuka, near the house in 1843. The house was built for Captain Fyfe's cooper, an important occupation at the time when whale oil was transported in wooden barrels. The original part of the house is unusual in that the piles are whale vertebrae rather than wood. Extended in 1860 by Robert's cousin, George Fyffe (his surname had two fs), the house is virtually unaltered from that time.

Kaikoura Peninsula Walks **

Walks begin at Point Kean at the eastern end of the peninsula.

Originally an island joined to the mainland by debris washed down from the Kaikoura mountains by the Hapuka and Kowhai rivers, the peninsula was long occupied by Maori with around fifteen pa sites identified. Sealers and whalers were attracted to the area early in the nineteenth century, and later came farmers. There are several short walks from Point Kean, though link tracks make it possible to walk to South Bay and back to the starting point (three to four hours). From the carpark to Point Kean Lookout is around 5 minutes, to Whalers Bay Lookout 35 minutes, and to Whalers Bay along the coast, around 45 minutes (this last walk is only possible at low- to mid-tide).

Kaikoura winery **

SH1, 2 km south of Kaikoura town

Cellar door open 10 a.m. to 5.30 p.m., tours on the hour until 4 p.m.

www.kaikourawines.co.nz

Perched on a limestone bluff overlooking both sea and mountains, this must be one of New Zealand's most scenic vineyards. In addition to being able to taste the locally grown pinot noir, pinot gris, and chardonnay, there are vineyard tours taking around 45 minutes, and plenty of space for you to bring a picnic.

Mt Fyffe Walkway ***

From SH1 north of Kaikoura, turn inland at Postmans Road and follow this road for a further 6 km to the carpark. The road is narrow and unsealed.

Following a broad 4WD track, the hike up to Mt Fyffe (1602 m) takes around seven hours and is rewarded by fantastic views of the lowland, Kaikoura Peninsula and the majestic Seaward Kaikoura Range to the west. If the summit seems just a bit too daunting then an alternative is the Fyffe hut at 1100 metres (five hours return).

Whale Watching ***

www.kaikoura.co.nz

The deep waters of the Kaikoura Canyon create a unique nutrient-rich environment which is home to a huge range of aquatic life including Hector's and Dusky dolphins, fur seals, sea birds, fish of every kind and, of course, whales. While a number of migratory whale species appear off the coast at different times of the year, in residence all year round are magnificent sperm whales which can grow up to 20 metres and weigh around 30 tonnes. The sperm whale is the deepest diver of the great whales and can descend to depths of over 1000 m and stay submerged for over an hour, though average dives are 20–50 minutes long and down to a depth of 400 m. Once hunted to near extinction, the whales are now protected, making this one of the most accessible and reliable whale-spotting areas in the world.

Whale Watch Ltd is the only operator licensed for on-water viewing (www.whalewatch.co.nz), though there are aerial viewing options available. Other operators cater for dolphin swimming and viewing, scuba diving and fishing.

Lewis Pass **

At 864 m, Lewis Pass is lower than Arthur's Pass and much less likely to be blocked by winter snow. The road follows an old Maori greenstone trail along the Lewis River south, and the Maruia River north of the pass, and is the main route from North Canterbury to the Buller region. The forest is predominantly beech, and the area tends to have fewer visitors than many other South Island regions.

There are a number of excellent short walks from the road and, for the more serious tramper, the 65-km St James Walkway (four to five days) is recommended.

Lake Daniels Track ***

Four km east of Springs Junction, a walk follows the Alfred River and Fraser Stream to this very pretty mountain lake. The track is well formed, easy walking and takes about two hours return. There is a large camping area at the beginning of the walk and near the entrance by the road is an intriguing fence, not to keep in stock, but to monitor any movement in the Alpine Fault.

Lewis Pass Lookout ***

From the pass, the 50-minute-return walk leads to a clearing with views of the Maruia River, Cannibal Gorge, Gloriana Peak and the Freyberg Range.

Waterfall Track **

Five km west of Maruia Springs this is a short bush walk to a 40-m waterfall.

Maruia Springs ***

Lewis Pass Road

www.maruia.co.nz

In direct contrast to the busy Hanmer hot springs, Maruia Springs is a unique blend of New Zealand high country and the best of Japan. Set in a forested mountain valley, the springs stand alone in a magnificent alpine setting, with the hot pools overlooking the Maruia River below. Under Japanese ownership for the past 10 years, the complex has private pools, a segregated Japanese-style bathhouse, outdoor rock pools styled to resemble a small mountain tarn, massage and a fine Japanese restaurant. The result combines Japanese elegance and style with relaxed high-country living.

In use for over 100 years, the pools draw from a natural hot spring from the other side of the river, and the water is piped untreated to the complex. Free from additives, it is high in mineral content and reputed to have healing properties, particularly for the skin. The pools are drained every day and can vary considerably in content and colour.

Waipara Valley

Pegasus Bay Winery ***

1 km south of Waipara turn into Stockgrove Road and the winery is 3 km down this road on the right.

Cellar door open daily 10.30 a.m. to 5 p.m.

www.pegasusbay.com

This family owned and operated vineyard was one of the first vineyards in the Waipara Valley which, with its hot dry summers and free draining gravelly soils, now produces some of the best pinot noir in the country. The rather plain road frontage hides the beautiful terrace restaurant overlooking gardens and a pond, and there are surprising views to the north.

Torlesse Wines *

SH1, Waipara

Open Friday to Sunday 11 a.m. to 5 p.m.

www.torlesse.co.nz

A small winery, set in a smart corrugated-iron building, carries out the entire winemaking process from crushing through to bottling on site. Producing a wide range of whites and reds, the company also 'handbatches' wines from other growers and recognises them as such on the label so that wine from particular vineyards is clearly identified.

Weka Pass Railway **

Glenmark Station, Glenmark Drive, Waipara

Trains run every first and third Sunday of each month, and every Sunday in January

www.wekapassrailway.co.nz

The Waiau Branch railway line was first opened in 1884 and was originally intended to be the main line north from Christchurch, but in 1945 it was replaced by the line via the coast. Not long after this branch line closed in 1978 local people together with railway enthusiasts joined together and acquired the track and much of the rolling stock to preserve this piece of rail heritage.

Today, using both diesel and steam engines, the Weka Pass Railway runs between Waipara and Waikari through the rugged open limestone country of the Weka Pass, a distance of nearly 13 km.

CANTERBURY &
ARTHUR'S PASS

Arthur's Pass Road ***

The most direct route from Canterbury to the West Coast, this road traverses some of the most dramatic mountain scenery in the country. From the dry tussock Canterbury region to the warm and very wet West Coast, the road in reality climbs two passes, with Porters Pass in the east at 942 m slightly higher than Arthur's Pass much further west at 920 m.

Arthur's Pass Township **

This pretty alpine village with its small corrugated-iron huts is a great base for walks in the Southern Alps. It has an excellent DoC office that provides updated weather and track information, and which should be your first call when planning any walks in the mountains. The weather is extremely changeable, and this area has taken a number of lives over the past few years.

For short walks there are the Cockayne Nature Walk (30 minutes return), Dobson Nature Walk (30 minutes return), Devil's Punchbowl (60 minutes return) and the Bridal Veil Falls (90 minutes return). The Temple Basin is two to three hours return, and for more advanced trampers, Mt Aiken, Avalanche Peak and Mt Bealey are six to eight hours return.

Castle Hill Walk **
SH73, 3 km east of Castle Hill

Weathered limestone rock formations, some over 10 m high, stand in the open grass country like some fantasy film landscape. The walk takes as long as you like, and the rocks are worth a close look as they are much more impressive close up than at a distance.

Cave Stream ***
SH73, 3 km west of Castle Hill

This cave, almost 600 m long, is part of limestone country in the Castle Hill area and is a great adventure for those with no caving experience, taking about an hour to work from one end to the other.

While easily accessible to any fit person, this cave is not to be taken lightly and every precaution should be taken before entering the system. You will get wet, and the water can be very cold, especially in winter, so warm clothing is essential, as is a torch (and back-up). Do not enter the cave after heavy rain or if the water is discoloured.

Otira Gorge ***

Originally a Maori trail through the mountains, the steep descent through the Otira Gorge below Arthur's Pass has been a great feat of road engineering. Work began in April 1865 but the road was not opened until 1886. At one stage during the construction, six men drowned in one week. The road continues to provide a challenge, especially around Candy's Bend and Starvation Point, where even now the road is covered by an open tunnel to protect it from water and loose rock in the very unstable terrain. On the 13-km stretch between Arthur's Pass and Otira township alone, there are 11 bridges. The Otira Viaduct, over 440 m long and opened in 1999, bypasses the worst of the road, and there is an excellent lookout point over the viaduct at Death's Corner, part of the old road.

Underground, the railway faced an equally big challenge. Begun in 1908, the tunnel wasn't opened until 1923, and at 8.55 km was, at the time, the longest railway tunnel outside of Europe.

At the foot of the gorge Otira township became an important rail centre, both during the tunnel construction and later as a service centre, though now only a few houses, a shabby pub and large railway sheds remain.

Porters Pass *

Lying between the treeless Torlesse and Big Ben ranges, Porters Pass is occasionally blocked by snow in winter. Just below the pass is Lake Lyndon, which in winter can freeze over.

Ashburton

Ashburton Aviation Museum *

Ashburton Airport, Seafield Road

Open Wednesday 10 a.m. to 4 p.m., Saturday 9 a.m. to 4 p.m., and first Sunday of each month 1.30 p.m. to 3.30 p.m.

www.ashburton.co.nz/aviation

Koha/donation

Based at the Ashburton airfield, which from 1942 to 1944 trained 1192 pilots, this museum with attached workshop features a partially restored Harrier jump jet, a 1942 German Weihe glider, and the only surviving example of a Cropmaster 25R, of which only 21 were built.

Ashford Handicrafts **

415 West Street

Open Monday to Friday 9 a.m. to 5 p.m , weekends and public holidays 10 a.m. to 4 p.m.

www.ashford.co.nz

In 1938 Walter Ashford invented a simple spinning wheel that revolutionised the home manufacture of knitting yarn. The business boomed during the Second World War when the demand for woollen garments for overseas servicemen peaked, only to succumb to the nylon revolution after the war. However, the fashion for home spinning and knitting was revived during the 1960s, and since that period Ashford Handicrafts has not looked back, producing over half a million spinning wheels for an international market.

The Ashford complex now houses a range of handicraft retail outlets, a cafe and, upstairs in the old house, a small collection of the historic spinning wheels including early Ashford designs. Just 500 m from Ashford Handicrafts is the 37-ha Ashburton Domain, noted for its extensive collection of exotic specimen trees.

Plains Vintage Railway and Historical Museum *

Tinwald Domain, Maronan Road, Tinwald

Open days are held every second Sunday of the month from October to June; can be accessed at all other times but displays limited

www.plainsrailway.co.nz

Entrance fee on open days, koha/donation at other times

Opened in 1973 on 3 km of track of the defunct Tinwald to Mt Somers branch railway line, this museum focuses on railway and rural history. A feature is the restored K88 Washington, a steam engine from the Vogel era of railway expansion in the 1870s.

Wheels Week **

www.wheelsweek.co.nz

First held in 1990, this festival, now held annually in May, attracts over 10,000 visitors and is supported by 30 local organisations. The festival has a loose 'wheels' theme, from cars and motorbikes through to spinning wheels and wheels on water, but the main focus is on vehicles, culminating in the street sprint finals on the last day.

Canterbury Foothills **

Just north of the Waimakariri River, these bush-covered foothills have a wide range of walks and picnic spots all within a short drive of downtown Christchurch. The beech forest and river valleys lush with ferns are alive with bellbirds and make an ideal day trip on a hot summer's day, while in winter the tops are frequently snow-covered. For the more active there are hikes up Mt Oxford (1364 m, eight hours return), Mt Richardson (1047 m, six-hour loop walk), Mt Thomas (1023 m, five hours return) and Mt Grey (934 m, three hours return), and for a more leisurely day out there are pretty picnic spots at the Ashley Gorge, Glentui waterfall and Lake Janet.

Glentunnel Library **

SH77, Glentunnel

At Glentunnel and at Coalgate, accessible coal provided the impetus for a lively pottery and brickmaking industry in the late nineteenth century that continued until the 1980s. Built in 1886, the Glentunnel Library, a tiny octagonal building complete with fireplace, is beautifully constructed of bricks and tiles made at the nearby Homebush Pottery. The library is also the beginning of the Millennium Walkway, which follows an old mine tramway and ends at the now closed Glentunnel mine.

Kaiapoi **

Tucked away just north of Christchurch on the banks of the Kaiapoi River, this attractive small town takes its name from a nearby pa, and means 'food depot'. Through the latter half of the nineteenth century Kaiapoi was a coastal trading port, and in the twentieth century it was strongly associated with the wool industry and in particular the manufacture of woollen blankets.

Today, the restored coastal trader MV *Tuhoe* is moored at the wharf just below the historic railway station and offers river cruises, while kayaking on the slow-moving river is a very popular pastime. Across the river is the unique Blackwells department store. Established in 1871, it is one of the oldest department stores in the country and one of the very few surviving in small towns today.

Methven Rodeo *

www.methveninfo.co.nz
Entrance fee

Held on Labour weekend each year at the Methven A&P Showgrounds, the rodeo attracts nearly 200 competitors and over 7000 spectators from all over the South Island. Events such as bareback riding, rope and tie, saddle bronc and bull riding are followed by lively entertainment during the evening.

Mt Hutt skifield ***

www.nzski.com

Just one hour's drive from Christchurch, Mt Hutt claims to be the skifield with the longest season in the southern hemisphere, with snowmaking starting as early as May. The field has an easy open terrain suitable for beginners through to advanced runs on the south face for extreme skiers and snowboarders. An added bonus is the superb view out over the Canterbury Plains to the sea.

Mt Somers **

SH72, 'Inland Scenic Route'

The cool beech forest of the Canterbury foothills round Mt Somers and Staveley are in direct contrast to the open plains below and the dry tussock mountain country inland. The high-country lakes Clearwater and Heron are noted for their fishing, and Mt Potts Station was the location of the fortress city of Edoras in *The Lord of the Rings*.

Two walks are particularly popular. The first is a short one-hour-return stroll following the Bowyers Stream through beech forest to the 7-metre-high Sharplin Falls. (The walk begins from the Bowyers carpark, sign-posted from Staveley.) The second is the more demanding full-day tramp to the summit of Mt Somers (1688 m), rewarding the tramper with a magnificent view of the plains to the east and the mountains to the west. (The walk begins from Coalminers Flat picnic area via Mt Somers village.)

Rakaia Gorge **

SH77

Broad terraces on both sides of the river lead down to a narrow gorge spanned by two bridges over a small rocky island in the middle of the river. A walkway upstream from the bridge takes around five hours return, but an appealing option is to take the jet boat, located just below the bridge, to the end of the track and walk back.

The Rakaia River leads deep into the mountains via the Lake Coleridge basin, and has good access to numerous fishing rivers with a reputation for small numbers of big fish, including brown and rainbow trout, and salmon.

Salmon fishing ***

www.rakaia.co.nz

The country's two best salmon-fishing rivers, the wide, multi-channelled or braided Rangitata and Rakaia, are both south of Christchurch. The season is from October through to the end of April, though the peak period is February and March, and the most fishing is on the river stretches between SH1 and the river mouths. The Rakaia Salmon Fishing Contest in February attracts a big crowd of anglers, guaranteed a good time regardless of the fishing prospects.

TranzAlpine Railway ***

www.tranzscenic.co.nz

Traversing some of New Zealand's best scenery, this leisurely train trip travels from Christchurch to Greymouth and return in a day. The geographical and climatic contrasts between the dry flat Canterbury Plains and the rugged lush mountains of the West Coast couldn't be more dramatic, and all within a half-day's travel. While Greymouth is hardly a 'to-die-for' destination there is enough to do there to fill in an hour, though if the weather is good it is worthwhile considering getting off the train at Moana at Lake Brunner and spending some time by the lake. The train itself has seen better days, but don't let that put you off a great day's travel over 223 km of New Zealand's best scenery on an historical railway line.

Waimakariri Gorge **

5 km north of Sheffield

The dramatic rock walls of the Waimakariri Gorge are spanned by an historic bridge built in 1876 and linking Oxford and Sheffield by rail. The piers of the bridge are over 30 m above the riverbed and are a very early example of the use of concrete in bridge construction.

The area is a very popular picnic spot, with good access to the river for boaties, kayakers and fishing folk.

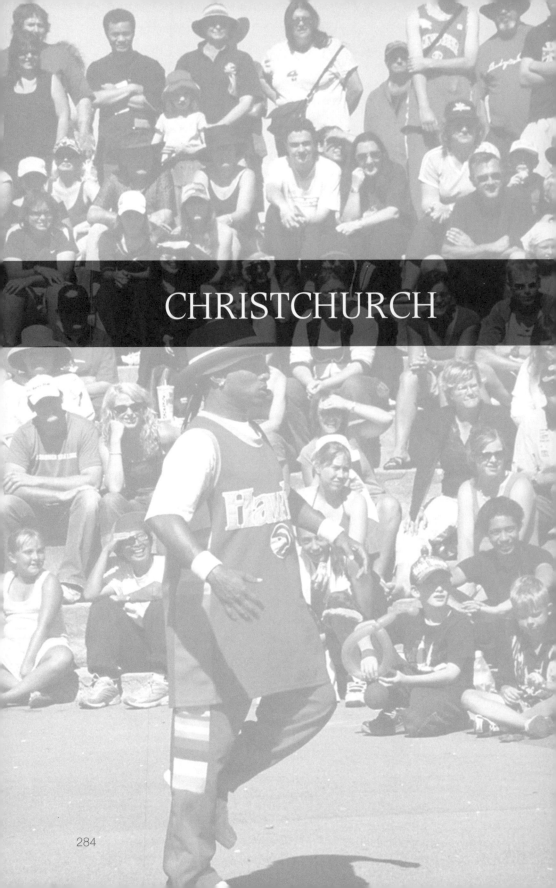

CHRISTCHURCH

Air Force Museum ★★★

Harvard Avenue, Hornby
Open daily 10 a.m. to 5 p.m. Closed Christmas Day
www.airforcemuseum.co.nz
Entrance fee

Located on a working airfield, this top-rate museum is a must for all aviation and military enthusiasts. The main gallery containing the aircraft has excellent displays enhanced by imaginative lighting and good use of models. Aircraft include a P51 D Mustang, Iroquois helicopter, Lockheed Hudson bomber, Supermarine Spitfire, Douglas Dakota DC3, Avro 626, English Electric Canberra, Vampire, A4 Skyhawk, and a Grumman Avenger with its distinctive folding wings that served in the Pacific.

This history gallery is thorough but not too overwhelming and includes good coverage of the First-World-War period and in particular the invention of interrupter gear that allowed synchronisation of a forward firing mechanism with propeller rotation. For the older generation the reconstruction of the wartime home will bring back many memories, fond or otherwise. Those wanting hands-on flying experience can try their hand in a Mosquito Flight Simulator.

From Monday to Friday, at 11 a.m. and 2 p.m., there are guided tours of the reconstruction hangar, where visitors can see work in progress and talk to the staff. (Hangar tours are also held during the weekends, but without restoration staff present.)

Antigua Boatsheds ★★★

2 Cambridge Terrace
Open daily, summer 9.30 a.m. to 5.30 p.m., winter 9.30 a.m. to 4 p.m.
www.boatsheds.co.nz

Built in 1882 by two boat builders, over 120 years later these beautiful green-and-white-striped sheds still hold boats for hire. From here you can canoe, boat or punt up the Avon River through the Botanic Gardens and Hagley Park, or just sit back in the cafe and watch life on the river slowly drift by. Even better, there is no need to worry about drowning — the Avon River at this point is shallow enough to stand up in.

Arts Centre ***

Worcester Boulevard

Information Centre open daily 9.30 a.m. to 5 p.m.

Free guided tours from 10 a.m. to 3.30 p.m.

Weekend Market Saturday and Sunday 10 a.m. to 4 p.m.

www.artscentre.org.nz

Originally the home of the University of Canterbury, as well as Christchurch Boys' and Girls' High Schools, the earliest buildings were constructed in 1887. Designed by Benjamin Mountfort, the stone buildings reflect the Gothic Revival style popular during the Victorian era. More buildings were added over the years, but the university rapidly outgrew the site during the 1950s and '60s, and in 1974 the last of the departments moved to the new campus at Ilam. Of particular note are The Great Hall, a restored classics lecture room, and the original college block and clock tower (facing Worcester Boulevard).

Now an attractive combination of retail and entertainment, the Arts Centre is home to a wide range of specialty shops, art galleries, live theatre, an art-house cinema, as well as bars and cafes. On the weekend a bustling market operates with great international food, fresh Canterbury produce, and unique New Zealand craft as well as live entertainment from noon to 2 p.m.

Rutherford's Den ***

Access through the Arts Centre Visitor Centre, Worcester Boulevard

Open daily 10 a.m. to 5 p.m.

Ernest Rutherford, born at Brightwater, Nelson in 1871, studied mathematics and physics at Canterbury University in the early 1890s and left New Zealand in 1895 to study at Cambridge University. Rutherford is best remembered for his work in nuclear science and is often called 'father of the atom'. He died in 1937 and is buried in Westminster Abbey near two other great scientists, Sir Isaac Newton and Lord Kelvin. Ernest Rutherford appears on the NZ$100 note.

At the Arts Centre there is a series of superbly preserved rooms that Rutherford once used that reflect university life in New Zealand around 1900. The lecture theatre comes complete with desks absolutely covered in student names and doodles carved in the wood over many decades, while downstairs is a tiny basement room where Rutherford conducted his experiments. On display are the replicas of the 36 medals awarded to Rutherford and gifted to the University of Canterbury for his contribution to science.

Canterbury Museum **

Rolleston Avenue

Open daily 9 a.m. to 5 p.m. April to September, and to 5.30 p.m. October to March

www.canterburymuseum.com

Koha/donation

One of New Zealand's oldest museums and founded in 1867, the museum has been housed in the present building since 1877 and has collected, over the years, more than two million items. Just inside the main entrance is a small room that has preserved the style and atmosphere of a nineteenth-century museum.

The Maori collection is extensive with rare pieces of South Island Maori art and a reconstructed southern moa hunter's camp.

Recently opened, the Hallett Station Antarctic exhibition re-creates life on the ice of the southernmost continent, including actual buildings from Cape Hallett Station, a joint NZ/US operation established in 1956.

The head of the triceratops attracts a lot of attention, as does the mummy in the Egyptian section. A noble woman, Tash pen Khasu was 25 years old when she died in 150 BC and her mummy comes complete with its own x-rays.

On Tuesdays and Thursdays there is a free guided tour around the museum at 3.30 p.m.

Canterbury Provincial Buildings ***

Corner Cambridge Terrace and Armagh Street

Open 10.30 a.m. to 3.30 p.m.

Christchurch's finest historical buildings, the Canterbury Provincial Council Buildings housed the Provincial Government from 1859 until 1876 when the system was abolished. Constructed in three distinct periods, the buildings are a mix of wood and stone, with the wooden, rather plain section being the oldest. Reflecting the increased prosperity of the new settlement, the second group of buildings was more elaborate, and displays the taste for Gothic Revival popular at that time. Continuing in the Gothic theme, the third section, built in 1861, was yet more ornate and includes the magnificent Stone Chamber. With beautiful stained-glass windows, kauri and rimu ceiling, and intricate stone carvings, the Stone Chamber should be on everyone's list of 'must see' in Christchurch. In addition to housing the provincial officials, the building was also, for a short period, home to the Canterbury Museum.

Canterbury Art Gallery **

Corner Worcester Boulevard and Montreal Streets

Open daily 10 a.m. to 5 p.m. and on Wednesday to 9 p.m. Closed Christmas Day

www.christchurchartgallery.org.nz

Purpose built, this modern stylish building seems just a bit too monumental for an art gallery. The building feels overly self-important and diminishes the art it contains. That said, the New Zealand collection of art is unmatched, with an outstanding representation of the country's key artists from the nineteenth century through to the present day. If you are short on time, make sure you visit this part of the gallery first. The rest of the collection is almost entirely painting focused, with little art that is challenging, and gives the interior a rather conservative feel in direct contrast to the contemporary exterior.

Cathedral of The Blessed Sacrament **

122 Barbadoes Street

Open daily 9 a.m. to 4 p.m.

Designed by Francis William Petre and opened in 1905, this is the most grand of all Petre's New Zealand churches. Built over a period of four years in the Roman Renaissance style, the massive dome rises more than 40 m above the city and the stained-glass windows come from both Chartres in France and Munich in Germany. Inside the church, the altar contains the relics of Saints Severinus, Lucidus, St Anthony Mary Zaccaria and Peter Chanel.

Centre for Contemporary Art **

66 Gloucester Street

Open Tuesday to Friday 10 a.m. to 5 p.m., Saturday and Sunday 12 p.m. to 4 p.m.

www.coca.org.nz

Jammed full of a wide range of contemporary art works, this gallery starts where the Christchurch Art Gallery, just around the corner, leaves off. Established in 1880, the exhibitions are constantly changing and the Centre is the very best place to see the latest in both New Zealand and international art expression. If you are also serious about buying New Zealand art, this should be your first call.

Christchurch Botanic Gardens ***

Rolleston Avenue

An oak tree planted in July 1863 commemorating the marriage of Prince Albert of Great Britain to Princess Alexandra of Denmark is regarded as the first official planting in the Christchurch Botanic Gardens.

Covering an area of 30 ha, mostly within a loop of the Avon River, these long-established gardens are reputed to contain more than 10,000 plants. Particularly impressive in summer are the fine herbaceous borders well suited to the southern climate, while grouped in the centre of the gardens are the tropical, cactus and orchid houses and a ponga-lined fern house. The elaborate Peacock Fountain, originally erected in 1911, and for many years dismantled and stored due to maintenance problems, was finally restored in 1996. Ornately Edwardian in style and made of cast iron, the fountain was made in the Coalbrookdale foundry in Shropshire, England.

ChristChurch Cathedral and Square *

Open daily 9 a.m. to 5 p.m.
www.christchurchcathedral.co.nz

This should be New Zealand's best public square, but unfortunately the city administrators forgot that people, not buildings, make a heart of a city lively. With the boisterous cafe strip located in Oxford Terrace, the square lacks any real warmth, especially at night.

Marooned in the middle of the square is ChristChurch Anglican Cathedral and it is the cathedral more than any other building that makes Christchurch appear so 'English'. It is the most traditional of buildings, constructed in the English Victorian Gothic style with a soaring nave, fine wall mosaics and stained-glass windows.

Building began on the cathedral in 1864, but after the foundations were laid funds quickly ran out, and when novelist Anthony Trollope visited in 1872 he described the 'vain foundations' as a 'huge record in failure'. However, by 1881 the nave was complete and opened, though the church was not finished until 1904. Of special interest are the fylfot motifs in the wall tiles laid in 1885. At first glance they appear to be a reversed swastika when they are, in fact, an ancient cross symbol which was purloined by the Nazis.

Guided tours are available and, for a small charge, you can climb the tower for panoramic views over the city.

Christchurch Marathon **

www.christchurchmarathon.co.nz

Held on Queen's Birthday weekend the race follows the course set for the 1974 Commonwealth Games. With a reputation for being flat and fast, the marathon attracts over 3500 New Zealand and international runners, and the event also includes a half marathon, 10-km Fun Run and Walk, an 18-km Social Walk and a kids' 2.5-km Mara'fun.

Christchurch Tramway **

Operating hours 9 a.m. to 6 p.m. April to October, 9 a.m. to 9 p.m. November to March

www.tram.co.nz

Pay as you board

These restored heritage trams cover a loop of 2.5 km that takes around 30 minutes to complete and links a number of inner-city attractions. Though, in all honesty, all the stops are in easy walking distance of the square, the appeal of the trams is in the lively and entertaining commentary of the drivers. For something different in the evening there is the option of dining on the move in a 1926 Melbourne tram known as the Tramway Restaurant.

City to Surf Run ***

www.adz.co.nz

This hugely popular run/walk attracts thousands of entrants to this 12-km course which begins at Cathedral Square and ends at Queen Elizabeth II Park. First held in 1975, the race is held annually in March.

Clearwater Golf Course ***

Clearwater Avenue, off Johns Road, Harewood

www.clearwaternz.com

Home of the New Zealand PGA Championship, this 18-hole golf course is regarded as one of the finest in the country. Covering an area of 188 ha, the par-72 course was designed by John Darby with assistance from Sir Bob Charles and also has a driving range and practice putting greens. In addition, the complex also includes hotel accommodation, two walking tracks, a tennis court and archery, as well as a restaurant and bars. Or try your hand at fly-fishing in the resort's lakes and stream, with coaching for beginners.

The course is open to casual visitors and bookings are recommended.

Dame Ngaio Marsh's House *

37 Valley Road, off Sherwood Lane, Cashmere

Guided tours daily (except Monday) by appointment only. Ph 03 337 9248

www.ngaio-marsh.org.nz

Entrance fee

Born in 1895, Dame Ngaio Marsh lived in this house from the age of 10 until her death in 1982. Best known for her detective fiction, she wrote over 30 novels from 1934 to 1978, and was also author of numerous articles, short stories, plays and works of non-fiction. An imposing figure, Ngaio Marsh dominated Canterbury literary and theatrical life, and her home is full of family treasures, books and paintings including a portrait by Olivia Spencer Bower painted in the early 1950s.

Ferrymead **

Ferrymead Park Road, off Bridal Path Road, Ferrymead

Open daily 10 a.m. to 4 p.m. Closed Christmas Day

www.ferrymead.org.nz

Entrance fee

Ferrymead is a combination of historical village and industrial and transport heritage, with a strong emphasis on railway history. The village area has an Edwardian emphasis, and, in 2007, the Colonial Home will open. The Hall of Flame houses the largest collection of fire engines in the southern hemisphere and the park is home to the Telecom National Collection. To really enjoy Ferrymead try and time your visit with special event days (see the website), when many of the exhibits become 'live', including the steam trains (which also run the first Sunday of the month and every Sunday in January).

The location of Ferrymead has strong historical links with the settlement of Christchurch. After crossing the Port Hills, settlers crossed the Heathcote at Ferrymead by way of a ferry, and small coastal vessels also unloaded their cargoes on the wharves at the same point. In 1863 New Zealand's first railway operated from Ferrymead to Christchurch. The ferry closed in 1864 with the construction of a bridge and the railway closed in 1867 with the opening of the Lyttelton rail tunnel.

Festival of Flowers and Romance *

www.festivalofflowers.co.nz

Initiated by the innovative former Mayor of Christchurch, Vicki Buck, as the Festival of Romance, the 'flowers' bit was added on later to tie in with Christchurch's reputation as the 'garden city'. In more recent years 'flowers' seems to have overwhelmed the 'romance' part of the festival. Held in February for a week, the city is festooned with all sorts of flower arrangements, from a floral carpet in the Cathedral and a Wearable Flowers Parade, to hanging baskets on the trams and numerous garden tours. Affairs of the heart are not entirely forgotten with a Valentines Ball For the Unattached, though the name sounds more desperate than romantic!

Hagley Park **

In 1850 surveyors included in the plan of early Christchurch a park of approximately 202 ha. It has been suggested that the sizeable park was designed to act as a buffer between the Anglicans led by John Godley in the centre of the settlement, and the staunchly Presbyterian Dean brothers who farmed at Riccarton. Now reduced in size to 161 ha, the park today is a mixture of gardens, woodland and sports fields, famous in spring for daffodils, bluebells and blossoming cherry trees along Harper Avenue. The Avon River forms a loop through the park around the Botanic Gardens, and the formerly swampy area north of the river has been transformed into two small lakes, Victoria and Albert.

The park takes its name from Hagley Park, the country seat of Lord Lyttelton, Chairman of the Canterbury Association.

International Antarctic Centre **

38 Orchard Road, Christchurch Airport
Open daily 9 a.m. to 5.30 p.m. May to September, 9 a.m. to 7 p.m. October to April
www.iceberg.co.nz
Entrance fee

Christchurch has had a long association with the Antarctic, beginning with Robert Scott who called into Lyttelton on his voyages south in both 1901 and 1910, and Ernest Shackleton who arrived in the *Nimrod* in 1907. From 1955 the airport has been the New Zealand base of the American 'Operation Deep Freeze'. Today the centre is home to a number of international Antarctic operations, as well as being an attraction in its own right.

In the centre visitors are able to experience real snow and ice along with sub-zero Antarctic temperatures as low as –18 degrees from the wind chill machine. The Penguin Encounter allows for both above- and below-water viewing of New Zealand's native little blue penguin, and a family favourite is a ride on the amazing Hagglund all-terrain vehicle.

Mona Vale **

63 Fendalton Road, Riccarton
Gardens open all year round
House restaurant open daily 9.30 a.m. to 4 p.m. October to April, Wednesday to Sunday only May to September

Situated in extensive gardens of over 5 ha along the Avon River, this grand house was designed by Christchurch architect JC Maddison for Frederick Waymouth, the Managing Director of the Canterbury Frozen Meat Company. Built 1899–1900, the house has Tudor overtones and is heavily influenced by the Arts and Craft Movement fashionable at the time. However, it was Annie Townend, who acquired the property in 1905 and named it Mona Vale, who was largely responsible for the style of the house and garden much admired today. Wealthy and energetic, Annie purchased extra land, planted the gardens, and added the fernery, gatehouse and the bathhouse (currently awaiting restoration).

Threatened with demolition in the 1960s, the house and garden were purchased by the City Council with the help of funds raised by the public.

New Brighton Pier *

Marine Parade, New Brighton

Strolling out on this pier has a strange attraction. Bare of any sideshows or distractions of any sort, the walk is a surprisingly pleasant way to pass the time, with views north and south along the coast and watching the occasional person optimistically fishing, and below, surfers braving the cold water. Jutting out 300 m into the sea, the pier actually replaces an older structure built in 1894 and demolished in 1964 despite efforts to save it. There is a cafe at the land end of the pier, and other cafes across the road by the rather forlorn New Brighton Mall. The library at the beginning of the pier must have the best view of any library in the country.

New Regent Street *

Built in the 1930s, New Regent Street is very rare in New Zealand in that the entire street is in the same Spanish mission style with the pastel-coloured buildings complementing the architecture. Originally a pedestrian mall, the narrow street was reopened to cars in the 1940s, and finally reverted back to a pedestrian precinct in recent years, with only the Christchurch tram running down the middle. While still retaining an aura of shabby chic, the street is now home to an eclectic and interesting mix of small shops and cafes.

Nurses' Chapel **

Riccarton Avenue near the Christchurch Hospital
Open daily 1 p.m. to 4 p.m.
Kohu/donation

This little gem tucked in front of the Christchurch Hospital has several times narrowly escaped demolition. Built in 1927, the chapel is the only memorial specifically to commemorate New Zealand women killed in war. The impetus for the chapel came from the deaths of three Christchurch nurses during the First World War when their ship the *Marquette* was torpedoed in 1915. Since then many other women have been remembered on windows and brass plaques on the chapel walls. The beautifully timbered interior with its fine parquet floor is complemented by stained-glass windows and a stunning modern aisle carpet designed by artist Nicola Jackson.

Orana Park **

McLeans Island Road
Open daily 10 a.m. to 5 p.m. Closed Christmas Day
www.oranawildlifepark.co.nz
Entrance fee

Set on 80 ha, Orana Park is an open-range zoo with more than 400 animals from over 70 species. The openness of the park might come as a surprise to people more used to the zoo and botanical garden combination of many city zoos, but the space allows animals the freedom not always found in smaller urban zoos.

The real secret to enjoying a visit to Orana Park is to time your visit to take advantage of the numerous animal encounters, as this is a great way to see the animals up close and learn more about them from the park's staff. The encounters are timed roughly 30–40 minutes apart so there is plenty of opportunity to see the animals and then stroll on to the next encounter. It is an amazing experience to hand-feed the giraffes, get within a metre of the massive rhinos, watch the 'cheetah chase', and, for the very young, pat and cuddle the farmyard animals. Go to the website and figure out what animals you want to see and time your visit accordingly, but start early as you are most likely to end up being at the park all day.

Operated by a charitable trust, the Park is also heavily involved in breeding programmes for both New Zealand and exotic endangered animals.

QE II Park **

171 Travis Road, New Brighton
Most facilities are open from 6 a.m. to 9 p.m. Monday to Friday and 7 a.m. to 8 p.m. Saturday and Sunday, but check the website details for the wave pool, slides, diving pool etc.
www.qeiipark.org.nz
Entrance fee

Completed in 1974 for the Tenth Commonwealth Games and named after Queen Elizabeth who opened the Games, the original complex had an athletic stadium, pool hall, squash courts, and weight-lifting facilities and could accommodate over 34,000 spectators.

Today, the QE II Park is best known for its extensive pool facilities with five hydroslides, wave pool, diving pool, two lap pools and a smaller pool for the very young. In addition to the pool complex, there are squash, basketball, netball and volleyball courts, a fitness centre and the outdoor all-weather athletic track.

Riccarton House and Bush/Dean's Cottage ***

Kahu Road, Riccarton
www.riccartonhouse.co.nz

Riccarton Bush is a small remnant of the kahikatea forests once common on the swampy plain around Christchurch, and some of the trees may well be over

600 years old. In addition to kahikatea, the bush also contains totara, rimu, matai and kowhai and is now firmly protected by a predator-free fence. The reserve is not large and the flat walk through the bush takes around 30 minutes.

Dean's Cottage is the oldest surviving building on the plain, and was built in 1843 to house the newly arrived settlers William and John Dean until resources allowed for a large house to be constructed. Timber from the bush near the house was used throughout, though originally the cottage stood closer to the road, and has since been moved to its present site.

Riccarton House is a large and grand Victorian home, and like many colonial houses it was built in several stages over many years as money became available. The first part of the house was completed in 1856, and the last stage, which gives the house its present character, in 1900. Riccarton House is open every day from 10 a.m. to 4 p.m. and serves an all-day menu.

Riccarton Market ***

Riccarton Racecourse, Racecourse Road
Every Sunday 9 a.m. to 2 p.m.

This large bustling market with over 300 stalls operates on a Sunday morning (except Easter Sunday when it operates on Easter Monday), and sells everything from fresh vegetables and food through to clothing and craft and a lot more besides. Unlike most other markets, Riccarton Market is not stuck in some ugly carpark, but situated in an attractive leafy park alongside Riccarton Racecourse with plenty of space and parking.

Science Alive *

392 Morehouse Ave
Open Sunday to Thursday 10 a.m. to 5 p.m., Friday and Saturday 10 a.m. to 9 p.m.
www.sciencealive.co.nz
Entrance fee

Totally hands on, Science Alive has a wide range of interactive exhibits designed to entertain and educate both young and old. Housed in the old Christchurch Railway Station the exhibits change on a regular basis and include an area for pre-school children and an indoor mini-golf range.

Show Week ★★★

www.nzcupandshow.co.nz

Held in November each year, Show Week is the most 'Canterbury' of all Christchurch events and unique in New Zealand. Combining racing with the traditional A&P Show (Agriculture and Produce), it means Christchurch is packed for the entire week — which also includes the public holiday of Canterbury Anniversary Day — and accommodation is at a premium.

The racing part of the week includes gallops and trotting, and greyhounds, at Riccarton and Addington racecourses, and the highlights are Guineas Day, New Zealand Trotting Cup Day, Mile Race Day and the grand finale, The New Zealand Cup Day.

The Canterbury A&P Show is held for three days at Canterbury Agriculture Park in Wigram Road and combines trade shows, produce and animal competitions, equestrian events and wood-chopping contests with the ever-popular carnival sideshows and rides.

Southern Encounter ★★

Cathedral Square, access through the Visitor Centre
Open 9 a.m. to 4.30 p.m.
www.southernencounter.co.nz
Entrance fee

The focus of this attractive modern aquarium is on southern fish species and, as well as the larger fish species such as wrasse, moki, snapper and trumpeter, the aquarium also includes trout, salmon, sea horses, crayfish and whitebait. The trout and salmon are fed at 1 p.m., the marine fish at 3 p.m. and, in addition, there is a touch pool containing marine life found on the rocky shore. The excellent kiwi house has supervised visits to protect the birds.

Sumner ★

Sheltered from southerly winds by the Port Hills and from the worst of the easterly by Sumner Head, this is Christchurch's most popular beach. At Shag Rock the broad estuary of the Heathcote and Avon rivers narrows considerably to a point where it is only a few hundred metres across to Spit Reserve on the north side. Cave Rock lives up to its name with a sea cave below, while on top of the rock is a great spot for watching the waves, especially in an easterly swell. A popular surf beach, there is also a large children's playground and paddling pool by the clock tower at the eastern end of the beach.

Tanks for Everything *

980 McLeans Island Road

www.tanksforeverything.co.nz

For something completely different, here is an opportunity to drive a wide range of military vehicles on a private off-road track. Vehicles include a Jeep, Land Rover 101, International 7-litre V8 Fire Engine, Ferret armoured scout car, Saracen 10-tonne personnel carrier, the amphibious Hagglund FV432 'battle taxi', and, the biggest of all, the 52-tonne 27-litre V12 Centurion tank. Full instructions are given and then you are off!

Taylor's Mistake **

A small beach lined with home-built cribs, Taylor's Mistake is best known for its lively surf (check out the live webcam www.taylorssurf.co.nz). The origin of the name is clouded by the astounding coincidence of three sea captains, all with the unlucky surname Taylor, coming to grief in this bay. Marked on maps as Taylor's Mistake as early as 1853, the name finally stuck after the unfortunate Captain Taylor of the American ship the *Volga* apparently mistook the bay for the entrance to Lyttelton Harbour in 1858.

It is also a start point for the popular Godley Head Walkway, and the Taylor's Mistake–Sumner walk via the dramatic coastal cliffs of the Giant's Nose, Whitewash Head and Sumner Head.

Willowbank Wildlife Reserve *

60 Hussey Road

Open daily 10 a.m. to 10 p.m.

www.willowbank.co.nz

Entrance fee

A curious mix of exotic and native animals, and halfway between a zoo and a farmyard, Willowbank offers an intimate animal experience. What also makes the reserve unique is that it is open in the evening, which is ideal for viewing nocturnal animals including the kiwi. At the same time, Willowbank also offers evening dining, and a Maori cultural show *Ko Tane*.

World Buskers Festival ***

Top busking acts from both New Zealand and around the world are drawn to Christchurch each January for a week of street entertainment that has gained a reputation as one of the best festivals of its type internationally. First held in 1994 under an initiative from the city council, led by the lively Mayor Vicki Buck, this festival now attracts up to 200,000 people into the central city to watch the most amazing variety of performances.

BANKS PENINSULA &
THE PORT HILLS

Akaroa ***

In 1838 Captain Langlois, a French sea captain who had visited Akaroa, established the Nanto-Bordelaise company, and in 1840 with a small contingent of French and German families set sail for New Zealand with the intention of establishing a French colony. By the time they arrived in August 1840 on the ship *Comte de Paris*, the Treaty of Waitangi had been signed, and the French found themselves arriving in what was now a British colony. Not wishing to return, the French and Germans established themselves around Akaroa Harbour and were later joined by British settlers.

Understandably, much is made today of the French settlement of Akaroa. In reality, however, very little distinctly French remains from this period, apart from place names and one or two buildings. Most 'French' establishments are likely to be less than 20 years old. That said, Akaroa is a very pleasant harbour settlement which, thankfully, has taken one French custom to heart — the provision of good food at the town's many cafes. Just don't come expecting a mini Paris.

The town has numerous historic buildings all within a short walking distance and the Rue Jolie and Rue Balguerie are particularly notable for their historic cottages. The only distinctive French building is the Langlois-Eteveneaux cottage which is now part of the excellent Akaroa Museum. Other important buildings include the wooden lighthouse built in 1880, The Gaiety Theatre (Rue Jolie), built in 1879 as a Masonic lodge, and the tiny Customs House (Rue Balguerie), built in 1858 to deter the smuggling of wine to avoid duty and complete with the original customs desk. For information on guided walks phone 03 304 7733.

Akaroa French Festival *

www.akaroa.com

In April each year Akaroa holds its French Festival, beginning the day with a re-enactment of the landing of the first French and German settlers, followed by a day of entertainment, music and food, all with a very French flavour. Bastille Day on 14 July is also celebrated with gusto in Akaroa.

Akaroa Museum/Te Whareroa ***

72 Rue Lavaud
Open daily 10.30 a.m. to 4 p.m.
Entrance fee

The main part of the museum is in Rue Lavaud and comprises the old Court House and the Langlois-Eteveneaux cottage, but also includes the old

Customs House a short walk away down the Rue Balguerie. The museum covers in depth local history from Maori settlement around 1000 AD to more modern times, including a period when collecting cocksfoot grass seed was an extensive and lucrative business on the peninsula. An excellent video presentation on the local history is worth a visit in itself.

One of the oldest buildings in Canterbury, the two-roomed Langlois-Eteveneaux cottage was built between 1841 and 1846 for Aimable Langlois, the brother of whaling Captain Langlois who first planned the colony. The pretty cottage has elements of French style particularly in regard to the windows which open inwards and have shutters, though there is some debate as to whether these features are original or were added later.

Linton Garden or The Giant's House **

68 Rue Balguerie

Open daily 2 p.m. to 4 p.m. October to June

www.linton.co.nz

Entrance fee

Linton, an historic house built for a local banker in 1881, is at the centre of a colourful mixture of mosaics, sculptures, and plants. Now owned by local artist Josie Martin, this garden playfully combines artworks and plants into a fantasy world that will not fail to delight young and old.

Akaroa Harbour ***

Younger than Lyttelton by three million years, the crater of Akaroa Harbour erupted eight million years ago and opened to the sea at Timutimu Head. As a Ngai Tahu stronghold, the main pa was on the Onawe Peninsula at the head of the harbour. Sealers used the Akaroa harbour as a base prior to 1800, and whalers followed in the early part of the nineteenth century.

For boat trips on the harbour there are three choices: catamaran, jet boat or sail on the historic *Fox II*, New Zealand's oldest ketch (with an option of helping crew the boat). Kayak and boat hire is available as well. Hector's dolphins are common in the summer and there is also an option of swimming with these rare creatures.

Barry's Bay Cheese Factory **

SH75, Barry's Bay

Ph 03 304 5809

Producing a wide variety of cheeses made in the traditional manner and using only natural ingredients, the Barry's Bay Cheese Factory is the only remaining dairy factory of the many that were once scattered around the peninsula. Every second day during the season, usually October to April, cheese making can be viewed through wide windows into the factory with helpful signs indicating the type of cheese being made. Available for tasting and purchase, the company makes a wide range of cheeses including cheddars, Canterbury Red, Maasdam, Havarti, and flavoured cheese.

French Farm Winery ***

12 Winery Road, French Farm Valley, French Farm Bay

Cellar door open daily 10 a.m. to 4 p.m.

www.frenchfarm.co.nz

A French-provincial style winery overlooking the sea, French Farm produces a small range of single-vineyard wines only available on site. There is formal and casual dining, both indoor (complete with open fireplace) and out, a petanque court, and a picnic area with plenty of space for kids to run about. Twice a month the vineyard hosts live theatre.

French Farm was known to early French settlers as Duke Decaze's Bay and was, from 1843 to 1847, the site of a French naval station farm. The name eventually contracted to French Farm.

Hotel Duvauchelle ***

SH75, Duvauchelle, 10 km from Akaroa

www.duvauchellehotel.co.nz

Built sometime before 1850 by Francois Le Leive, and called The Travellers Rest, the hotel has had numerous names since, including the Somerset, the Crown, the Bricks, Hotel des Pecheurs, and even The Robbers Return in the early 1970s. Inside the cosy pub the walls are lined with historic photographs, and across the road the old shearers' quarters now provide backpacker accommodation.

Le Race ***

www.lerace.co.nz

A demanding and hilly cycle race, the course begins in Cathedral Square and quickly climbs the Port Hills to the Sign of the Kiwi, and then follows the Summit Road to Gebbies Pass and down to the flat at Motukarara. From here it heads through Little River and up to Hilltop picking up the Summit Road again for a further 40 km through to the finish at the Akaroa Domain. Attracting over 1000 cyclists, the race can be completed as an individual or as a team.

Okains Bay ***

Settled by Europeans in the early 1850s, Okains Bay flourished on the back of a timber industry supplying the growing town of Christchurch. Farming followed on from timber, but the isolation of the bay led to a declining population and to the small seaside settlement that it is today. Unspoiled Okains Bay has a very good swimming beach and, near the beach, two large caves large enough to picnic in. The historic library, now restored, was first opened in 1865.

Okains Bay Maori and Colonial Museum originally began as the private collection of Murray Thacker and is now housed in the old Cheese Factory. This is one of the most extraordinary collections anywhere in the country. The Maori collection alone rivals any of New Zealand's major museums and, in addition to a complete meeting house, includes an 1840 kareto or puppet, a sacred god stick dating back to 1410, a pre-European waka huia from the east coast, superb greenstone tiki, and even a Chatham Islands dendroglyph — human figures carved into the bark of a tree.

Murray has also been busy collecting buildings; the old Akaroa Grandstand, a totara slab cottage built in 1884, and a complete 1871 blacksmith's workshop. The Colonial Room houses artefacts relating to the history of the bay, and among a vast array of items is an impressive collection of tobacco-related objects such as match boxes, cigarette packets and tobacco tins. The museum is open 10 a.m. to 5 p.m. (closed Christmas Day).

Onawe Peninsula **

Onawe Peninsula, rising to a height of 100 m, juts out well into the upper harbour and is only linked to the mainland by a narrow strip of land which is virtually under water at high tide. An ideal position for a fortified pa, the

Snowboarding, Mt Hutt

Polyfilla Villa, Cosy Nook, Southland

South West Bay, Ulva Island, Patterson Inlet, Stewart Island

Ngati Toa chief Te Rauparaha used local captives to trick his way into the pa leading to a terrible massacre of the inhabitants, followed by a cannibal feast at Barry's Bay. There is a track onto the peninsula which takes around one hour return.

Summit Road **

This road follows the spine of the peninsula and runs up from Akaroa town and rejoins SH75 at Hilltop. There are fantastic views over the harbour and, from this road, trips can be made to Okains Bay, Little Akaloa, and Le Bons and Pigeon bays, all small and fascinating with a history of their own. While the roads down to the bays are narrow and winding, any roads linking the bays are even narrower, more winding and unsealed. An interesting alternative to driving is to join a Mail Run Tour. These tours are no tourist gimmick, but actually do deliver mail to peninsula households along the way. Visit www.akaroamailrun.com

Lyttelton **

Christchurch's port, Lyttelton quickly became an important settlement when the only access over the steep Port Hills was by a difficult road. A rail tunnel was vital and this was opened in 1867, though a road tunnel had to wait almost 100 years and was eventually opened in 1964. The town has many historic buildings, including Canterbury's oldest church, The Church of the Most Holy Trinity (built 1860), Grubb Cottage (built 1851) and the unique Timeball Station (built 1860). A small museum has a good display on local history and the movie *The Frighteners* was filmed here. The Information Centre has a guide to the historic buildings and a location map for *The Frighteners*.

Torpedo Boat Museum **

Charlotte Jane Quay

Open 1 p.m. to 3 p.m. Saturday, Sunday, Tuesday and Thursday in summer and Saturday and Sunday in winter.

Entrance fee

Sitting in Lyttelton Harbour is a curious slice of naval history. Torpedo boats had their heyday in the late nineteenth century, and were a small semi-submerged vessel equipped with a charge that was designed to explode against a ship, below the water line. With much fanfare New Zealand acquired four such boats in 1884 in response to the Russian scare and one, HMS *Defender*, was stationed at Lyttelton. But the technology was not a great success and by 1900 they were no longer required. Eventually sold off, the *Defender* lay abandoned on Purau Beach for many years until recently rescued and is now partially restored and housed in the old Powder Magazine Building (built 1874).

Timeball Station ★★★

2 Reserve Terrace

Open daily 10 a.m. to 5.30 p.m. October to April, Wednesday to Sunday 10 a.m. to 5.30 p.m. May to September

Entrance fee

One of the few such buildings left in the world, these stations were vital for early shipping to obtain Greenwich Mean Time, necessary to accurately calculate longitude at sea. Ships adjusted their clocks at the time the ball dropped. The Lyttelton Timeball Station operated from 1876 to 1934 and today the ball is dropped at 1 p.m.

Lyttelton Harbour *

Like Akaroa, Lyttelton Harbour is the crater of a very ancient volcano formed 12 million years ago, and the rugged hills and dramatic sea cliffs are testament to aeons of geological turbulence. The area around the harbour has been occupied for over 1000 years, first by the Waitaha people, and later by Ngati Mamoe and then Ngai Tahu. Quail Island in the upper harbour was for a considerable period the quarantine station, and even at one time, in the early 1920s, a leper colony. The island is named after a native quail found only on the island but now extinct. Tiny Ripara Island is an historic pa site and at the end of the nineteenth century was fortified against attack from Russia, which was at that time expanding into the Pacific. The rare Hector's dolphin is frequently seen both in the harbour and around the entire Banks Peninsula.

Black Cat Cruises offer a range of excursions on the harbour in addition to operating the ferry service to Diamond Harbour across from Lyttelton (www. blackcat.co.nz). For something a bit different, take a trip on the historic steam tug *Lyttelton*. Built in Glasgow in 1907, and originally called the *Canterbury,* a local preservation group run Sunday-afternoon cruises at 2 p.m. from September to June. Ph 03 322 8911.

Diamond Harbour *

Originally called Stoddart's Bay and linked by ferry to Lyttelton (25 km by road), Diamond Harbour is a pleasant and sunny coastal village. A short loop track from the reserve just below historic Godley House (built 1880 and now a restaurant) leads to a lookout point with views across the harbour. Nearby is Stoddart's cottage, built in 1860 and in which Mark and Margaret Stoddart raised six children. Originally just one room, the house was imported in kitset form from Melbourne, Australia and the wooden walls are packed with rammed earth to provide better insulation. In a surprisingly humble act, it was Mark Stoddart who renamed the bay Diamond as the glittering water in the bay reminded him of the precious stone.

Godley Head Walkway ***

The usual starting point is from the carpark at Taylor's Mistake, but the track is also accessible from the carpark at the end of Summit Road.

This well-formed track leads along the coast through open grass and tussockland, and gradually rises above the rocky shore to Godley Head. From Godley Head, the track zigzags down a short steep hillside to the Second World War gun emplacements, and includes a100-m tunnel access right at sea level. The views from the track are exceptional in every direction, and the entire loop back to Taylor's Mistake will take around three hours.

Mt Herbert Walkway ***
Diamond Harbour

The highest point on the peninsula at 919 m, Mt Herbert has commanding views of Canterbury and, in particular, Lyttelton Harbour. The peak is frequently snow-covered in winter. The walk begins at Diamond Harbour and ends at Charteris Bay about 5 km from the start of the track. Needless to say, it is a steep climb, though the track is well marked and well formed and takes six to seven hours return.

The Port Hills

Bridal Path Walkway **
The Christchurch end begins at Bridle Path Road, Heathcote

In 1851 this track was the main access from Lyttelton to the fledgling Christchurch settlement and, today, the Bridal Path is still a challenging walk.

For the early settlers laden with baggage this track must have been daunting indeed and a monument commemorating the endurance of pioneer women can be found on the summit. An alternative to walking the uphill track is to take the gondola to the top and walk back down to either the Heathcote Valley or Lyttelton where the track ends near the entrance to the road tunnel.

Christchurch Gondola **

10 Bridal Path Road, Heathcote Valley
Open daily 10 a.m. to 9 p.m.
www.gondola.co.nz
Entrance fee

Rising to almost 500 m, the 1-km-long gondola carries passengers to a great viewpoint over Lyttelton Harbour to the south, the city and coast to the north, and the plains and Southern Alps to the west. At the top, in addition to the cafe and restaurant, there is the Heritage Time Tunnel, a journey back in time to when the peninsula was a fiery volcano, through Maori mythology, to life on board an immigrant ship.

There are a number of short walks around the summit or you can even stride out and walk back downhill to either the Heathcote Valley or Lyttelton.

Crater Rim Walkway *

Victoria Park Road, above the Sign of the Takahe

No one seems to be able to agree where this walk begins or ends. Some have it start at the Sign of the Takahe and through to Cooper's Knob, while others start at Godley Head and end at the bottom of the Rapaki Track. Most walkers tend to start from the Sign of the Kiwi at the top of Dyers Pass Road and then walk the section through to the Ahuriri Reserve just beyond Cooper's Knob, more or less following the Summit Road. With easy access off the Summit Road, this walk can also be undertaken in short stages.

Despite the rocky and rugged nature of the landscape, the walking is relatively flat and easy on good tracks and passes through native bush remnants, a reminder that the peninsula was once heavily forested. The views are superb in all directions, but be aware that runners and mountain bikers also use these tracks.

Port Hill Rest Houses **

Henry Ell, an early-twentieth-century Liberal politician, envisaged a series of rest houses along the Summit Road as stopping points for walkers and travellers, though only four were ever built. The Sign of the Takahe completed in 1949, long after Henry died, was the most ambitious of the rest houses. Constructed of volcanic stone with stained-glass windows in the ornate Victorian Gothic style, the Sign of the Takahe is now a restaurant. The Sign of the Kiwi at the summit of Dyers Pass Road is a more modest structure and is now a tearooms, but the Sign of the Bellbird in Kennedy's Bush, and the Sign of the Packhorse at Mt Bradley are little more than stone shelters.

Victoria Park *

Dyers Pass Road, Cashmere

This park of 260 ha and planted in a wide variety of both native and exotic trees is a maze of walking and mountain bike tracks, and the popular Bowendale Mountain Bike Track starts here. Located on a steep hillside, the best walk is to begin at the top and stroll down through the trees (the fit can always do it the other way round). While the name of the park celebrates Queen Victoria's Golden Jubilee in 1897, the park was first established as early as 1870 with formal planting under way in the 1880s. The park was the scene of one of New Zealand's most famous murders when, on 22 June 1954, Pauline Parker, aged 16, and Juliet Hulme, aged 15, bashed Pauline's mother to death with a brick.

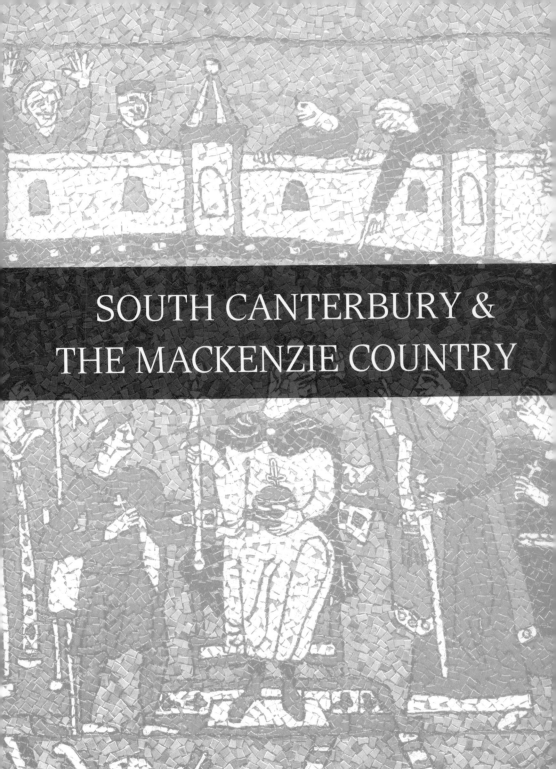

SOUTH CANTERBURY &
THE MACKENZIE COUNTRY

Geraldine

1066: A Medieval Mosaic **

10 Wilson Street (The Giant Jersey)

Open daily Monday to Friday 9 a.m. to 5 p.m., Saturday and Sunday 10 a.m. to 4 p.m.

www.1066.co.nz

Entrance fee

This recreation of the Bayeux tapestry is nothing short of extraordinary. Created by Michael Linton and his daughter Rachel using the teeth of knitting machine pattern discs, the mosaic is 42 m long, took 25 years to complete and is made up of 2,000,000 pieces. While that in itself is impressive, Michael has also extended the story of the Norman Conquest, which in the original tapestry ends at the coronation of William the Conqueror.

To make things even more interesting the mosaic contains an alphametic puzzle code, as yet unbroken. While all this may sound weird, the result is plain fascinating and well worth a visit.

The knitting shop, The Giant Jersey, which houses the 1066 Mosaic, is also the home of the largest knitted jersey in the world, measuring over 2 m high and 5 m across.

Vintage Car and Machinery Museum **

178 Talbot Street

Open daily 10 a.m. to 4 p.m. October to June, weekends only July to September

Entrance fee

This extensive collection has a strong emphasis on tractors and farm implements, with a good range of vintage cars and just one aeroplane, the rare English-built 1929 Spartan. Other highlights of the museum include an 1877 horse-drawn fire engine, a 1913 Sanderson and Mills tractor, and a 1929 International truck restored and rebuilt by John Britten as a gypsy caravan. Then there is the amazing 'Wilcox Special' made to 'plough the unploughable'. Built by Reid and Gray in Invercargill in 1939, this enormous plough was designed to work swamp and scrubland into usable farmland.

The Mackenzie Country

Black stilt country **

The black stilt, found only in New Zealand, is one of our most endangered birds and its habitat is now severely restricted to a number of rivers in the Mackenzie basin. In 1981 the birds numbered 23, and in 2005 the population had risen to a mere 55 adults. The jet-black plumage and long red legs of the adult bird are very distinctive, and while the birds are rare, there is a very good chance of spotting one as they are not shy and feed in shallow water throughout the basin including the hydro canals.

Church of the Good Shepherd ***
Tekapo

In January 1935 the Duke of Gloucester, the third son of King George V and Queen Mary, laid the foundation stone for this tiny church during a tour of New Zealand. The Church of the Good Shepherd was built as a memorial to the European settlers of the district, and the famous window behind the altar, which frames a view of the lake, was an original feature of the building. So as to make as little impact as possible on the grand high-country landscape, the church was built of local stone, and even the area around the church has been left in its natural state, with only uncultivated high-country plants.

The nearby statue of a sheep dog is not the legendary James McKenzie's dog, Friday, but was erected in 1968 by local farmers in recognition of the contribution made to farming by the humble working dog.

Gliding at Omarama ***

A combination of geography and weather patterns makes Omarama one of the best gliding locations in the world. A mixture of frontal systems, mountain thermals, valley convergences and alpine ridges found at Omarama creates the uplift necessary to power a glider, also known as 'soarable energy'. The soaring season is from September to April, and a number of operators in the small township cater for every level of interest from beginner to professional. An added attraction is the awesome high-country scenery.

American aviation adventurer Steve Fossett has used Omarama as a base for attempts to crack a number of world records, including the highest glider flight. In 2002 Fossett broke the 1000-km gliding world record here with an average speed of 166.46 kph.

Lake Tekapo ***

www.laketekapountouched.co.nz

Fed by the icy waters of the Godley River, Lake Tekapo is quickly becoming an alternative holiday destination to the more commercial Queenstown and Wanaka. At 700 m the climate is definitely alpine but the rainfall is low, the sunshine hours high and in summer it can be very hot. Motuariki Island in the middle of the lake is a popular picnic spot and noted for its plantation of pines with giant cones.

Tekapo is famous for ultra-clear night skies, especially in winter, and the University of Canterbury operates an astronomical observatory on Mt John just west of Tekapo village (tours arranged through Earth and Sky, www. earthandsky.co.nz). The views from the top of Mt John (1031 m), a two-hour walk, are dramatic.

East of Tekapo is the Mt Dobson skifield, becoming increasingly popular with the recent improvement of access to the field including the triple chair lift up the West Valley (www.dobson.co.nz).

Lindis Pass **

Linking Central Otago to the Mackenzie basin, the Lindis Pass reaches a height of 490 m, and winds its way through classic New Zealand high country. Open, rocky, tussock land, the view from the top is expansive and particularly attractive in autumn when the spare trees in the valleys turn golden.

Mackenzie Pass *

While the usual route to the Mackenzie Country from Canterbury is via Burkes Pass, the pass through which James McKenzie drove his stolen sheep lies on a rugged stretch of road just to the south.

Born in Ross Shire, Scotland, McKenzie (better known as Jock) immigrated first to Australia and then came on to New Zealand. He came to fame in March 1885 when he 'acquired' a flock of 1000 sheep. According to McKenzie he came by the flock by legitimate means, but not so according to the law, and he was apprehended near a pass leading to a previously unknown high-country basin. McKenzie's dog, Friday, was equally legendary, and apparently capable of moving the entire flock of sheep without command. McKenzie, whose native tongue was Gaelic and who sat silently throughout the trial, was found guilty and sent to jail. He twice escaped before vanishing from history altogether. Both the pass and the basin now bear his name (though spelt differently) and a plaque in the pass written in English, Gaelic and Maori commemorates McKenzie's exploits.

Mt Cook/Aoraki ★★★

New Zealand's highest mountain at 3754 m, and known in Maori as Aoraki, or 'the sky piercer', sits at the head of a dramatic glacial valley. The mountain is at the heart of Mount Cook National Park, covering an area over 70,000 ha and containing all but one of New Zealand's peaks over 3000 m. The first successful ascent of the mountain was on Christmas Day 1894, and the area is a magnet for serious mountain climbers. Mt Cook/Aoraki is not to be treated lightly, though, as it has taken numerous lives.

The road to the mountain first follows Lake Pukaki, then the broad Tasman River valley, to the area known as the Hermitage. For most, this is the usual stopping point, especially for camera-happy tourists. While the spectacular mountain views alone are worth the visit, there are some excellent short walks in the area, though check with the Department of Conservation (DoC) office for updated weather and track conditions before setting out. Short walks from the Mount Cook village include Bowens Bush Walk (10 minutes return), Glencoe Walk (30 minutes return), Governors Bush Walk (one hour return), and Red Tarn Track (two hours return). From the Whitehorse carpark in the Hooker Valley there are three other walks: the Kea Point Walk (one hour return), Sealy Tarns Track (two hours return), and the Hooker Valley track to the lake (three to four hours return).

With Aoraki stealing the show, it is easy to overlook the Tasman Glacier, which, at almost 30 km, is the longest glacier in the country. The Tasman Valley Road (turn right off the main Mount Cook road just before the village) leads a short distance (8 km) to the Blue Lakes carpark, the starting point for two short walks with views of the glacier. The Blue Lakes and Tasman Glacier View walk is 40 minutes return and Tasman Glacier Lake Walk is one hour return.

Upper Waitaki Power Project ★

www.twizel.com

This extensive power project, begun in 1968, links lakes Tekapo, Pukaki, Ruataniwha and Ohau through a series of massive canals and power stations to Lake Benmore. The town of Twizel, taking its name from the nearby Twizel River, was created to service the project and was, at the time, the most modern of all the hydro towns. The intention was to remove the town once the project was completed, but it survived and is now the centre of a thriving tourist industry. The hydro lakes have become destinations in themselves, popular for fishing and boating, and Mt Cook/Aoraki is not far away.

The best place to get an idea of the extensive nature of the Upper Waitaki scheme is just south of the town, where a viewpoint overlooks the complex of canals and one of the power stations.

Opihi Vineyard ★★★

Opihi Road, Hanging Rock (off SH8 from Pleasant Point)
Open Tuesday to Sunday 11 a.m. to 4 p.m. September to May, closed June to August
www.opihi.co.nz

Worth a trip to South Canterbury in itself, this boutique vineyard on the slopes above the Opihi River produces a fine line of white wines including pinot gris, chardonnay, riesling and muller thurgau. In addition to wine tasting, the winery offers cafe dining in the historic stone homestead with an expanse of lawn with plenty of room for children to run around. From the winery there is easy access to a notable Maori rock art drawing of a taniwha, and down to the river to Hanging Rock. To make a day of it, close by is the historic Kakahu lime kiln (built 1876), the limestone bluffs of the Kakahu escarpment and, at Waitohi, the Richard Pearse Memorial. The area is also home to the only east coast colonies of the rare long-tailed bat.

Peel Forest Park ★★★

Covering over 700 ha on the southern bank of the Rangitata River in the foothills of the Southern Alps, Peel Forest Park is a remnant of a much larger forest. The area has a climate distinct from the plains, with a much higher rainfall and heavy snowfalls in the winter, and supporting a rich and diverse flora and fauna — including a large number of native birds and giant totara, matai and kahikatea trees. (The Big Tree Walk leads to a 1000-year-old totara, 31 m tall and with a girth of 8.5 m.) The variety of ferns is especially surprising, and a third of all native fern types can be found here.

The park has a wide range of walking tracks, and jet boat and raft companies provide trips through the Rangitata Gorge. The walking tracks start at two main areas, Blandswood and Te Wanahu, both clearly sign-posted and within 2 km of Mt Peel village. Walks from Blandswood include Dennistoun Bush (one-and-a-half hours return), Emily Falls (one-and-a-half hours return), Rata Falls (two hours return), Kaikawaka Track (20 minutes return), Deer Spur (two hours return) and Little Mt Peel Track (five hours return). From Te Wanahu carpark there is the Big Tree Walk (30 minutes return), Allan's Track (three hours return), Fern Walk (one-and-a-half hours one way), and Ackland Falls Track (one-and-a-half hours return).

Pleasant Point Railway **

Main Road, Pleasant Point
Open one Sunday a month and public holidays
www.timaru.com/railway
Entrance fee

Operating along a 2-km stretch of the old Fairlie branch line, the exhibits at this museum are in excellent restored condition compared with those in other similar institutions. The main station at Pleasant Point was built in 1875 and houses a railway museum, while at the Keenes Crossing end of the short line there is a fully restored locomotive turntable and a vintage movie theatre. Rolling stock includes an 1878 D16 engine, a 1922 Ab 699 engine, an 1895 birdcage carriage and a 1925 Model T Ford Railcar, the only surviving example in the world.

The opening hours are limited so, if you are keen to visit, you really need to plan carefully. Details of opening hours and timetables are available on the website.

Timaru

Aigantighe Art Museum ***

49 Wai-iti Road
Open Tuesday to Friday 10 a.m. to 4 p.m., Saturday and Sunday 12 noon to 4 p.m.
Koha/donation

Pronounced 'egg-and-tie' and meaning 'at home' in Scottish Gaelic, this lively gallery houses a substantial art collection and is worth a trip to Timaru on its own. In addition to an extensive European collection, Aigantighe has a significant holding of works by New Zealand artists including CF Goldie, Frances Hodgkins, Petrus Van der Velden and Colin McCahon — who was born in Timaru and whose parents lived in Geraldine.

The gallery hosts innovative art from both New Zealand and around the world, and takes pride in providing each artwork with an extensive caption, making the art very accessible to the layperson. A particularly appealing aspect of gallery exhibitions is the way it arranges a wide range of art types and styles around a particular theme, enabling the viewer to appreciate differing views on that theme. Housed in an historic 1908 home belonging to the original benefactors, the gallery has a substantial collection of sculptures in the garden surrounding the house, which are open to view at all times.

Caroline Bay **

In 1890 the creation of a lengthy breakwater for Timaru Harbour changed the sea currents sufficiently to start washing sand of pulverised shingle from the harbour entrance into Caroline Bay, creating, in a short time, a safe sandy beach. In 1911 the Caroline Bay Association was formed to popularise the bay as a resort along European lines. To this end, formal gardens, promenades, a sound shell and playgrounds were built linked to a piazza on a bluff above the bay. Today the area still retains its original Edwardian flavour, but with many more attractions designed to appeal to newer generations. The piazza has recently been redeveloped into a lively cafe strip.

Caroline Bay Carnival **

www.carolinebay.org.nz

First held in 1911, the Caroline Bay Carnival is a major annual event beginning on Boxing Day. The Carnival draws people from all over the South Island attracted by two weeks of non-stop seaside entertainment, ranging from ever-popular talent quests through to sideshows and, of course, the Miss Caroline Bay competition. In the past, Caroline Bay was always up there with Whangamata and Mt Maunganui as a New Year 'hot spot'. Now much more a family festival, the Carnival highlight is the New Year's Eve concert and spectacular fireworks display.

Long a part of the Carnival is the historic merry-go-round, now restored and the only one of its kind in New Zealand. Built in France in 1920 by a showman named La Retle, the ride has carved German horses, a German organ and hand-painted roundings. The merry-go-round was first shipped to

England for the Crystal Palace Show in the early 1920s, then transported first to Australia, finally arriving in New Zealand in 1928. Acquired by the Caroline Bay Association in 1973, the merry-go-round is such a Carnival institution that parents who rode on it as children are now bringing their children back to experience the unique showground ride.

Dashing Rocks **
Track begins corner of Pacific and Westcote Streets

This is a 30-minute loop walk along a coastal bluff just north of Caroline Bay, with wide views back to the city and along the coast. The name is obvious when a heavy swell is running, and the highlight of the trip is a small but attractive arch of weathered rock.

The Landing Services Building ***
George Street

This fine building of bluestone (lava) was constructed in 1870 to facilitate the landing and storage of goods unloaded by longboats from ships offshore prior to a sheltered harbour being built. The building was located right on the beach prior to reclamation and it is the only example left in the southern hemisphere of this type. Now housing a pub and the Timaru Information Centre, the Landing Services Building is one of many historic buildings in the port area.

Sacred Heart Basilica *
Craigie Avenue

This is another grand Catholic church designed by FW Petre, and built in 1910. Constructed of red brick and white stone, the church has particularly fine stained-glass windows and a 1912 Arthur Hobday pipe organ.

South Canterbury Museum **
Perth Street
Open Tuesday to Friday 10 a.m. to 4.30 p.m., Saturday, Sunday and public holidays 1.30 p.m. to 4.30 p.m.
Koha/donation

This compact museum houses excellent displays on local history including a great photographic exhibition of the Caroline Bay Carnival, complete with a

1953 archive film, and a display of cartoon characters Tim and Ru. Created by the Timaru Brewing Company in 1920 to promote their beer, the stylish 'men about town' were highly popular right through to the late 1950s with corny jokes such as, Tim: 'Why is Africa called the Dark Continent?' Ru: 'Because there is no Timaru there.' Though the jokes may have dated, the spare elegant style of the cartoons has not.

Rightfully in pride of place is a replica of Richard Pearse's aeroplane, designed and built by him from bamboo and calico (his nickname was 'Bamboo Dick'). While the debate will never be finally settled, all true New Zealanders know that Richard Pearse flew before the Wright brothers, and that the argument really only hinges on whether or not it was 'controlled' flight. Born and raised in Upper Waitohi, about 18 km northwest of Timaru, Pearse was an inveterate inventor but was considered by many locals to be a crank (his other nickname was 'Mad Pearse'). While he worked away at other inventions, flight was his passion, though developments in aviation quickly overtook Pearse's backyard efforts. He died in 1953 in relative obscurity, his achievements recognised only long after his death.

Timaru Botanic Gardens *
Corner of King and Queen Streets

Tucked away south of the city centre, these surprisingly large gardens contain formal flower beds, an aviary, a fern house, rose gardens, and a very grand war memorial. The former tea kiosk is delightfully remembered as 'Erected in 1923 by the Floral Fete Committee', while the band rotunda was built in 1911 to celebrate the coronation of King George V and Queen Mary.

Waimate

The Hunters Hills *

The White Horse Monument high on Mt John (446 m), and dedicated to the work of the humble Clydesdale horse, is best appreciated from a distance. A quaint piece of New Zealand folk art, it owes more to Kiwi enthusiasm than to art, and it is easy to see that the materials to construct the horse cost only $240. The views are worth the effort whether you come by road, via the walkway or on mountain bike.

Kelceys Bush is a small bush remnant of the extensive forests that once covered these hills. The forest was destroyed in a disastrous fire that swept the hills in 1878 and burnt down 70 homes and a Maori settlement and permanently ruined the flourishing timber industry. A short track leads through the bush to the modest Sanders Falls.

The hills are also home to the Bennetts wallaby, released in 1875 to foster a fur industry. Now considered a pest, they are much sought after by hunters and for an up-close view there is a wallaby enclosure in Victoria Park in town.

Mountain biking trails in the hills are popular, as is the annual Pub to Pub Mountainbike Ride from the Waiho Forks Hotel to the Hakataramea Hotel via the Meyers Pass.

St Augustine's Church **
John Street

This extremely attractive church was built in 1872 of locally milled matai and totara on land donated by settler Michael Studholme. The very handsome lantern tower was added in 1883, giving the church a distinctive and unusual roof line. The stand-alone bell tower was added in front of the church in 1903, and a rare stained-glass window features Sir Galahad's vision of the Holy Grail, which in this case is a chalice.

St Patricks Church *
Timaru Road

Built in 1909, this church seems far too big for a town the size of Waimate. Tall and grand in style, the design is distinctly the work of FW Petre, who built several other Catholic churches in the South Island. The three bells of the church were cast in Belgium in 1922, the largest weighing over half a tonne, and the organ was one of the last built by renowned organ builder Arthur Hobday, in 1916.

Waimate Museum **
28 Shearman Street
Open Monday to Friday 1.30 p.m. to 4.30 p.m., Sunday and public holidays 2 p.m. to 4 p.m.
Entrance fee

Housed in the old Waimate Court House, the museum is worth visiting for the building alone. One of the country's most appealing small buildings, the court house was constructed in 1879 and still contains the magistrate's bench. Alongside the museum is a cob cottage, and a pit-sawn totara cottage and jail, both built around 1880.

NORTH OTAGO

Macraes Gold Mine **

Macraes Flat, off SH85, 80 km north of Dunedin

Tours most days 10 a.m. and 2 p.m. (bookings essential)

www.oceanagoldtours.com

Ph 0800 465 386

New Zealand's largest goldmine, Macraes produces, on average, 100 kg of gold per week, which is over 50 per cent of the country's production.

Gold was discovered here in the 1860s and small-scale mining continued through to 1954 when all operations closed down. Then in the 1980s, when the price of gold escalated, the area was investigated for a new mining operation, which eventually opened in 1990. There are six pits in all, over 200-m deep, and the operation is set to expand further in the next few years. The two-hour tour of the mine includes the heritage mining sites, viewing the giant Frasers open-cast pit and the maintenance area with its huge machinery used in the mine.

Moeraki **

The Moeraki boulders are an unusual geological formation known as septarian concretions. They are the result of erosion exposing this more resistant stone in the shape of almost perfect round boulders which now lie scattered along Moeraki beach. In Maori legend the boulders are the gourds washed overboard from the voyaging waka *Araiteuru* which arrived here around 1000 years ago.

While most people stop by the beach and go for a quick walk and then move on, an alternative is to drive into the small picturesque fishing village of Moeraki and park at the beginning of the Millennium Track. From here it is an hour return to the boulders on the beach (best seen at low tide), and in the other direction the walk leads up to a lookout point over the village and the coast (also one hour return). Moeraki has a long association with Maori with an old pa site, Onekakara, located above the township, and further on, a small Maori church built in 1862 with stained-glass windows, made in Rome, depicting Christ, the Mother and Child, and local Maori chief Matiaha Tiramorehu. Moeraki was also an early whaling station, established by John Hughes in 1836.

Oamaru

Blue Penguin Colony ***

Waterfront Road (by the harbour)

9 am to viewing time just before dusk

www.penguins.co.nz

Entrance fee to the viewing stand

It will come as a surprise that the penguin colony, now a major attraction in the area, was established only relatively recently, with only 33 breeding pairs in 1992, and now numbering over 120 pairs. The smallest of all the penguins, the blue penguin is common throughout New Zealand and Australia, but Oamaru is the only place where the numbers are reasonably large and the birds easy to see as they make their way at dusk from the sea to nests in the old quarry.

The Visitor Centre at the colony has superb information on the birds and the natural history of the area, with a special viewing stand built to give visitors an excellent yet undisturbed view of the birds. There is an entrance fee to the stand which opens for viewing time just before sundown when the birds come ashore for the night. Numbers vary considerably depending on the time of year so check when buying tickets as to how many penguins are likely to come ashore that evening.

Historic Harbour Street ***

The working area for the port, Harbour Street, is totally Victorian in character and has an appealing intimate feel. The buildings here are warehouses, port offices and grain stores in contrast to the grand buildings on Thames Street and now house galleries and craft shops, and tucked down a side alley, the famous Penguin Club, with a reputation as one of the best music venues in the country (www.penguinclub.co.nz).

Historic buildings in the harbour area include Smith's Grain Store (1881), Union Bank (1878), New Zealand Loan and Mercantile Warehouse (1882), Customs House (1883), Harbour Board Office (1876) and the Criterion Hotel (1877).

Historic Thames Street ***

Oamaru has, without a doubt, the finest collection of Victorian buildings in New Zealand and the grandest of these are along a short section of Thames Street. Most were built between 1870 and 1885 when the town flourished as an important port. Eventually improved rail links replaced the port as a means of transport and the town became a quiet backwater. With a small and stable population throughout the twentieth century, the lack of development in the town through this period no doubt saved these fine buildings. What also makes the town unique is that local Oamaru stone was almost the exclusive construction material, giving the town a uniform look uncommon in New Zealand.

The friendly information centre (corner Thames and Itchen Streets) has a detailed brochure on all the historic buildings, which are in easy walking distance of each other and include Bank of New South Wales (1883 and now the Forrester Gallery), National Bank (1871), St Lukes Anglican Church (1876), First Post Office (1864 and now a restaurant), Post Office (1883 and now the Waitaki Council offices), Courthouse (1882) and Athenaeum (1882 and now housing the very fine North Otago Museum).

Janet Frame House **

56 Eden Street

Open daily November to April 2 p.m. to 4 p.m.

Janet Frame, one of New Zealand's best-known authors, lived in this house between 1931 and 1943 and she attended Oamaru North School and Waitaki Girls' High School. Her time in Oamaru made a deep impact on the young writer and her three-part autobiography beginning with *To The Is-land* is particularly worthwhile reading. The house contains memorabilia and, recently, a collection of childhood writings was found concealed under the floorboards, hidden away for over 65 years.

Masquerade ***

Held annually in July, this fabulous winter festival focuses on a street parade down Thames Street to Tyne Street with hundreds of people wearing marvellous masks that they have created, ending up at the equally fabulous Grainstore Gallery. For information contact Donna Demente at the Grainstore Gallery, 9 Tyne Street, Oamaru.

Oamaru Harbour *

Naturally sheltered from the worst of the southerly weather by Cape Wanbrow, Oamaru attracted early Maori and was also home to sealers and whalers in the first half of the nineteenth century. With the construction of the breakwater beginning in 1871 Oamaru quickly became an important port town, especially after the development of refrigerated export meat shipments in 1884. The rocks for the breakwater came from the quarry that is home to the Blue Penguin colony, and the picturesque harbour is now shelter to a small fishing fleet.

Oamaru Victorian Heritage Celebrations ***

www.historicoamaru.co.nz

In keeping with the town's Victorian style, Oamaru has, over the years, developed one of the best heritage festivals in the country. Held in November over a number of days the festival features a wide range of events such as The Servants and Swaggers Dance, the National Stone-Sawing competition, a Victorian High Tea, the highly entertaining New Zealand Penny-farthing Championships, the Grand Victorian Street Parade, the Garden Party and the Victorian Ball and, on the final Sunday, the whole historic area is closed off for the Victorian Fete.

Parkside Limestone Quarry *

Airedale Road, Weston

www.oamarustone.co.nz

Ph 03 433 1134

Entrance fee

Creamy white in colour and very even in texture, Oamaru stone is soft enough to be sawn into blocks, but hardens with age making the stone an ideal building material. This quarry, opened in 1906, is now the only one producing building stone from limestone in a seam over 40 m thick. Initially the stone is cut in 2-tonne blocks by a massive double chainsaw mounted on rails, and then transported to the cutting shed to be reduced to smaller building blocks by circular saws. Tours of the quarry and limeworks are on Tuesday and Thursday mornings at 10.15 a.m. and take an hour.

Totara Estate **

SH1, 2 km south of Oamaru

Open Wednesday to Sunday 1 p.m. to 4 p.m. and school and public holidays 10 a.m. to 4 p.m.

www.totaraestate.co.nz

Comprised of four historic farm buildings constructed of Oamaru stone, three of these buildings date from the 1860s, and the carcass shed from 1881. It was from here that the first cargo of sheep meat was prepared to be sent frozen to Britain on the ship *Dunedin* in 1882, though the meat was frozen on board, and the ship left from Port Chalmers, not Oamaru.

In addition to the restored nineteenth-century farm buildings, there are early New Zealand sheep breeds and an audiovisual presentation on the New Zealand meat industry. The Estate also hosts the Harvest Home Festival, a traditional autumn harvest festival, though with modern twists such as lambburgers.

Whitestone Cheese **

3 Torridge Street
Open daily 9 a.m. to 5 p.m.
www.whitestonecheese.co.nz

Established in 1987, this award-winning organic cheese maker offers cheese tasting and a viewing area to watch cheeses (from both cow and sheep milk) being made. Whitestone won the 2006 Champion of Champions Award with its outstanding Windsor Blue which had already collected nine trophies and 10 gold medals. Its cafe also offers Otago wines to match the 18 varieties of cheese made by Whitestone.

Yellow-eyed Penguin Colony *

Bushy Beach. From the town, follow Tyne Street to Bushy Beach Road, then to the carpark at the end of the road.

The hoiho or yellow-eyed penguin is much larger than the blue and much less sociable, preferring nesting spots isolated from other penguin neighbours. At Bushy Beach a small colony of these rare birds has established itself in the low-growing vegetation above the beach and a special hide has been constructed to allow public viewing. These penguins come ashore late in the afternoon (the blue penguin comes ashore at dusk) and the beach is closed after 3 p.m. as the birds will not come ashore if they are disturbed by people placing themselves on the beach between the sea and their nests.

Puketapu Summit — Palmerston *

The track begins from carpark, sign-posted from SH1 in Palmerston

A steep climb leads to an unusual monument erected on the summit of Puketapu (343 m) in the memory of local politician Sir John McKenzie. McKenzie was a champion of the small farmer and, as a politician, instrumental in breaking up the huge landholdings of the late nineteenth century. Built in 1931 (an earlier monument collapsed) of local bluestone, the cairn is 13 m high and has an internal staircase. The walk is two hours return and the view from the top is spectacular. For the very fit, a race to the top is held in October in memory of Albert Kelly the local policeman, who during the Second World War, hiked to the top of the hill every day to scout out the local coastline for signs of the enemy.

Waitaki Valley **

The valley follows the broad Waitaki River from near Oamaru up to the Mackenzie Country and the following entries are along SH83 driving east to west.

Dansey's Pass **

If you are looking for an 'off the beaten track' experience then a trip over the Dansey's Pass is for you. This road from the Waitaki Valley through to Naseby was originally the coach road supplying the gold fields of the Maniatoto basin. Winding first through the limestone farmland along the Maerewhenua River, the road then climbs to the pass, reaching a height of 934 m, and passes through stunning wild tussock country before dropping down into Naseby. On the north side of the pass, near Naseby, is the historic Dansey's Pass Coach Inn built of local stone and beautifully restored, a popular stopping point offering refreshments and accommodation. The Inn serviced the Kyeburn Diggings, a gold field that at one stage supported a population of 2000 people. The Inn was built in 1862 and legend has it that the stonework was paid for in beer.

The road is narrow, winding and unsealed, dusty in summer and frequently closed by snow in winter, but don't let that put you off the trip. There is a camping ground 14 km from Duntroon.

Duntroon

Maori Rock Art ★★

North Otago and South Canterbury are home to hundreds of sites containing Maori rock art, though much of it is very hard to see and even harder to access. At Duntroon there are two sites that are both accessible and easy to see. The first site at Maerewhenua is just south of Duntroon about half a kilometre on the road to Dansey's Pass. There is a bit of a scramble uphill to an extensive limestone overhang which has drawings along its entire length. The second site, Takiroa, is just 3 km west of Duntroon on SH83 and contains substantial drawings in both red and black, some of which are pre-European.

Vanished World Centre ★★★

SH83, Duntroon

Open daily 10 a.m. to 4 p.m. October to June, Saturday and Sunday only
11 a.m. to 3 p.m. July to October

www.vanishedworld.co.nz

Entrance fee

North Otago has some of New Zealand's most interesting geology and, around Duntroon in particular, there are fascinating rock formations and fossils that are easily accessible from the road. The Vanished World Centre is an excellent starting point with a collection of impressive fossils up to 30 million years old and including ancient penguins, whales and dolphins, some species of which are unknown to science. Even better, the centre has a kids' table where youngsters (why do they have all the fun?) can crack open rocks and find their own fossils to keep. Available for purchase from the centre is a brochure 'Vanished World Fossil Trail' which details a self-guided tour of the most interesting geological sites in North Otago. And don't forget to check out the mysterious 'rattling rocks'.

A short loop drive from the Centre at Duntroon takes around two hours including walking and these are some of the highlights:

- Anatini Whale Fossil
  A short walk from the road through a landscape looking like a movie set takes you to the fossil of a baleen whale. The fossil is very clear and protected by perspex from prying fingers and has an interpretive board explaining which parts of the whale are visible.

- Elephant Rocks
  Fascinating limestone formations shaped by erosion stand out starkly in the open farmland.

- Awamoko Stream — Valley of the Whales
  Exposed limestone contains the fossils of whales, dolphins and shells.

- Earthquakes
  Huge rocks have broken away from the cliffs to expose fossils of an ancient seabed. Take care as rocks still fall and there are crevices in the area.

Nichol's Forge

Open when the Flying Pig cafe next door is open — usually 10 a.m. to 4 p.m.

Established in 1898 this original forge comes complete with the tools of trade of the blacksmith and is just ready for the smithy to walk in and start work. Even the tiny office in the front looks the part and comes complete with an ancient typewriter.

Kurow Hill Walk *

From SH83 in Kurow go past the shops in the town and then turn left into Grey Street and the track begins from the end of the street.

A short but steep walk climbing to 250 m leads to a fantastic lookout point over the Waitaki Valley and the surrounding mountains (one hour return). If walking is not for you then the local area also has some excellent mountain bike trails and a leaflet is available from the Kurow Information Centre. And if both walking and cycling are tame, then the famous 'That Dam Run' offers a choice of running 100 km, a marathon and a half marathon either as an individual or as part of a team.

Benmore Dam *

Benmore Information Centre open daily 10.30 a.m. to 4.30 p.m. from mid-October to end May. From June to mid-October open 10.30 a.m. to 4.30 p.m. weekends only. Tours are at 11 a.m., 1 p.m. and 3 p.m. Not recommended for people with pacemakers.
Ph 03 438 9212
Entrance fee

The Waitaki River has the fourth-largest water flow of any New Zealand river and the narrow valley of the upper Waitaki River was ideal for the construction of hydro-electric power schemes. There are, in all, three hydro lakes, Waitaki, Aviemore and Benmore, the latter dam being the largest of the three. The oldest dam, Waitaki, was begun in 1928 and completed in 1934. The last dam in New Zealand to be built using picks and shovels, before the advent of earthmoving machinery, over 1200 workers were on site at the peak of construction. The Aviemore dam, built in 1968, is a combination of earth and concrete and features a 1-km-long spawning race that allows fish to migrate upstream.

Benmore, built between two natural rock outcrops, was begun in 1958 and completed in 1965 and is the largest earth dam in New Zealand. Constructed of clay-like gravel and supported by two shoulders of river gravel, the volume of water behind the dam is one-and-a-half times the capacity of Wellington Harbour. The Benmore Track begins at the carpark above the dam and is a short climb to a viewpoint over the Waitaki Valley and to the mountains, including Mt Cook.

The area is fast becoming a popular holiday destination, especially for boating and fishing both in the lakes and on nearby rivers.

Trotters Gorge *

Turnoff is 2 km south of Moeraki on SH1 into Horse Range Road and the picnic area is on the right (but not well sign-posted, so it is easy to drive past).

A 152-ha reserve on the southern end of Horse Range, Trotters Gorge is a popular picnic spot and walking area. From the picnic area the main track follows Trotters Creek along the valley floor through native bush and is flanked by rocky bluffs that look like limestone but are in fact a greywacke/breccia conglomerate. The walk to a hut is around two hours return.

CENTRAL OTAGO

Alexandra

Alexandra Blossom Festival **

www.blossom.co.nz

Always held on the last Saturday in September, this festival began in 1957 to raise money for the local swimming pool and quickly became one of New Zealand's iconic events. The highlight of the festival is the famous parade of floats, some decorated with over 20,000 blossoms, followed by a day of sport and entertainment at Pioneer Park.

Earnscleugh Historic Tailings *

Cross the bridge heading south out of town, turn right into Earnscleugh Road and then, after 3 km, turn right into Marshalls Road.

This must win the prize for the most bizarre tourist attraction, but is actually fascinating in its own right. Hectare after hectare of piles of shingle and stone are all that remain of an industry that boomed in the early twentieth century. Gold was discovered here in 1862 and, once the easily worked gold was exhausted, dredges moved into the riverbed, with varying degrees of success. In 1895 the invention of the tailings elevator allowed dredges to stack the tailings behind them and therefore work into the river bank rather than just the riverbed. At the goldrush height, 20 dredges worked the riverbed between Alexandra and Clyde leaving behind a moonscape of shingle and stone. The tailings are part of the Otago 50th Anniversary Walkway that runs from Alexandra to Clyde.

Flat Top Hill and Butchers Dam **

On SH8, 5 km south of Alexandra

Flat Top Hill is a rare example of dry short-tussock grassland and has its very own natural history with distinctive plants, animal life and geology adapted to this harsh environment. Gold was discovered at Butchers Gully in 1862 and the dam itself was built in 1935 to 1937 for irrigation. A loop walk takes around 30 minutes with excellent interpretive panels along the way, but it is worth continuing further up the slope to the summit of Flat Top Hill from which there are great views over Alexandra and the Clutha River.

Great Alexandra Lions Easter Bunny Hunt **

First began in 1991 this hunt is held over a 24-hour period from Friday to Saturday of Easter weekend and, in some years, can bag as many as 26,000 rabbits. For a variety of reasons the numbers are limited and, to join the hunt, a person can request their name to be entered into a secret ballot. Once chosen, individuals then combine into teams of twelve. A further ballot allots the area for each team, and the winning team is decided by the number of rabbits shot. Teamwork and tactics are essential and while, at one level, the hunt can be viewed as sport, on another level, the reduction in rabbit numbers has a significant impact on the viability of farming in the district. To get on the mailing list for the ballot write to: PO Box 139, Alexandra.

Arrowtown **

www.arrowtown.org.nz

Like Queenstown, this town is one of those 'love it or hate it' places. A mixture of historical gems and touristy shops and cafes, Arrowtown can be crowded during the holiday period, but it is still easy to get away from the crowd and enjoy the natural beauty of the area.

Gold was discovered in the riverbed in 1862 by shearer Jack Tewa, and a shanty town was quickly established close to the river, only to be washed away in a flood the following year. Rebuilt on higher ground, the town had a population of over 7000 with further settlements at Macetown, Skippers and Bullendale. Over 60 buildings remain from the goldmining period including a row of quaint miners' cottages dwarfed by huge old trees. The cool Central Otago climate is one of the few places in New Zealand to have spectacular autumn colour, and this is one of the best times to visit the area, being between the summer tourist peak, and the winter ski season. The riverbed below the main street was the scene of the famous chase through the ford in the first *Lord of the Rings* movie. Surely New Zealand towns must soon promote themselves as NOT a *Lord of the Rings* location!

The excellent museum in the middle of the main street (Buckingham Street) is located in several heritage buildings, including the old Bank of New Zealand, and is well worth a visit.

Arrowtown Walks **

Around Arrowtown are several good walks of varying lengths and they all start by the river behind the shops.

Arrowtown War Memorial

Well away from the crowds in the main street, this hill, crowned by the local war memorial, has a great view over the town and surrounding countryside. To get there continue uphill through the Chinese settlement to the road and then turn left to the memorial (the historic Arrowtown cemetery is opposite the memorial). To return to the town, turn down Wiltshire Street and into Buckingham Street. The entire walk will take only 30 minutes.

Big Hill Track

A good day's walk of around seven hours on a loop track that was originally the main access route to Macetown. The track is steep in parts.

Gully Loop Track

A three-hour loop track that includes old goldmine workings and a monument to William Fox who started the rush for gold on the Arrow River.

Otago 150th Anniversary Walkway

A pleasant 4.2-km walkway (one hour) along the willow-shaded Arrow River.

Tobins Track

About an hour-return walk to the Crown Terrace with views over the town and the surrounding mountains.

Chinese Settlement **

The Chinese miners of the gold fields occupied the margins of society both socially and physically and very little remains of their humble homes. At Arrowtown, the Chinese section of town has been preserved, and in some places reconstructed, to provide the best overview of the life of the Chinese miner on a New Zealand gold field.

Millbrook Golf Course ★★★

www.millbrook.co.nz

With The Remarkables mountains forming a dramatic backdrop, Millbrook is considered to be one of the best alpine golf courses in the world. Designed by champion New Zealand golfer Sir Bob Charles, the course takes advantage of its position with several elevated tees, but it is more than just pretty scenery. The 18-hole, par-72 course has over 60 bunkers, and each hole has a challenge of its own.

In addition to the golf course, Millbrook offers luxury accommodation, restaurant and bar facilities, golf coaching, a driving range, putting greens and excellent equipment for hire. Open to visitors, it is best to book ahead.

The Brass Monkey Motorcycle Rally ★★

www.brassmonkeyrally.org.nz

A motorcycling institution, this rally is held annually at Queen's Birthday Weekend at the Ida Dam, near Oturehua north of Alexandra. The location was chosen for its extremely cold winter temperatures (nearby Ophir recorded New Zealand's lowest temperature of −22°C), and despite the cold (or because of it) the event attracts over 3500 motorcyclists to this mad winter campout. The Brass Monkey is famous for the most ingenious inventions to keep warm and a large continuous bonfire is the natural heart of the rally.

Central Otago Skifields ★★★

The cold clear winters, coupled with the high elevation, have provided Central Otago with some of the best and most scenic skifields in New Zealand. Their easy accessibility and good facilities make up for the sometimes fickle snow conditions.

Cardrona Alpine Resort

www.cardrona.com

Located halfway between Queenstown and Wanaka the three basins of the Cardona Skifield offer excellent dry snow and open slopes on a range of terrain that will suit everyone from beginners to more advanced. The field is particularly popular with free-style skiers and snowboarders, and frequently hosts snowboarding championships.

Coronet Peak

www.skinz.com

New Zealand's first skifield established in 1947, Coronet Peak is less than half-an-hour's drive from Queenstown. South facing and with snow-making machines, this is one of New Zealand's more reliable skifields. Three lifts provide good access to the undulating terrain, and night skiing on Friday and Saturday nights during the middle of winter are an added bonus.

The Remarkables

www.skinz.com

This skifield, high on the dramatic Remarkables mountains, has a sunny north-facing aspect with a wide range of slopes to suit all levels of ability. Particularly beginner- and family-friendly, this field includes a children-only handle tow.

Treble Cone

www.treblecone.co.nz

Located just 20 km south of Wanaka, this is New Zealand's largest skifield with fantastic views of Lake Wanaka and the Southern Alps. Triple Treat is the longest run (3.5 km), and the field is particularly popular with snowboarders and more advanced skiers looking for a challenge.

Waiorau Snow Farm

www.snowfarmnz.com

Situated high in the Pisa Range above the Cardrona Valley, this is the only skifield in New Zealand dedicated to cross-country skiing. With over 50 km of groomed trails suited for both classic and skate skiing, the snow farm also has dedicated snow tubing areas and is ideal for a family day out. Held in August each year is the Snowfarm Infinity Merino Muster Ski Marathon which includes 42-, 21-, and 7-km races.

Central Otago Vineyards ***

When the first vineyard was established in the Gibbston Valley, the venture was treated with much scepticism, but now Central Otago is producing some of New Zealand's best wines and has, without a doubt, some of the most scenic vineyards in the country. In addition to the stark and rugged terrain, the weather is by New Zealand standards extreme; hot and dry in the summer, and very cold in winter. While pinot noir is the area's signature wine, Central Otago also produces some award-winning white wines including chardonnay, pinot gris and riesling. The two main areas for wine production are at Bannockburn near Cromwell, and the Gibbston Valley in the Kawarau Gorge. Highly recommended as the first stop on any wine tour of Central Otago is the Big Picture in Cromwell. Located on SH6, the Big Picture offers an introduction to wine through its unique Aroma Room and tasting experience. Combining a cinematic overview of a vineyard and a winemaker with wine tasting, this is the ideal place to start a wine tour whether you are a complete novice or a wine connoisseur. In addition to wine tasting, the Big Picture has a fantastic selection of Central Otago wines for sale and a restaurant and cafe.

Bannockburn Vineyards

Akarua
Cairnmuir Road, Bannockburn
Cellar door open Monday to Friday 10 a.m. to 5 p.m., weekend 11 a.m. to 4 p.m.
www.akarua.com

In addition to wine tasting, Akarua offers winery and vineyard tours by arrangement and also brews three types of beer on the premises, under the Wild Spaniard label. The popular Lazy Dog Cafe and Wine Bar has both indoor and outdoor dining in a great courtyard atmosphere.

Carrick
Cairnmuir Road, Bannockburn
Cellar door open daily 11 a.m. to 5 p.m.
www.carrick.co.nz

Located on the Cairnmuir Terraces this smart modern winery produces whites in addition to pinot noir, and offers wine tasting and food in a stylish cafe looking out to the Carrick Range.

Mt Difficulty
Felton Road, Bannockburn
Cellar door sales 10.30 a.m. to 4.30 p.m. and to 5 p.m. in the summer.
Cafe open 12 noon to 3 p.m. Labour Weekend to Easter.
www.mtdifficulty.co.nz

This beautifully situated vineyard has a fantastic outlook north over Cromwell and beyond from the broad terrace in front of the cafe. In addition to award-winning pinot noir the winery also offers some excellent white wines.

Olssen's Garden Vineyard
306 Felton Road, Bannockburn
Cellar door open 10.30 a.m. to 5 p.m.
www.olssens.co.nz

The first vineyard in the Bannockburn area, Olssen's has an individual and homely atmosphere, just the place to try their wines or enjoy a picnic lunch under the trees or down by the ponds.

Kawarau Gorge Vineyards

Amisfield Winery
10 Lake Hayes Road, Queenstown
Cellar door open daily 10 a.m. to 8 p.m., bistro closed Monday
www.amisfield.co.nz

The closest vineyard to Queenstown, Amisfield is a stunning modern winery overlooking Lake Hayes, with sophisticated indoor and outdoor dining as well as a gallery for local artists. The bistro at Amisfield won the 2006 Vineyard Restaurant of the Year Award and, in addition to excellent pinot noir, the vineyard also produces pinot gris, dessert wine and méthode traditionnelle.

Chard Farm Winery
Chard Farm Road, off SH6, Gibbston
Cellar door open Monday to Friday 10 a.m. to 5 p.m., Saturday and Sunday 11 a.m. to 5 p.m.
www.chardfarm.co.nz

The setting for this vineyard is spectacular with the grapes planted to the very edge of the wild Kawarau River gorge and steep rocky hills creating a towering backdrop to the French-style winery. The narrow road is a trip in itself and is like a mini 'Road to Skippers' and was, during the nineteenth century, the main road through the gorge. It does have an advantage in that the road is so narrow that tour buses can't fit through!! Like other Central Otago vineyards, Chard Farm offers chardonnay and riesling, in addition to its award-winning pinot noir.

Gibbston Valley Wines
SH6, Gibbston

Cellar door open 10 a.m. to 5 p.m.

www.gibbstonvalley.co.nz

Gibbston Valley Wines were the pioneer vineyard of the area with plantings as early as 1981 and their first commercial wine bottled in 1987. Their pinot noir has over the years won numerous awards and recently their Gibbston Valley 2005 Riesling won the New Zealand Champion Trophy. In addition to wine tasting, Gibbston Valley has a superb cafe in a garden setting and right next door is the Gibbston Valley Cheese Company which produces boutique varieties from both cow's and sheep's milk using traditional methods.

Peregrine Wines
Kawarau Gorge Road, Gibbston

Cellar door open daily 10 a.m. to 5 p.m.

www.peregrinewines.co.nz

A spectacular modern vineyard, the award-winning building was designed by Wellington architect Chris Kelly and complements Peregrine's award-winning pinot noir.

Wanaka Vineyards

Rippon Vineyard
Mt Aspiring Road, Wanaka

Cellar door open 11 a.m. to 5 p.m. December to April, 1.30 p.m. to 4 p.m. July to November. Closed May and June.

www.rippon.co.nz

One of the earliest vineyards in Central Otago, the Department of Scientific and Industrial Research (DSIR) first started experimental plantings here in 1975 and by 1981 the vineyard was already extensively planted. Pinot noir is the signature wine but varietals include chardonnay, riesling, merlot, shiraz, osteiner and gewürztraminer.

With its spectacular site above Lake Wanaka, Rippon is famous for its vistas over the rows of grapes down to the lake, especially attractive in autumn when the yellowing leaves of the vines contrast with the bright blue of the lake. Rippon doesn't have a cafe but is a great place to bring a picnic. The vineyard is home to the Rippon Music Festival held every two years (even numbers) and focusing on contemporary music from hip-hop and dance to reggae and rock.

Clyde and the Clyde Dam **

Like most Central Otago towns, Clyde was established in response to a goldrush in the 1860s only to slowly decline through the first half of the twentieth century, leaving the town virtually untouched for the past 100 years. Formerly known as Dunstan (changing the name of the town must have been fashionable in Central Otago as most mining towns seem to have changed their names at least once), the town today has a number of handsome well-proportioned wooden and stone buildings including the Post Office, hotel, and the Vincent County Council Chambers, now the local museum. Two of the town's more popular events are the Clyde Annual Wine and Food Festival and, for the super fit, the multi-sport race, Goldrush. The festival attracts big crowds to the town each Easter Sunday and the gruelling Goldrush in March involves road and mountain biking, running and kayaking 375 km through Central Otago back country (www.goldrush.co.nz).

The town is now dominated by the massive 100-m high Clyde Dam built between 1977 and 1989, though it was belatedly discovered to be very vulnerable to earthquakes, which must have done wonders for the property prices in Clyde just below the dam! Lake Dunstan, created by the dam, extends well upriver though it doesn't broaden out until above Cromwell and is now a popular destination for boating and fishing (brown trout).

Cromwell

www.cromwell.org.nz

Cromwell Old Town **

At the confluence of the Kawarau and Clutha rivers, Cromwell was originally known as The Junction and in 1862 gold was discovered in the river below the town, leading to the inevitable population boom characteristic of Central Otago settlement. Following the same pattern of gold towns worldwide, Cromwell declined once the gold ran out, but, unlike most gold towns, eventually survived as a service town for the district.

When the Clyde Dam was proposed there was considerable opposition in Cromwell as the scenic gorge below the town as well as the central business area was to go under water. However, the government pushed ahead with the project and the old town was flooded in 1993. Fortunately, the best of the historic buildings were dismantled and then faithfully reconstructed on higher ground. Today, this small complex of buildings is one of our better 'historic villages'. Here you can spend a pleasant 30 to 60 minutes wandering around old stables, shops and stone cottages, and finish off the walk with a pleasant stop in the cafe overlooking the lake.

Mountain Bike Racing ***

The open dry country of Central Otago, directly contrasting with the wet and mud of most of New Zealand, is a mountain biker's heaven and throughout the region there are numerous excellent mountain bike tracks (information centres will have details).

Cromwell is home to several bike races, most of which, strangely, seem to focus on the historic Bannockburn pub. In late December each year is the Bannockburn Mountain Bike Classic with options of 35-, 22- and 10-km distances starting from the Bannockburn pub. For the very adventurous, is the 31-km Carricktown Crusher which includes a climb over the 1300-m Duffer Saddle to the old gold towns of Carricktown and Quartzville (and starting and finishing at the Bannockburn pub). The Garston to Bannockburn Pub to Pub Adventure Crazy Gutbuster is a 75.4-km race held in November that crosses the Hector Mountains from Garston and then follows the Nevis River to Bannockburn. For road cyclists there is, in mid-January, the Lake Dunstan Challenge, a virtually flat 92-km ride around the lake.

Real Fruit Ice Cream Cromwell ***

Central Otago is famous for its flavoursome apricots, cherries, nectarines and peaches which flourish in hot dry summers. Numerous roadside stalls offer fruit for sale direct from the orchard but for a real treat try real fruit ice cream where the fruit is whipped into the ice cream while you wait, at either Jones Family Orchard or the Freeway Orchard, both on the main road.

The Sluicings **

Felton Road, Bannockburn

In the late nineteenth century technology enabled gravelly soils to be worked with high-pressure sluicing hoses which resulted in a drastic revision of the landscape. In this area the terrain has been altered into a fantasy world of pinnacles, gulches and canyons, with very little growing in the barren soil. The walk takes less than an hour though you can also explore old goldmines in the area (you will need a torch). This is a great place to work up an appetite, or walk off your lunch from the vineyards close by.

Glenorchy *

www.glenorchyinformationcentre.co.nz

The old adage that 'it is better to travel than to arrive' very much applies to Glenorchy. While the small village of Glenorchy isn't up to much, the trip along the lake from Queenstown has magnificent vistas both of the mountains across the lake and up the Dart River into the heart of Fiordland. There are a number of excellent walks along the road from Queenstown and further up the Dart River Valley, including access to the famous Routeburn, Caples and Greenstone Tracks. The area is also notable as yet another *Lord of the Rings* location and jet-boating on the Dart is famous for both the thrill and the scenic backdrop.

For railway buffs, the village does have the curious attraction of an old red railway goods shed, though no railway ever reached Glenorchy. The shed is a reminder of the era when transport on the lake was once part of the New Zealand Railways network.

Hayes Engineering Works **

Ida Valley — Omakau Road, Oturehua
Open Saturday and Sunday 11 a.m. to 4 p.m. August to May

The modest mud-brick and corrugated-iron buildings that form Hayes Engineering are representative of the Kiwi knack of being able to make anything. From this remote workshop, established by Ernest Hayes in 1895, came a wide range of simple but effective agriculture inventions that, by Ernest's death in 1933, had gained a worldwide reputation. In particular, the Hayes wire strainer, invented in 1905, was widely exported internationally. The company moved to Christchurch in 1952 and is still operated and owned by the Hayes family, and, today, this unique collection of buildings is much the same as when it was fully operational in the 1930s.

Kingston Flyer **

Operates daily 1 October to 30 April

www.kingstonflyer.co.nz

Originally running between Gore and Kingston Bay from 1878 through to the 1950s, the Kingston Flyer connected with a steamer which ferried passengers and freight across Lake Wakatipu to Queenstown. Today the train rattles along 14 km of track from the lake down to Fairlight, with vintage carriages pulled by a New Zealand-built Ab Pacific-class steam locomotive. The return trip takes an hour and a half and is great fun.

Lakes Hayes **

Much loved by calendar companies and landscape artists, Lake Hayes is famous for the autumn colours of the willows and poplars along its shores. On the northern side of the lake is an extensive picnic area with large shady trees along the shore edge and, as the shallow waters of Lake Hayes are not as cold as the deeper mountain lakes, this is the place to be on a hot summer's day.

Naseby ***

If you have ever wondered what Arrowtown was like before all the tourists, then Naseby is the place for you. Situated in the northern Maniatoto under the Kakanui Mountains, gold was discovered in the Hogburn in May 1863, and by the end of the year the diggings were home to over 5000 men. Four years later the rush was over, but gold could still be extracted by hydraulic sluicing — effective, but with a ruinous effect on the landscape. Fortunately, conifers were later planted over the old tailings and, today, Naseby is an attractive forested town.

Originally the area was known as Parkers, after two brothers involved in the initial gold discovery, and later changed to Mt Ida, and finally to Naseby.

The small cosy town has a number of historic buildings including two of Central Otago's oldest pubs, both of which were built in 1863. The oldest pub is The Ancient Briton, an atmospheric old stone building, while just around the corner is the fine wooden Royal Hotel, built just a few months later.

For something completely different and surprising, a few kilometres out of town on the Dansey's Pass road is the Eden Hoare Fashion Museum. Here is a collection of over 200 frocks designed by New Zealand designer Eden Hoare in the 1970s, and, if that isn't enough, there is also a collection of over 400 Jim Beam decanters!

Ophir Post Office *

Swindon Street, Ophir

Open Monday to Friday 9 a.m. to 12 p.m.

A gold boom-town named after the biblical King Solomon's mine, gold was discovered here in 1863, and the population quickly rose to 1000 people. Originally known as Blacks, only a handful of buildings remain, including the Court House, Police Station and the Post Office. The Post Office is particularly notable and is now owned by the Historic Places Trust. Built of schist stone in 1863 it still has most of its original furnishings, and the internal configuration is unchanged from the time it was built. Today, the building still functions as a post office for the tiny population of only 50 people, and by a strange twist of history has been run by women since the 1890s.

Ophir has the unenviable fame of having the coldest recorded temperature in New Zealand, a teeth-chattering −22°C recorded in July 1995.

Otago Central Rail Trail ***

www.otagocentralrailtrail.co.nz

Whoever it was within the Department of Conservation (DoC) who promoted this rail trail in the first place deserves a medal. Despite early opposition to the idea, the rail trail now attracts thousands of visitors to Central Otago to cycle, walk or horse-ride all or part of this 150-km stretch of the old Clyde to Middlemarch railway line. Operating for over 80 years, the line was closed in 1990 and acquired by DoC in 1993, finally to reopen in 2000 as the Central Otago Rail Trail.

The trail is in six sections, each between 19 and 32 km in length, and along the way passes through tunnels, over bridges and viaducts and through some of New Zealand's most dramatic landscape. The most popular way to travel is by bike, and both bike hire and bike transport can be arranged locally through the website or from the beginning of the trail at Clyde. Accommodation along the trail is limited, so you need to book well in advance, especially for autumn which is the most popular time to hit the trail.

If time is critical then the most scenic section is the 23-km stretch from Lauder to Oturehua which includes several tunnels as well as the longest bridge over the Manuherikia River.

Queenstown

Definitely not the place to get away from it all, Queenstown is a lively tourist town beautifully situated on the shores of Lake Wakatipu. Over the years the town has redefined itself several times from an old goldmining settlement through to ski resort and, in more recent times, New Zealand's 'Adventure Capital'. And, when you are not jumping, floating, skiing, or flying, Queenstown has every sort of place to eat, drink and party. By New Zealand standards Queenstown is expensive and runs the risk of being 'over sold'. If you are looking for unspoiled New Zealand, Queenstown is not the place, but if you are looking for a town that buzzes with activity night and day then this is the place for you.

Eichardt's Hotel *

Marine Parade, Queenstown

www.eichardtshotel.co.nz

Very little remains of old Queenstown, and even Eichardt's Hotel, with its long association with the town, has undergone as many changes as the town itself.

The area was originally settled by William Rees and Nicholas von Tunselmann in 1859, and Rees built a large woolshed on the shores of Lake Wakatipu where the hotel now stands. With the discovery of gold, people poured into the Wakatipu basin, and in 1863, Rees, recognising a business opportunity, quickly turned the woolshed into an hotel called the Queen's Arms. Completely rebuilding the hotel in local stone, Rees entered into a partnership with the former Prussian guard Albert Eichardt in 1866, who became the sole owner in 1869. Renamed Eichardt's Hotel, it was Albert and his wife Julia who turned the establishment into a Queenstown legend with first-class accommodation and even electricity 30 years before the town had a supply.

Today, the hotel continues in the same tradition and is a small luxury establishment on the lakefront.

Queenstown Adventure Activities ***

Queenstown is the home of every sort of adventure activity, none of it cheap and every year the choice becoming even more mind-boggling. There is bungy jumping, paragliding, quad biking, four-wheel-driving, kayaking, mountain biking, abseiling, paraponting, horse trekking, whitewater rafting, jet-boating, heli-skiing, snowboarding, gravity swinging, river surfing, rock climbing, off-road touring, canyoning, diving, ballooning, high-wire flying, skydiving, hang gliding and more things not yet invented. And, if that is not enough, there are at least five companies offering *Lord of the Rings* location tours!

The good thing is that there are very few 'rip off' merchants in New Zealand. It is a small country, word gets around fast and bad operators don't tend to last long, but a few hints will help make your 'adventure' more successful:

- It helps if you have a good idea regarding what you want to do before you arrive, and, that way, you are less likely to be dazzled by what's on offer when you get there. Most of the companies have good websites so check them out before you arrive if you can.
- Ask locals or other travellers for advice and their experiences regarding individual operators, though remember locals (especially hotels) may have a vested interest or a financial arrangement with an operator.
- Obtain precise information about what you get for your money. For example, an activity may be advertised as taking three hours, but a large proportion of that might be taken up with travelling or other incidental activities.
- Ask how long the company has been operating, as some companies go out of business quickly while the better ones survive on their reputation.
- Check if the activity is weather dependent or if you can cancel (and get your money back) if the weather is not to your liking — whether or not the activity goes ahead.
- Ask about safety equipment and safety standards. Many of the activities are exciting because they are dangerous, and while New Zealand has an excellent safety record accidents do happen.
- Decide what risks you are prepared to take. There is no point in blaming the operator if the activity is a lot more exciting than you had bargained for.
- Finally check any 'money back' options if the trip is cancelled or postponed especially if you are on a tight time schedule.

For most people the 'big three' are bungy jumping, whitewater rafting and jet-boating and although that narrows the options down considerably, there is still plenty of choice.

Jet-boating

It is hard to go past the Shotover River for sheer jet-boat excitement and here the choice is easy as Shotover Jet are the only operators on the river (www. shotoverjet.com). If it is a combination of scenery and excitement you are after then consider the Dart River as a jet-boating option.

Whitewater Rafting

The Kawarau River is considered to be one of the best rivers for whitewater rafting, with quiet stretches to catch your breath between the wild rapids, though there are also options on the Shotover River.

Bungy Jumping

Queenstown is the home of the bungy jump with endless variation on a theme. AJ Hackett operates the oldest bungy-jump site, off the historic Kawarau Bridge (43 m), and the highest bungy jump in New Zealand, over the Nevis River (134 m). Visit www.AJHackett.com

Queenstown Gardens *

Set on a peninsula, this park with unspoiled views over the lake to the mountains is just the place to walk off that dinner or lunch or, if you prefer, play a game of tennis or go ice skating.

Queenstown Walks **

If you are in the mood for a good walk, there are several excellent tracks around Queenstown that quickly take you away from the crowds and into some surprising magnificent landscapes.

Ben Lomond Track/One Mile Creek Trail

Both these tracks begin at the One Mile Powerhouse carpark on Lake Esplanade, a short distance from Queenstown on the Glenorchy Road.

The One Mile Creek Trail is a loop track up one side of the creek and down the other and takes around one hour.

Ben Lomond, on the other hand, is a day's tramp that requires a good degree of fitness along with the appropriate clothing and food. The summit (1748 m) is definitely subalpine and has spectacular views, not only over The Remarkables and Lake Wakatipu, but west into the mountains of Fiordland, and north as far as Mt Aspiring. The trip to the summit takes around seven hours but a short option to the Ben Lomond Saddle (1310 m) takes around three-and-a-half hours. The section from the Saddle to the summit is a grunt, though the track is good and there is the option of starting the tramp from the top of the Gondola which will cut out around 400 vertical metres from the climb.

Frankton Arm Walk

Following the shore of the lake east from central Queenstown through the gardens, this track links several small beaches and takes around 90 minutes return.

Queenstown Hill Walkway

Beginning at Belfast Street in the town, this walk is a good steady climb to the top of Queenstown Hill (907 m) with the reward of great views over the town and lake. The walk will take around two to three hours.

Sunshine Bay Walk

This track follows the shoreline of the lake west from the town centre to the small beach at Sunshine Bay. The walk includes great views over the lake, passes through some small tracts of beech forest and takes around 90 minutes return.

Queenstown Winter Festival **

www.winterfestival.co.nz

Held towards the end of June every year since 1975, the 10-day Queenstown Winter Festival has become one of Central Otago's big party events. Unfortunately, in warm years, the festival has often lacked the essential ingredient of snow, but that hasn't deterred the hardy from participating in over 60 events including the 'flying' birdman competition, the downhill dog racing and Queenstown's own special version of 'drag racing'. At night-time the fun continues, so never mind the cold, just wrap up warm and party on.

Skyline Gondola ***

Brecon Street

Opens 9 a.m. to late

www.skyline.co.nz

Entrance fee

A very popular visitor attraction, the Gondola rises 450 m to Bob's Peak with great views over the town and the lake. To keep you amused at the top there is the Skyline Restaurant, the AJ Hackett Ledge bungy jump and swing, and the Skyline Luge. At the bottom there is a bird park with a kiwi house, an indoor mini-golf course and, across the road, the historic Queenstown cemetery. For the fit, there is a track to the top just to the left of the ticket office.

TSS *Earnslaw* ★★

www.realjourneys.co.nz

Constructed in Dunedin in 1911 by shipbuilders John McGregor and Co., the *Earnslaw* was then dismantled and transported to Kingston in pieces by rail. After a six-month period to rebuild the vessel, the TSS *Earnslaw* sailed on her maiden voyage to Queenstown in February 1912. Along with three other vessels, the *Ben Lomond*, *Antrim* and *Mountaineer*, the *Earnslaw* transported people and cargo from Queenstown to Kingston, Glenorchy and the high-country stations across the lake.

Fully restored in 1984, the vessel is still powered by a coal-fired steam engine and now offers lake cruises, including trips to Walter Peak sheep station across the lake. During the survey period from late May to early July 2007 the TSS *Earnslaw* is out of service and boat trips on the lake are by launch.

Race To The Sky ★★★

www.racetothesky.co.nz

Cardrona Valley

Held for two days every Easter, Race To The Sky is New Zealand's top hill-climb event, attracting over 100 competitors and thousands of spectators. The uphill gravel course climbs 3500 m over 15 km and around 137 bends with an average gradient of 1:1. There are races for cars, trucks, motorbikes and quads. The rules are simple — the fastest to the top wins! Long dominated by the late Peter 'Possum' Bourne, a statue in his honour has been erected on the course which claimed his life in 2003.

Accommodation is at a premium during this event especially when it coincides with Warbirds Over Wanaka which is held every two years.

Ranfurly Art Deco *

www.ruralartdeco.co.nz

Located on SH85 in the northern Maniatoto, Ranfurly must be given full marks for trying hard. Once an important railway town, a series of arson attacks in the 1930s destroyed many of Ranfurly's most significant buildings. Rebuilt in the art deco style, today the town has only about 10 buildings that could be described as art deco, though these include the very stylish Centennial Milk Bar, and the Ranfurly Lion Hotel. The town hosts a lively art deco festival in February each year.

Roxburgh

Bullock Track Walk *

The track begins 2 km north of Roxburgh on SH8.

This five-hour return tramp leads to a tussock-covered summit with fantastic views over the Teviot Valley, the Clutha River and beyond to the Lammerlaw Ranges.

Lake Onslow **

Tucked away only 22 km east of Roxburgh, this manmade lake set in high tussock country has a unique natural beauty. The open nature of the surrounding countryside gives this an unusual feel compared to the lakes in more mountainous country. The area was once appealingly called 'The Dismal Swamp' until flooded in 1888 to provide water for mining operations. The dam waters were later raised several times and, from 1924, provided water for irrigation and power. Now covering an area of over 800 ha, the lake has excellent fishing (brown trout) and boating facilities.

Somebodies Darling **

From SH8 turn over the Clutha at Millers Flat then turn right and follow the river for 9 km, the last section down Beaumont Station Road is unsealed.

According to popular legend, in February 1865 an unidentified body of a young man was found washed up on the river bank by a local man William Rigney. Rigney then buried the drowned man not far from the river bank and provided a headboard for the grave inscribed 'Somebodies Darling Lies Buried Here'. When Rigney died in 1912 he was buried next to Somebodies Darling with his inscription reading, 'Here Lies the Body of William Rigney The Man Who Buried Somebodies Darling'. In fact, William Rigney never claimed to have either found the body or to have buried it, but merely provided the gravestone. And as for being unidentified, the dead man was believed to be Charles Alms, a butcher from the Nevis Valley who drowned in the Clutha on 25 January and was subsequently washed downstream. So much for romantic legend.

The Road to Skippers ***

One of New Zealand's legendary roads, the road to Skippers has hardly changed since it was built in the 1860s to service the goldmining settlements along the Shotover River. Unsealed and very narrow, the road is more suited to 4WD or at least vehicles with a reasonably high wheel base. Definitely not for the faint-hearted, with huge drops into the Shotover River, the road also requires considerable backing skills if another vehicle comes the other way, as much of the road is only one way.

All that remains of the Long Gully Pub, built in 1863 and burnt down in 1951, is the fireplace and chimneys and at the end of the road is a camping ground, the restored stone school house and the Mt Aurum homestead. Historic Skippers suspension bridge was built in 1901, while an even older bridge over the Shotover was built in 1864 and is now used for bungy jumps. If you don't want to drive, several operators run 4WD tours along the road.

Wanaka ***

While not as frantic as Queenstown, Wanaka has, in recent years, changed from a quiet lakeside backwater to a sophisticated alpine town with smart shops, luxury accommodation and modern cafes. Still, it is not hard to get away from the crowds, either on the lake or in nearby Mt Aspiring National Park.

Glendhu Bay Motor Camp Ground **
Mt Aspiring Road
Phone 03 443 7243

Glendhu Bay, just west of Wanaka on the road to Mt Aspiring, is an iconic New Zealand camping ground. Situated right on the shores of the lake (with a boat ramp), the camping ground has this magnificent bay all to itself and is an ideal spot, whether in a tent, caravan or a campervan.

Motutapu Gorge *

Motutapu Gorge Road opposite the Glendhu Bay Motor Camp

In stopping at the lookout at the end of the road by the gorge you will wonder why you even came here, but a short walk to the wooden bridge allows a view deep into the impressive limestone gorge below.

New Zealand Fighter Pilots Museum and Warbirds Over Wanaka ***

Wanaka Airport, SH6

Open daily 9 a.m. to 4 p.m.

www.nzfpm.co.nz

Entrance fee

On Easter Weekend 1988 military aviation enthusiast Sir Tim Wallis held an airshow called Warbirds On Parade at the Wanaka Airport ideally situated on a terrace high above the Clutha River. Such was the success of the show, that it was decided to repeat the event every two years and, within a decade, under the new name Warbirds Over Wanaka, the show became one of the best aviation displays in the southern hemisphere. Now attracting over 100,000 visitors, each show has a unique theme featuring rare aircraft from around the globe in all-day non-stop aviation action. In addition to the displays in the air, on the ground there are vintage machinery, military vehicles and an aviation trade expo (www.warbirdsoverwanaka.com).

In 1993 the New Zealand Alpine Fighter Pilots Museum opened at Wanaka Airport and now has an exceptional display of classic fighter planes, including the Supermarine Mk XVI Spitfire, Hawker Hurricane, de Havilland FB5 Vampire, Polikarpov 1-16 Ishak and the de Havilland Tiger Moth.

The Puzzling World of Stuart Landsborough **

2 km from the lakefront on the Queenstown Road

Open daily 8.30 a.m. to 5 p.m.

www.puzzlingworld.co.nz

Entrance fee

Just the place to visit when the weather is not great, the Puzzling World is a series of rooms each with their own illusions, and is guaranteed to be a hit with young and old alike. There is an impressive two-storey maze with over 1.5 km of passages; the cafe has puzzles on each table (just the place if you are sick of chatting in the car); and the public toilets (free) are an entertaining destination in their own right with their recreation of a Roman latrine.

Wanaka Walks ***

Diamond Lake Lookout

Twenty km from Wanaka on the Mt Aspiring Road, the turnoff to the track is just before the bridge over the Motutapu River.

After skirting the small Diamond Lake, the track steadily climbs uphill through rock outcrops and bush, to an excellent lookout over Lake Wanaka and the Matukituki River. The trip to the lookout takes about one hour return, though there is a further option of continuing uphill to the top of Rocky Mountain (775 m) which takes three hours return.

Mt Aspiring Rob Roy Glacier Walk

The track starts from the Raspberry Creek carpark in Mt Aspiring National Park.

This walk traverses a wide range of terrain beginning in the open grassland of the Matukituki Valley before entering beech forest along a mountain stream, and gradually rising out of the bush into an alpine tussock basin with views of the Rob Roy Glacier, waterfalls and the mountains beyond. Keep a close eye on the keas around here as they can be very pushy and will steal anything once your back is turned.

Mt Iron

2 km from Wanaka on SH6

A popular two-hour loop walk to the top of Mt Iron (548 m) will give you good views over Wanaka lake and the town. The mountain bears the scars of earlier glacial action.

Roys Peak

5 km from Wanaka on the Mt Aspiring Road

Climbing up the 1200 m to the summit of Roys Peak (1578 m) is a slog, but the views from the top are spectacular. Spread out below is Lake Wanaka and, glimpsed beyond that, is Lake Hawea, while to the west are Mt Aspiring and the Southern Alps. The zigzag track is in good condition and is a steady rather than very steep grade. The return trip to the summit is around six hours, though a two-hour return walk will take you to a good viewpoint. Closed for lambing during October and the first half of November.

DUNEDIN

Baldwin Street **

Off North Road, Northeast Valley

In a city of steep streets (34 Dunedin streets have a gradient steeper than 1:6), Baldwin Street, with a 1:2.8 gradient, reigns supreme (in other words the street rises 1 m for every 2.8 m travelled horizontally). More than a few motorists have come to grief on Baldwin Street. Only 200-m long, it is not advisable to drive up the street as it is a cul-de-sac with very little room to turn at the top. In 2001 two students decided to travel down the street in a wheeled rubbish bin, but hit a parked trailer with one student being killed instantly, and the other sustaining serious head injuries. On a lighter note, the street holds the annual Baldwin Street Gutbuster in February, a running race to the top and back with the fastest time around two minutes, while in July it is the venue for the charity Jaffa race, where over 10,000 sponsored Jaffas roll down the street with a prize for the winner.

Cadbury World ***

280 Cumberland Street, Dunedin
Open daily 9 a.m. to 4 p.m. Tours every half hour. Closed 25 and 26 December, 1 and 2 January.
www.cadburyworld.co.nz
Entrance fee

One of Dunedin's most popular tourist attractions, Cadbury have been in Dunedin for over 70 years and produce 85 per cent of New Zealand's chocolate. A must for all Willy Wonka fans, the tour takes around 75 minutes including the factory and the chance to sample the product. For those not wanting to do the tour, the extensive entry foyer is open to the public and has an excellent and comprehensive display covering the history of chocolate and the Cadbury company.

However, the factory part of the tour is not included on Sundays and public holidays (and it can be closed at other times) so check the details before you book.

The popular Cadbury Chocolate Carnival is held in July and includes the Jaffa Race down Baldwin Street, a Choc Art Exhibition, and the Choc Bomb also known as 'silly things to do with chocolate'.

Carisbrook *

Burns Street

One of New Zealand's oldest sports grounds, Carisbrook began life as a cricket venue in the 1870s. The first international cricket game was held there in 1883 (Otago and Tasmania), and the first rugby international in 1908 (New Zealand and England/Wales). The ground is better known as 'The Brook, or, more colourfully, as 'The House of Pain', in reference to the tough games of rugby that visiting teams can expect when playing here. With a capacity of 35,000, the ground also has a reputation for boisterous students, especially on the terraces. Until recently any game could be viewed from the road above the ground, appropriately named 'The Scotsman's Grandstand'.

Dunedin Botanic Gardens ***

Cumberland Street

The oldest botanical gardens in New Zealand and established in 1863, these gardens fall naturally into two parts. The original gardens are flat and laid out in a formal fashion with some of the best herbaceous borders in the country, a rose garden, an Edwardian Winter House, a children's playground complete with Peter Pan statue and a duck pond with free duck food (now how kind is that!).

The stunning perennial long borders are themed in colours: white, blue, yellow, violet and red and are at their peak in December to February. On Sunday afternoons in summer there is live music in the band rotunda. The ornate Wolfe Haven Fountain was built in 1898 and originally stood in the Queens Gardens by the railway station. During the New Zealand and South Seas Exhibition held in Dunedin in 1925, the fountain graced the foyer of the Grand Court after which it was moved yet again, this time to the Botanic Gardens where it has finally stayed put.

The upper and larger section of garden, across the Water of Leith, is quite different; the planting is less formal, with larger tree and shrub collections. Just across the stream the hill has been landscaped into broad terraces with seating and a rock garden, the perfect spot to view the garden, listen to the music or just read a book and watch the world go by. This part of the garden has a 4-ha rhododendron and azalea garden and is at the heart of the springtime Dunedin Rhododendron Festival.

Further up the hill and well worth the short hike are very attractive new aviaries (Dunedin doesn't have a zoo), and, among other birds, there are the

New Zealand native parrots kea, kaka and yellow-fronted, red-crowned and the rare Antipodes Island kakariki. As well as the birds being on show to the public, the aviaries also have a breeding programme for endangered native birds.

Dunedin City Art Gallery ***

30 The Octagon
Open daily 10 a.m. to 5 p.m. Closed Christmas Day and Good Friday
Koha/donation

Formerly the old DIC department store, this immensely stylish art gallery was opened in 1996, and is big enough to be interesting, and yet small enough to be welcoming. The gallery itself holds a wide collection of New Zealand and European art, and in recent years has attracted some exceptional international art exhibitions to Dunedin.

There is a permanent exhibition room for Dunedin-born artist Frances Hodgkins (1869–1947), internationally recognised as one of New Zealand's most significant Neo-Romantic painters of the 1930s and '40s.

Dunedin Fashion Week **

www.id-dunedinfashion.com

Dunedin is home to a number of small innovative fashion houses, and attracts visitors from all over the country to the highly regarded id Dunedin Fashion Week each year in March. Held in the fabulous Dunedin Railway Station, with a claim to having New Zealand's longest catwalk, the two main events are the Vodafone id Dunedin Emerging Designer Awards, and the Vodafone id Dunedin Fashion Show. For visitors outside of Fashion Week the Information Centre has a leaflet with the details of the local fashion houses.

Dunedin Gasworks Museum **

20 Braemar Street, South Dunedin
Open 12 noon to 4 p.m. on the first weekend of each month
Entrance fee

First opened in 1863, and closed only in 1987, the remaining gasworks buildings are largely Edwardian, though the 24-metre-high boiler house chimney is believed to date back to the 1880s. One of only three such museums in the world, the highlights are the stationary steam engines that at one time pumped coal gas to Dunedin households.

Dunedin Railway Station ***

Anzac Avenue

Built in 1906 in the Flemish Renaissance style, the station was, at the time, the largest and busiest railway station in the country. The two-storey building is constructed of dark volcanic stone and Oamaru limestone with Royal Doulton porcelain tiles in the foyer. The beautiful mosaic floor in the foyer is complete with rail motifs, and NZR insignia feature over the ornate ticket windows. Overlooking the foyer are magnificent stained-glass windows featuring a front-on view of a train in full steam. Along the platform, the Edwardian ironwork is all original, and it is from here that the Taieri Gorge train departs.

First Church of Otago ***

415 Moray Place

Set on a lawn in a quiet side street this church has one of the most beautiful exteriors of any religious building in New Zealand. The original site was a hill that was lowered 13 m by convict labour and the spoil used to reclaim the harbour which, at that time, was just below the bluff on which the church was built. Opened in November 1873, the church is constructed of Oamuru stone on a base of Port Chalmers volcanic rock with a slate roof and timber ceilings of Baltic pine. The interior is naturally lit by huge stained-glass windows and on the outside are gargoyles, not with the usual grotesque faces, but with gentle human features.

The church was designed by Robert Lawson and the Visitor Centre at the back of the church has displayed the beautiful original architectural drawings, as well as historic photographs taken during construction.

Historic Dunedin ***

Very much the boom-town during the second half of the nineteenth century on the back of Central Otago gold, growth in Dunedin in the twentieth century has been far more modest and has meant that the city has retained many of its fine Victorian buildings. Most of the historic buildings are clustered around the Octagon and along Princes Street, once the heart of the business district. All are within easy walking distance of the central city and the Otago Settlers Museum offers a range of excellent guided walks led by knowledgeable locals.

Some highlights are as follows:

ANZ Bank
Princes Street

Built of Oamaru stone in 1874, the bank was designed by Robert Lawson who was at the time a very influential and prolific architect in Dunedin.

Bank of New Zealand
Corner Rattray and Princes Streets

Opened in 1883 this grand bank typifies the prosperity of nineteenth-century Dunedin.

Crown Milling Company
Manor Place

The flour mill was originally built in 1867 with the fifth floor added in the 1890s.

Dunedin Prison
Lower High Street

Definitely not open for tours, it is surprising to find a prison in the heart of the city. Built of brick in 1896, the design was heavily influenced by the New Scotland Yard building in London.

Law Courts
Stuart Street

Built in 1899 and designed by John Campbell, the government architect, the Flemish Renaissance style is similar to the nearby railway station. The building has four courtrooms, including the very grand and ornate High Court.

Municipal Buildings
The Octagon

Designed by Robert Lawson and completed in 1880, the building was considerably altered in 1939, and again in 1963 when the bell tower was removed. Restored in 1989, the building is yet again resplendent with its 40-m-high clock tower.

National Bank
Princes Street

Built in the Modern Classic style in 1912. the construction is of ferro-concrete and faced in stone.

New Zealand Rail Road Services
Cumberland Street

Now part of the Otago Settlers Museum, this building is a substantial art deco structure (built 1939) and rare in mainly Victorian Dunedin.

Old Post Office
Corner Water and Princes Streets

This huge imposing building was built in 1937, much later than the other historic buildings in the area.

Savoy Tearooms
Princes Street

The Haynes Building housed the legendary Savoy Tearooms on the first floor. Now an Italian restaurant, all the best architectural features of the Edwardian tearooms are retained including the leadlight windows.

St Joseph's Roman Catholic Cathedral
Corner Rattray and Smith Streets

In contrast to his more Romanesque-style churches (Invercargill, Christchurch, Waimate), renowned church architect FW Petre designed this church in the Gothic Revival style. Built of bluestone, the church was opened in 1886.

The Exchange
Princes Street

Once the economic heart of Dunedin, The Exchange has at its centre the elaborate Cargill Memorial built in 1863 to honour founding settler William Cargill. Originally in the Octagon, it was moved to the Exchange in 1872 and converted into a very grand drinking fountain.

Union Bank

Corner Princes and Liverpool Streets

Built in 1874 of Port Chalmers breccia and Oamaru stone, the bank was designed by Robert Lawson and is now a nightclub.

Wains Hotel

Princes Street

Now part of the Mercure Hotel group, Wains was built in 1878 and the elaborate facade has been recently restored.

Huriawa Pa Karitane Beach ***

Follow the road to the beach then turn left at the beach along Sulisker Street and continue 500 m uphill to the entrance.

Volcanic in origin, Huriawa Peninsula was the perfect location for a fortitfied pa. With steep cliffs and sea on three sides, defenders of the pa had exceptional views along the coast both north and south, and east over the flat estuary. A Ngai Tahu stronghold, the pa was the scene of a protracted battle where the defenders successfully held out for over six months. Today the entrance is through a carved gateway with paths leading to the end of the peninsula with views over the blowholes to the beaches beyond. Hooker's sea lions and fur seals are common along these shores.

Karitane was also the site of an early whaling station in 1837 and the home of Dr Truby King who founded Plunket — an institution dedicated to the health of newborn babies and which was hugely successful in lowering the infant mortality rate in New Zealand in the early twentieth century. The name 'Karitane Yellow' is the popular name give to any colour similar to that of a baby's soiled nappy.

Mount Cargill **

Take Pine Hill Road (off SH1) to Cowans Road which leads to the top.

The heights of this 676-m peak with huge 360-degree views are often mist-shrouded and the vegetation and climate are definitely subalpine. For such a prominent lookout point the last section of road is surprisingly rough and unsealed, but for those feeling fit, the Bethune's Gully Walkway from Norwood Street in the Northeast Valley is a healthy alternative to driving.

New Zealand Sports Hall of Fame **

Dunedin Railway Station, Anzac Avenue
Open daily 10 a.m. to 4 p.m. Closed Christmas Day
www.nzhalloffame.co.nz
Entrance fee

The Hall of Fame is dedicated to New Zealand's greatest sports performers and is crammed full of the most amazing sports memorabilia guaranteed to delight and surprise sports and non-sports fans alike. Covering virtually every sport, the displays include New Zealand's first Olympic medal won by boxer Ted Morgan at the 1928 Amsterdam games, jockey Bill Skelton's riding kit, and a reconstructed long-jump pit showing Yvette Williams' amazing jump at the Helsinki games in 1952.

Octagon **

Much improved over the past few years, the Octagon is now a great public space with cafes, the city art galley and picture theatres. Dominating the Octagon is St Paul's Anglican Cathedral with its broad flight of steps leading up to the Gothic interior, with a rather odd modern extension tacked on to the back of the church. Originally the cathedral was planned for the middle of the Octagon, but the fiercely Presbyterian Scottish settlers were having none of that, and the Anglicans finally had to settle for a position on the higher east side. Next to the Cathedral is the beautifully restored Town Hall (Information Centre on the ground floor), and alongside that, the only blemish on the Octagon, the very ugly 1970s Civic Administration Building. At the heart of the Octagon is a statue of the Scottish poet Robert Burns, unveiled in 1886 to a crowd of over 8000, and venue for poetry-reading contests on the bard's birthday, 25 January.

Olveston ***

42 Royal Terrace
Open daily, tour times 9.30 a.m., 10.45 a.m., 12 noon, 1.30 p.m., 2.45 p.m., 4 p.m.
www.olveston.co.nz

While not among New Zealand's oldest buildings, Olveston is without a doubt one of the best 'old house' experiences in the country. What makes this house special is that it is crammed full of fascinating furniture and ornaments with so little changed since the house was built. If your time is short in Dunedin, put a visit to this house on the top of your list.

Completed in 1906 the house was commissioned by David Theomin, a Jewish immigrant who developed a very successful music business in Dunedin in the latter half of the nineteenth century. Designed by London architect Sir Ernest George, no expense was spared in the construction and in the house, including every modern convenience from a central heating system and telephone, through to a shower and heated towel rail in the bathroom.

Unfortunately for the family the only son, Edward, died at an early age, and the daughter, Dorothy, died childless in 1966. Dorothy left the house to Dunedin City which, at the time, was not particularly thrilled to receive such a gift even though it realised what a great asset this house is to the city.

So little has been altered over the last 100 years that it appears that the Theomins have just gone out for the day, and are due back at any moment. In the kitchen are complete dinner sets, personal ornaments still sit on the dressing tables in the bedroom, and the only thing missing in the billiard room is the cigar smoke.

Otago Museum ***

419 Great King Street
Open daily 10 a.m. to 5 p.m. Closed Christmas Day
www.otagomuseum.govt.nz
Koha/donation

Established in 1869 (the specially commissioned building dates from 1877), this is one of New Zealand's oldest museums and is a testament to the value that the early Scottish settlers placed on learning. Holding nearly two million items, the museum has some outstanding collections and it is not surprising that it has won a number of tourism awards.

The Maori collection is exceptional with material from all over the country, including several Ngati Porou carvings dating from the 1870s, and *Te Paranihi* a waka taua built for the Whanganui chief, Paturoma, around 1840. The recreation of the Shag River Settlement north of Dunedin is a graphic illustration of how Maori survived in the cooler climates of the south.

The Pacific collection is equally superb with a Moai from Easter Island complete with his balancing hat, a cape of red and yellow feathers which belonged to Liliuokakalani, the last queen of Hawaii, and a rare stone figure from the mysterious Polynesian occupants of Pitcairn Island.

The natural history section has an impressive range of moa skeletons of various sizes, a complete skeleton of the extinct Haast eagle, the largest eagle in the world, and New Zealand's largest fossil of a plesiosaur.

The Classical collection must rank as one of the best in New Zealand with the museum holding almost 10,000 ancient objects, including a complete Egyptian mummy dating back to 1300 BC, and a very impressive collection of Greek pottery.

Otago Peninsula ***

www.otago-peninsula.co.nz

An old volcano, the peninsula has a character all of its own and no visit to Dunedin would be complete without touring here. On the north side, the road follows the coast, weaving in and out of small bays with colourful boat sheds, ideal for sailing, swimming and windsurfing. Another road follows the high ridges of this rugged peninsula with spectacular views in every direction. An excellent alternative to driving is to take a harbour boat trip on the *Monarch* which offers a variety of excursions from one-hour to all-day. Visit www.wildlife.co.nz

The following is based on a trip out to Taiaroa Head out along the coast and back to the city via the high road.

Glenfalloch Woodland Garden **

430 Portobello Road

Open daylight hours. Cafe and wine bar open September to April 11 a.m. to 3.30 p.m.

www.glenfalloch.org.nz

Entrance fee

Glenfalloch, meaning 'hidden valley' in Gaelic, was established by George Russell in 1871, and was accessible, at the time, only by sea. The homestead, constructed of kauri and Baltic pine, still survives in the garden where some of the trees date from 1872. Over the years extensive and diverse tree planting continued, and in 1917 Glenfalloch was sold to Philip Barling, who over the next 40 years set about creating an idyllic English garden. Philip's son, John, inherited the garden in 1956 and planted the rhododendrons and azaleas. Now open to the public, the gardens are especially appealing in summer (the cafe is open as well) but worth visiting all year round.

New Zealand Marine Studies Aquarium *

Turn left opposite the Portobello Hotel and drive for 1.5 km — don't be put off by the road.

Open daily 12 noon to 4.30 p.m. Closed Christmas Day

www.marine.ac.nz

This small aquarium with the focus on southern sealife is part of the University of Otago marine research facility. Here you can see pig fish, sea horses and an octopus with a 1-m arm spread, as well as dabble in the popular Touch Pool. The aquarium also has a great view of the harbour and of Quarantine Island/ St Martins Island just offshore. For those especially interested in marine life, the personalised tour at 10.30 a.m. is highly recommended.

Otakau Marae *

Harrington Point Road

Koha/donation

Built in 1946, this marae complex consists of the wharenui Tamatea and a small Maori church. While the wharenui has an unusually high gable and shallow porch, what makes the marae really different is that the buildings at a distance appear to be wood, when in fact the entire construction, including 'carvings', is entirely of concrete.

Royal Albatross Colony **

Open 9 a.m. to 6 p.m., May to mid-September 10 a.m. to 4 p.m. Tours every half hour.

Entrance fee

These magnificent birds with wing spans of up to 3 m and flying speeds of over 100 kph, first established themselves on Taiaroa Head between 1914 and 1919. From the first chick in 1938, the colony has slowly grown, especially in recent years when protection from predators has been more rigorous. While the albatross are the stars of the show, the reserve is also home to 11 bird species including the rare Stewart Island shag.

There are albatross here all year, though numbers vary considerably and the colony itself is closed during the breeding season mid-September to mid-November (though there is every chance of seeing birds flying). Best time to see birds is from December to February and you are more likely to see the birds flying when the weather is rough and windy. The only access to the colony is by guided tour and bookings are recommended as this is a very popular spot to visit (check the prices as well).

Penguins **

Otago Peninsula is home to both the blue and yellow-eyed/hoiho penguins, and there are hides especially constructed for viewing at Sandfly Bay and Pilots Beach. In recent years the popularity of penguin watching has put stress on the birds with visitors unintentionally diminishing the very wildlife they come to see. Less than 4000 hoiho remain, and penguins are easily deterred by people on the beach between them and their nests. If disturbed they will return to the sea leaving their chicks unfed, so if you don't want starving penguin chicks on your conscience use the hides or sit quietly back from the beach.

An alternative is to visit the Penguin Place (ph 03 478 0286). A working farm with a breeding colony of rare yellow-eyed penguins, as well as some blues, the Penguin Place offers a one-and-a-half-hour tour of the breeding colony using specially constructed hides that allow very close viewing of the birds. Hoiho are not social birds and like to keep their distance from neighbours by nesting in thick scrub. While the Penguin Place has substantially replanted the dunes, they have, in the meantime, provided private nesting boxes for the birds, and the tours are in groups of no more than 15 people (if there are no penguins the tours don't go). In winter there is only afternoon and early evening viewing with all-day tours from October to Easter. Chicks can be seen November to February.

Larnach Castle **

Camp Road, Highcliff

Open 9 a.m. to 5 p.m., (the gardens are open to 7 p.m. in the summer)

www.larnachcastle.co.nz

Entrance fee

The house, modestly named The Camp, was built of local stone in 1871 for the dodgy Dunedin businessman William Larnach. Later Larnach became a politician and after finding himself in deep financial trouble, committed suicide in a committee room at Parliament in 1898. The family was also a deeply troubled one, and the castle is said to be haunted by Larnach's unhappy first wife Eliza (after she died, William married her sister) and the ghost of Larnach himself. Donald Larnach, William's son, in keeping with a family tradition, also shot himself but this time much closer to home at the Grand Hotel in Princes Street (now the Southern Cross).

The grand castle has been meticulously restored after years of neglect and even, at one time, functioned as a nightclub. The garden surrounding Larnach Castle is classified as a Garden of National Significance and there is an option to visit just the gardens. Accommodation is also available.

Sandymount Walks **

Sandymount Road off Highcliff Road

The Otago Peninsula is well endowed with walks of varying length, and three of the best short walks are from Sandymount on the central southern side of the peninsula. While the rest of the country tends to overdo signage, Dunedin seems to have taken a different approach, and appears to have an abhorrence of good signage for visitors. Walks are seldom clearly marked and there is little to indicate walk times.

From Sandymount, appropriately named, as this is a sand dune high on a hill, the walk to the dramatic cliffs of The Chasm takes around 30 minutes return, to Lover's Leap 60 minutes return, and to Sandfly Bay, where there is a hide for penguin watching, 60 minutes return (an alternative short walk to Sandfly Bay is off Ridge Road).

Otago Settlers Museum *

31 Queens Gardens

Open daily 10 a.m. to 5 p.m. Closed Christmas Day and Good Friday

vwww.otago.settlers.museum

Entrance fee

This collection began in 1898 when the Otago Settlers Association began accumulating documents and portraits for the fiftieth anniversary of the founding of Dunedin city. Hundreds of these portraits, of the mainly staunch Scots pioneers, still hang in the Smith Gallery. In addition to the Scottish history of the city, the museum covers Maori and Chinese histories, as well as the social and economic background of Otago province. The museum retains its original Edwardian galleries, and is linked to the old art deco NZR Transport Building, which appropriately holds the transport collection. On display outside the museum are two locomotives, JA1274, the last steam engine to be built in New Zealand, and 'Josephine' a Class E double-ended Fairlie locomotive, one of only four left in the world and New Zealand's oldest steam engine (arrived at Port Chalmers in 1872).

Port Chalmers **

www.portchalmers.com

While Dunedin itself lies at the head of Otago Harbour, the harbour is too shallow and narrow for substantial shipping and from early days Port Chalmers was developed as the deep-water port for the city. New Zealand's third-oldest town (founded in 1844), Port Chalmers has many fine stone buildings, most of them constructed between 1874 and 1880. Stonemasons from the Isle of Portland were employed building the dry dock in 1872, then the biggest in the country, and when that was completed sought other work locally. Historic buildings include the Port stables built 1867, National Bank 1877, The Municipal Buildings 1889, Iona Church 1883, and Holy Trinity Church 1874.

It was from Port Chalmers that New Zealand's first cargo of frozen sheep meat left for Britain on the clipper *Dunedin* in 1882.

Aramoana *

10 km from Port Chalmers

This beautiful sweep of white sandy beach is just the place for a long quiet walk and a stroll out onto the long breakwater to watch ships coming and going from the harbour or to catch a view of seals and albatross. Tiny old-fashioned cribs shelter behind the dunes, and the tidal area just inside the harbour entrance is a favourite spot for wading birds, including godwits. Fortunately plans to build an aluminium smelter here in the 1970s came to nothing.

Port Chalmers Hotels ***

No port town is complete without pubs and Port Chalmers has more than its share of historic hotels some of which still offer accommodation as well as food and drink.

Carey's Bay Hotel

17 Macandrew Road

This attractive stone pub built in 1874 and originally called The Crescent, has in recent years been beautifully restored and is famous for its extensive collection of paintings by Dunedin artist Ralph Hotere.

Chicks Hotel
2 Mount Street

Built in 1876 by Harry Dench and originally named the Jerusalem Hotel, it was taken over by George and Ellen Chick in the 1880s.

Port Chalmers Hotel
Beach Street

The oldest hotel in Port Chalmers it was originally opened as the Surveyors Arms in 1846.

Port Chalmers Museum **
Open 9 a.m. to 3 p.m. Monday to Friday and 1.30 p.m. to 4.30 p.m. weekends and public holidays

Jam-packed with fascinating objects, this great small museum feels more like an antique shop than a museum. No fancy lighting or interactive display for bored kids here. Strong on maritime history, the Painting Room has a huge canvas of nineteenth-century Port Chalmers, and there is a massive old diver's suit, along with cannons from the perfectly named pirate ship *The Don Juan* which was built in 1857 and the remains of which are still visible at low tide at Deborah Bay. The stone building was originally the post office, opened in 1877.

Signal Flagstaff Hill *
Constitution Street

Yet another pirate ship, the *Cincinnati* supplied the mast that was erected here in 1864 and used to carry signal flags and lamps to guide ships to the port. The hill is a great spot to watch the busy wharves just below.

Signal Hill *

Signal Hill Road

The Cargill Lookout on Signal Hill, to the north of the city, has fine views over Otago Harbour and the central business district. The massive Centennial Monument, built in 1940, has chunky Tolkienesque statues of a woman with a skein of wool and a man holding a book.

St Clair and St Kilda Beaches **

These magnificent beaches lie along the south coast of Dunedin city and there is nothing between them and the Antarctic. Nevertheless these white sandy shores are both popular for swimming and, at the St Clair end of the beach, for surfing. The beach front at St Clair has a promenade with the restored Hydro Hotel as its centrepiece.

St Clair Hot Saltwater Pool *

The Esplanade, St Clair
Open Labour Weekend until March Monday to Friday 6 a.m. to 7 p.m., weekends 8 a.m. to 7 p.m.
Entrance fee

Situated with waves crashing on the rocks below and a great view along the beach, a pool has been on this site since 1884, though thankfully heated since the early 1960s. Recently renovated and including the addition of a very pleasant cafe, the pools are closed in winter.

Speight's Brewery Tour ***

200 Rattray Street
Shop open daily Monday to Thursday 9.30 a.m. to 7 p.m., Friday to Sunday 9.30 a.m. to 5 p.m.
Tours Monday to Thursday 10 a.m., 12 noon, 2 p.m. and 7 p.m., Friday to Saturday 10 a.m., 12 noon, 2 p.m. and 4 p.m. Charge for tours.
www.speights.co.nz

Along with the chocolate factory, one of Dunedin's most popular tours, Speight's have brewed beer in Dunedin since 1876. For a long time a regional brew, Speight's became popular throughout the country on the back of its famous 'Southern Man' and 'Pride of the South' advertising campaigns. The tours of the brewery include beer tastings and take one-and-a-half hours, but they are very popular so book ahead. If you can't make a tour the shop sells distinctive Speight's merchandise including a six-pack sampler of each of its beers, and right next door are the Ale House bar and restaurant.

Taieri Gorge Train ***

www.taieri.co.nz

Departing from Dunedin's historic railway station, the train, complete with refurbished and comfortable 1920s carriages, wends it way through the dry and rugged schist country of the Taieri Gorge. On the original line to Alexandra constructed between 1879 and 1891, the train either stops at Pukerangi (literally in the middle of nowhere and an odd sort of place to stop) or Middlemarch, where the line now ends. You can begin the Central Otago Rail Trail from here. Along the way the line crosses numerous bridges and viaducts, travels through tunnels and cuttings, and for much of the way hugs the banks of the scenic Taieri River.

The railway also operates, in summer only, the *Seasider*, which travels 66 km north along the coast to Palmerston with the option of returning via the Macraes Gold Mine to Pukerangi, and back by train to the city via the Taieri Gorge (selected days only).

Tunnel Beach Track ***

From St Clair follow the Black Head road towards Green Island. Where Green Island Bush Road goes right, turn left and the carpark is 300 m down this road.

A short walk of around one hour return leads over farmland to a wild seascape of dramatic cliffs, a sandy cove and a natural arch. The tunnel was constructed by John Cargill, son of the prominent settler William Cargill, as private access to the beach for his daughters, away from prying eyes on the public St Clair Beach. Unfortunately one of his daughters later drowned there. Not safe for swimming.

University of Otago **

Most direct access, across the Water of Leith off Union Place

New Zealand's oldest university and established in 1869, the first building, that includes the clock tower, was designed by Maxwell Bury, and completed in 1878. Other buildings that followed took their lead from his design, creating a complex of buildings with a unified style that is unlike any other New Zealand university. With a student population of 20,000 out of a city population of 120,000, Dunedin is more influenced by its students than any other university city in New Zealand. Most of the students also live within a short distance of the university fostering a central-city atmosphere of great cafes, music stores, bookshops and a very lively pub culture.

SOUTH OTAGO & THE CATLINS

Clutha Punt — Tuapeka Mouth **

Operates 8 a.m. to 10 a.m. and 4 p.m. to 6 p.m. weekdays only

Operating since 1896, and the only such punt remaining in the southern hemisphere, this unique craft uses the prow of the punt and large rudders to direct the flow of the current to propel the punt across the river on overhead wires.

In early days on the river a regular shipping service ran between Tuapeka Mouth and Balclutha (Clutha is the ancient Gaelic name of the Clyde River in Scotland), as this point was the closest access on the Clutha to the gold field just to the north. Check the operating hours to avoid disappointment.

Lawrence **

Once a prosperous gold town, Lawrence in 1862 had a population of 11,000 (Dunedin at the time had a population of 6000) and was then known as The Junction, as the town was located on the junction of the Tuapeka and Wetherstons streams. Now a popular stopping point on the road between Central Otago and Dunedin, the town still retains numerous historic buildings ranging from the grand Bank of New Zealand (now a cafe) through to the more modest Athenaeum (combination library and educational facility) and the Chinese Joss House (now a private home). Lawrence is also the home of J Wood who composed the national anthem *God Defend New Zealand*, first played in Dunedin on Christmas Day 1876 (Thomas Bracken wrote the words). A walking map of the historic buildings is available from the Information Centre in the main street which also houses the local museum with displays of mining equipment, the history of the Chinese mining community and a reconstruction of the interior of a tiny miner's cottage.

Gabriel's Gully *

4 km from Lawerence

The site of New Zealand's first major goldrush, Tasmanian prospector Gabriel Read discovered gold here in May 1861, and by September that year over 6000 miners had set up camp in the Gully looking to make their fortune. The easy alluvial gold was quickly exhausted, but other discoveries were made nearby, including at Blue Spur, Waitahuna, Munro's Gully and Adams. The overall area was known as the Tuapeka Goldfields. A popular folk song of the time had as its chorus, 'Bright fine gold, Bright fine gold, One a pecker, Tuapeka, Bright red gold'.

Today not much remains of the bustling gold field. A loop walk of around 90 minutes takes the visitor through the most important sites interspersed with excellent information boards. There is an attractive picnic area by a pond another 250 m further on from the beginning of the walk.

Manuka Gorge Tunnel Track *

On SH8, 13 km from the SH1 turnoff at Milton

30 minutes return

The brick-lined Mt Stuart tunnel is 442 m long and was part of a railway opened in 1876 from Milton to Alexandra linking the coast with the gold fields further inland. The walk is flat and glow-worms can be seen at the wetter eastern end of the tunnel. A torch is helpful, if not essential.

Sinclair Wetland **

854 Berwick Claredon Road, South Taieri. This road runs west of lakes Waihola and Waipori just off SH1 south of Mosgiel.

Phone 03 486 2654

Koha/donation

Wetlands suffer from bad PR and the very name just sounds damp, muddy and unpleasant. Even the old name 'swamp' at least had an air of mystery and intrigue. By their nature, wetlands are flat and it is often hard to actually see anything. The Sinclair Wetlands, however, are fortunate in having two small islands, linked by a high causeway, both of which have excellent views over the entire reserve.

Covering 315 ha, and adjoining lakes Waihola and Waipori, these wetlands are all that remains of the huge swamp that covered most of the Taieri Plain, which has long since been drained for farmland. This wetland has survived only because of the vision of Horrie (Horace) Sinclair who purchased land in 1960 and allowed it to revert back to its original state, thus saving one of the country's most important wetlands. In addition to 40 bird species that breed here, another 45 bird species have been recorded in the wetland. There is camping and backpacker accommodation on site.

The Catlins ***

For years the southeastern corner of the South Island was very much a remote destination, but in recent years it has become one of the more popular driving trips in the country, though fortunately it does not yet attract bus tourist trade. Apart from one small stretch, SH92 is sealed, there are good facilities and accommodation both at Balclutha and Owaka, and a very helpful Information Centre at Owaka. Especially attractive is the fact that most of the sights along this road are just a short side trip off SH92.

However, before Southlanders object to this region appearing in the South Otago section, the Catlins appear in this part of the book only because most visitors travel here in a southward direction. The author fully acknowledges that the last entries in this section (ordered from north to south) are part of Southland and not Otago.

Nugget Point ***

From Balclutha drive to Port Molyneux and then on to Kaka Point and follow the unsealed coast road for 8 km to Nugget Point.

Wild and windswept Nugget Point is named after the group of jagged rocks just offshore and this track leads out to the most spectacular views both north and south along the coast. The historic lighthouse on the point was built in 1870 when Port Molyneux, just to the north, was an important port and the rugged Catlins coast took a high toll on shipping.

Just before the lighthouse a steep track leads down to Roaring Bay (10 minutes one way) where there is a hide to watch both blue and yellow-eyed penguins which come ashore to nest late in the day. On the rocks below the point is a unique seal contain, as this is the only location in New Zealand where elephant seals, fur seals and Hooker's sea lions share the same colony. The seals are hard to see because the track is 130 m above the sea and the animals blend easily with the colour of the rocks. Binoculars are very useful. The walk takes around 30 minutes return and the track is largely flat and well formed.

Tunnel Hill **

3 km south of Owaka on SH92

Constructed with pick and shovel, this 250-metre-long rail tunnel on the Catlins branch line was opened in 1895 and closed in 1971. A torch is useful and for those interested in railway history an old railway station and goods shed still stand at Maclennan further to the south.

Cannibal Bay **

A magnificent sweep of deserted beach, Cannibal Bay is one of the Catlins' best surf beaches and home to sea lions which are fairly common along this coast. While sea lions may appear awkward, they can be very aggressive and move surprisingly fast, so it is best to keep a good distance. From Cannibal Bay it is a 30-minute walk south along the beach to False Islet and Surat Bay.

Jacks Beach and Blowhole **

The turnoff to Jacks Beach is just before Owaka off SH92.

Real Kiwi cribs snuggle along the shore of this beautiful beach dominated by the cliffs of Catlins Heads. From the southern end of the beach an easy track across private farmland leads to the dramatic Jacks Blowhole. Over 200 m from the sea, the hole is 55 m deep and the boom of the blowhole at high tide is especially impressive. The walk is one hour return (donation requested) and is closed for lambing in September and October.

Pounawea **

There is something bucolic and timeless about Pounawea — the sort of place where you fish off the wharf and it doesn't matter if you catch anything, kayak when the tide is right or just laze about reading in a tent.

There is an excellent nature walk through a 38-ha stand of fine coastal bush that is accessed through the camping ground, and located in the estuary is an historic 'dolphin', a simple wooden structure that assists boats to turn in the narrow confines of the river channel. Built in 1882 at the cost of 25 pounds few of these structures survive today.

Purakaunui Falls ***

Well sign-posted off SH92 south of Owaka, the falls are 9 km off the main road just past the Catlins River bridge.

The waterfalls in the Catlins area are not especially high or dramatic, but are more like picturesque water features set in the bush. Purakaunui Falls are one of the most popular falls in the Catlins and gently cascade down a rock face, though the best view is from the lower lookout accessed by a short flight of steps. The walk takes around 20 minutes return and is through an especially fine forest of beech, ferns and mosses.

Old Coach Track *

On SH92 on the north side of the bridge over the Tahakopa River just before Papatowai.

A flat walk following an old coach road leads through magnificent coastal beech and totara forest to the beach, once a moa hunters' camp. The walk takes one hour return.

Picnic Point/King Rock **

Sign-posted off SH92 south of the Papatowai village

This 30-minute loop walk starts out along the beach and then returns through native forest of kamahi, matai and rimu. Further south along the coast is Kings Rock, an eroded pillar of stone looking like a chess piece, and only accessible at low tide.

Florence Hill Lookout ***

SH92, 2 km south of Papatowai

At almost 200 m, Florence Hill lookout has spectacular views south over the pristine Tautuku Bay, the Rainbow Isles and Tautuku Peninsula and, to the north, the blowholes at Long Point are just visible.

Lake Wilkie **

SH92, 5 km south of Papatowai

The lake sits in a hollow below an escarpment and is fringed by mature podocarp trees. In summer the rata in flower is particularly impressive. It is only five minutes to the lookout over the lake and a further five minutes to the lake's edge and boardwalk.

Traills Tractor **

The track begins on the southern side of the Fleming River bridge on SH92.

In contrast to the natural beauty of the region, this walk has human history as its focus and, in particular, the extensive timber-milling industry in the Catlins. Just 10 minutes return, the walk leads to the site of the Cooks sawmill and the restored Traills Tractor. This is a Fordson tractor adapted to run on

SOUTH ISLAND

SOUTH OTAGO & THE CATLINS

rails which either pushed or pulled log-laden carriages from the bush to the mill. At intervals along the track are signs indicating where buildings once stood, though nothing remains today.

Cathedral Caves ***

2 km south of the Tautuku River on SH92

Entrance fee

A series of spectacular sea caves, the main cave is over 30 m high and some go deep into the cliff so a torch is necessary if you want to explore. Only accessible at low tide and, even then, you might get your feet wet, the walk is around one hour return, or longer depending on how many caves you explore. Tide timetables are helpfully posted on the gate and the gate is closed if the tide is not right, so to avoid disappointment, check tide times before setting out.

McLean Falls **

1 km south of the Cathedral Caves

The most spectacular of the waterfalls in the Catlins area (this southern section of the coast is more correctly known as Chaslands), the McLean Falls are over 20 m high and the walk takes around 45 minutes return through bush.

Niagara Falls and Waikawa *

These tiny falls in the Waikawa River were named in jest by an early surveyor who had visited the more impressive Niagara Falls in North America. At Waikawa, originally a whaling station, is a small local museum in the old school packed with historic photographs, old Maori adzes, moa bones and a curious embroidery made by a local man, Herbert Campbell, while a prisoner of war during the First World War. Nearby Porpoise Bay is home to rare Hector's dolphins (which are less than half the size of the more common bottlenose dolphin).

Curio Bay ***

12 km off SH92 from the Waikawa turnoff

The fossilised stumps and trunks of trees, up to 160 million years old, are clearly identifiable on the rocky flat shelf that is Curio Bay. The trees are subtropical in origin, including kauri and cycads and were felled in a single

379

cataclysmic event, most likely a volcanic eruption. The preserved forest is best seen at low tide.

Curio Bay is also home to a colony of yellow-eyed penguins who pop out of the surf late in the day and shuffle slowly over the rocky ledge to their nests in the flax and shrubs above the bay. Sit quietly and you can get very close to these rare birds.

Slope Point *

6 km south of Haldane

While Bluff may feel like the most southerly point of the South Island, that honour belongs to Slope Point at 46.4 degrees south. Windswept and often bleak, the Point has great coastal views and is also famous for its wind-sculptured trees. The Point is a 20-minute-return walk from the end of the road and is closed for lambing 1 September to 1 November.

Waipapa Point **

5 km south of Otara

This attractive beach, often frequented by sea lions, is dominated by an historic lighthouse built in 1884, the last wooden lighthouse to be built in the country. The light was built in response to New Zealand's worst shipping disaster which occurred in the early hours of 29 April 1881 when the *Tararua*, sailing from Dunedin to Bluff, struck the Otara reef just to the north of Waipapa Point. Although the weather was fair, the seas became rough on the incoming tide and several lifeboats were swamped as soon as they were launched. Eventually the ship broke in two and, despite being clearly visible from shore, few survived the wild surf. Many of the 131 who perished are buried in the 'Tararua Acre' just to the east of the point.

SOUTHLAND &
STEWART ISLAND

Bluff

Bluff Hill **

Access off Lee Street

At 265 m above sea level, the views from the top are superb, south to Stewart Island, far inland, and to the mountains of Fiordland to the west. Across the estuary from Bluff is the gigantic Tiwai Point aluminium smelter opened in 1971 producing over 350,000 tonnes of aluminium a year. Tours of the smelter are available most weekdays at 10 a.m. but bookings are essential (ph 03 218 5440).

Bluff Maritime Museum **

241 Foreshore Road

Open daily Monday to Friday 10 a.m. to 4.30 p.m., weekends 1 p.m. to 5 p.m.

Entrance fee

Bluff is one of New Zealand's oldest settlements (locals claim it is the oldest), and this excellent small museum focuses on the history of the town, and, in particular, its long connection to the sea. There are displays on whaling, the oyster industry and shipwrecks all accompanied by extensive historical photographs. The museum has a working steam engine from the tugboat TST *Awarua*, and, outside, a real oyster boat the *Monica II* which you can go inside.

Bluff Oyster and Southland Seafood Festival ***

www.bluffoysterfest.co.nz

The oysters, dredged from the floor of the Foveaux Strait, and known as Bluff oysters, are internationally renowned for their delicate and succulent taste. This popular festival, held in April, begins with the traditional piping in of the Bluff Oyster and is followed by a day of entertainment and great local seafood. Crowds pack the usually quiet, and somewhat run-down port town, for festivities that include Oyster Opening competitions, the Oyster Sack Fashion Parade and an Oyster Eating Competition, the title currently held by local Invercargill man, Tom Sawyer.

Paua Shell House **

258 Marine Parade

Open daily 9 a.m. to 5 p.m.

Entrance fee

For years Fred and Myrtle Flutey welcomed thousands of visitors from all around the world to their amazing home decorated with every conceivable version of paua ornamentation. Although the couple are now deceased the Flutey house has become a New Zealand icon, a tribute to the idea that ordinary people can do extraordinary things.

Stirling Point **

The much-photographed Stirling Point signpost points to various cities around the globe and marks the beginning of State Highway One. For most people this is their most southerly destination in the South Island, though Slope Point further east is a few degrees south of Bluff. But who cares, standing on that windswept point, Bluff feels as far south as you would want to go. The Point is also the starting point of the popular Foveaux Walkway around the coast with a side track that leads to the top of Bluff Hill.

Clifden Suspension Bridge *

Built across limestone narrows over the Waiau River in 1899, this bridge in Western Southland replaced a punt, and at 115 m long was, at that time, the longest span of any bridge in New Zealand. Now open only to pedestrians, it remained in use as a traffic bridge until 1978. Below the bridge by the river is a very pleasant picnic spot.

Cosy Nook/Mullet Bay **

Sign-posted 5 km east of Orepuki and 5 km from SH99

Mullet Bay, better known as Cosy Nook, is a tiny rocky haven on the wild southern coastline. Once supporting a large Maori population, Matariki, the largest of the offshore islands was at one time a fortified pa. In more recent years the cove was home to a small fishing fleet and, while most of the old fishing huts have gone, a handful of small cottages remain of which the 'Polyfilla Villa' is a classic.

Crank It Up Day **

Edendale Recreation Grounds, Edendale

Held on the last weekend of January and hosted by the Edendale Vintage Machinery Club, Crank It Up Day has a most amazing collection of working vintage farming machinery, guaranteed to provide a great day's family entertainment.

Forest Hill and Tussock Creek Reserves *

Central Southland

Though Southland place names have numerous references to the vast forest that once covered this plain (e.g. Heddon Bush, Ryal Bush, Gummies Bush, Centre Bush), hardly a native tree is left standing. These two adjoining reserves, just southwest of Winton, contain the only native bush left in Central Southland, and even this was milled for the larger trees. The contrast between the dense bush, the open farmland of the plains and the stark grassy hills could not be greater. However, this bush contains a surprising number of native birds, a cave complete with cave wetas, a giant rata tree, huge native tree fuchsias and a good lookout point over the plain. There are two entrances, one off Forest Hill Road, 7 km south of Winton and the second off Tussock Creek Road a bit further south. To walk the whole length of both reserves takes around two hours one way, though there are short walks from both entry points.

Gore

Croydon Aircraft Company **

SH94, Mandeville

www.croydonaircraft.com

Koha/donation

An airfield has existed here since the 1920s so it is appropriate that the Croydon Aircraft Company has based an international business here, restoring biplanes and, in particular, the de Havilland Tiger Moth. The very friendly people here allow visitors to see a range of projects in various stages of restoration, or you can take a flight in a Tiger Moth, or just lunch at the adjoining restaurant appropriately named The Moth.

Eastern Southland Gallery ***

Hokonui Drive opposite the Information Centre

Open Monday to Friday 10 a.m. to 4.30 p.m., weekends and public holidays 1 p.m. to 4 p.m. Closed Christmas Day, Boxing Day, New Years Day and Good Friday.

Koha/donation

One of the finest art galleries in the country and nicknamed the Goreggenheim, the gallery received a major boost with the gift of a collection from John

Money, an ex-New Zealander now living in Baltimore. In addition, finance was provided to completely redevelop the gallery (housed in the historic Carnegie library, built 1910) into a modern facility to hold fine collections by New Zealand artists such as Ralph Hotere, Rita Angus, and Theo Schoon. However, the most impressive is the 'jaw dropping' collection of African art, the likes of which you will not see elsewhere in New Zealand.

Fleming's Creamoata Mill *
Gorton Street

Dominating the centre of town is the Creamoata Mill complete with the iconic 'Sergeant Dan The Creamoata Man', an advertising device from the 1920s designed to promote Creamoata porridge made from locally grown oats. The main building was constructed in 1892 while the 30-m chimney dates from 1912. The building is classified Category One by the Historic Places Trust.

Gore Golden Guitar Awards ***
www.goldenguitars.co.nz

The Gore Golden Guitar Awards draw over 15 000 visitors to the town for a week of entertainment attended by the best New Zealand country musicians. Established in 1973, the festival is held annually during the week prior to Queen's Birthday Weekend with tickets selling fast once they go on sale in early April. The awards attract over 700 competitors to a variety of events including Songwriting awards, the Golden Queens contest, Busking awards, and, of course, the main event, the New Zealand Country Music Awards. Early in the week is a 'Walk Up' concert for anyone who wants to 'give it a go', and on the last weekend there is a Truck Parade through the main street of the town.

Hokonui Fashion Awards **
www.hokonuifashion.com

First held in 1988, these awards are now recognised as the top event for New Zealand's amateur fashion designers to showcase their talents in front of high-profile judges as well as an audience of over 700 people.

Hokonui Moonshine Museum ***

Hokonui Drive SH98 (the Moonshine museum, Gore Heritage Centre and Information Office are all in the same building)

Open Monday to Friday 8.30 a.m. to 4.30 p.m., weekends and public holidays 9.30 a.m. to 3.30 p.m. (summer) and 1 p.m. to 3.30 p.m. (winter). Closed Christmas Day, New Year's Day and Good Friday.

Entrance fee to Moonshine Museum

Gore Heritage Centre free

Miss this museum and you miss one of the best museum experiences in the country.

The Hokonui Moonshine Museum tells the story of the famous illegal brewing of whisky through the prohibition era in the early twentieth century. What makes this museum hugely appealing is that it is both informative and entertaining in a way most museums try to, but seldom achieve. Here you will find a recreation of an illegal bush still and the story of the people behind the stills, and the law enforcers who set out to catch them. The display also outlines the history of the Temperance Movement and its strong connection with the early politicisation of women. At one point in the museum, visitors have to choose between the Bar and Temperance Hall, though those who choose the Bar eventually find themselves back in the Temperance Hall. Don't be mean, pay the small entrance fee and enjoy the experience.

Moonshine Festival ***

www.gorenz.com

Held on the last weekend of February, crowds pack the Heritage Precinct to enjoy this celebration of food, music and, of course, the famous Hokonui whisky. With the advent of prohibition in 1900 locals set up illegal stills in the nearby bush-cloaked Hokonui Hills and for over 50 years (and 30 arrests) produced what was regarded as the best bush whisky in the country. In particular, the McRae family, originally a clan from the Scottish Highlands who settled in the district in the 1870s, managed to dodge the law, producing fine whisky for over 80 years. Whisky from the original MacRae recipe is now produced legally and for sale at the Information Centre along with Hokonui Whisky chocolates.

Trout Fishing ***

Gore lies at the heart of a network of streams and rivers that boast some of the best brown trout fishing in the country, if not the world. The fishing for these highly regarded sporting fish is by sight in clear waters of the Mataura River and its numerous tributaries. The season is from 1 October to 1 April and there is good access to fishing spots throughout the district. Gear can be hired locally and professional guiding is also available (www.bbsports.co.nz).

Invercargill

Anderson Park Art Gallery *

91 McIvor Road, North Invercargill
Open daily 10.30 a.m. to 5 p.m. Closed Christmas Day
Koha/donation

This attractive art gallery with its excellent collection of New Zealand art was originally built in 1926 as the home for local businessman Sir Robert Anderson. Gifted to the city in 1951, along with its park-like gardens, Anderson Park is a favourite spot for locals and visitors alike.

Historic Invercargill *

Established in 1856, Invercargill has a small number of historically important buildings all within a short walk of the central city. These include:

The Water Tower
Queens Drive at the end of Leet Street

Built in 1889 this highly decorative brick water tower with its Romanesque windows is over 42 m high and has commanding views of this flat city (open Sunday afternoons).

Provincial Chambers
Esk Street

This small building is a rare survivor of the early days when Southland was a separate province. Built in 1864, and first used as a Masonic Lodge, the Provincial Government worked from here from 1866 to 1870 when it reunited with Otago Province after its financially disastrous experiment with a wooden railway line.

First Church
Tay Street

This unusual Presbyterian church, constructed of brick, was opened in 1915 and has strikingly Romanesque lines that still look modern today.

St Mary's Basilica
Tyne Street

Designed by renowned church architect FW Petre, the dome of St Mary's dominates the skyline of south Invercargill. Built in 1905, the ground-floor plan is surprisingly small for such an imposing building.

Dee Street Hospital
Dee Street

Believed to be New Zealand's oldest hospital building on its original site, the main building was constructed in 1876, while the former Porter's Lodge, also part of the hospital complex and dating from 1866, is Invercargill's oldest building.

Oreti Beach **

While swimming in the sea is not necessarily closely associated with the cooler Southland climate, this is a fine stretch of sandy beach just 10 km from Invercargill and is also regarded as one of the best surfing beaches in the region. For those not willing to brave the water, Oreti Beach is just the place for those idyllic long walks (though the shallower water here is not as cold as on the more open sea beaches).

Queen's Park **
Gala Street

The elegant Feldwick Gates lead into one of the finest public parks in the country. The 80-ha park is a combination of sports fields and a golf course together with gardens including formal flower beds, a rose garden, tropical Winter Gardens, azalea and rhododendron gardens and a bird aviary — in short, something for everyone.

Shearing South *

55 Dee Street

Open daily Monday to Friday 10 a.m. to 4 p.m., weekends 1 p.m. to 4 p.m.

www.shearingsouth.co.nz

Entrance fee

Established by international shearer Kevin Stevenson, this is a comprehensive look at the demanding world of shearing and also the vital part that sheep farming has played in the development of the Southland province. A short video introduces the visitor to the world of the shearer, along with a recreation of the 1950s woolshed, a shearing hall of fame and even an art gallery.

Southland Museum and Art Gallery ***

108 Gala Street

Open daily 9 a.m. to 5 p.m. Monday to Friday and 10 a.m. to 5 p.m. Saturday and Sunday

www.southlandmuseum.com

Koha/donation

Invercargill's 'must see', this museum is world famous for it tuatara breeding programme and is the best place in New Zealand to see this unusual reptile. Tuatara are ancient animals dating back to the dinosaur age and, like most reptiles, they can sit still for a very long time and in fact looked more stuffed than alive. However, when food is on offer they can move surprisingly fast and have a very strong bite. The star of the show is Henry, over 100 years old; and weighing in at 1.2 kg, he is possibly the heaviest tuatara in the world. For after-hours viewing, the museum has a large glass window that looks on to the tuatara enclosure from the outside. Now how thoughtful is that!

But this museum is more than just the place to see tuatara. The excellent display 'Beyond the Roaring Forties' tells the human and natural history of New Zealand's sub-Antarctic islands including the intriguing story of the gold-laden *General Grant* which sank in the Auckland Islands in 1866. There is a moving ship deck popular with children, and the original lighthouse from Waipapa Point. The well-presented Maori section has a very fine and rare bow piece for a Maori waka, carved around 1600 in the shape of a whale.

Monkey Island *

1 km off SH99 southeast of Tuatapere

Once a thriving port settlement supplying local settlers and goldminers in the nearby Longwood Range, the origins of its name are unclear and today nothing remains of the township. The tiny offshore island is accessible at low tide and this is the easiest access point to a wide sweep of wild beach. There are spectacular views across Te Waewae Bay to Humpback Ridge and the Princess Mountains.

Otautau War Memorial *

Main Street, Otautau

Country districts all over New Zealand often have substantial war memorials for both world wars, and more rarely, the South African War. These memorials seem disproportionately large to districts where the population over the years has drifted away and nowhere is this more noticeable than in country areas of the South Island. Otautau is a pretty small town on the banks of the Aparima River, and has, as its local war memorial, two First World War field guns, one Turkish and one German. How these were acquired is anyone's guess, but they were presented to the town in 1921 and temporarily 'borrowed' during the Second World War to train gunners.

Stewart Island/Rakiura ***

www.stewartisland.co.nz

New Zealand's third-largest island is home to the country's newest National Park, Rakiura, created in 2002 and covering 85 per cent of the total island. The island has an exceptional unspoiled landscape of untouched bush, hidden bays, and rugged mountain ranges (the highest point is Mt Anglem at 980 m). With only 25 km of road and fewer than 400 people (and most of those are in the main settlement of Oban), the island has a gentle relaxed feel (cellphone coverage is minimal) but it does have a good range of accommodation, a great pub and a handful of good places to eat. The ferry is modern and fast, taking just an hour from Bluff to Oban, but be warned that Foveaux Strait has a reputation as a wild stretch of water. However, the ferry is fairly small and is frequently booked out especially in summer, so make sure you book ahead. The ferry company, Stewart Island Experience, also runs a number of short trips out of Oban for day visitors (www.stewartislandexperience.co.nz). While a day trip is worth the effort, especially if the weather is good, once on the island the place weaves its own magic that makes you just want to stay. There are also scheduled flights from Invercargill to Oban.

Kiwi Watching ***

The island has a substantial brown kiwi population of around 20,000 birds (40 times the human population) some of which have developed unusual habits. Here the usually solitary kiwi sometimes form family groups, and are often active during the day as well as at night, while at Mason's Bay the kiwi come down to the beach at night to feed on sand hoppers. There are several operators on the island who organise kiwi viewing trips.

Stewart Island Museum **

Open 10 a.m. to 12 noon Monday to Saturday, 12 noon to 2 p.m. Sunday
Entrance fee

This tiny one-room museum holds some surprising treasures relating to the long history of this island important to both Maori and Pakeha. Among the Maori displays are two rare necklaces of indeterminate age, one of bone and the other more unusually made of dolphins' teeth. Maritime history is well covered with examples of scrimshaw, but the most remarkable item of all is an extremely rare globe (one of two in the world) based on Cook's maps of New Zealand showing Stewart Island as a peninsula linked to the mainland — along with Banks Peninsula shown as an island, these are two of Cook's very rare mistakes.

Ulva Island **

This island wildlife sanctuary lies in Patterson Inlet just around the corner from Half Moon Bay where Oban is situated, and is a popular destination especially for day trippers. Now cleared of pests, the island is small and relatively flat with a network of excellent tracks linking a number of very attractive beaches (Sydney Cove is the most attractive beach though South West Beach is well worth the walk). Just a short water-taxi ride from Golden Bay (a 20-minute walk from the wharf, but there is transport as well), the island is promoted as a haven for wildlife, but you will be disappointed if you are expecting the bush to be alive with rare native birds. As yet, the birdlife is not so prolific though the cheeky weka is common, especially on the beaches.

Walking Tracks ***

Stewart Island is a walker's dream and, in all, there are 250 km of tracks, 10 times longer than the roads. The bush is superb, with stunning coastal vistas and surprising wildlife — in addition to the native wildlife keep an eye out for the shy white-tailed deer. The Rakiura Track is a three-day circuit on the northern third of the island, mainly following the coast, and is one of New Zealand's Great Walks. Other walks, a little less demanding and all close to Oban, are Horseshoe Point (three hours return), Fern Gully (two hours return), Moturau Moana (one hour return), and for those on a day trip to Ulva Island there are several excellent short walks of less than 30 minutes on the road to the wharf at Golden Bay.

Tour of Southland **

www.tourofsouthland.com

New Zealand's top cycle road race, the Tour of Southland, is a gruelling five-day circuit of the province in a number of stages of varying lengths. Attracting the best cyclists from New Zealand, the event starts and finishes at the velodrome in Invercargill, and the unpredictable November weather often proves just as challenging as the course itself.

FIORDLAND

Fiordland National Park

www.fiordland.org.nz

New Zealand's largest National Park, established in 1952, and over 1,252,000 ha in size, contains some of the country's most dramatic and unspoiled landscapes. In 1984 the park was recognised as a World Heritage Area. Much of the park is rugged, mountainous and has a hard and very wet climate, but this untouched part of New Zealand is spectacular and is home to some of the rarest plants and birds in the world. The park also contains the Sutherland Falls which, at 580 m, is one of the highest waterfalls in the world. For the average visitor the park is accessible only at the fringes, though specialist tour operators offer a wide range of options for those wanting something more adventurous. The only public roads through the park are the Milford and Hollyford roads.

The park has a wide range of tramps and walks that will suit most levels of fitness and the excellent Information Centres at Tuatapere and Te Anau have up-to-date track and weather information. Serious consideration should be given to blowing the budget on a scenic flight over the park as this is an alternative — for appreciating the scale of this magnificent wilderness — to taking some very long hikes.

Doubtful Sound ***

Doubtful Sound is, after Milford, the most accessible of the Fiordland sounds and with far fewer visitors than at Milford Sound, it has a much more unspoiled feel. Home to fur seals, crested penguins and bottle-nosed dolphins, the 40-km long fiord (Milford is 16 km) is also the deepest at 400 m.

Several operators run a variety of trips across Lake Manapouri to the West Arm, then by bus over the Wilmot Pass and down to Deep Cove on Doubtful Sound. These can include visiting the Manapouri Power Station and are either day or overnight trips. The largest operator is Real Journeys www.realjourneys. co.nz

Fiordland Major Walking Tracks ***

Fiordland has some of the best walking tracks in the country, but for these you need a good level of fitness and good equipment as the terrain is mountainous and the weather changeable, unpredictable and usually very wet. Some of the tracks are very popular and can get crowded over the peak summer period.

The Milford Track, for instance, is booked out months in advance. Bookings open on 1 July and can be arranged on line or through any DoC office (www.doc.govt. nz). Before setting out on any tramp check the excellent DoC office in Te Anau for up-to-date track and weather information.

Caples River and Greenstone River Tracks

Although these tracks can be done separately, together they form a loop track from the Lake Wakatipu-to-Milford Sound road around the Ailsa Mountains linked via the McKellar Saddle. The track emcompasses alpine scenery, and the two river valleys are quite different in character — the Caples is more open and tussock-clad while the Greenstone is narrower and bush-lined. The round trip takes four to five days and is less demanding than some of the other Fiordland tracks. A further option is to return on the Routeburn Track.

Dusky Track

This is the most challenging track in the National Park, taking eight to nine days to complete and covering 84 km via Dusky Sound. With the starting points at Lake Hauroko and Lake Manapouri (neither easy to access), this track is for experienced trampers only, reaching deep into the heart of the Fiordland mountains and traversing untouched wildness like no other Fiordland walk. There are numerous river crossings, some with wire bridges, and the terrain is mountainous with Centre Pass reaching a height of 1051 m.

Hollyford Track

From the heart of the Fiordland mountains the track follows the Hollyford River to Lakes Alabaster and McKerrow and through to the mouth of the Hollyford River at Martins Bay. Among the many highlights are excellent views of Fiordland's highest mountain, Mt Tutoko.

From the end of the Hollyford Road the track is 56 km long with the only options of getting out, to either walk back or fly out. The trip takes four days, but as the Hollyford Valley is at a low altitude, this track is less affected by seasonal weather than the other Fiordland tracks. However, there are numerous river and creek crossings on this track and in bad weather trampers can be stuck for days.

Hump Ridge Track

Originally known as the 'Hump Track'(so named after its most prominent geological feature), but later changed to the more delicate Hump Ridge Track, this walk in the southern part of the park combines coastal vistas and wildlife with one of the few human landscapes in Fiordland National Park (parts of this track are through private land). A highlight is the spectacular Percy Burn Viaduct, the largest wooden viaduct in New Zealand and the remains of Port Craig, once a lively sawmilling town. To walk the entire track takes three to four days but for those who do not want to, helicopter and boat options can shorten the trip.

Track information and permits are available from the Information Centre in Tuatapere (www.humpridgetrack.co.nz), which also houses the Bushman's museum with a focus on the local early sawmilling industry. Tautapere is also famous for its sausages, available at the LL Butchery just down the road from the Information Centre.

Kepler Track

A popular loop track through the Jackson Peaks, this 60-km walk takes three to four days, accessed either from Rainbow Reach near Lake Manapouri or the Dock Bay Control Gates at Te Anau (a track along the Waiau River also links these two points).

Traversing beech forest and alpine terrain, this medium-grade track has spectacular views over Lakes Manapouri and Te Anau as well as the mountains to the west. The highest point on the track is 1472 m, at Mt Luxmore, which can be very exposed in windy weather.

Milford Track

The oldest, most famous of the Fiordland tracks, and the most popular, the Milford Track is a four-day, 53-km walk from the north end of Lake Te Anau through to Milford Sound. To control numbers, only 40 people are allowed to start the track each day. However, for very hardy and experienced trampers, bookings are not required through the winter (May to October) though hut tickets are still required. However, at this time of the year, the track is often closed, with snow and avalanches a constant danger.

The track traverses very diverse terrain, from the less wet eastern side over the spectacular Mackinnon Pass (at 950 metres the most demanding section of the track) and down into the very wet, but more scenic Milford Sound part of the track. There is also an option of a short side trip to the Sutherland Falls, a 580-m tiered waterfall with the main drop of 270 m.

Routeburn Track

The most popular track after the Milford, the Routeburn Track starts (or ends) from The Divide on the Milford Road and ends at the Routeburn Shelter north of Glenorchy near Queenstown. The track is 32 km long and takes three days through spectacular alpine terrain crossing the Harris Saddle (at 1255 m, the highest point on the track) and then following the Routeburn River to the road end. Rather than the road trip back, many trampers return via the Caples or Greenstone tracks. Another option is a two-day return tramp from the Milford Road to the Harris Shelter which encompasses the best scenery on the track.

Lake Hauroko ***

One of the few accessible points in the southern area of the park, Lake Hauroko is the deepest New Zealand lake, at a depth of 462 m, and one of the ten deepest lakes in the world. Beautiful, wild and undeveloped, access to the lake is along a 32-km road (20 km are gravel) off SH99 just 12 km north of Tuatapere. There is a three-hour walk through beech forest on the northern side of the lake to a great lookout point.

While there is a boat launching ramp, the lake is subject to very high winds and can quickly become extremely rough. In 1968 the remains of a high-born Maori woman was found in a cave on Mary Island in the lake. Believed to have been placed there in 1600, she was found buried in a sitting position.

Dusky Track begins from the head of the lake and can be accessed by boat (prearranged) or by guided walk.

Lake Manapouri ***

Much less developed than Te Anau, this, New Zealand's second-deepest lake (440 m) has a great air of mystery with over 34 small islands and numerous bays leading into the heart of the Fiordland mountains.

In 1970 the lake was at the heart of one of New Zealand's greatest conservation battles, the Save Manapouri Campaign which opposed plans to raise the level of the lake by 30 m to increase power generation. Over a quarter of a million New Zealanders signed a petition to save the lake and the issue had a significant impact on the 1972 general election which saw a Labour Government elected on a platform that included leaving the lake level unchanged.

Several operators offer boat trips from the very pretty Pearl Harbour, where kayaks are also available for hire.

Two good short walks, one north and the other south of the lake, are as follows.

Pearl Harbour return via the Circle Track ***

This three-hour walk begins along the Waiau river, follows the lake and then leads uphill to two lookouts giving great views over Hope Arm, Garnock Burn and Mt Titiroa. Transport across the river is necessary and either water taxi or rowboat hire can be arranged through Adventure Manapouri, ph 03 249 8070.

Rainbow Reach to Shallow Bay **

Part of the Kepler Track, accessed 11 km south of Te Anau.

A swing-bridge across the Waiau leads to the track through mountain beech to Shallow Bay on Lake Manapouri. Moturau Hut and Shallow Bay Hut offer shelter and toilets on the way, before the return to the bridge. Around three hours.

Lake Te Anau ***

Covering an area of 344 sq km and at 65 km long, Te Anau is the largest lake in the South Island and the second-largest in the country after Lake Taupo. The east and west sides of the lake could not contrast more. To the west, the rugged Kepler, Murchison and Stuart mountain ranges rise to over 1500 m and are snow-clad in winter and bush-clad at the shore line — three arms of the lake, unimaginatively named South, Middle and North Fiords reach deep into the mountains — while, to the east, the landscape is flat, open and much drier.

The Murchison Mountains, between the South and Middle Fiords, are the last natural mainland bastion of the rare takahe. There were only four sightings of the bird between 1800 and 1900 so by the early twentieth century the takahe was thought to be extinct. Then in November 1948 ornithologist Dr Geoffery Orbell rediscovered the birds in the Murchison Mountains, though numbers have dropped considerably, mainly due to predation by stoats.

Te Anau Glow-worm Caves ★★★

www.realjourneys.co.nz

The glow-worm caves lie directly across the lake from the Te Anau township, and are the most impressive outside of Waitomo. A combination boat and cave trip, operated by Real Journeys, takes two and half hours, starting with the boat trip to the western side of the lake, followed by a short walk through bush, then a trip in a small boat on an underground river through the caves themselves to the glow-worm grotto.

Te Anau Wildlife Centre ★

Te Anau Manapouri Road, 1 km south of the Te Anau Shopping Centre

An open park on the lakeside with various aviaries contains native birds, some of which are not easily seen in the wild, including takahe, weka, kaka, kea and parakeets.

Manapouri Power Station ★★

www.meridianenergy.co.nz

Manapouri Power Station is unusual in New Zealand in that it relies on the natural 178-m height difference between Lake Manapouri and Deep Cove in Doubtful Sound, rather than a dam, to harness water for power generation. The difficult terrain and harsh climate made the construction of the power station particularly challenging, and although investigated as a power source as early as the 1920s, it wasn't until 1964 that work began. The project took eight years to complete, including the underground power station and a 10-km tailrace tunnel through hard granite and gneiss rock. During this period, 16 men died both underground and during the construction of the road over the Wilmot Pass. In May 1998 work began on a second 10-km tailrace tunnel which was completed in 2002, this time with no loss of life.

Several tour operators offer tours that include the power station.

Milford Road ★★★

The road from Te Anau to Milford Sound covers some of New Zealand's most spectacular scenery and is the only road to give access through Fiordland National Park. While most visitors tend to travel directly to Milford Sound, take the boat trip and then return, it is worthwhile planning for some short excursions along the way. The road is sealed and in excellent condition, though it is subject to road closures during winter, mainly due to snow and ice conditions around the Homer Tunnel. Make sure you have a full tank of fuel before leaving Te Anau and you will need to carry chains in winter (available for hire in Te Anau). Cellphone coverage is limited to Te Anau and Milford Sound (if that) and facilities and accommodation at Milford itself are very limited.

The road is very busy in the mornings with buses aiming to catch the mid-day boat trips so, if you want to avoid the worst of the crowds, leave before 8 a.m. Up to 100 coaches per day use the road in the peak of the season but, fortunately, most of the traffic travels in the same direction.

The following highlights are based on travelling from Te Anau to Milford Sound.

Eglinton Valley **

Flat and grassy with steep bush-clad hills on either side of the Eglinton River, this is the quintessential glacial valley with views deep into the mountains. The best views are from Mackay Creek at the southern end of the valley.

Mirror Lakes *

Several flax-fringed tarn lakes alongside the road reflect the mountains beyond and are a very popular short stop for bus tours.

Key Summit ***

For those not contemplating walking a major alpine track, this three-hour-return walk to Key Summit (918 m) is an excellent option as the track includes beech forest, subalpine terrain, and, at the top, spectacular views of the Hollyford, Greenstone and Eglinton Valleys. The track begins at The Divide, which, at 531 m, is the lowest east-west pass through the Southern Alps.

Hollyford Valley ***

If there is time, the Hollyford Valley is an attractive side trip, and while the road is unsealed it is flat for almost its entire length and in good condition.

Lake Marion and Marion Falls ***

A three-hour-return trip to a small alpine lake above the bush line with superb views of the Darran Mountains. The falls are a gushing rocky cascade through beech forest, and are only 20 minutes return from the Hollyford Road.

Gunn's Camp ★★★

No cellphone coverage, no electricity (generators provide power until 10 p.m.) and no phone lines, this camping ground alongside the Hollyford River is the place to get away from it all. In addition to camping and camper sites, there is accommodation in old Public Works huts, the larger of which originally housed families, and they come complete with a range for cooking and heating. The camp was established by Murray Hunt, who lived in the valley for over 50 years until the age of 81 when he retired to Te Anau. However, his larger-than-life personality lives on in his collection of Hollyford memorabilia at the small museum (part of the store), and while you are at the store don't miss checking out 'Murray's Fridge'. If you want to stay here you can take a chance and just turn up or write a letter, (yes a letter!) to Bill and Helen, Hollyford Museum Trust Board, Private Bag, Hollyford, Te Anau.

Hollyford Airstrip ★★

This is the ultimate bush airstrip, a narrow and very short 'runway' of sorts, with the bushes each side of the strip trimmed back just enough to clear the wings. If there wasn't a sign indicating this was an airstrip, it would be easily mistaken for a short stretch of road. Don't even go and look if you are scared of flying. You can, however, to actually see planes land and take off from this amazing 'airport', check with the friendly people at Gunn's Camp store who might know when planes are due.

Humboldt Falls ★★

The total height of these falls is 275 m, though they fall in three stages, of which the tallest single drop is 134 m. Of course they are much more impressive after heavy rain. The walk is an easy 30 minutes return through bush, but the view of the falls is quite distant across the Humboldt Creek.

Homer Tunnel ★★

Prior to construction of the tunnel, the only access to Milford Sound was either on foot via the Milford track, or by sea, so there was considerable pressure on the government to build a tunnel through the Homer Saddle to open up the area to tourism. Government work schemes during The Depression provided a ready source of labour, and work began on the road in 1929, and on the tunnel in 1935. Progress in the harsh environment was slow and dangerous, and although the breakthrough was achieved, work on the tunnel was halted during the war years. Work resumed after the war with the tunnel finally completed in 1953. The road on the western side of the tunnel is dramatic with its sheer cliffs and hairpin bends that drop steeply down to Milford Sound. The single-lane tunnel is 1.2 km long, slopes steeply down towards the Milford end with a gradient of 1 in 10, and is controlled by traffic lights (though the wait isn't usually too long).

The Chasm ***

The Cleddau River is forced through a narrow gorge creating an impressive torrent of water that, over thousands of years, has worn the rock into smooth sculptured formations. The walk is flat and twenty minutes return.

Milford Sound ***

Milford Sound is one case where reality exceeds expectation, no matter how many photographs of Mitre Peak you have seen. The long arm of the sound reaches 16 km inland from the sea with peaks rising dramatically out of the water to over 1500 m. What makes Milford even more remarkable is that the drop below water continues to depths of over 300 m, though, at the entrance, the water depth is only 27 m. No matter how many tourists pack in here, the landscape dwarfs them all.

Geologically speaking, Milford Sound is a fiord formed by glacial action rather than a drowned river valley as in the Marlborough Sounds. The spectacular Bowen Falls plunge 165 m from a hanging valley into the sea while, further along the sound toward the sea, the Stirling Falls drop 156 m. Both are spectacular after heavy rain.

The sound is home to a large seal population, the rare Fiordland crested penguin and Dusky and bottlenose dolphins, while underwater black coral grows just 10 m below the surface (rather than the usual 40 m) as the surface water here is heavy with dark tannins creating the illusion of much deeper water.

There are at least four boat operators offering various day-trip options on the sound. These can be booked on line, in Te Anau, Queenstown or at the modern Visitor Terminal in Milford itself. In addition to the day trips there are also overnight boat trips, kayaking and diving trips on offer. The Milford Deep Underwater Observatory has an underwater viewing facility.

Index